Routledge Reviva

The English Book Trade

Originally published in 1938, and as a third edition in 1974, this volume presents the results of original research into the economic aspects of the transition from the medieval manuscript to the modern printed book. It discusses the problems of supply of materials and labour created by the introduction of machinery and the growth of the literary market. The social evolution of the printing crafts is portrayed, focussing first upon the Stationers' Company and later upon the trade union. The book traces the development of the author-printer-publisher relationship, and its bearing on the question of copyright and reviews, inter alia the organisation and price policy of bookselling from the days of legal maximum prices to the net book agreement. The 3rd edition contains sections on Public Lending Right, paperbacks, photocopying in its relation to publishing and the rise of international publishing.

The English Book Trade

An Economic History of the Making and Sale of Books

Marjorie Plant

Third revised edition published in 1974 by George Allen & Unwin Ltd.

This edition first published in 2024 by Routledge
4 Park Square, Milton Park, Abingdon, Oxon, OX14 4RN
and by Routledge
605 Third Avenue, New York, NY 10158.

Routledge is an imprint of the Taylor & Francis Group, an informa business

ISBN 13: 978-1-032-89824-7 (hbk)
ISBN 13: 978-1-003-54486-9 (ebk)
ISBN 13: 978-1-032-89843-8 (pbk)
Book DOI 10.4324/9781003544869

TRANSCRIPTION OF THE FRONTISPIECE

FYNES FOR DEFAUTIS FOR PRYNTYNGE WITHOUTE LYCENSE

Johnne Tysdayle for pryntinge without lycense The A.B.C. and a nother suche lyk for bothe he ys fyned iiijs viijd	
Rycharde harvy for byndynge of greate bokes in shepes Lether ys fyned at	xijd
Randall Tyerer for byndynge of mediante bokes in shepes Lether ys fyned at	iiijd
Williame greffeth for that he prynted a medisine made by doctour owyn withoute Lycense was fyned at	xijd
Henry Sutton for takynge of a straunger Contrary to the orders of this howse ys fyned to paye	xijd
Williame pekerynge and Williame greffeth for contensious wordis betwene thame had for convaynge awaye of a Copye of doctor owyns medysine ys fyned at vjd le pece	xijd

ffynes for defaute for
pryntynge wtoute lycense

John Tysdayle for pryntinge wtout lycense the A. B. C. and a nother suche lyke for bothe he ys fyned [illegible]

Rycharde harvy for byndynge of greate bokes in shepes lether ys fyned at — xijd

Randall Tyrer for byndynge of medians bokes in shepes lether ys fyned at — iiijd

William greffeth for that he prynted a medisine made by doctor owyn wtoute lycense was fyned at — xijd

henry Sutton for takynge of a strannger contrary to the orders of this howse ys fyned to paye — xijd

William peckerynge and william greffeth for contensious words betwene them had for conveyinge awaye of a Copye of doctor owyns medysine ys fyned at vjd le pece — xijd

FINES IMPOSED BY THE STATIONERS' COMPANY, 1558–9
Reproduced by permission of the Stationers' and Newspaper Makers' Company from a page of the Wardens' Accounts
(For transcription please see previous page)

THE ENGLISH BOOK TRADE

An Economic History of the Making and Sale of Books

BY

MARJORIE PLANT

D.SC.(ECON.), F.L.A.

LONDON

GEORGE ALLEN & UNWIN LTD

Ruskin House Museum Street

FIRST PUBLISHED IN 1939
SECOND EDITION 1965
THIRD EDITION 1974

ISBN 0 04 655012 7

PRINTED IN GREAT BRITAIN
in 11-Point Fournier Type
BY UNWIN BROTHERS LIMITED
OLD WOKING SURREY

Preface to the First Edition

This study of the English book trade is designed as a contribution to the economic history of Great Britain. It is a strangely neglected chapter. The history of the printed book has attracted much attention from scholars other than economic historians, from bibliographers and students of literature, from historians of political movements and ideas, of censorship and of freedom of the Press. The economic and social significance of the invention of printing and of its introduction into this country is universally recognised, and yet the history of the economic development of the English book trade itself, the structural form which it gradually evolved, the problems of supply and demand which it encountered and overcame, the techniques which it adopted and discarded, the social and economic relationships which arose between masters and men, have not hitherto been described and appraised.

The account has been carried from the introduction of printing down to modern times, but only the main trends of twentieth-century development have been indicated. It is no part of the work of the economic historian to analyse present-day business problems within the industry, to appraise the merits of rival techniques, or to judge matters which are the subject of current controversy within the trade. Nor has any attempt been made to provide a history of the technology of the industry, details of which have been confined strictly to the elementary needs of the student of economic trends.

I am aware of many inevitable shortcomings in this volume. There would have been many more had it not been for the generous assistance which I have received in many quarters. My thanks are due particularly to Professor R. H. Tawney for his encouragement and advice through all the stages of research, and to Professor Arnold Plant for reading the manuscript and making many suggestions. Mr. L. J. Cumner, Assistant Secretary of the British Federation of Master Printers, has generously supplied information on matters of present-day organisation. Among the specialist libraries which it has been my privilege to consult I have benefited particularly from the collections of the St. Bride's Institute Technical Library and the British Library of Political and Economic Science. To my chief, Dr. W. C. Dickinson, Librarian of the latter institution, I am especially indebted for much kindly interest and assistance. Finally, I tender thanks to the Master and Wardens of the Stationers' and Newspaper Makers' Company for permission to reproduce the page from the Wardens' Accounts for the year 1558–9 which forms the frontispiece.

1939 MARJORIE PLANT

NOTE TO THE THIRD EDITION

The general scope of this book remains unchanged, but various statistical and other data have been brought up to 1970 or after. Fuller treatment has been given of certain subjects, notably trade unions and sales promotion, which have acquired greater significance since the Second World War, and sections on photocopying in its relations to the book trade, Public Lending Right, the paperback industry and international publishing are included for the first time.

Readers who wish to pursue individual topics in greater detail will find it worth while to consult the extensive *Classified Catalogue of a Collection of Works on Publishing and Bookselling in the British Library of Political and Economic Science*, British Library of Political and Economic Science (London School of Economics and Political Science).

I am indebted to Professor Sir Arnold Plant for reading my additions in manuscript and checking my interpretation of economic developments.

1973 M.P.

CONTENTS

PART ONE
THE AGE OF HAND-PRINTING

Contents

LIST OF ILLUSTRATIONS

PART ONE

THE AGE OF HAND PRINTING

CHAPTER I

Introduction

OVER two thousand years before the birth of Gutenberg a reviewer of his times observed that "Of making many books there is no end." The discovery of the art of typography, which was to have so vital an influence on the growth of culture, was therefore not at first of such importance in industrial organisation as might be imagined. In an industry which had for generations been satisfying the needs of the scholar, tradition weighed heavily against any innovation, however momentous.

The Manuscript Book

The most perfect organisation of the book market in ancient times was to be found in the Roman Empire. The book at that time took the form of the "volumen," or roll, consisting of parchment or papyrus with writing on only one side, as distinct from the later "codex"; but the same general discussions as to the function of the entrepreneur, his relations with the author and with his customers, are relevant here as at the present day. There was only one essential difference: after the original outlay labour was to the Roman publisher a relatively free factor of production; the abundance of slaves specially trained for the work of copying manuscripts would have rendered the printing-press unnecessary even had it been known, for it was claimed that a whole edition of a work could be finished within a day of the delivery of the copy. The edition, which ranged as a rule from five hundred to a thousand copies, was thus produced without any charge to the publisher for type-metals, founding, composing or press-work; the only expenses on the mechanical side were for the provision of simple writing-materials and for the bare maintenance of the slaves. On a more up-to-date problem, as to whether the author received any payment for his work, opinions are divided. There is sufficient evidence to show that as a rule he did not sell his work outright to the publisher; the only doubt is as to whether he received royalties. From general reasoning that would appear unlikely: the purchaser of a single copy of a work was in a position to have as many manuscript copies made from it as he desired, and these could be put on the market with too little indication of their source for the author to be able to claim compensation. It is not surprising, then, that Roman books were noted for their cheapness, and secured a wide demand. Trade with districts far afield was rendered possible by an excellent road system extending throughout the Empire. Until the end of the fourth century there was a well-organised book trade between Rome and the whole of the civilised world. This in great part collapsed with the fall of the Empire, yet for some centuries to come Rome was to be the only true book market in the world. The day of monastic book production had arrived, yet even the wants of the monasteries were satisfied to some extent from Rome; Benedict Biscop, for instance, made several journeys there to buy books for the abbeys of Wearmouth and Jarrow, founded by him in the seventh century.

From the year 529, when St. Benedict founded the monastery of Monte Cassino, until the end of the twelfth century, the main activity both in the production and the distribution of books was centred in the monasteries. The Benedictines and later orders bound themselves to keep the rules of poverty, chastity, obedience and also of labour, and in the constitutions given to the Benedictine monasteries of the province of Canterbury, in 1277, it is specifically stated that "The abbots may allow their cloistered monks, in place of manual labour, according to their ability in other occupations, to employ themselves in studying, in writing, in correcting, in illuminating, and in binding books." Nor were these books intended entirely or even mainly for use within the monastery in question. The Benedictine monasteries at home and on the Continent seem to have been publishing centres in the accepted trade sense. The copies of works in the monastic library were to some extent given in exchange for copies of other texts; others were sold through the agency of travelling monks; others were bargained for cattle or land, thus adding directly to the material wealth of the monastery. Here, as in the Roman Empire, there was an abundance of labour, making for cheap output. But as the market widened it was found profitable to employ paid scribes who were not monks. Thus in St. Albans, one of the most important mediaeval literary centres in England, the Abbot Paul about the year 1100 collected funds from his friends for the payment of daily wages to his scribes. By the thirteenth century paid scribes did much of the transcribing in the English monasteries, while among the other lay brethren there was usually a bookbinder. The question of payment for authorship did not arise, for the monastic transcribers, when not engaged upon their own chronicles and service books, confined their attention to the classics and to the works of the Fathers.

The advantages of division of labour were realised from an early date in the monasteries. It seems to have been rare for one monk to undertake all the processes necessary for the production of a book. The usual procedure was for one monk to prepare the parchment by rubbing it with powdered pumice-stone and cutting it into sheets of the required size; he would pass it on to the scribe, who would copy his text on to it, leaving the initial letters and coloured borders to be added by the illuminator; the manuscript was then ready to be handed on for the final process, binding. By the close of the Middle Ages some of these stages had been subdivided. At the end of the fifteenth century, for instance, Trithemius, Abbot of Spanheim, gave detailed instructions to the monks who were entrusted with the binding of his books: "Let that one fasten the leaves together and bind the book with boards; you prepare those boards; you dress the leather, you the metal plates which are to adorn the binding."[1]

Even the transcribing of a single manuscript came to be the work of more than one scribe: a text was commonly divided into sections in order that several monks could work upon it at the same time, their copies afterwards being sewn in correct order by the binder. But this was nothing to the efficiency attained as the manuscript rose to importance as an article of commerce. The method described by Alcuin of York as early as the eighth century seems to have been widely adopted in later years: "The young monks file into the *scriptorium* and one of them is given the precious parchment volume containing a work of Bede or Isidore or Augustine, or else some portion of the Latin Scriptures, or even a heathen author. He reads slowly and clearly at a measured rate while all the others, seated at their desks, take down his words; thus perhaps a score of copies are made at once."[2] Some idea of the output of a body of monks working steadily to dictation may be formed from the record that Jacob of Breslau had by the time of his death in 1480 written so many volumes that six horses were required to carry them.

From the last decade of the twelfth century the universities joined the monasteries in the work of producing books. The University of Bologna in 1259 led the way in appointing official "stationarii," whose duty it was to stock prescribed textbooks and lend them to students and teachers at fixed rates. One effect must have been to lower the demand for copies. The trade in manuscripts was hampered by a city statute which limited the amount of commission to be taken by the stationarii to 2½ per cent. A further prohibition in force in most universities against taking any book out of the university town probably tended to increase the total net output. The bookseller's connection with the university assured him of a steady trade, but set narrow bounds to his enterprise. The stationers of Paris, for instance, were for centuries organised as a guild within the university, subject to strict censorship and price regulation, even though there was from the thirteenth century a general European demand for the products of the Parisian scribes.

The English universities exercised far less supervision over their stationarii than did those on the Continent. The main irksome provision binding the booksellers of Oxford and Cambridge in the fourteenth and fifteenth centuries was that their wares had to be passed by the Chancellor as being free from heretical statements. So attractive did Oxford become to the bookselling fraternity that in 1374 it was found necessary to decree that none except the sworn university stationers or their deputies should sell any book greater in value than half a mark. In spite of that, forty years later the university booksellers still seemed to be feeling the strain of competition: in 1411 the edict was issued that "as the duties of the university stationers are laborious and anxious, every one on graduation shall give clothes to one of the stationers."[3] The stationers were not of course alone in finding it difficult to pay their way; there are many instances already in the fifteenth century Oxford records of the pawning of books by lecturers and students.

By the beginning of the fifteenth century there was an active trade in manuscripts outside the universities. Italy was the centre of the trade, Venice being the headquarters by virtue of its geographical position: the city was well situated for the collection of Eastern texts and for the sale of transcripts to other European towns; it was easily accessible to enterprising scribes from Constantinople; greatest advantage of all, the city could not be surrounded in time of war, and its markets could not be cut off. Next in importance to Venice came Florence and Milan. At about this time manuscripts began to take their place among the goods sold at the fairs of Frankfort and Nordlingen. The English fairs, notably those of St. Giles and Stourbridge, also had their manuscript dealers. But as a whole the details of the English mediaeval trade in manuscripts are obscure. It is certain that there was some efficient means of book distribution, for even Wyclif's prohibited version of the Bible found its way into all parts of the country before the end of the fifteenth century. Pedlars probably played an important part as booksellers in country districts, but the vigorous London trade in manuscripts from the middle of the fourteenth century was carried on mainly by the grocers and mercers, who also sold writing materials.

The Continued Production of Manuscript Volumes during the First Century of Printing

At the time of the introduction of printing into France there were more than ten thousand copyists in Paris and Orléans alone. What was their fate? The answer depends partly on the extent of the demand for the work of the scribe in fields other than book production, and partly on the rate at which the printed book ousted the manuscript. With regard to the first point, there was from the end of the fifteenth century a rapid rise of commercial enterprise; writing was by no means a general accomplishment, and a considerable number of business houses were springing up to whom the services of a scribe were essential for the keeping of accounts. Moreover, as the printing-press, with its cheapening of books, contributed to the spread of education, the services of the writing-master came more and more into demand.

In considering the second point, the rate at which the manuscript was superseded by the printed book, it must be remembered that a large proportion of the scribes of the fifteenth century were monks, who would not in any case be thrown on the mercy of the world owing to a change in the popular taste. As it happened, there was no sudden change in demand. There has always been a type of customer to whom a machine-made article is abhorrent; the mechanically-made book had to survive years of contempt before it came to be recognised as fully respectable. Evidence of this is to be found in a description of the library of the Duke of Urbino written by Vespasiano, a noted though clearly biased manuscript dealer, in 1482: "In this library all the volumes are of perfect beauty, all written, by skilled scribes, on parchment and many of them adorned with exquisite miniatures. The collection contains no single printed book. The Duke would be ashamed to have a printed book in his library."[4] So great was the preference of the older scholars for the manuscript volume that it was known for scribes to prepare their manuscripts from printed copy. It may have been to pander to this taste that the first printers cast their type to imitate as closely as possible the written form of the letter, even prolonging the use of those tiresome abbreviations which were no longer of real service.

Scepticism as to the permanence of the new form of book was another element tending to prolong the employment of the copyist. In 1492 the Abbot of Spanheim wrote a letter entitled "De laude scriptorum manualium" in which he earnestly exhorted the monastic scribes not to give up their work; while, he argued, a work written on parchment could be preserved for a thousand years, it was very unlikely that any volume printed on paper would last for more than two centuries. A large number of important works, he urged, had not been printed at all, so that any copies of these which were wanted must be written by scribes; the scribe, therefore, who stopped work because of the invention of the printing-press could be no true lover of books, or he would give more thought to the intellectual needs of the future.

The writing of service books in the monasteries did actually continue long after the invention of printing, probably as a traditional religious exercise rather than for any economic cause, except where difficulty of communication with a printing centre was a contributing factor. But it is interesting to note that in Germany many of the Benedictine monasteries came to be furnished with printing-presses of their own. There was at least one similar case in England: the monastery of Tavistock, in Devonshire, was the source of two printed works, *The boke of comfort* (1525), and a *Confirmation of the charter, perteyninge to all the tynners wythyn the countey of Devonshyre* (1534).

The employment of the scrivener in copying books survived longer in England than in any other country, owing to the exigencies of fashion. In the Elizabethan period it was considered beneath the dignity of a gentleman to have any dealings with a publisher; it was therefore customary for courtiers to circulate manuscript copies of their works among their friends. By that time the productions of the Parisian scribes were limited to such manuscripts as could be sold as works of art. For these there was a steady demand in a luxury-loving age.

During the sixteenth century there were still two classes of work in which the manuscript was a more economical form of production than the printed book. The first group consisted of Greek works. Until about 1550 there were few printers who cared to risk the expense of providing Greek founts of type for the satisfaction of a very limited market, and in any case the journeyman printer had not as a rule as great familiarity with the Greek language as was commonly possessed by the scribes. The second category was composed of works for which the publisher could not gauge the demand. Certain Latin texts were definitely needed by all university students, whereas the great body of classics were required only by an occasional scholar. Rather than lose on an undertaking the publisher would naturally leave it alone. So there was still employment for the copyists in satisfying special needs.

To some extent the copyists may have been absorbed into the printed book industry. We have seen that the ideal at which the first printers aimed was a perfect imitation of the manuscript; there was accordingly a demand for scribes to design the face of the new type, a demand strictly limited, it is true; there was also a call for the services of the rubricator, for the mediaeval practice of leaving initials to be filled in as a supplementary process was continued during the first twenty years of typography. The more enterprising workers, of course, gave up their old methods and adopted the new; some of the early printers had been trained as scribes, illuminators or metal workers. The Stationers' Company itself, which on its incorporation in 1557 was granted the national monopoly of printing, seems to have been the natural descendant of a fourteenth-century body of London scriveners known as the Writers of the Court Hand and Text Letters.

The World Setting of the English Book Industry

During this long period of manuscript production there evolved some degree of specialisation. Italy, the home of the wonderful libraries of Greek and Latin manuscripts collected by Cosmo de Medici and others, was the main source of classical works. The university quarters of Paris followed closely in importance. But the main activity of the French scribes was in the production of service books, for which they possessed a virtual European monopoly. The Renaissance, which had brought to Italy and France a revival of classical scholarship, had the effect in Germany of rousing scientific interests. A revived interest in mathematics came concurrently with the discovery of Greek and Roman astronomical and mathematical treatises and with the new attention to navigation.

Geography and astronomy began to take an important place in intellectual life, fostered by the work of such scientists as Regiomontanus, the fifteenth-century citizen of Nuremberg. As the knowledge of typography spread from Mainz throughout Europe in the years following 1462 it caused no revolution in publishers' choice of material. There were, for instance, sixty-four main printed editions of Latin works before 1500; of these, five were published in Germany, one in France and all the rest in Italy. Similarly with regard to Greek authors, sixty-two editions appeared in Italy before 1530, not one having been issued from a press of any other country. But the spread of learning was to alter the balance. By 1550 Italy was losing her premier position: between 1532 and 1544 only two editions were published in Italy as against seven at Basel; between 1545 and 1557 six came from Italy, eight from Paris, one from Basel and one from Zürich. England had no place at all in this branch of output. Much the same is true of service books. Out of a hundred-and-five editions of the Sarum missal in the British Museum printed before 1540 only twenty-four are of English origin, sixty-seven of them are French, and many even of the English ones are embellished with ornaments borrowed from France.

The truth was that at the time of the invention of printing England was economically of little importance. She was a mainly agricultural country, still behind the Netherlands and France in her greatest manufacturing industry, cloth-making, and relying on her raw wool as the chief means of commercial intercourse. She had no town to compare with the great cities of Venice and Genoa. She had taken no part as yet in the new voyages of discovery. In the matter of material wealth she came far after Italy and Spain. The revival of learning, spreading northwards and westwards from Italy, reached her after the rest of Europe had become readjusted to the new intellectual spirit. Thus when Caxton set up his press at Westminster in 1476 he had to find some sheltered branch of the trade from which he could confront a well-established foreign competition. There was a very small market for works of classical scholarship, and in any case the fact of England's being off the main trade routes caused a relative difficulty in procuring manuscripts. Caxton therefore devoted himself to satisfying the surest home demand, which at this time was for romance literature. Of the hundred or more works which he published before his death in 1491 the most famous are the *Canterbury Tales*, the *Morte d'Arthur*, *Aesop's Fables*, *Reynard the Fox* and the *Golden Legend*. His success in these undertakings was assured through the patronage of the well-to-do; his early appointments as Governor to the English Nation at Bruges and as steward to Margaret, Duchess of Burgundy, together with his close connection with the Mercers' Company, provided him with influential friends in his publishing career, so that we find him issuing the *Golden Legend*, for instance, at the desire of the Earl of Arundel, who promised to buy several copies and also to pay him an annuity of a buck in summer and a doe in winter.

Caxton's business was carried on after his death by his foreman, Wynkyn de Worde, who produced about eight hundred works in the forty years of his career. Most of them were small pamphlets, so that in the aggregate his output was not very great. Actually, at the opening of the sixteenth century the English printing industry had still to develop. It has been estimated that the number of printers in the world during the fifteenth century was about fifteen hundred, in about two hundred and thirty-six places.[5] Italy accounted for seventy-one of these towns, Germany for fifty, France for thirty-six, Spain for twenty-six, Holland for fourteen. The largest individual firm was that of Anthoni Koberger, of Nuremberg, who in 1500 had over a hundred employees engaged in printing Bibles and theological works; he had agencies in Frankfurt, Paris and Lyons, and carried on business in the Netherlands, France, Italy, Austria, Poland and, to some extent, in England. During the fifteenth century there were only four presses in the whole of England, in London, Oxford and St. Albans. In 1500 there were three master printers, all in London, and all aliens. The first Oxford University Press had come to an end in 1485, and the second, destined to last for only three years, was not set up until 1517. Scotland and Ireland were still without presses. It was not until 1507 that James IV of Scotland gave leave to Walter Chepman and Andrew Myllar to import a printing-press and type to print law books, breviaries and other works associated with the office of a king's printer. Irish printing seems to have begun in 1550. In that year Humphrey Powell was authorised to set up his press.[6]

Whereas the supremacy of Italian printing in the fifteenth century could be partly attributed to freedom from Government restrictions, the French position was attained through deliberate encouragement by the State. In 1369 Charles V of France granted exemption from all taxation to every person engaged in making or selling books, including even such specialists as illuminators and parchment-makers. The possibilities of tax evasion thus opened up were too tempting; in 1384 further regulations were needed to except from this privilege any book dealers who carried on for gain any other occupation. This policy continued even after the introduction of printing. In 1553 Henry II freed all books from customs duties and the *octroi*.

The English fifteenth-century attitude to the book trade was liberal at a time when a mercantile policy was developing in other industrial fields. In 1463, for instance, the importation of woollen cloth and of certain other manufactured goods was prohibited in the supposed interests of home industry. The policy in regard to book production was different simply because there was as yet nothing to protect. An Act of 1484 for the regulation of conditions under which foreigners carried on business in England, therefore, contained a clause which established free trade in books: "this Act or any parcel thereof, or any other Act made or to be made in this said parliament, shall not extend, or be in prejudice, disturbance, damage or impediment to any artificer or merchant stranger, of what nation or country he be, or shall be of, for bringing into this realm, or selling by retail or otherwise, any books written or printed, or for inhabiting within this said realm for the same intent, or any scrivener, illuminor, binder or printer of such books, which he hath or shall have to sell by way of merchandise, or for their dwelling within this said realm for the exercise of the said occupations." Approximately two-thirds of the persons connected with the English book trade until about 1535 were aliens, and except for William Caxton and Thomas Hunte of Oxford no Englishman issued a single book until about 1516.[7] The official King's Printers to Henry VII, William Faques and his successor, Richard Pynson, were themselves both Normans.

The success of foreign printers was not to continue unchallenged in an age when a new national consciousness was arising. The growing jealousy of aliens made itself felt against printers as against other craftsmen; Pynson was only one of those who suffered ceaseless opposition. As the possibilities of the new industry came to be realised the free-trade policy gradually gave way to one of protection. The alien was handicapped at the outset by having to pay double subsidies, but in 1523 a Bill was passed which affected him more vitally; this Act forbade any alien to take any but English-born apprentices or to keep more than two foreign journeymen; it also put every alien under the control of the warden of his craft. There was already a custom whereby the members of the Craft of Stationers were debarred from taking foreigners as apprentices; thus it happened that it became impossible for an alien to be apprenticed to the printing trade, or, consequently, to become a member of the Stationers' Company. An Act of 1529 was directed against undenizened aliens, that is, those who had not obtained the right to live and trade as natives, forbidding them for the future to set up "any house, shop or chambre wherein they shall occupy any handy craft within this realm." It was the Act "for prynters and Bynders of Bokes," 1534, which really brought the book industry under national control; it began by repealing the Act I. Ric. III. c.9, which had allowed the free importation of books, and ordained that "noo person or persones recyant or inhabytaunt within this Realme . . . shall bye to sell agayn any prynted bokes brought frome any partes out of the Kynges obeysaunce redy bounden in bourdes lether or perchement"; its next ruling was that "no person . . . shall by within this Realme of any Stranger borne out of the Kynges obedyence other than of denyzens, any maner of pryntyd bokes brought frome any the parties behonde the See, except only by engrose and not by retayle." If we add to these restrictions the order issued in 1555 by the Mayor and Commonalty of London to the effect that no citizen should employ a foreigner except in certain trades, which did not include printing or bookselling, the essentially English character of the names of the freemen enrolled in 1557 in the charter of the Stationers' Company is in no way surprising.

In this way the English printer lost that foreign rivalry which might have compelled technical improvement. English sixteenth-century printing was lamentably bad in comparison with the products of the press of Aldus Manutius at Venice, Johann Froben at Basel, the Estiennes in Paris, or Christophe Plantin at Antwerp. In exceptional cases the employment of aliens had to be allowed to make up for the deficiencies of the native workman; in 1574, for instance, Thomas Vautrollier was granted letters patent to print seven works in Latin, with the special privilege of engaging "six woorkemen Frenchmen or Duchemen, or suche lyke, for the sayd space and terme of tenne yeres wythout any lett or dysturbance."[8] With regard to bookbinders there were fewer restrictions, and all the best binding during the sixteenth century was done by foreigners, of whom Thomas Berthelet was the most noteworthy. Even here jealousy arose by the end of the century. In 1597 the freemen bookbinders of London complained to the Lord Mayor about this competition, and consequently the Court of Aldermen decreed that every alien who had served as a journeyman bookbinder should be allowed to serve as a journeyman for the rest of his life, but should never keep a shop or work for himself as a binder.[9]

The effect of this narrow policy was not, after all, to foster English industry, but rather to drive some of the best work abroad. A case in point was the printing of Matthews's Bible in 1538: Grafton and Whitchurch, who held the royal patent, obtained special permission to print this edition in Paris, because there were in France better printers and better paper than could be had in England. The Inquisition put a stop to the work for a time, but the Bible was completed by 1539 through the bringing over of French workmen and materials to London. Sir Thomas More submitted his works to a Basel firm for the sake of securing skilled production and a wider circulation for his books. Cardinal Wolsey himself, on founding a school at Ipswich in 1524, allowed its Latin grammar to be supplied from the press of Arnold Birckmann at Antwerp.[10]

Our importation of books was directly dependent on the religious views of the governing classes. The English books printed in Basel, Geneva, Zürich, Augsburg, Cologne, Nuremberg and other continental towns in the sixteenth century were mainly theological. As we have seen, in the first part of the century service books were mostly produced abroad. The progress of the Reformation and the accompanying suppression of Catholic devotional works had therefore a serious effect on the continental printers who specialised in this trade. In Paris not a single Sarum missal was printed between 1534 and 1554. From that date there was a brief revival ending with the reign of the Catholic Queen Mary. The bitter religious controversies of this period were carried on by the exchange of pamphlets between temporarily orthodox writers and holders of the opposite views who found it expedient to seek printers abroad. There was a large sale for this imported literature, in spite of a proclamation of 1542 commanding that "no person shall bring into the realm any English book printed beyond sea concerning Christian religion, nor shall sell any English book printed beyond sea without the King's special license."[11] The works of Knox were published mainly in Geneva until the accession of Elizabeth. From then it was the Catholics who published abroad, the main activity being in answers to the "Apologia Ecclesiae Anglicanae" of Bishop Jewel. These were issued from Antwerp and Louvain. After the sacking of Antwerp by Spanish troops in 1576 the town lost its supremacy in printing as in all its other economic activities, and Louvain and Douay were from this time the chief publishing centres for Catholic works. By the end of the century there existed another party of religious refugees, the extreme Puritans. Their works were mostly printed at Middelburg.

While it was unsafe for a printer to attempt to supply theological works without being sure of the Government attitude, in the case of purely political treatises he had to be still more wary. Throughout the Tudor period the great aim of the Council was to maintain peace; the fear of popular risings caused the Government to deal severely with any suggestion of sedition. Hidden meanings were looked for in the most innocent of publications, so that the printer who was considering the issue of a new work had to calculate not only the risks of monetary failure but also the possibility of losing his life as a result of his project. The Act of 1534, though directed against aliens, was ostensibly concerned with them especially as being possible introducers of seditious literature. Even the granting of a charter to the Stationers' Company in 1557 appears to have been in large measure an attempt to ensure full governmental control over the products of the printing-press. From this time the printer was more sure of his position, as by submitting a work to the wardens of the Company and having it entered in their register he secured permission to print it and passed on the responsibility to the Company as a whole. In 1586 a Star Chamber decree forbade the printing of a book by anybody except the Queen's Printer until it had been read by the Archbishop of Canterbury or the Bishop of London, or both of them, except in the case of law books, which were to be licensed by the two Chief Justices and the Chief Baron, or any two of them. This policy was essentially political in import, but it had definite economic repercussions. The printer-publisher was given a surer idea as to the field in which it was safe to compete. But, on the other hand, the delay involved by licensing, often amounting to three months and sometimes to two or three years, must seriously have diminished the sales and therefore the publication of works of a more fleeting interest. As for those so-called seditious works which it was intended to suppress, experience showed that import restrictions were not so rigorously observed as to hinder them from being printed abroad.

By the beginning of the seventeenth century the English printers could meet their continental rivals on more even terms, but this was not due to progress at home so much as to a falling from the previously high standard abroad. The earlier European printers had also been scholars. One of the most notable, Johann Froben (Frobenius) of Basel, who published from 1491 to 1528, gathered round him a band of learned advisers, including Erasmus himself, who lived in the publisher's house; these acted as general editors and press correctors. Aldus Manutius, who set up his printing-house in Venice in 1494, also maintained a number of assistants competent to edit Greek texts. Robert and Henri Estienne, of Paris and Geneva, and Christophe Plantin, of Antwerp, especially call for mention in considering these fifteenth- to sixteenth-century scholar-printers. England could boast of no names such as these. The only really outstanding printer here was John Day, who published about three hundred important works between 1546 and 1584 under the patronage of Archbishop Parker, and who is noteworthy as having cut the first fount of Anglo-Saxon type. From about 1600 it was the purely commercial printer who was predominant, abroad as well as at home. The Elzevirs, it is true, issued handy editions of the classics from Leyden and Amsterdam throughout the seventeenth century, but they apparently had not sufficient depth of learning to publish any but the already well-known texts. In quality of production the Continent had sunk to the English level, while in quantity of output England had gained ground. As contrasted with the one or two master printers in business at the opening of the sixteenth century there were in 1635 twenty-three; and, as we shall see, this number was artificially low.

The prosperity of any branch of economic activity is directly affected by the prevalence of war, and this is surely nowhere more true than in the case of the book industry. In Mr. G. H. Putnam's opinion[12] certain classes of works, such as philosophy and poetry, need to be read at leisure; there is little demand for them in times of civil and religious strife; hence the decline in such publications in Germany during the Reformation period. We have seen that Venice attained its publishing supremacy largely owing to its immunity from war influences. In Germany, on the other hand, the book trade of such important centres as Frankfurt and Leipzig

Typographus. Der Buchdrucker.

ARte mea reliquas illuſtro Typographus artes,
Imprimo dum varios ære micante libros.
Quæ prius aucta ſitu, quæ puluere plena iacebant,
Vidimus obſcura nocte ſepulta premi.

Hæc veterum renouo neglecta volumina Patrum
Atq; ſcolis curo publica facta legi.
Artem prima nouam reperiſſe Moguntia fertur,
Vrbs grauis, & multis ingenioſa modis.
Qua nihil vtilius videt, aut precioſius orbis,
Vix melius quicquam ſecla futura dabunt.

THE HAND-PRESS
From *De Artibus Mechanicis* (drawn by Jost Amman)

was completely disorganised by the Thirty Years' War (1618–1648). In England the comparatively peaceful sixteenth century allowed for a steady output of belles-lettres as well as of theological and devotional works, but the Civil War brought complete chaos to the industry. The abolition of the Star Chamber in 1641 meant the lapse of its decrees, and left the printing industry suddenly freed from restrictions. The unprivileged classes of stationers seized this new opportunity to infringe patents; licensing rules were ignored, and publications succeeded one another rapidly without any corresponding increase in the number of entries in the Stationers' Register. Parliament became alarmed at the nature of the new pamphlets, and in 1643 issued a reactionary ordinance authorising the master and wardens of the Stationers' Company, the Serjeant of the House of Commons, and others, to search for and seize unlicensed printing-presses, and instituting a new and more rigorous system of censorship. It was the working of this ordinance which brought Milton to write his *Areopagitica, or Speech for the liberty of unlicensed printing* (1644), in the issue of which he disregarded all publishing decrees by neglecting to have it licensed or to mention the name of the printer. Times were too troubled for parliamentary interference to have much effect in keeping down the number of controversial pamphlets and news sheets. In the eagerness to publish, everything was sacrificed to speed. As far as the art of printing is concerned, these are the worst years in history; the existing type was too scarce for this suddenly increased output of books, and thus we find many founts used indiscriminately in the same work. Although the restrictions on type-founding had lapsed with the rest, the knowledge that on the restoration of order they would probably be reimposed may have discouraged the multiplication of type. In addition, the small printers who rushed in were apparently men of little learning or taste. Apart from Humphry Moseley's editions of the works of such writers as Milton, Shakespeare, Beaumont and Fletcher, there was little which was not marred by careless workmanship.

Thus the middle of the seventeenth century found the English book industry in a broken-down condition. Its recovery was hindered by further catastrophes. In 1662 a Licensing Bill was passed by which the Crown usurped the authority of the Stationers' Company, following this in 1663 with the creation of a new office, the Surveyorship of the Imprimery and Printing Presses. This was a complete departure from the traditional method of press regulation. Hitherto the Crown had always used the Company as the instrument for carrying out its policy, not without some consideration for the interests of that body; but under the surveyorship of Roger L'Estrange the Company lost all administrative power. Two years later there came the plague, which, besides causing the death of many of those connected with the trade, meant the almost entire closing down of bookshops. The culminating disaster was the Great Fire of 1666: this not only involved the destruction of printing-presses and stores of paper in various parts of the city, but also completely destroyed the chief bookselling quarter, St. Paul's Churchyard, together with great stocks of books which had been carried into the Church for safety. Pepys, writing in his diary on the 26th of September of that year, estimated the loss of books alone to amount to about £150,000. Not until the eighteenth century was there a real revival of the industry. The Oxford University Press was alone in maintaining a good standard of production during the second half of the seventeenth century, and the output even of this firm averaged only about thirty books a year.

CHAPTER II

The Demand for Books

"Laymen," wrote Richard de Bury, Bishop of Durham, "to whom it matters not whether they look at a book turned wrong side upwards or spread before them in its natural order, are altogether unworthy of any communion with books."[1] Fortunately for the book trade, the century and a half which elapsed before the introduction of printing saw a notable improvement in the literacy of the lay population.

The Educational Background

The educational institutions of mediaeval England had, it is true, been designed to train their pupils for one of the learned professions; if not for the Church, then for law or medicine, rather than for production and trade. But education was not confined to the universities and schools. The feudal lords may have had no need for classical scholarship, but preparation for knighthood involved education of a more general kind. The centre for this training in chivalry was the castle. Here from the age of seven to fourteen the children of the higher families were gathered to learn a little religion, to learn to read, if their mothers had not already taught them, and, for the rest, to be instructed in all those sports and social arts which were to form so large a part of their adult life. This more spectacular side of the life of the man of rank may have blinded the eyes of Bishop de Bury to his quieter cultural aspects. There is little doubt that the sixteenth-century men of fashion who delighted in writing amorous verse were keeping alive a tradition formed by earlier poets of chivalry.[2]

The rest of the rural population, consisting for the most part of peasantry, had little opportunity to improve their station in life. The Statute of Apprentices of 1406 was designed to keep them in their places; it forbade them, unless they owned a specified amount of land, to apprentice their children to trades and manufactures in the towns. But one thing it did allow. No matter what his rank, any man was to be free to send his sons and daughters to any school he pleased to learn "literature," which we may take to mean Latin.

By the fifteenth century there was arising a practical need for knowledge of at least reading and writing. Moreover, it was almost as essential to understand Latin as English. This was true not only of priests, physicians and lawyers, but also of many of those who had no connection with the learned professions. To the merchant Latin provided a medium for transactions at the international fairs. Even at home it was the language in which the shopkeeper ordinarily kept his accounts; the earliest complete bookseller's account-book which has been discovered, that of John Dorne of Oxford (1520), has most of its items entered in Latin, although a few amusing lapses into Dutch rather interfere with the accuracy of his totals. Fifteenth-century tradesmen, too, had kept written accounts. A number of the bills presented to New College, Oxford, during several years in that century are evidence that artisans and quite small men of business knew how to write, and could therefore read.[3] The craftsman, liable to be elected to office in his small local gild, was not fitted for his task unless he could read and help to keep the records of his fraternity, which, again, might be in Latin.

Whatever benefits the printing-press has conferred upon modern education there is no doubt that the English educational system was well established by the time Gutenberg performed his miracle. Of the universities, Oxford dates from the early twelfth century and Cambridge from the thirteenth; and a writ of Henry III dated 1231 refers to the "multitude" of students at Cambridge.[4] The history of the public schools begins a century and a half after this: Winchester College was founded in 1387, followed by Eton College in 1441, and, about the same time, by St. Anthony's, the chief London school of the fifteenth and sixteenth centuries. During the Wars of the Roses there was a slight setback: part of the Eton endowment was taken away in 1463, and the college was

annexed to St. George's, Windsor; it was re-established four years later, but with revenues so diminished that for the future it was impossible to reserve the school for the poor and needy for whom it had been originally endowed. During the sixteenth century a number of other public schools were established: St. Paul's, the Mercers', Christ's Hospital, Westminster (refounded in 1540), Merchant Taylors', Rugby and Harrow. Dean Colet's ruling as to the admission of boys to St. Paul's School shows that they were expected to be able to read and write already: "If your chylde can rede and wryte his own lessons, then he shalbe admytted into the schole for a scholer."[5]

Whatever the original plan of the public schools they came after a time to be associated with the wealthier classes. For the new middle class, the families of rising merchants, there were the city grammar schools. There was an ample supply of them. It has been estimated that in the late fourteenth century there were already at least ten such schools to each county. For the whole population of roughly two and a quarter millions, that is to say, there were about four hundred.[6] As regards grammar schools, indeed, the country was better provided then than in modern times. The Government inquiry into chantries and the continuance of schools (1546) brought to light the fact that there was approximately one school for every 8,300 people. In 1865 the report of the Schools Inquiry Commission showed that the population had outstripped the rate of increase in schools so that there was now only one school for every 23,000 people. London, for its population of 44,000, had in the year 1546 at least three schools besides St. Paul's: St. Anthony's, St. Martin's-le-Grand and St. Mary-le-Bow. The term "grammar school" denoted any one of seven types of school, being either independent or connected respectively with cathedral churches, monasteries, collegiate churches, hospitals, gilds or chantries.[7] The fees were usually so low as to draw not only the younger sons of the nobility but also the children of tradesmen and small landowners. For instance, the chantry certificate for Blabroke, in the parish of Newland, Gloucester, stated that the chantry was founded "to the entent to manteigne a discrete priest, beyng sufficiently lerned in the arte of Gramer, to Kepe a Gramer scoole half Free; that ys to seye, taking of scolers lerning gramer, 8d. the quarter, and of others lerning to rede, 4d. the quarter."[8] It is not surprising to read that this particular school was "very well Haunted." In fact, the school attendance rolls of some of the most remote districts would compare favourably with those of many country schools of the present day. The grammar school of Campden, Gloucester, is recorded by the Commissioners as having usually between sixty and eighty scholars. The parishes of Chesterford, Gosfield and Walden, Essex, had about twenty, forty and sixty school-children respectively, while Blisworth, Northamptonshire, had thirty.

The existence of these schools throughout the country ensured a steady demand for certain textbooks. Greatest of all was the demand for Latin Grammars. The curriculum of the public school and grammar school alike consisted of Latin, dialectic and rhetoric, being planned to enable the boys to proceed to a university or enter one of the professions when about sixteen years old. It was hardly calculated to fill them with a love of reading for its own sake. Dean Colet, in building up St. Paul's School, had no time for such works as "ratheyr may be called blotterature thenne literature," which, he ruled with emphasis, "I utterly abbanysh and exclude oute of this scole, and charge the Maisters that they teche [always what] is the best and instruct the chyldren in greke and laten, in Redyng unto them suych auctours that hathe with wisdome joyned the pure chaste eloquence."[9] The exclusion of "blotterature," although it may have discouraged the supply of light reading, did in the meantime provide the bookseller with a safe field of enterprise. The publication of one of the prescribed classics or grammars was one of the least speculative branches of the book industry. Between 1518 and 1533, for instance, Robert Whittington produced thirteen Latin grammars, and they all ran into several editions. At Ipswich Grammar School, which may be taken as typical, the prescribed authors were Aesop, Terence, Virgil, Cicero, Sallust, Caesar, Horace and Ovid, to be supplemented by Lily's Grammar and the Donatus. A popular schoolbook of the late sixteenth and early seventeenth centuries was the *Bucolica* of Mantuanus, which was prescribed as a textbook in the original statutes of St. Paul's, St. Bees' and Durham schools.

All of this makes one wonder whether the schoolboys of the sixteenth century could have been really human. John Stow reassures us, although his intention is to describe the learned debates which were carried on every year on St. Bartholomew's Eve by scholars from the various grammar schools. They took place in the priory churchyard at Smithfield in the presence of the masters and other scholars. It happened for many years that St. Anthony's Hospital won the contest, so that by Elizabeth's reign the boys of St. Paul's felt bound to prove their natural superiority. Therefore, "the schollers of Paules meeting with them of S. Anthonies, would call them Anthonie pigs and they againe would call the other pigeons of Paules, because many pigeons were bred in Paules church, and Saint Anthonie was always figured with a pig following him, and, mindfull of the former usage, did for a long season disorderly in the open streete provoke one another with *salve tu quoque! placet tibi mecum disputare. Placet.* And so proceeding from this to questions in grammar, they usually fell from wordes to blows, with their satchels full of bookes, many times in great heaps that they troubled the streets and passengers; so that finally they were restrained with the decay of St. Anthonies schole."[10] There was little risk, evidently, that one copy of a textbook would serve for succeeding generations of boys!

There was ample provision for learning to read for all those who wished for it. Those who had not the means to attend the grammar schools were catered for in free schools or by the teaching of the local priest. Of the 259 schools mentioned in the warrants for the continuance of schools, 1546–8, forty-five provided only a rudimentary education. The village schoolmaster was usually well advanced in years. Thus the chantry certificate for Launceston, Cornwall, puts on record "13s. 4d. yerly distributed to an aged man chosen by the mayre to teache yonge chylderne the ABC."[11]

In dealing with the city of Hereford, again, mention is made of "Sir Phylipe Hye, of the age of 4 score yeres, incombent, beinge a ryght honest man indyfferently lerned, and taketh paynes in kepying of a scole and bryngyng up of chylderne."[12] The textbook which for many years was in general use was *The ABC and Little Catechism*, for which John Day was granted a publishing patent. Some idea of the demand for this book may be gathered from the fact that in 1585 Thomas Dunn and Robert Robinson disposed of ten thousand copies of it within eight months.[13] But it is doubtful whether there was any great thirst for knowledge among the poor. An eighty-year-old incumbent was hardly the person to make the learning of the alphabet attractive to young children. The Commissioners of 1546 seem at times almost to have despaired of the rural intellect. In writing of the parish of Bodmin, Cornwall, which had a population of two thousand, they remark that part of the duty of the priest is to teach children grammar, and comment feelingly, "A very meate place for a learned man to be . . . goodes worde, for the lorde knoweth the said twoo thousand people are Very Ignoraunt."[14]

The biggest demand for editions of the classics was to be expected from the universities, which were still influenced by the opinion of Roger Bacon and others that true learning consisted of the accurate knowledge of a text. There were, according to William Harrison (1577), about three thousand students at a time in the universities of Oxford and Cambridge, and, from his account, many of them seem to have looked upon their higher education as a life work: "From our entrance into the university unto the last degree received is commonly eighteen or twenty years, in which time, if a student has not obtained sufficient learning thereby to serve his own turn and benefit his commonwealth, let him never look by tarrying longer to come by any more. For after this time, and forty years of age, the most part of students do commonly give over their wonted diligence, and live like drone bees on the fat of colleges, withholding better wits from the possession of their places, and yet doing little good in their own vocation and calling."[15] A large body of students and fellows keeping up their "wonted diligence" until the age of forty should have had quite an appreciable effect on the book market.

Besides the purchases of books by individual students there were, of course, those of the college libraries. In common with the monastery and cathedral libraries the university collections suffered severe losses at the time of the Reformation, the books belonging to Corpus Christi, Trinity Hall, King's and St. Catherine's Colleges, Cambridge, being almost entirely destroyed. From about 1545 onwards Archbishop Parker and others worked at their restoration, Parker finally bequeathing the whole of his own library to Corpus Christi College, Cambridge. The work of Sir Thomas Bodley in building up his great library at Oxford during the closing years of the sixteenth century is too well known to need more than a passing mention. But despite all the interest taken in the reconstruction of these university collections, it cannot be claimed that the colleges had much direct influence on the book trade. Their libraries were built up almost entirely through private bequests. During the reign of Mary, indeed, apart from service books not a single work was bought for any of the Oxford or Cambridge colleges.[16] By the college authorities the library seems to have been valued as a convenient gaol rather than as a store of learning. There was a case at Lincoln College, Oxford, in the year 1611, which illustrates this point: "Whereas Sir Baber was found corrigible . . . for his disobedience and misdemenor . . . the Rector did injoyne him the punishment in forme following, viz., to studie in the Librarie every day in the week, except Saterday or holy daye, or his answering daye, for the space of two howers in the day, viz., from 8 till 9 in the forenoone, and from 1 till 2 in the afternoone, and this for the space of a moneth."[17] Thirteen years later a certain Matthew Watson, of the same college, was in trouble for his "notorious inebriety." Although he argued that "to err is human, that if he daily took water, the strength of his body would be diminished," the verdict ran that he was "either to bring a certificate of his good behaviour from the place where hee then abode, or else presently to returne to the college, and to bee confined to the librarie."[18]

Purchasing Power in the Sixteenth and Seventeenth Centuries

Given the general ability to read, the demand for books on the part of private individuals was obviously determined above all else by the state of their finances. This was, unfortunately, specially poor in the case of clergy and teachers. The annual stipend of a priest (who frequently acted also as schoolmaster) ranged in general from about £10 to £20, with the surrender of a year's income to the Crown on his induction to a living and an annual tax of one-tenth thereafter. The chantry certificate for Blabroke, Gloucester (1546), describes the incumbent and schoolmaster as having "no other lyving then in the seid chauntry, which ys yerely, £11." The incumbent of the chantry of Bishop Alcock, Kingston-upon-Hull, was granted £10 a year and was specifically forbidden to accept payment from his pupils. The priest of St. Michael's, Cornhill, received only £8 a year. Payment was little better at the universities: the income of the Vice-Chancellor of St. John's College, Cambridge, in the middle of the sixteenth century was £12, while the fellows of King's College, Cambridge, received only about £5 13s. 4d. a year. The average pay of a schoolmaster at that time was £6 9s. 6d.[19] The schoolmaster at Wotton Underhedge, Gloucester, received the remarkable sum of £10 1s. 7¼d., being a few pence more than the amount paid to the master of Eton College. The salary of the master of the College of Jesu, Rotherham, is set down as "for his stipend, £10; for his gowne clothe 12s.; for fyre to his chamber, 3s. 4d.; his barber and launder free."[20] It might be thought that these low incomes could be explained entirely in terms of differences in the value of money between the sixteenth century and the present day. That this is not so is clear from the terms of appointment of Christopher Ocland to the headmastership of St. Olave's, Southwark, in 1571: he was engaged at the comparatively high salary of twenty marks (£13 6s. 8d.), but was allowed to add to his income by taking boarders, "for that twenty marks was not sufficiente lyving."[21]

The bookseller's custom arising from these professions was, therefore, very limited. But, in any case, we must not take too idealistic a view of the learning of the English clergy at this time. According to contemporary evidence (1577) it left much to be desired. It seems to have been quite a usual practice for livings to be given to servants in place of wages: some patrons "do bestow advowsons of benefices upon their bakers, butlers, cooks, good archers, falconers, and horsekeepers, instead of other recompense, for their long and faithful service."[22] In part this may be accounted for by the religious uncertainties of the century: a theological argument accepted as orthodox in one decade might lead to the stake in the next. It was no wonder that the traditional type of intellectual priest was giving way to a body of apathetic ministers who had no opinions to express. When the number of vacant livings was so great that a hundred and fifty priests had to be ordained in one day, as happened in 1559, selection from among the candidates was out of the question.

This quotation incidentally illustrates a further point—the poverty of the nobility. They were notoriously in debt. Elizabeth herself was reduced to rewarding her favourites and paying her servants by appointing them to office or granting them patents of monopoly; her Stuart successors were in worse straits. The difficulty of the nobles in obtaining the repayment of their loans to the Crown, added to their general impoverishment through the Wars of the Roses, the debasing of the coinage, and their own wild extravagance, made it equally impossible for them to pay their own retainers. Their lack of means was specially regrettable from our point of view in that the courtiers formed probably the most intellectual class of the day. "It is a rare thing with us now to hear of a courtier which hath but his own language," writes Harrison; "and to say how many gentlemen and ladies there are that besides sound knowledge of the Greek and Latin tongues are thereto no less skilful in the Spanish, Italian, and French, or in some one of them, it resteth not in me."[23] Sir Walter Raleigh was not the only traveller who always carried a trunk full of books on his voyages. It was unfortunate for the book trade that this class of all others was finding it necessary to economise, although the custom whereby the courtier circulated manuscript copies of his literary works must in any case have diminished to some extent the demand for the printed book. Against this it must be agreed that the Government servant, at least, must have felt the need of a knowledge of the more important publications of the day. His income was usually high in comparison with that of the schoolmaster or priest: Thomas Edmonds, for instance, was appointed Secretary for the French Tongue in 1596 at a salary of £66 13s. 4d.; but by virtue of his public office his expenses would, no doubt, be correspondingly high.

According to Harrison, the one truly wealthy class consisted of the lawyers, "of whom some one having practised little above thirteen or fourteen years is able to buy a purchase of so many one thousand pounds." There was, in fact, a bigger market for law books than for any others among the more serious works. Certain books, such as the *Year-books, The Great Abridgment of the Statutes* and Lyttelton's *Tenures* were the indispensable tools of the profession. Merchants and yeomen farmers, too, were among the more prosperous men of the day, although in certain districts the yeomen were threatened with ruin by the workings of the agrarian revolution; but a demand for books was not implied in the same way by the nature of their calling.

As regards the working-classes, there seems to have been little to spare for anything beyond the bare necessities of life. Wage-earners were still in the minority in this period, but such wages as were paid were rigidly restricted by law or by gild regulations. The Act 6 Hen. VIII. ch. III., for instance, limited the payment of the bailiff of husbandry to 26s. 8d. a year together with meat, drink and 5s. for clothing; the shepherd was to receive 20s. a year, 4s. for clothing, and meat and drink; carpenters, masons and bricklayers were given from Easter to Michaelmas a maximum of 4d. a day with, or 6d. without, food, and a penny a day less for the rest of the year.

It is quite clear, then, that apart from school texts the publishing trade had to cater for a very limited market. Robert Copland, compiler and printer of *The Seven Sorowes that Women have when theyr Husbandes be Deade* (1525), may have been recording an actual experience when, in the course of an imaginary conversation with Quidam, he offered him a certain book for 4d.: Quidam's reply was, "A peny I trow is ynough on bokes. It is not so soon goten, as this world lokes."[24]

So far it has been assumed that all those who could read and had money to spare would choose to buy books. Actually this was no more true of the sixteenth and seventeenth centuries than it is of the present day. Copland took a very mournful view of the popular taste: the prologue to *The Castell of Pleasure* (1518) runs:

Author: ". . . Emprynt this boke, Copland, at my request,
And put it forth to every maner state."
Copland: "At your instaunce I shall it gladly impresse,
But the utterance, I thynke, will be but small.
Bokes be not set by: there tymes is past, I gesse;
The dyse and cardes, in drynkynge wyne and ale,
Tables, cayles, and balles, they be now sette a sale.
Men lete theyr chyldren use all such harlotry,
That byenge of bokes they utterly deny."

There were two main reasons for the neglect of reading. In the first place, it demands leisure, and working hours in those times were long. The Act of 1514, already mentioned, regulated not only wages but also hours of work, ordering that "every artificer and laborer be at werke between the myddle of the moneth of Marche and the myddle of the moneth of September before V. of the Cloke in the mornyng, And that he have but half an hower for his brekefast, and an houre and half for his dyner at suche tyme as he hath season for slepe to hym appoynted by the said estatute; And that he departe not from his werke betwene the myddle of the seid monethes of Marche and September till betwene vij and viij of the Clok in the evenyng . . .; And that from the myddle of September to the myddle of Marche every Artificer and laborer be at their Werke in the spryngyng of the day and departe not till nyght of the same day; And that the seid Artificers and laborers slepe not by day but only from the myddle of the moneth of May unto the myddell of August." Taking into consideration also the workman's gild activities, unless he dispensed with his midday nap he could have had little time to devote to reading. Nor was it only the manual workers who began their work early: shops were open by seven o'clock, and the Privy Council met at eight.

Counter-attractions to Reading

The second cause of slackness in the book trade was the existence of counter-attractions to reading. These were almost as varied as at the present day. As regards the wealthy, the ideal very often aimed at was magnificence in dress and food, involving reckless expenditure of both money and time. The more vigorous could spend their leisure in hunting, hawking, archery, dancing, or in ball games, of which tennis appealed specially to the aristocrats and golf and hockey to the poorer classes. This, too, was the period of the formal garden, whose cultivation provided an engrossing interest for many of the nobility, although the less patient among them tried to take a short cut by using coloured soils. The great social asset of rich and poor alike was music; the singing of madrigals filled many of the hours that the customs of another age might have given up to reading, while, to judge from the advertisements issued by the city of London regarding the qualifications of boys educated in Bridewell and Christ's Hospital, musical ability was regarded as a recommendation even for employment as a servant or husbandman. In competition with music and with books was the drama. The gild-pageant was losing its power of attraction, but only in favour of the more elaborate masque and the professional stage. Moreover, play-going was a cheap pastime: admission to a London theatre could be secured for a penny. But none of these pursuits provided that thrill of adventure essential to a restless age. This was found by the more valiant in voyages of discovery, in piracy, or in highway robbery. The rest found their excitement in gambling. Card-playing and dice-throwing were rife in all grades of society, and had such an upsetting influence that it was thought necessary to make them illegal in the case of servants and craftsmen except during the Christmas season.

The Demand for News

There is one form of publication which can always compete with even the lightest of amusements—the newspaper. The gossip-lovers of to-day had their counterpart in the sixteenth and seventeenth centuries. Unfortunately, Tudor caution would not allow the issue of any domestic news, while care had to be taken in describing happenings abroad. So great were the risks that until 1622 few publishers ventured to print any news except in occasional pamphlets, such as *Newes out of Holland* (1619). The first real journals were the *Corantos*, issued from 1622 onwards. These appeared weekly, or twice a week if sufficient news arrived, but, as the public were unaccustomed as yet to the idea of a regular newspaper, each *Coranto* was given a fresh title; this made it clear that the information was different from that in the preceding number. Such as they were, these journals met with an immediate welcome. "Custom" (wrote the author of one of them) "is so predominant in everything that both the Reader and the Printer of these Pamphlets agree in their expectation of Weekly Newes, so that if the Printer have not wherewithall to afford satisfaction, yet will the Reader come and aske every day for new Newes; not out of curiosity or wantonness, but pretending a necessity either to please themselves or satisfie their Customers." But the publication of the *Corantos* was not allowed an uninterrupted run: in 1632 the Star Chamber suspended them, owing to a complaint by the Spanish ambassador; and it was not until 1638 that they were revived by letters patent. The publication of home news was prohibited until 1641. In that year the House of Commons authorised the issue of the first of the *Diurnalls:* "The heads of severall proceedings in this present Parliament from the 22 of November to the 29, 1641." The *Diurnalls* were followed during the next few years by *Weekly Accounts*, *Mercuries*, *Intelligencers* and other accounts of the progress of the Civil War, but there was nothing in the nature of a modern newspaper until the first publication of the *London Gazette*, in 1665.

It is easy enough to prohibit the publication of newspapers as such. It is not so easy to prevent the publisher from attempting to satisfy in some other way the most certain demand of his public. The safest way of doing this was to issue news in the form of fiction. This presented few difficulties, for the news most eagerly welcomed concerned, not abstruse points from parliamentary debates, but murders, fires, monstrous births and such like. Accounts of such events could be given as vividly in ballad form as in any other, and a study of the entries in the Stationers' Register will show that this type of publication far outnumbered all others. Any incident promising to make good copy was promptly registered as the subject of a new ballad. In August 1605, for instance, tales were on foot of the murders committed by a certain John Fitz; within a month three separate versions of the proceedings had been licensed to different printers: "A narration of the bloody murthers Comitted by the handes of Sir John Fyghtes a knight of Devonshire," "A ballett uppon the Lamentable Murthers of Sir John Fytz executed uppon himself and others," and "Sir John Fitz his ghost, or the dolefull Dreames of Lusty Jack his chief Associate and companion in mischief." What modern newspaper could provide more sensational news than this of 1622: "A Discourse of Newes from Prague in Bohemia, of an Husband who by witchcraft had murthered xviij wives, and of a wife who had likewise murthered xix husbands"?

Even bigger than the market for these accounts of amazing events of the past was that for forecasts of still more astounding things to come. The revival of the study of astronomy by the scientists was accompanied by a widespread belief in astrology among the unlearned. To the publisher, therefore, "prognosticating almanacs" came to be "readier money than ale or cakes."[25]

The preponderance of this nonsensical type of literature did not escape the criticism of the more thoughtful men of the day. William Lambarde complained that the whole art of printing was abused by the production of "sundrie bookes, pamfletes, Poesies, ditties, songes, and other woorkes . . . serving . . . to let in a mayne Sea of wickednesse . . . and to no small or sufferable wast[e] of the treasure of this Realme which is thearby consumed and spent in paper, being of it selfe a forrein and chargeable comoditie";[26]

as a remedy he suggested the setting up of a body of twelve men to be called the Governors of the English print, with licensing powers.

It is easy to exaggerate the poor taste of the reading public. To regard the working of the Renaissance in England as entirely without effect would be to belittle the work of Colet, Lily, Latimer, Grocyn and More in the spread of classical knowledge, or of Linacre, physician to Henry VII and Henry VIII, in fostering the science of medicine. It was, in fact, during the sixteenth century that there was founded the first society for the study of English history and antiquities; it met weekly from 1572 to 1604, its members including Archbishop Parker, Sir William Cecil, Sir Nicholas Bacon, Thynne, Camden, Cotton and William Herbert, Earl of Pembroke, besides a number of tradesmen, country gentlemen, schoolmasters, lawyers and clergymen.[27] The Reformation, as one would expect, stimulated the demand for religious works. Caxton, a shrewd business man, was probably right in judging that there would be little sale for Bibles or for theological works in his day. By 1526 there was a definite demand for them: in that year Tyndale published his New Testament, and, although its sale was prohibited by the Council, six editions were exhausted by 1530. From this time a very large proportion of the more serious publications consisted of works of religious controversy.

Nevertheless, the general attitude to books was anything but encouraging to the bookseller. It is aptly illustrated in Bale's preface to *Leland's Journey* (1549): in speaking of the destruction of the monastic libraries he says, "A great number of them which purchased those superstitious mansions, reserved of those library books, some to scour their candlesticks, and some to rub their boots; some they sold to the grocers and soap-sellers; some they sent over sea to the bookbinders, not in small numbers, but at times whole ships full, to the wondering of the foreign nations. . . . I know a merchant man . . . that bought the contents of two noble libraries for forty shillings price; a shame it is to be spoken. This stuff hath he occupied in the stead of grey paper, by the space of more than ten years, and yet he hath store enough for as many years to come!"

Compulsory Demand for Books

This state of affairs was not to be endured by the printer without protest. It seemed to him that if the public could not show a natural interest in books it was the duty of the Government to produce a compulsory demand for them. All unconsciously he was advocating a return to the methods employed in the mediaeval monasteries. In the statutes drawn up by Archbishop Lanfranc for the English Benedictines (1070) was the ruling that "On the Monday after the first Sunday in Lent, before Brethren come into the Chapter House, the librarian shall have a carpet laid down and all the books got together upon it, except those which the year previous had been assigned for reading. These the brethren are to bring with them, when they come into the Chapter House, each his book in his hand. Then the librarian shall read a statement as to the manner in which Brethren have had books during the past year. As each Brother hears his name pronounced, he is to give back the book which had been entrusted to him for reading; and he whose conscience accuses him of not having read through the book which he had received, is to fall on his face, confess his fault, and entreat forgiveness. The librarian shall then make a fresh distribution of books, namely a different volume to each Brother for his reading." It seems improbable that a choice of reading was allowed.

On examination, then, one finds that the orders during the sixteenth century that a copy of the Bible should be placed in every parish church were issued at the behest of the printer, and not through any anxiety as to the religious welfare of the people. When Grafton printed his "Matthew's Bible" in 1537 he wrote to Cromwell asking that it should be commanded "that every curate have one of them, that they may learn to know God and to instruct their parishioners. Yea, and that every abbey should have six, to be laid in six several places"![28] In reply to his request it was ordered that a copy should be placed in every parish church; this guaranteed him a sale of at least fifty-two copies in London alone. Four years later a like order was issued regarding the "Great Bible" of 1540. In this case Anthony Marler, who financed its publication, had sent a petition to the Privy Council in which he laid no claim to a missionary spirit but frankly stated that unless his Bibles were sold he would be ruined.[29] Again, when Archbishop Parker wrote to Cecil in 1568 on sending the Queen the first copy of the "Bishops' Bible" he suggested that "the Printer [Jugge] hath honestlie done his Diligence. Yf your honour wold obteine of the Quenes highnes, that this edicon might be Licensed and only [solely] comended in publike reading in churches . . . yt weare no greate cost to the most parishes and a Relief to him for his great charges susteined."[30] One is left to wonder whether there was any ulterior motive for the Queen's injunction of 1559 that the *Paraphrases of Erasmus* should be bought for every church, the cost being borne by the priest and his parishioners, or for the Act of the Privy Council of April 21, 1582, whereby the study of two poems of Christopher Ocland was made compulsory in all the schools of the realm.

In one direction the attitude of the Government was to become less favourable to the publisher. The growth of Puritanism was accompanied by a decline of the drama, and in 1642 Parliament closed all theatres. Officially they remained closed until 1660, and although the rule was not strictly enforced play-reading fell inevitably out of fashion. Fortunately for the printer, the ban on news publication had been raised in time to provide an even more profitable outlet for his energies.

The New Intellectual Interests of the Seventeenth Century

The greater number of the more serious publications of the first half of the seventeenth century were works of political or religious controversy. Nevertheless, in spite of the general preoccupation with constitutional matters and with arguments between Anglican and Puritan, there was a growing body of writers of scientific interests. In between the quarrels of James I and his Parliament Sir Francis Bacon found time to write his *Novum Organum*. William Harvey, in the meantime, was developing his theory of the circulation of the blood. From now onwards more and more of the entries in the Stationers' Register bear witness to a growing interest in astronomy, mathematics, physiology and mechanics. These divergent interests were brought together by the incorporation of the Royal Society in 1662. The new investigations were not confined to pure science. From 1621, when Thomas Mun published his *Discourse of Trade unto the East Indies*, and more especially from 1664, when he issued his *England's Treasure by Forraign Trade*, the minds of the rising merchants were turned to the problem of the favourable trade balance. Sir William Petty expounded yet another new science in his *Essay concerning Multiplication of Mankind* (1682) and his *Political Arithmetic* (1690).

Access to books had by now become a necessity to the man of the world. Pepys had collected so many of them by 1666 that they were piled on chairs, an inconvenience which, he confessed, prevented him from reading any but the topmost.[31] The Rev. Richard Baxter, by 1691, had gathered together a library of 1,448 volumes.[32] Among them, no doubt, were some of those publications of John Dunton which seem so unaccountably to have become best sellers. One of them, according to Dunton, sold well through being published "at the critical time": it was Jay's *Daniel in the Den*; or, *The Lord President's Imprisonment and Miraculous Deliverance*, issued on the acquittal of Lord Shaftesbury. It seems more difficult to account for the success of the other two works which he printed about the same time (1680): the *Sermon Preached by the Reverend Mr. John Shower at the Funeral of Madam Anne Barnardiston*, which went into three editions, and *The House of Weeping*, a collection of funeral discourses preached by Dunton's father. Dunton's possibly most successful publication was one of the seven which he repented of having printed at all—*The Second Spira* (1693). It had been imposed upon him as the authentic memoirs of a clergyman of the Church of England. In spite of the "deep despair on every page," or perhaps because of it, he sold about thirty thousand copies in six weeks.[33] Any work of a religious nature seemed assured of a market. The whole impression of Ness's *The Life of Pope Innocent XI* sold off in a fortnight,[34] and Dunton printed ten thousand copies both of Lukin's *Practice of*

Godliness and of Keach's *Travels of True Godliness* without recording any regret.

Recalling how serious were the majority of Dunton's publications it is strange to find him rebuked for unseemly frivolity. In 1718 a friend saw fit to remonstrate with him on his growing levity. "Pray look on the title of your Platonic Wedding again," he wrote, "and consider whether any person of common sense, or that knows the polite part of the world, would buy it; and it is they are the greatest readers. Frolic and merry conceits are despised in this nice age. The mentioning the 'Athenian Oracles' will do your Works an injury; for you know they are condemned to long oblivion. What I speak is not in the least to affront you; but if you have Essays or Letters that are valuable, call them Essays and Letters in short and plain language; and if you have any thing writ by men of sense, and on subjects of consequence, it may sell without your name to it; but pray leave out that, and all your female trumpery; for I am in too public a rank not to know the taste of the age; and I can assure you the mentioning of female correspondents and she-wits would ruin the sale of the best Authors we have."[35]

The seventeenth century had seen considerable intellectual growth. But one must beware of attributing the great achievements of what was, after all, a quite small body of enthusiasts to the nation at large. The schools seem to have ignored the new developments altogether. Teaching in the grammar schools was still mainly confined to Latin and Greek, with perhaps a little Hebrew.[36] The founders of local schools for the poor, although they increased in number during the seventeenth century, seem to have been equally lacking in imagination. It was not until 1699, when the Society for Promoting Christian Knowledge set up its charity schools, that the modern type of elementary education began, with its insistence upon "the three R's" as the first essential.

The Eighteenth Century

During the first half of the eighteenth century the charity schools catered for a large section of the community. In 1707 there were already 69 of them in or near London, teaching 2,813 children.[37] Their influence grew steadily for the next twenty years, so that by 1727 there were 1,389 charity schools in England and Wales with 27,854 children attending them. For some reason there was a setback to their activities from this time onwards, and it was not until 1780, when Sunday schools were first established for religious and general education, that the educational needs of the masses again began to receive a little attention. Five years later the Sunday Schools Union was formed to carry on the work on a larger scale, but the rapidly growing population was too much for its valiant efforts. Charles Knight, writing of his childhood in the early nineteenth century, tells us that "not many of the working people could then read the newspapers."[38]

The decline in the numbers of pupils in the middle of the eighteenth century was not confined to the charity schools. In 1751 Winchester had only 8 commoners instead of the 93 in residence in 1737. Westminster from 1765 to the end of the century had only 250 to 300 boys as compared with 434 in 1727, while the numbers at Eton dropped from 500 to 230. Admissions to the universities were necessarily fewer in consequence; the students registered at Oxford fell from the 300 or more of the beginning of the century to below 200.[39] The rising middle class questioned the practical use of the traditional curriculum of the public schools and the universities, but the demand for a modern type of education was met only in part by private academies and boarding schools of doubtful efficiency.

The state of eighteenth-century education was thus hardly sufficient in itself to create a reading public. Nor was the general scale of wages as yet high enough to leave a book-buying surplus. As late as the third quarter of the century twelve pounds a year were still thought sufficient for the year's pay of a schoolteacher,[40] who of all others might be expected to show an interest in literature. Wages were certainly higher than they had been: "it may be affirmed in general," says Josiah Tucker in 1757, "that the Wages of Men . . . is for the most Part, from 1s. to 2s. 6d. per Day: and the Wages of Women from 4d. to 1s. throughout the

Kingdom."[41] At the same time it must be remembered that the cost of living had also increased, so that unless books could be produced at very low prices they would ill be afforded by the working man. The specialisation of industry, with the resultant crop of textbooks to worry the aspiring apprentice, was still a long way ahead.

There was, of course, by this time a wealthy class of considerable size. Whether its members were also book-lovers is another matter. Some of them obviously were. Others, like David Papillon, built up a good library because it was by now the correct accompaniment to a large estate. It is recorded of Papillon that he arranged for a bookseller to supply him with two hundred pounds' worth of books at twopence each. Their subjects did not matter in the least; the only stipulation was that all the books should be in a good state of preservation and that there should be no duplicates.[42] It was for such libraries as those that Sir Hildebrand Jacob, eighteenth-century poet and scholar, spent his summers in searching: "As soon as the roads became pretty good, and the fine weather began to set in, his man was ordered to pack up a few things in a portmanteau, and with these his master and himself set off, without knowing whither they were going. When it drew towards evening, they inquired at the first village they saw, whether the great man in it was a lover of books, and had a fine library. If the answer was in the negative, they went on farther; if in the affirmative, Sir Hildebrand sent his compliments, that he was come to see him; and there he used to stay till time or curiosity induced him to move elsewhere."[43]

There were by now a number of private libraries large enough to attract such a book-lover. Antony Collins, the free-thinker, had collected 6,893 works, in English, Greek, Latin, French and Spanish, covering divinity, history, philosophy and travel. In 1726 the library of John Bridges, late of Lincoln's Inn, was sold for £3,730. In the middle of the century two other important collections were sold, that of Dr. Mead, for £5,496 15s., and the library of Martin Folkes, president of the Royal Society, which brought in £3,091 5s.[44] But the catalogues of these sales give the impression that the contemporary printer was receiving little encouragement from the book-collecting enthusiasts. Dr. Mead's library was largely made up of incunabula and of works printed on vellum. One of them, a large paper Olivet's *Cicero*, was bought by Dr. Askew for £14 14s. to be sold again for £36 15s. The library of Martin Folkes contained similar treasures. This sale, too, was attended by Dr. Askew, and the two fifteenth-century editions of Pliny which he bought there for £11 11s. and £7 17s. 6d. respectively he was able to sell later on for £43 and £23. Was there, perhaps, some truth in Pope's satire on the book-collector of his day?

> His Study! with what Authors is it stor'd?
> In Books, not Authors, curious is my Lord;
> To all their dated Backs he turns you round:
> These Aldus printed, those Du Sueil has bound.
> Lo some are Vellum, and the rest as good
> For all his Lordship knows, but they are Wood.
> For Locke or Milton 'tis in vain to look,
> These shelves admit not any modern book.[45]

It is reassuring to find one eighteenth-century library evidently intended to be read. James West, in his turn president of the Royal Society, possessed 1,200 volumes on divinity, 700 on education and languages, 750 volumes of English poetry and romances and 560 on philosophy, mathematics, agriculture and medicine, as well as about 100 on chemistry and natural history, and a large number on history, heraldry and topography.[46]

The demand for news was still a sure one. No matter how the general habit of reading might change, any newspaper which could offer thrills or anything which would serve for gossip was sure of a wide circulation—as no doubt it always will be. There were in 1724 three daily papers, seven which were published three times a week and six weekly ones, their circulation running into thousands.[47] The Government, casting around for new sources of revenue, had in 1712 imposed a stamp duty upon newspapers, so far with no apparent check to the demand for them. Nevertheless, the money and time devoted to the newspaper must have reduced the amount of each available for the book. James Lackington, one of the few booksellers of the century who managed to make a fortune, was quite sure of it. "The best time for bookselling," he said, "is when there is no kind of news stirring; then many of those who for months would have done nothing but talk of war or peace, revolutions, and counter-revolutions, etc. etc. for want of other amusement, will have recourse to books; so that I have often experienced that the report of a war, or the trial of a great man, or indeed any subject that attracts the public attention, has been some hundreds of pounds out of my pocket in a few weeks."[48]

Next in popularity to the newspaper was the literary periodical. *The Gentleman's Magazine*, first issued in 1731, had in a little more than ten years secured for itself a circulation of 15,000. *The Tatler* and *The Spectator* had been successful from the beginning. In the tenth number of *The Spectator* Addison makes a joyful calculation: "My publisher tells me, that there are already three thousand of them distributed every day; so that if I allow twenty readers to every paper, which I look upon as a modest computation, I may reckon about threescore thousand disciples in London and Westminster."

In spite of the low general level of education, there was evidently by this time a good potential demand for reading-matter if only the bookseller could offer the right material. It was his business to forecast what this right material would be. He was on fairly safe ground where the newest form of literature, the novel, was concerned. "Novels," so it was said in 1757, "are a pretty light summer reading, and do very well at Tunbridge, Bristol, and other watering-places; no bad commodity either for the West India trade."[49] Richardson and Fielding had a large public eagerly awaiting another *Pamela* or another *Joseph Andrews*. As novels increased in number so did the new circulating libraries, and, a point of the first importance to the book trade, the reading habit spread to women. The £1,600 which Millar paid Fielding for *Tom Jones* and *Amelia* turned out to be a most remunerative investment. Here at last was a type of publication which would appeal to all classes, rich or poor, learned or ignorant. "I suppose," says Lackington towards the end of the century, "that more than four times the number of books are sold now than were sold twenty years since. The poorer sort of farmers, and even the poor country people in general, who before that period spent their winter evenings in relating stories of witches, ghosts, hobgoblins, &c. now shorten the winter nights by hearing their sons and daughters read tales, romances, &c. and on entering their houses, you may see *Tom Jones*, *Roderick Random*, and other entertaining books, stuck up on their bacon-racks, &c."[50]

Throughout this period of hand-production, therefore, from the days of Caxton to the end of the eighteenth century, the publication of fiction was a fairly safe undertaking. Even the Puritanical disapproval of light literature could not altogether destroy the craving for romance. But from the beginning there had been a demand even more insatiable, for news. From being merely an idle pastime it had become, as a result of the industrial revolution, one of the necessities of life. It was, indeed, the inability of the hand-press to keep pace with the reporting of current events to a growing population which was to bring the period of hand-printing to a close.

CHAPTER III

The Division of Labour in the Book Industry

A GENERAL tendency in industrial development is towards increased specialisation by the individual firm for the furtherance of cheap and efficient production. In some cases, on the contrary, it is found more economical to gather into one concern a number of processes which are mutually dependent, safeguarding the position still further by securing control of markets and transport facilities. Or alternatively, technical conditions may be such as to favour backward integration, whereby the firm controls its supplies of raw materials. The evolution of the book industry has taken the more normal course, that of gradually increasing specialisation.

There are several distinct processes contributing to the production of books. Some of them one might expect to find combined with one or more of the others; the rest stand apart as more specialised. In view of the comparatively small amount of ink required in the production of any one work it would seem unlikely that the book printer would make his own. In the case of type, too, it might be more economical to rely on an outside source. As regards paper the case is rather different: it is conceivable that the publisher on a large scale might be willing to take over the management of a paper-mill in order to ensure against delay. We should not suggest that an author or translator should publish his own books, although we might feel no surprise at learning that a single firm undertook the printing, publishing and even binding of them. Yet, according to an experienced publisher, the combination even of printing and publishing is uneconomic: "Many authors think it is a great advantage to a publisher to possess his own printing works. This is a delusion. It may even be a positive disadvantage. To be run economically and therefore profitably a printing plant needs an even supply of manuscripts to print. No one firm, however large, can ensure that the supply will arrive sufficiently regularly to keep all the machinery steadily employed. If there is a lull, either the machinery is idle or, in order to make full use of his plant, the publisher is tempted to embark on some new publication which he would otherwise have declined. There is thus a perpetual conflict between the requirements of the printing and publishing sides of the business."[1] In the light of this argument the early book-producing concerns would appear to have come far short of efficiency, were it not that the publisher had no alternative but to undertake his own printing.

In fifteenth-century Italy the whole industry turned on the activities of the paper-makers: in order to create a demand for their paper they employed staffs of scribes to write upon it. After the invention of printing they established printing and publishing concerns, still, perhaps, with the object of finding a use for their primary product. In the infancy of the printing industry, for instance, Bonaccorsi and Montali turned their respective paper-mills into general printing offices and book manufactories. Even in the early sixteenth century an important Florentine printer-publisher, Francis Cartolajo, was by his chief occupation a paper manufacturer. In Germany, again, the printer who undertook much of Luther's work, Lucas Cranach, managed a paper-warehouse and bookshop as well as his printing works. The great Christophe Plantin of Antwerp entered the industry at another point: he began his career as a binder; from this he proceeded to bookselling; by 1555 he was also a printer and publisher. Whatever their approach to the industry the chief continental book producers of the fifteenth and early sixteenth centuries all combined at least the functions of printer, publisher and bookseller, selling at least their own publications at the retail stage.

There is no instance of an early English printer's attempting to make his own paper, but, in all other respects, for the first fifty years or more of the English printing industry the position agreed with that on the Continent: the printer published and sold books. Usually he also bound them. This fact has been established from the internal evidence of the books themselves: the boards composing the binding are frequently found to consist of waste sheets from the printing works which issued the book. Pynson's earliest bindings, for instance, were commonly lined with leaves printed by Machlinia, whom he succeeded about the year 1488. Among those known to have controlled binderies as well as printing works were Julian Notary, working in London from 1498 to about 1520, and John Reynes, printing between 1527 and 1544. Wynkyn de Worde, who took over Caxton's business, employed a binder at home but seems to have sent out some of the work, for in his will he left to "Nowel, the bookbinder, in Shoe Lane (Fleet Street), XX.s. in books; and to Alard, bookbinder, my servant, vj.*l.* xiv.s. iiij.d."

It would, perhaps, be untrue to say that every printer of the early sixteenth century founded his own type, but one can at least infer from the complete silence on the subject until the end of the century that there was no separate industry of type-founding. It seems possible that the early printer lent his type to others; unless the type used by Pynson, De Worde and Notary had been cast from the same bad matrices there is no other way of accounting for the general similarity of their printing and the identically irregular letters appearing in their work.

The early printing-publishing house, then, regularly saw books through all stages from printing, or even the making of the type, to marketing. But there were curious complications. Although each firm carried on all these various processes, the individual book seems on occasion to have wandered backwards and forwards between one publishing-house and another. Robert Wyer, for example, published at his house at the sign of St. John the Evangelist, near Charing Cross, works on theology and medicine which were largely sold for him by other printers; he printed for John Gough, Richard Bankes and others, although they themselves ran printing-presses; but the works which he sold had often been printed by Pynson, Laurence Andrewe or Richard Faques.

As if it were not enough to combine all the mechanical processes of book production in one firm, it frequently happened that the master printer began at the first stage of all and actually wrote or translated the works which he was to print. Thus John Rastell, printing at the sign of the Mermaid, Cheapside, between 1517 and 1533, wrote as well as published the *Natura naturata*, *Canones astrologici* and abridgments of the statutes; he also translated works from the French. Thomas Gibson published five works between 1533 and 1539, one of which, the first concordance to the English New Testament, he had compiled himself. Robert Copland, printing and publishing between 1510 and 1547, translated *The Kalendar of Shepherdes* and other works, and wrote such verse as *The Seven Sorowes that Women have when theyr Husbandes be Deade.* Robert Crowley, vicar of St. Giles, Cripplegate, from 1566–88, is far better known as the writer of vigorous denunciations of social injustice than as a printer; yet the fact remains that throughout the reign of Edward VI he was printing in Ely Rents, Holborn, where he published and sold *The Vision of Piers Plowman*, his own book *The Way to Wealth*, and about twenty other works.

The Growth of Specialisation

By the middle of the seventeenth century the various processes in the industry had become clearly defined and their control, generally speaking, divided between a greater number of entrepreneurs. This development was mainly a natural one arising from the general increase in the volume of publications, but political influences had also played their part. To take first the case of type-founding: one may gather from the Star Chamber decree of 1586, which mentions every other branch of the industry but this, that there had not yet arisen a special class of letter-founders. The distinction arose during the next ten years, for in 1597 the Stationers' Company caused Benjamin Sympson, a type-founder, to enter into a bond of £40 not to cast any type without giving previous notice to the master and wardens. The Star Chamber, in an effort to stem the growth of illicit printing, in 1637 limited the number of founders for the whole kingdom to four.* This was not so drastic an order

* July 11, 1637. Second decree concerning printing: ". . . XXVII. *Item*, the Court doth order and declare, that there shall be foure Founders of letters for printing allowed, and no more." [Vacancies to be filled by the Archbishop of Canterbury or Bishop of London, with six other High Commissioners.]

as might be thought; Arthur Nicholls, one of the four appointed, petitioned the Archbishop of Canterbury for permission to print, on the ground that the making of type would not keep four men fully occupied: "Of soe small benefitt hath his art bine, that for 4 yeares worke and practice he hath not taken above 48 *l.*, and had it not bine for other imploymente he might have perrisht."[2] This in no way reflects on the size of the printing industry itself, but merely illustrates the fact that now that printers were not making their own type they preferred to import the more artistic founts from the Netherlands: the country was dependent upon Dutch type from about this time to 1720, when its importation was prohibited.

The divorce between printing and publishing was gradually coming into effect before any Government action was taken on the matter. Towards the middle of the sixteenth century there were several who, though ostensibly printer-publishers, devoted most of their attention to the publishing side of the business and arranged for other firms to undertake the printing. The charter of incorporation granted to the Stationers' Company in 1557 helped to widen the chasm: the monopoly of printing for the whole of the kingdom was from henceforth to be vested in the members of the Company and such other persons as should be specially licensed, but no restrictions were made with regard to publishing or bookselling. This meant that non-members of the Company who were too old to be apprenticed would probably never print, although they might publish and sell books. From 1586 onwards the Star Chamber limited the number even of members of the Company who were allowed to become master printers, so that the rest had either to spend the remainder of their careers as journeymen or else to turn their attention to the other branches of the trade. As a further development, the smaller publishers did not keep shops of their own, but issued works in their own names while really employed by other stationers. Others continued to sell books after they had stopped printing or publishing.

Although certain publishers were no longer entitled to print, any printer might still publish. Moreover, although the Licensing Act of 1662 repeated the order limiting the number allowed to print, it was openly ignored. There was still scope for the man intent on publishing as well as printing. Joseph Moxon makes it clear, in 1683, that a printer may still be undertaking the whole of the work in connection with the distribution of a book: he speaks of the collater piling the finished books into the press, and leaving them there for a day and a night; then, he says, "As he takes each number of *Books*, he Tyes them up with Packthred, lays a Waste Paper under and upon each *Bundle*; and if the *Master-Printer* Printed the *Impression* for Himself, he writes the *Title* of the *Book*, and number of the *Books* on the uppermost Waste Paper, and sets them by square and orderly on the Shelves in the *Warehouse*, to deliver them out according to the *Master-Printer's* order. But if the *Impression* were printed for an Author, or a Bookseller, he sends them to the Authors or Booksellers, without writing on the uppermost Waste Paper."[3] One still occasionally finds books, such as Sir Robert Filmer's *Patriarcha* (1680), described as printed and sold by "Walter Davis, bookbinder, in Amen Corner." Two of the best-known publishers of the late seventeenth and early eighteenth centuries were also printers and bookbinders—Richard Baldwin, publishing between 1681 and 1698, and Jacob Tonson II, working from about 1700 to 1735. The book industry in the provinces was of later development, so that as far ahead as 1751 John Almon was to write, with respect to the Liverpool bookseller to whom he was apprenticed, that, "as is not uncommon with booksellers in provincial towns," he carried on also the trades of bookbinder and printer.[4]

In spite of cases such as these, the tendency was, as we have said, to specialise. By 1700 there appear to have been, in London, 188 persons calling themselves booksellers (or publishers), 42 who were printers, and only 25 who were both printer and publisher. There were still 7 acting as both bookseller and binder, as distinct from 4 who were full-time binders. In the provinces there were about 55 publishers, 8 printers, and apparently only 2 who combined the trades.[5] Fifty years later London had 86 described as "bookseller and publisher," 42 "booksellers" (some of whom seem to have been publishers), 28 printers, and 15 printer-publishers.

A FIFTEENTH-CENTURY BIBLIOMANIAC
From *The Ship of Fools*

JOHN DAY

The provinces by this time had 26 printers and about 120 in the confused category of booksellers and publishers, of whom a few were also printers.[6] These proportions probably bear some resemblance to those of the present day; the little class of printer-publishers has never wholly disappeared.

The question arises as to which of the two, printer or publisher, employed the bookbinder after the division of the industry. The association, already mentioned, between a particular binding and a particular press is not in evidence in books published since about 1550. From that time to the end of the century it appears that the publisher bound only those volumes which he was exhibiting in his own bookshop; the rest he would pass on in sheet form to the bookseller, who had them bound in accordance with his customers' requirements. During the first half of the seventeenth century the responsibility for binding (where a whole edition was bound) seems to have been assumed by the publisher: from this time, instead of each known copy of a work being in a different kind of binding, all copies came to be uniformly bound. The statistics given above show that a few publishers still had their own binding equipment. Even in the early eighteenth century, John Brindley, publisher of Jethro Tull's *Horse-Hoeing Husbandry* and other works, described himself on his trade card as "Bookseller and Stationer at the King's Arms in New Bond Street, Bookbinder to Her Majesty and His Royal Highness the Prince of Wales."[7] These were comparatively rare instances. In the normal course of events the books were sent to a separate establishment to be bound, a Stationers' Company decree of October 21, 1577, ordering the bookbinder to return the work within three days of the date appointed, on pain of imprisonment.

As was to be expected, the division of the book trade was accompanied by jealousy between its two main parts: printer and publisher (usually known as stationer at this time) each strove for pre-eminence. This was the ground of a complaint of journeymen printers in 1614: "the Stationers by an agreement among themselves will reta[i]le no new copies [i.e. books], vnlesse they be of their owne. For be it neuer so Religious, Learned, or profitable, if it be a Printers, either by purchase, or by free gift, they will not sell the same: but the Printer must loose his labour, his Paper and expence, if he will not sell them at their rate; by which meanes the Stationer hath all the profit both by Printing and Bookeselling."[8] George Wither amplified this complaint: "The Printers mystery is ingenious, paynefull and profitable: the Bookebinders necessary; the Claspe-makers vsefull. And indeed, the retailer of bookes, commonly called a Booke-seller, is a Trade, which being wel gouerned, and lymited within certaine bounds, might become somewhat seruiceable to the rest. But as it is now (for the most part abused) the Bookeseller hath not onely made the Printer, the Binder, and the Claspmaker a slaue to him: but hath brought Authors, yea the whole Commonwealth, and all the liberall Sciences into bondage. For he make all professers of Art, labour for his profit, at his owne price, and vtters it to the Common-wealth in such fashion, and at those rates, which please himselfe."[9] For the first century of printing the printer had been supreme. The ascendancy of the bookseller, or publisher, was a seventeenth-century development which reached its height in the eighteenth. Things had come to such a pass by 1739 that Dr. Johnson wrote in the *Gentleman's Magazine*, "We can produce some who threatened printers with their highest displeasure, for having dared to print books for those who wrote them." One can sympathise with Edward Clarke's comment to William Bowyer about twenty-five years later, when Bowyer was thinking of taking over the management of the Cambridge University Press: after mentioning a few arguments against the idea, he says, "There are certainly two objects in view in this proposal, which, if these objections did not lie in the way, would to me be great inducements. The thought of *governing the Booksellers*, either for gain or glory, would give me a greater pleasure than any other object in trade. In that respect I think just as you do."[10]

The Function of the Bookseller

A certain confusion will have been noticed between the terms "bookseller" and "publisher." In the early years it came about naturally enough that the man who printed a work both published it and sold it by retail: "bookselling" therefore described each of these activities. As the market developed the individual trader found the advantage of varying his stock, and to this end exchanged the works which he had printed for those from other presses—hence the familiar form of the seventeenth century title-page: "printed by A, and may be had of B, C and D." John Dunton availed himself of this device when he began to print in the second half of the century, for he records, "The very first Copy I would venture to print was written by the Reverend Mr. Doolittle, and intituled, *The Sufferings of Christ*. This book fully answered my end; for, exchanging it through the whole Trade, it furnished my Shop with all sorts of Books saleable at that Time."[11] Dunton here shows himself acting in two different capacities: in the first instance he has had personal dealings with the author, has helped to plan the final form of the book, and has arranged for and taken the financial risks involved in its printing and circulation; in the other he is merely offering for sale various works produced quite independently of him. Here we have the essential difference between publishing and bookselling; but for a long period no such difference was recognised in common speech.

By the eighteenth century the term "publisher" had come into use. Even so, the old idea lingered, and the new word served merely as an alternative for the old. The humble bookseller who made no pretence to be more than a salesman for other men's products must have been awakened with something of a shock in the year 1770 to realise what this haphazard means of description might involve for him. A case had arisen in which J. Miller, a printer of Paternoster Row, had advertised one of his pamphlets, the *London Museum*, as being also on sale at the shop of J. Almon in Piccadilly. Almon had given him no authority for doing this, but it was "pretty much the custom (since the metropolis has become so large and populous) for booksellers residing in one part of the town to advertise their books, &c. to be had *also* of booksellers residing in *another* part of the town."[12] Unfortunately for Almon, this particular pamphlet contained one of the ill-famed letters of Junius, and the wretched bookseller found himself faced with a trial for publishing a seditious libel. Judge and witnesses alike agreed that Almon was guilty of publishing the work, whether in ignorance or not. The judge, Lord Mansfield, held that "As to the *publication*, there is nothing more certain, more clear, nor more established, than that the publication—a sale at a man's shop—and a sale *therein*, by his servant, is evidence, and not contradicted, and explained, is evidence to convict the *master of publication*; because, whatever any man does by *another*, he does it *himself*. . . . As to the publication, here are two witnesses that swear to the fact: *Bibbins* swears, that being led by an advertisement, that such a pamphlet was published and sold at the defendant's, in *Piccadilly*, that he went there, asked for it publicly. . . . There is another witness, *Crowder*, who likewise swears, that he asked publicly for one, and that was sold him by the defendant's man."[13] Mr. Justice Aston was of the same opinion: "I take it for a rule, that the buying a book or libel in a bookseller's shop is sufficient evidence to charge the master with a publication, though it does not appear in evidence that he knew the contents, or of the book being there."[14] Where the law holds that "a sale at a man's shop" is publication the bibliographer must simply recognise a distinction between the economic and legal connotation of the verb "to publish."

The Position of the Author

The person who was of no account whatever in the early years of the book industry was the author. It was not until the eighteenth century that he came into his own. The power of the "stationer" over the mere writer is illustrated by a remarkable undertaking secured by the Stationers' Company from Gervase Markham in 1617: "Memorandum That I Gervase Markham of London gent do promise hereafter Neuer to write any more book or bookes to be printed of *the Deseases or cures of any Cattle, as Horse, Oxe, Cowe, sheepe, Swine and Goates &c.*"[15] Markham's prolific output during the preceding four or five years must seriously have interfered with the booksellers' policy of price maintenance. But in spite of the comparative unimportance of the author in the book industry, there existed a far greater degree of intimacy between him and the printer than would be possible under present-day conditions. Just as Erasmus is known to have lived for many years in Basel with Froben, his publisher, so it was that the English stationer frequently provided lodging for the writer whose work he was publishing. Thus Doctor Fulke with two of his men and their horses were maintained for about nine months by his publisher, Bishop, while he was writing his *Confutation of the Rhemish Testament*, about 1590, and Bishop supplied him with all the books he needed for his work. Gabriel Harvey was another who was so maintained. The author might be a professional servant or even employee of the publisher.

Proof Correcting

The close proximity between author and printer-publisher allowed for constant supervision of the press by the author, and accounts for those variations in the text of different copies of the same edition which have proved so perplexing to students of sixteenth-century literature; in those days of leisurely hand-printing it was perfectly simple to make minor alterations in wording between the pulling off of one copy and the next. Not only was this supervision by the author borne with by the printer, it was expected. It was understood that the writer should pay regular visits to the printing-house in order to correct the proofs. Foxe called once a week at John Day's house to superintend the printing of his *Actes and Monumentes*, in 1563; other writers made these journeys daily. It is then no matter for wonder that the printer considered himself absolved from all errors, and that we find such introductory notes as this, from the printer to the reader:

> Mend the Printer's faults, as thou doest them espy,
> For the Author lies in Goal [*sic*], but knows not why.[16]

It was all very well to blame the author for every misprint. Did the printer, then, take no responsibility at all for the mistakes of his journeymen? If not, there had been a sad falling away from the conscientiousness of the pioneers in printing. Caxton, we know from the prefaces of some of his books, always read through the whole text after it was finally printed off, marking in red ink any mistakes which he found. One of his journeymen was then given the task of making these alterations in every copy of the impression, after which the zealous master compared them with his own version to make sure that none of his corrections had been overlooked. The same method was adopted by several of his contemporaries abroad; it was not until later that it occurred to one of them to print a list of errata on some of the blank leaves of the book.[17]

The sixteenth century certainly shows a slight tendency towards more slipshod work in this respect. Wynkyn de Worde was admittedly content with a generally lower standard of printing than that of his master, Caxton. As printing became a more everyday affair it was perhaps natural that absolute accuracy should have been regarded as a luxury beyond the means of the ordinary small printer. The typical English printer during the sixteenth century was a poor man, and the professional press corrector was an expensive workman. Abroad there might be a few printer-publishers like Robert Estienne, who "was so exact and solicitous after perfection, that, in a noble contempt of gain, he used to expose his proofs to public view with offer of a reward to those who should discover any faults."[18] The man who was printing for his livelihood simply could not afford this. So it was that throughout Europe abuses were rife for the want of good correctors; "persons of that class were thought too chargeable by many Printers."[19] This state of affairs could not continue for very long. In Spain the Government, finding that the sarcastic comments of the learned had no effect, took matters into its own hands: it ordered that before a book was offered for sale the work should be examined by specially appointed censors, and compared with the original manuscript; any errors noticed were to be listed on the first leaf, and the censors were then to certify that, these faults excepted, the book had been faithfully printed.[20] In England it seems to have been thought more convenient to give the author access to the press and then to blame him for any imperfections.

There were, of course, certain cases in which the master printer had to make special arrangements for proof correcting. For classical works he would either assume the responsibility himself, if he were a scholar, or he would employ press correctors. By

Moxon's time (1683) the corrector was regularly established in the printing-office, and blame for such misprints as had escaped notice naturally fell to his lot; "Thus you see," says Moxon, "it behoves him to be very careful as well as skilful; and indeed it is his own interest to be both: For if by his neglect an *Heap* be spoiled, he is obliged to make Reparation."[21] Whether this meant that he might have to pay for a whole section to be set up again is uncertain.

Even when the official press corrector had charge of the work stray comments show that the proud author still at times visited the printing-works, anxious that his creation should receive due care. On the whole, though, it was usual by the end of the seventeenth century for proofs to be sent to the author rather than for him to call at the office to read them; as trade expanded it would have been an impossible state of affairs to have the printing-house developing into a social club for authors. Nevertheless, even though the author might be kept off the premises, he could not disavow all responsibility. This was recognised in an advertisement which appeared in 1711:[22] "If any author that is absent desires to have the press accurately corrected according to his copy, whether it be English, Latin, Greek, Hebrew, or French, let the printer leave the sheets at Mr. Cliffe's at the Bible and Three Crowns in Cheapside, Mr. Phillips at the Black Bull in Cornhill over against Sweeting's Alley, or Mr. Tracy at the Three Bibles on London Bridge, and it shall be done with all possible care and despatch by a person well read in Arts and Languages, who may be heard of at all these book-sellers as occasion shall require." William Bowyer, the noted eighteenth-century printer, had difficulty with several authors over this question. Possibly the most trying writer with whom he had to deal was William Warburton, Bishop of Gloucester. When his edition of Pope's work was going through the press, from 1749 to 1751, Warburton was anything but complimentary on the progress of the work; "I am surprized," he wrote, "I have not yet had a proof of the first sheet, which I delivered when I was in London to be re-printed; and think myself very ill-used by the neglect.—I expect what I order to be done, to be done out of hand." Later, in agitating again for a quicker supply of proofs, he complained, "Sure you know the post comes every day." His impatience apparently turned Bowyer obstinate, for over a year later he was still writing with regard to the same publication, "Mr. Bowyer, I take it extremely ill of you for not sending me two copies of all the reprinted leaves, prefaces, title-pages, &c. before I left town, as I ordered. If I thought what I said would be any way regarded by you I would have sent them by Leake's parcel."[23] Bowyer seems to have suffered beyond endurance from this author during the following ten years, and when, to crown his former insults, Warburton in 1762 chose another printer for the second edition of *The Doctrine of Grace*, he relieved his feelings as follows: "Your Lordship will say, you removed your book to another Printer, because I had printed the first edition of it very incorrectly. I answer, my Lord, that you saw every proof-sheet yourself, and ought to share with me at least in the imputation of incorrectness. You said, indeed, at first setting out, *that you would not be my Corrector*; but then, my Lord, you should not be your own. When sheets are hurried away to an impatient Author late at night by the post, the Printer is precluded from reviewing them with that accuracy he otherwise should bestow upon them. In the canceled Leaves which your Lordship complains of, there were no less than six faults in one page, viz. p. 151; only one of which, upon the return of the sheet, was corrected by your Lordship. . . . In short, my Lord, you have prescribed a law to me, by which no other Printer will ever be bound, viz. that I should suffer for every error of the press which you leave uncorrected."[24] Having given himself the satisfaction of writing these words, Bowyer put the letter away and never sent it.

For all that, it was not only authors who were careless proof-readers. Horace Walpole was always being chided by his friends for his lack of patience in correcting the books which he published. This did not seem to worry him in the least. In fact he once said, optimistically, "I hope future edition-mongers will say of those of Strawberry Hill, they have all the beautiful negligence of a gentleman."[25]

The Division of Labour in the Book Industry

The Author-Printer-Publisher Relationship

The peremptory manner in which Bishop Warburton wrote to his printer was the outcome of a far different relationship between author and printer from the one typical of earlier times. In the sixteenth and seventeenth centuries the printer-publisher had shown a somewhat contemptuous attitude to the author which was perhaps explainable by the cheapness of literary work. The author had no bargaining power whatever. It was largely, no doubt, owing to custom that payment was non-existent or miserably small: the writer still tended to look towards a patron rather than to a publisher for maintenance, feeling it less of an indignity to be provided with an annuity by some noble family than to become the employee of a bookseller. The patron was undertaking no light task in fostering literature: so great was Sir Robert Drury's zeal that he housed John Donne and his whole family for five years; Ascham and Jonson both secured patronage lasting for the greater part of their career. As versification came more and more into fashion in the reign of Elizabeth regular patronage had to give way to infrequent gifts of money, but the author remained unwilling to become a professional writer even though he might have fallen into dire want. A similar condition had existed in Germany in the Reformation period: a number of writers in support of the Roman doctrine had professed horror at the idea of accepting payment from a bookseller for their defence of the Church, but had raised no objection to receiving rewards from the Pope or his cardinals. In Germany as in England the attempts to force patronage by dedicating works to some exalted personage were becoming ineffectual on account of their frequency. Thus in 1594 the magistrates of Leipzig announced that they had been overburdened with dedications, and could accept no more. When the publisher found himself so well stocked with manuscripts for which somebody else had paid, it was not to be expected that he should offer large sums for professional work.

If the publisher found himself insufficiently provided with free material he was inclined to help himself. According to sixteenth- and seventeenth-century reasoning, all rights in a manuscript were vested in its present holder, no matter how the work had come into his possession. George Wither felt bitterly on the treatment accorded to the author: the bad bookseller, he says, "makes no scruple to put out the right Authors Name, and insert another in the second edition of a Booke; And when the impression of some pamphlet lyes vpon his hands, to imprint new Titles for yt (and so take mens moneyes twice or thrice, for the same matter vnder diuerse names) is no iniury in his opinion. If he get any written Coppy into his powre, likely to be vendible, whether the Author be willing or no, he will publish it; And it shall be contriued and named alsoe, according to his owne pleasure: which is the reason, so many good Bookes come forth imperfect, and with foolish titles."[26] Incidentally, the courtier sometimes found this weakness of the publisher rather an advantage than otherwise. It provided an easy way of getting his literary outpourings printed without any loss to his dignity: having secretly arranged for his manuscript to be stolen and delivered to a publisher he could afterwards profess surprise and annoyance at the whole proceedings.

There were, of course, publishers whose dealings were above reproach. There were also authors who quite frankly wanted their work printed and were anxious to be paid for it. But, by reason of the flooding of the market by the methods related above, the rate of payment was low. For John Stow's great life-work, the *Survey of London*, which John Wolfe published in 1598, the payment was only £3 and forty copies of the work; for his *Brief Chronicle* he received £1 and fifty copies. Round about the year 1620 the payment for pamphlets and small collections of poems was £2. The agreement between Milton and his publisher with regard to *Paradise Lost* (1667) is often quoted: Samuel Simmons promised to pay him £5 down, a further £5 when the first edition was exhausted, and the same amount on the sale of the second and third editions, if these were called for. The second edition was demanded in 1669, and the £5 duly paid, but in 1680, six years after Milton's death, his widow gave up the full copyright to Simmons for another £8.[27] On the whole, the author was well-advised to write plays rather than verse: these he could sell straight to the theatre for anything between £6 and £20, together with the profits from one performance. The worst-paid work of all was translation, for which the recompense was commonly a few copies of the work.

Authors, expected from their profession to be able to write convincingly, are well qualified to show their publishers in a poor light. But the publisher, too, had his point of view. John Dunton, in his numerous dealings with authors during the second half of the seventeenth century, found some of them so exacting that they wanted to become "half-booksellers," or else they demanded such a large sum for their copy that the sale of the whole impression would scarcely cover the bare cost of production.[28] When he did find a generous author Dunton was unstinting in his praise, as, "Mr. Ridpath . . . has written much; his style is excellent; and his humility and his honesty have established his reputation. He scorns to receive a farthing of *Copy-money*, till he knows what numbers are sold off."[29] Still, even Dunton liked to obtain his copy free of charge: with regard to what he called his "fifth project," *The New Practice of Piety*, he wrote, "To render this Book the more acceptable to the curious Reader; if any ingenious Querist has conceived in his own mind (or met in his reading with) any new or uncommon Thoughts, if he will send them to Smith's Coffee-house, directed to the Athenian Society, they shall not fail of a place in this *nice Undertaking*."[30]

There seems by this time to have been a recognised market price for certain classes of work. Jacob Tonson remonstrated with Dryden in the year 1693 for sending him too little copy, although there had been no definite agreement as to the quantity: he felt ill-used that Dryden had sent him only 1,446 lines of translation of Ovid for fifty guineas, but had sent another bookseller 1,518 lines of a translation for forty guineas.[31] If one man could reckon, so could the other. Dryden, discussing payment on another occasion, and bearing in mind the depreciated state of the currency, said, "I expect fifty pounds in good silver: not such as I have had formerly."[32]

At the opening of the eighteenth century the author with a gift for flattery still had little need to worry about payment from the publisher: patronage was at its height in the days of Queen Anne. It was quite usual to give an author from five to ten guineas for the dedication of a play.[33] It was not only flattery, moreover, nor the desire to be thought a man of taste, which influenced the patron at this time. Such men as Harley, Halifax and St. John were genuinely anxious to encourage the author of small means. But the accession of George I was to change all this. It was useless now to look to the Court to patronise the mere writer; there were more important political issues at stake. It is fortunate that the chief writers of the first half of the century—Johnson, Pope and the rest—were in any case intent on remaining independent, and that market conditions were by then such that they could rely for their livelihood on their own bargaining power with the publishers.

It must have been difficult enough to make a living from authorship at the beginning of the century. From Bernard Lintot's memorandum book, which came into the possession of John Nichols, the printer, it appears that £4 or £5 would often buy the copyright of an author's work: in 1710, for instance, Lintot paid £4 for the right to publish Elsum's *Book of Painting*, and in 1716 £5 7s. 6d. for David Edward's *Journals of Parliament.*[34] Lintot's payments to Pope were rather higher: for the first book of *Statius* (1712), £16 2s. 6d.; for *The Rape of the Lock* (1712), £7; for *Windsor Forest* (1713), £32 5s.; these were typical amounts. Pope's *Homer* was a much more paying proposition. This was published by subscription, and Lintot agreed to provide at his own expense all the subscription and presentation copies, and to pay the author £200 for each of the six volumes. Altogether Pope realised £5,324 4s. from this work. Some of Lintot's payments were very small, possibly owing to the slight nature of the material he was buying; thus he gave Dr. Sewel only £1 1s. 6d. "for writing observations on the tragedy of Jane Shore."[35] One has to remember that these figures still require adjustment before they can be compared with modern conditions: Johnson estimated the cost of living, about 1730, to be in the neighbourhood of £30 a year.[36]

The value of a work in the eyes of a publisher naturally depended to some extent on the popularity of the author, which in turn depended either on the writer's previous publications or on his social position. This was perhaps why Johnson, being now well known, received £125 for *Rasselas* (1749), while Goldsmith, having still neither fame nor social position, in 1762 received only sixty guineas for *The Vicar of Wakefield*; and why Fielding's payment rose from £183 10s. for *Joseph Andrews* to £700 for *Tom Jones*, and £1,000 for *Amelia*. It was not unknown for an author of no reputation and therefore of little worth to the publisher to borrow a name which would stand him in better stead. Robert Sanders was a case in point: "his principal work was the notes he wrote for the Bible, which was published, 1773, under the name of Dr. Henry Southwell. This was no fictitious name, but the real name of a Clergyman, who received a considerable gratuity (I believe a hundred guineas) for the liberty of using it, while the writer of the notes was paid the poor pittance of twenty-five or twenty-six shillings a sheet: such was the difference between the real and the reputed author."[37]

As the century advanced publishers were able and willing to be more liberal, but authors were still inclined to distrust their good intentions. John Wilkes, during his stay in Paris (1767), asked for five hundred guineas for his *History of England*, and when John Almon appeared anything but anxious to pay so large a sum he wrote in argumentative terms: "I hear from London, that Lord Lyttelton has received from Sandby and Dodsley three thousand pounds for his History of Henry II. . . . You see, therefore, you are mistaken when you say five hundred guineas are more than ever were given for such a volume."[38] Wilkes seems to have won the day, as Almon formally agreed to pay him £400 and to accept a bill drawn in favour of a third person. According to James Lackington, famous as the first dealer in "remainders," the complaints made against publishers were usually groundless. Were it not for these men, he pointed out rather unnecessarily, the public would never have seen Johnson's Dictionary, not to mention the works of Pope, Sir John Hawkins, Hume, Gibbon and the rest. As to their meanness, "the late Mr. Elliot, bookseller, of Edinburgh, gave Mr. Smellie a thousand pounds for his Philosophy of Natural History, when only the heads of the chapters were wrote. Hume received only £200 for one part of the History of Britain, but for the remainder of that work he had £500. Dr. Robertson was paid for his History of Scotland but £600, but for his Charles V he received £4,500. . . . It is confidently asserted that the late Dr. Hawkesworth received £6,000 for his Compilation of Voyages."[39]

The only time when publishers were apt to become inattentive, according to Lackington, was when authors refused to sell their copyrights; they were envious of success which was not to be their own.[40] In spite of this theory, the publisher at times deserved sympathy. Authors could be most exasperating. No one was better aware of this than William Bowyer, who frequently undertook to print for private publication. One at least of these ventures ended in a childish squabble: Bowyer had agreed to print five hundred copies of Dr. Thomas Morell's version of the *Prometheus Vinctus*, half of them for Eton College and the rest for Morell's benefit, but before long a bitter correspondence began; in October 1766, Bowyer wrote to Morell, "Rev. Sir, As you own yourself a bad oeconomist, it is one step to your ceasing to be so. To the same purpose I must beg leave to tell you, I do not chuse to print your book, unless you find the paper for it; as Booksellers always send in the paper for the books in which they have the property. I would advise you, by way of oeconomy, to get subscriptions, and put the money by in a drawer, to pay your Printer." Two months later it was Morell's turn: "Sir, Half a sheet in two months, and that a very indifferent one, far beneath your usual care and great abilities, is what, I believe, no one would submit to with patience. I own I cannot. It would have been more just in you, at first, instead of sending me an impertinent letter, about getting subscriptions . . . to have told me that you wanted either leisure or inclination to serve me. . . . If you doubted your pay, I told you the money should be advanced beforehand, or at least by the sheet."[41] Perhaps it was all to the good that Bowyer broke off the arrangement at this stage. Happily, many of his contacts with writers were of a pleasanter nature. Daines Barrington, for one, explained his unwillingness to hand over the copyright of his *Observations on the Statutes* (1768) on the grounds that he did not wish Bowyer to lose by the undertaking. When he found that there was little risk of this he offered Bowyer the publishing rights of a second edition, which the printer willingly accepted.[42] John Murray would scarcely have believed in such generosity. Writing to Professor Millar of Glasgow about twenty years later he complained that most authors first applied to a publisher for his offer and then used it as a means of bargaining for better terms elsewhere.[43]

By the middle of the eighteenth century, therefore, authors had acquired a bargaining power unknown in the early days of printing. In part the improvement in their position was due to a growth in the popular demand for books, but a more important factor was the changed legal conception of literary property. At the end of the seventeenth century the author had still no redress for the unauthorised publication of his work. By the Copyright Act of 1709, as we shall see, definite rights were secured to him.

CHAPTER IV

The Structure of the Industry in the Period of Hand-Production

The Location and Size of the Industry

THE early location of the industry, at home and on the Continent, was determined by the situation of the mediaeval manuscript markets. Throughout northern Europe these were normally in the precincts of the cathedral or the parish church. The London manuscript trade had become established in Paternoster Row, and it was here that the trade in printed books began.

Although the earliest London printing was not carried on in Westminster Abbey itself, as the imprints of some of Caxton's books imply, it was actually performed in the almonry of the abbey, in the tenement known as the "Red Pale." Apart from the two university presses, the printing-houses established in England during the first century of typography were almost without exception in the vicinity of ecclesiastical buildings. Outside the cities of London and Westminster they were as follows:[1] there were in Southwark four printers working consecutively from 1514 to about 1556; in St. Albans a schoolmaster, who remains unidentified, was printing from 1480 to 1486, after which there is a gap until the time of John Hertford or Herford, 1534–8; in York the first known press, that of Hugo Goes, was established in 1509, being followed by one or two others of short duration; the monastery of Tavistock, Devonshire, was the source of two printed works, issued in 1525 and 1534 respectively; there were three printers in Ipswich in 1548, but in the same year one of them, John Oswen, moved to Worcester, where he was licensed to print service books; from 1549 or before to 1556 John Mychell was printing in Canterbury; finally, in 1570 a press was set up in Norwich by Anthony de Solmpne, one of the Flemish refugees, but, as far as is known, only one work issued from it. The only other presses outside London were the private ones used surreptitiously in connection with religious controversy. One of these, used by Martin Marprelate and other Puritans, was moved from Moulsey, near Kingston, Surrey, to Fawsley, Northamptonshire; next it was taken to Norton and Coventry, and finally, by way of Woolston in Warwickshire, to Manchester. The private press used by the Roman Catholic Party had also to be moved secretly from one place to another.

What would have been the natural headquarters of book production by the end of the sixteenth century is a matter for conjecture, for in 1586 all provincial printing was abruptly ended by a decree of the Star Chamber. In an effort towards effectual regulation of the press it was ordered on June 23rd that "no printer of bookes, nor any other person, or persons whatsoever, shall sett up, keepe, or mayntein, any presse or presses, or any other instrument, or instruments, for imprinting of bookes, ballades, chartes, pourtraictures, or any other thing, or things whatsoever, but onelye in the cittie of London, or the suburbs thereof (except one presse in the universitie of Cambridge, and one other presse in the universitie of Oxforde, and no more) and that no person shall hereafter erect, sett up, or maynteyne in any secrett, or obscure corner, or place, any suche presse." Until the relaxing of vigilance during the Civil War and the falling of this decree into abeyance with the Court of Star Chamber there was, then, no printing outside London, Oxford and Cambridge except of a clandestine nature.

In London the industry was at first concentrated in the district stretching from St. Paul's Churchyard to Fleet Street. Wynkyn de Worde moved from Caxton's house in Westminster to the Sun in Fleet Street in about the year 1501. Two years later, Richard Pynson, King's Printer, settled near St. Dunstan's Church, Fleet Street. Julian Notary, printing from approximately 1498 to 1520, worked successively at Westminster, Temple Bar and St. Paul's Churchyard. Robert Copland, John Butler, Laurence Andrewe and Thomas Berthelet were other early sixteenth-century printers whose headquarters were in Fleet Street, while among their contemporaries in St. Paul's Churchyard were John Raynes, Thomas Petit, Thomas

Raynald and Robert Toye. So great was the competition for premises in St. Paul's Churchyard, the main bookselling quarter, that by the middle of the century it was usual for a printer-bookseller to rent only a small shop or stall in the churchyard and to carry on his printing in a larger house on a less valuable site on the outskirts of the city. Christopher Barker, printer to Queen Elizabeth, was one of those who so divided the two branches of his business: his bookshop was at the sign of the Tiger's Head in St. Paul's Churchyard; his printing-house was in Foster Lane. In the year 1560 there were two bookstalls in the churchyard, one at the middle north door and one at the west. There were also sixteen houses round the churchyard, bearing such names as the Bible, the Brazen Serpent, the Cock, the Crane, the Hedgehog and the Holy Ghost. Besides these there were twenty-two other business houses, situated in Paternoster Row, Aldersgate, Little Britain, Smithfield, Blackfriars, Fleet Street, Cannon Street, Thames Street, Knight Riders Street, Foster Lane, Golden Lane, Poultry, Cheapside and Lombard Street. In 1600 the general localisation of the industry remained unchanged, but by now there were four stalls and thirty-one houses round the churchyard and fifty-nine other business houses. St. Paul's Churchyard continued to be the headquarters of the trade until the reign of Queen Anne, when Paternoster Row took the leading place, although in about 1630 Archbishop Laud had the stalls cleared away from the church doors. A westward movement began in the early seventeenth century with the opening of bookshops in Holborn and the Strand, while towards the middle of the century London Bridge became noteworthy as the centre of the trade in nautical books. The gates of the city came to be used: Alders Gate was for a time the printing-house of John Day; Temple Bar was, between 1566 and 1578, the printing-house of William How and, from 1596 to 1597, the bookshop of Hugh Jackson.

Even before limits were set to the printing industry its size in the provinces was, as we have seen, so small as to make it almost unworthy of mention. London enterprise was not much more extensive. From the beginning of the sixteenth century, the period of De Worde and Pynson, until well into its second quarter, there were rarely more than two or three printers at a time who were noted either for quality of work or for output. Only thirty-six men are known to have printed in London between 1500 and 1550, and all of these except twelve belong entirely to the period following 1530. The book entries in the Stationers' Register for the years following 1557 give some idea of the number of printers actively following their occupation: the number to whom "copies" were granted rose steadily from thirteen in 1557–8 to thirty-four in 1562–3; the number fell in 1563–4 (a plague year) to twenty-one, but by 1576–7 it had risen to forty. In the five years from 1590 to 1595 books were licensed to ninety-seven printers. These were the numbers of printers as distinct from printing-houses. Christopher Barker stated in 1582—not, perhaps, without some of the prejudice natural in one of the chief patent-holders—"There are 22 printing-howses in London, where 8 or 10 at the most would suffise for all England, yea and Scotland too, but if no man were allowed to be a Master Printer, but such whose behaviour were well knowne, and auctorised by warrant from her Maiestie, the arte would be most excellently executed in England, and many frivolous and vnfruitfull Copies kepte back, which are dayly thrust oute in prynt, greatly corrupting the youth, and preiudiciall to the Comon wealth manye wayes."[2] It may be that Barker used his influence as Queen's Printer to prevent the rise of further competition, for in 1586 the Star Chamber decreed "that no Prynter, nor other person or persons whatsoever, that hath sett up any presse or Instrument for ymprintinge within six monethes last past, shall hereafter use or occupye the same, nor any person or persons shall hereafter erect or sett up any presse or other instrument of pryntinge, tyll the excessive multytude of Prynters havinge presses already sett up, be abated" to such a number as the Archbishop of Canterbury and the Bishop of London should think sufficient.[3] In 1615 an order was made by the Court of the Stationers' Company that only twenty-two printers should exercise their craft in the City of London, and in 1637 the Star Chamber decreed that as any vacancy arose a new master printer should be appointed by the Archbishop of Canterbury, or the Bishop of London, with six other high commissioners. One of the printers so recommended was John Raworth, of whom it was naïvely reported that he was "said to be an honest man and may come in in steed of his father Richard Raworth yat is an Arrant knave."[4] There was still a way by which the stationer could turn printer without special influence: he had only to marry his master's daughter, whereby he would automatically succeed to the business, or, alternatively, to marry a printer's widow. In more than one instance a printer's widow married a second and third husband: thus John Kingston's widow married George Robinson and Thomas Orwin, each of whom in turn came into possession of Kingston's printing-house.

Notwithstanding these various decrees, there were by 1649 far more than twenty-two printers at work in London. In that year certain printers were ordered by the Council of State to enter into recognisances not to print seditious books. Sixty printers in London and the two universities made this undertaking, and this number obviously does not account for the various clandestine presses, the real founts of seditious publications. During the Commonwealth period few extra presses seem to have arisen: according to Sir Roger L'Estrange[5] there were still, in 1660, about sixty printers at work in London, with about 160 apprentices and a large number of journeymen. Being no lover of the Press he proposed that the number of printers should at once be reduced to twenty with a corresponding reduction in the employment of apprentices and journeymen.

The Licensing Act of 1662 went some way towards legalising L'Estrange's suggested orders, although for some reason it failed to enforce them. After various clauses establishing licensing authorities came one which provided that there should be no more master printers until the number had fallen to twenty. The Act might have been more effectual if certain specified printers had been ordered to stop work, drastic though such a step would have been. As it was, it was openly ignored, and new men set up whenever it appeared to them profitable—but still, with few exceptions, in London.

One small development had been sanctioned by the Act of 1662: York was now expressly mentioned as a place where printing might be carried on. One is tempted to infer from the fact that still, after two centuries, there had been no real attempt to break bounds and set up a press wherever there was a population large enough to justify it that the trade was not generally profitable. And yet, strangely enough, Sorbière was struck at this very time by the apparent prosperity of the trade. "I am not to forget," he writes, "the vast number of booksellers' shops I have observed in London; for besides those who are set up here and there in the City, they have their particular quarters, such as St. Paul's Churchyard and Little Britain, where there is twice as many as in the Rue Saint Jacque in Paris, and who have each of them two or three warehouses."[6] Admittedly, these were booksellers, not necessarily printers; but even booksellers outside London were few and far between. Boswell mentions in his *Life of Johnson* that in the early eighteenth century Dr. Johnson's father, Michael, was a bookseller at Lichfield, and that in those days "booksellers' shops in the provincial towns of England were very rare, so that there was not one even in Birmingham, in which town old Mr. Johnson used to open a shop every market-day."

When the Licensing Act lapsed, in 1695, and the trade was thus freed from restrictions, there were at last a few attempts to establish printing-presses in the provinces. Thomas Jones, a London bookseller, had set up one in Shrewsbury by 1696, and in that year Jourdaine established the first Plymouth press.[7] By 1725 there were presses in Manchester, Birmingham, Liverpool, Bristol, Cirencester, Exeter, Worcester, Norwich, Canterbury, Tunbridge Wells, York, Newcastle, Nottingham—in fact, in every town of any size. They were not on the whole very prosperous concerns. Some of them, such as the press of Hugh Grove at Portsmouth and that of William Ward at Nottingham, are known only for the printing of a few sermons.[8] T. Goolding, of Newcastle-upon-Tyne, is known only for one small book, *Honesto Willo* (1715).[9] But in any case the industry as a whole was still of no remarkable size. In 1724 Samuel Negus drew up a list of all the printing-houses in the kingdom, and these amounted to twenty-eight in the provinces and seventy-five in London. The London ones he subdivided into thirty-four "known to be well affected to King George," three "Nonjurors," thirty-four "said to be High Flyers," and four "Roman Catholicks."[10] These were printers. Publishers and booksellers were more numerous. By 1750 there were about 120 of them in the provinces and about 128 in London.[11] Macky, in his *Journey through England* (1724), found that there had been a regrouping of the London trade: "The booksellers of ancient books in all languages are in Little Britain and Paternoster Row; those for divinity and the classics on the north side of St. Paul's Cathedral; law, history, and plays about Temple Bar; and the French booksellers in the Strand. It seems, then, that the bookselling business has been gradually resuming its original situation near this Cathedral ever since the beginning of George I, while the neighbourhood of Duck Lane and Little Britain has been proportionately falling into disuse."

The Size of the Firm

Statistics of the number of printing-houses give little idea of the size of the industry unless the capacity of the individual firm is known. It must be admitted that never throughout this period was any English printing-house commensurate with its chief continental rivals. In the opening years of the sixteenth century Anthoni Koberger, of Nuremberg, was using twenty-four presses and giving employment to over a hundred workmen. Johann Froben of Basel had seven presses at work in the year 1504. By 1576 Christophe Plantin of Antwerp had twenty-five presses and employed about a hundred and fifty workers. Yet Christopher Barker, printer to Queen Elizabeth and owner of one of the most considerable English businesses of the century, ran only five presses. The fear of competition led to a formal complaint of the master printers to the Court of Star Chamber in 1615 that too many presses had been erected, and to the consequent limitation of their number: the King's Printer was not mentioned, but of the remaining nineteen printers, fourteen were restricted to two presses each and the other five to one.[12] (In direct contrast to this policy is the order issued in 1618 by the Provost of Paris, on the advice of the Gild of Publishers, Printers and Binders, that each master printer should keep not less than two presses in running order.) The regulation of 1615 was somewhat modified by the seventeenth clause of the second Star Chamber Decree concerning printing (1637): "That no allowed Printer shall keep above two Presses, unlesse he hath been Master or upper Warden of his Company, who are thereby allowed to keep three Presses and no more, under paine of being disabled for ever after to keepe or use any Presse at all, unlesse for some great and speciall occasion for the publique, he or they have for a time leave of the Lord Arch-Bishop of Canterbury, or Lord Bishop of London for the time being, to have or use one, or more above the foresaid number, as their Lordships, or either of them shall thinke fit."[13] This order lapsed during the Civil War but was confirmed by the Licensing Act of 1662. We still find, therefore, in a survey of printing-presses of the year 1668 that the largest employer, James Fletcher, kept only five presses and employed only thirteen workmen and two apprentices; next in importance was Thomas Newcomb, with three presses and a proof press, twelve workmen and one apprentice; Thomas Leach, at the other end of the scale, had one press, not his own, and one workman.[14] It seems almost incredible that our Elizabethan and early Stuart literature should have issued from between fifty and sixty presses, a number, of course, exceeded in many a single printing establishment of the present day.

The university presses were rather more favoured than the rest. In 1636 Laud secured for the Oxford University Press a royal charter granting it the right to employ three printers, each of them being allowed two presses and two apprentices.[15] The Cambridge Press, too, had six printing-presses in the year 1689, according to the diary of Samuel Sewell, an American judge.[16] Their advantage was of short duration, as it happened; after 1695 there was no official hindrance to the number of presses any printer might use. It was not every printer who could afford an extra press, in any case. Some of the early provincial printing-houses, as we have seen, were very small. It is not surprising to find that the master of one of these had frequently to do most of the work himself. For many years Andrew Brice, the eighteenth-century Exeter printer, carried on "all and every offices of a Master Printer, Corrector, &c.," and was sometimes "actually forced to work at the Composition Part of the Occupation even at Midnight."[17] The mere lapse of an Act obviously did not force such a firm as this to extend. What it did was to allow each individual printing-house to develop to its best economic size. For many firms this was a size much larger than would previously have been allowed. The firm of Jacob Tonson and John Watts, for instance, was employing about fifty workmen in 1730, according to Benjamin Franklin's autobiography. Samuel Richardson by the middle of the century was setting his forty employees to work in three separate printing-houses.[18]

Output

The difference in size between the English firm and the continental is reflected in their relative output. Between 1473 and 1513 Anthoni Koberger of Nuremberg issued 236 separate works, many of them being in several volumes. Froben of Basel printed 257 large works between 1491 and 1528. In Leyden Louis Elzevir published about 100 books in the 34 years from 1583 to 1617, while John Elzevir issued 112 in the 6 years from 1655 to 1661. There is no exact means of estimating the volume of Caxton's output (1476–91) as his work, being mainly romance literature of a popular appeal, was not of the type to be preserved in the collections of contemporary scholars. According to William Blades, 98 works have been definitely identified as Caxton's, and there are about 10 more which may be his. His foreman and successor, Wynkyn de Worde, produced about 800 pieces in the 40 years to 1534, but these consist almost entirely of small pamphlets, so that his total output was actually far below that of Koberger or Froben. The only sixteenth-century printer whose type of work is comparable with that of the continental scholar-printer was Reynolde Wolfe, King's Printer in Latin, Greek and Hebrew, but he issued only 73 works between 1542 and 1573. The largest output and the best printing during the sixteenth century must be credited to John Day, whose publications from 1546 to 1584 amounted to about 275. Next must be ranked the royal printers: Richard Pynson printed about 180 works in the 35 years to 1528, including *The Canterbury Tales* and *The Shepherd's Calendar*; Thomas Berthelet issued about 250 between 1529 and 1554, notably Fitzherbert's *Book of Husbandry* and *Surveying* and the *Golden Book* of Marcus Aurelius; Christopher Barker published about 120 between 1574 and the end of the century. The output of the great majority of printers fell far below these figures, even allowing for the elasticity of the term "work." Julian Notary, one of the best-known of the early sixteenth-century printers, issued only about 20 books in as many years. William Faques, King's Printer, is recorded as having issued only 2 volumes and a broadside in 1504, another broadside in the following year and 3 deeds in 1508. William Bonham, one of the original members of the Stationers' Company, is known for only 7 publications. Such instances might be multiplied.

As regards annual output there was no English printer who equalled the 40 works issued from Plantin's house in Antwerp in 1587. If we disregard Richard Grafton, whose 30 publications of 1549 included a number of proclamations, the record for the century belongs to John Wolf, who published, among other works, *The Shepherd's Calendar* and Stow's *Survey of London*, and who issued 20 works in the year 1589, 18 in 1590 and 17 in 1591. With the exception of Wolf, Berthelet and Day few printers exceeded an output of 6 works in any year, while for many the average may be given as 2 volumes a year, or even less.

Actually, this low annual output was all that could be expected from the sixteenth- or seventeenth-century printing-house with its one or two hand-presses. Charles Knight, who had experience of this type of press, calculated that two men, working eight hours a day each, would print from it 1,000 sheets a day, so that it would take 200 days, or about threequarters of a year, to produce an edition of 10,000 copies of a schoolbook of 20 sheets (equivalent to 320 octavo pages), the normal size.[19] In confirmation of this, there is among the State Papers of

Henry VIII an indenture of 1523 between John Palsgrave and Pynson for printing 750 copies of *Lesclarcissement de la Lange Francoyse*: in this Pynson undertook to print a sheet on both sides each day. The printing of the *Bodleian Catalogue*, too, was carried on at the rate of a sheet a day. The main catalogue was printed between July 30 and October 10, 1604, and the Appendix between April 29 and June 4, 1605.[20] It may be that the journeymen did not keep up the rate of a sheet a day unless they were driven to it, for in 1732 Dr. William Webster advised Dr. Zachary Grey, after much experience of the trials of publishing, "If you think of publishing the MS. against the Rights of the Christian Church, with the Quakers' Bill . . . I believe you would think it most proper to have them printed in London, where they are *much more expeditious* than the Cambridge presses."[21]

It seems impossible to find out how much work was done by individual printers during the second half of the seventeenth century, for most of the volumes issued during this time bear the name of the bookseller but not of the printer. John Dunton, fortunately, did anticipate our curiosity, and obligingly told us that by 1698 he had printed 600 books, of which, as he remarks, "it would be strange if all should be alike good."[22] This was a total not reached by some well-known publishers even of the eighteenth century. The firm of Newbery, noted specially for children's books, issued only about 300 works between 1740 and 1802.[23] It seems, though, that a rather higher output was now usual, Robert Dodsley issued over 900 works in the course of his career between 1729 and 1764,[24] and Edmund Curll, of ill-repute, sent out over 1,000 between 1706 and 1746.[25] Both of these publishers at various times issued more than 50 new works in a single year.

The low output of the individual firm during the first two centuries, combined with the restrictions on the size of the industry as a whole, prevented the attainment of a large aggregate production. One may gain some idea of the volume of sixteenth-century publications from the researches of Joseph Ames as revised by William Herbert (1785), although the statistics to be compiled from their *Typographical Antiquities* should not be taken as complete. For the year 1510 the total number of works recorded by Herbert was 13; for 1530 it was 28; for 1550, 87. From 1557 we are provided with more complete statistics in the book entries in the Stationers' Register, although even these do not give an absolutely accurate record: the register is a list of works authorised to be printed, not of those actually produced, and on this account an attempted estimate of total production may be too high; on the other hand, the compulsory enrolment of copies was not extended to works for which a royal patent had been granted, while it was obviously not enforced in the case of clandestinely-printed political tracts or the numerous "pirated" editions of literary works. Of the 89 book entries in the register for 1560–1, 20 relate to mere ballads, which were usually so small that they may be almost disregarded. For 1580–1 the number of entries rose to 219, but quite one-quarter of these, again, were ballads. The figures remain remarkably constant from this time until the year 1639–40, when 355 copies were entered, about 100 of them being ballads. With the outbreak of the Civil War restrictions were of no avail: the collection of Thomason tracts in the British Museum bears witness to the prolific output during the following years. Nevertheless, with the restoration of order the volume of production resumed approximately its former size. One of the earliest catalogues published in England, "of all books printed in England since the dreadful fire, 1666, to the end of Trinity term, 1680" shows that 3,550 books were printed during these years, about one-half being single sermons or tracts. Disregarding such small works as these it may be estimated that, on an average, about 100 new books were issued annually. Yet in Germany, according to the statistics collected by Panzer and others, 571 works were printed as early as the year 1520 and 944 in 1523!

To the twentieth-century critic, used to an annual output of more than 10,000 new books alone, a total of 100 for the whole kingdom may seem pitiably small. It will perhaps readjust our ideas to read a sentence or two from the preface to Ralph

Lever's *The Art of Reason*, printed by Henry Bynneman in 1573: "If ye consider the bookes, that are now printed, and compare them with the bookes, that were printed at the first, Lord, what a diversity is there, and how much do the last exceed the first! yet if you will compare the first and the last printer together, and seek whether deserveth more praise and commendation, ye shall find that the first did farre exceede the last: for the last had help of manye, and the first had help of none. So that the first lighteth the candle of knowledge (as it were) and the second doth but snuff it."

In spite of the breakdown of restrictions at the end of the seventeenth century there seems to have been no increase in the average output of the trade as a whole during the eighteenth. The *Complete Catalogue of Modern Books, Published from the Beginning of the Century to 1756* shows a yearly average of 93 works excluding pamphlets. It is possible that the catalogue was not really complete, but this number is far higher than could have been expected from the entries at Stationers' Hall. Between 1714 and 1774 there was only one year in which more than 100 works were registered by the Stationers, and the average was under 50.[26] In order to realise to the full our international unimportance as producers of books during the whole of this period we have only to glance at the statistics of new works shown at the Leipzig fair. At the 1616 fair there were 731 new works. Most of these were German, naturally enough; but there were also 57 from Venice, 47 from France, 38 from Holland, 22 from Switzerland—and 4 from England. In 1716 the total had fallen to 558, but in 1789 it had risen to 2,115; these included 91 from Switzerland, 52 from France, 45 from Denmark, 12 each from Poland and Hungary, 9 each from Riga and Holland, 6 from Italy—and 2 from England.[27] Was this to be explained entirely by our national diffidence?

The Size of the Edition

A discussion of output involves consideration not only of the number of works issued and of their average size but also of the number of copies of each work. From 1587 the size of the edition of most publications was limited by a regulation of the Stationers' Company. The intention behind the decree was to provide extra work for the compositor by limiting the number of copies which might be taken from any forme: a series of small editions, the type being reset for each, although giving extra expense to the printer, was held to be socially more desirable than one large edition for which the type had to be set only once. In practice the order could hardly have had much effect. The number at any impression was limited to 1,250 or 1,500 except in the case of grammars, prayer books and catechisms, of which there might be four impressions annually, each of 2,500 or 3,000, "and except also *the statutes* and *proclamacons* with all other bookes belonginge to ye office of her maiesties printer which by reason of her maiesties affayres are to be limited to no numbers. And except all *Calenders* printed Red and black and also except all *Almanackes* and *prognostications*."[28] One would think that 10,000 new copies of a grammar annually would more than satisfy the demands of a population totalling only between two and three millions, although it had certainly been claimed in the Star Chamber case of R. Day *v*. T. Dunn, R. Robinson and others (1585) that Dunn and Robinson had printed and disposed of 10,000 copies of *The ABC with the lyttell Catechisme* (Day's patent) in eight months. The attempt to help the journeyman could have been made far more effective by extending the restrictions to almanacs and prognostications, for which the demand was enormous. Very seldom did the edition of works which were limited to 1,250 copies reach even 1,000 in practice. In the case of certain books, such as John Dee's *General and rare memorials pertaining to the art of navigation* (1577), only 100 copies were printed. Even the Shakespeare quartos did not exceed 1,000 copies to the edition. Probably the publishers' uncertainty of the market had a greater effect than any order of the Company in keeping down the numbers. It is noticeable that in 1635, by which time the demand for books could be gauged more easily, the printer was allowed a greater output. The order of that year was "that noe Bookes printed of the Nonpariell Letter exceed aboue the number of 5,000. And of the Brevier 3,000. Except the

Priviledge granted to the Company and the *Testament*, belonging to the Kinges Printers Commonly called Cheekes *Testament*, and of that 6,000, at the most. But yf occasions shall require to have a greater number than the said 2,000. That then uppon good reasons shewed to the Master and Wardeins, the said Master and Wardeins may permitt to be printed 3,000, but noe greater number in any wise."[29]

Two thousand copies to an edition were probably ample in most cases. It is interesting to find that a large proportion of John Newbery's publications, in the eighteenth century, were issued in an edition of this size. The truth was that the public was not yet really greedy for books. When its interest was at last aroused, with the coming of the novel, a far bigger edition would scarcely meet the demand. The first edition of *Rob Roy*, 10,000 copies in all, was sold out in three weeks, and a second edition of 3,000 was embarked upon straight away. After that success it would have been unthinkable to issue a Scott novel in anything under 10,000 copies. After all, had not John Dunton, a century before, printed 10,000 copies of Lukin's *Practice of Godliness*?[30]

To judge by contemporary criticisms, the tendency during the eighteenth century was not to issue too large editions, but too frequent ones. It was complained that within a few months of buying a book the reader found that it was already out of date owing to the issue of a revised edition. In 1737 a Copyright Bill was introduced with the part object of removing this grievance: one of its clauses specified that a second edition of a work costing more than 5s. would be protected only if the amendments were issued also in separate sheets, so that the owner of a copy of the first edition could buy the supplementary material without the rest. The Bill passed the Commons, but was rejected in the House of Lords.

Rather than issue a large uniform edition the publisher often finds it more profitable to publish the same work in a variety of forms, calculated to attract all manner of buyers. This practice was already being followed in the eighteenth century. John Newbery, in advertising his *Letters on the Most Common as well as Important*

Occasions in Life (1758), calls attention to the choice now open to his readers: "The regard which the public has been pleased to pay to this volume of Letters has induced the Editor to print it in three different sizes. That is to say, the above edition on a new elzevir letter at eighteenpence; an Edition in Twelves on a larger letter at two shillings, and a small edition for those who are very young at one shilling.''[31]

Secondary Occupations

In spite of complaints of too frequently revised editions, the eighteenth-century publisher was not always fully occupied by his profession. Book production, from quite early days, was often carried on in conjunction with some other trade, or with one of the learned professions. Crowley has already been mentioned in this connection. William Rastell, as well as being a printer, was an eminent lawyer who rose to be a justice of the Queen's Bench in Mary's reign. Thomas Raynald printed about thirty books between 1540 and 1555 and was at the same time a physician. William Baldwin was primarily a minister and schoolmaster, but he added printing to his work towards the middle of the sixteenth century in order to further the Reformation. It was in order to join in religious controversy that William Dugard, the Royalist headmaster of Merchant Taylors' School, set up a printing-press there in 1644.

The secondary occupation was not always connected with scholarship. James Askew, a London stationer, was also described in the register of the Stationers' Company (1593) as "one of the merchauntes of Barbarie, Spaine, Portugall and the East Cuntreies." Conrad Myllar and Garbrand Harkes, stationers at Oxford, were licensed to sell ale and wine; in this they were following the example of Lotter, who had kept a wine shop and an inn as well as undertaking some of the earliest printing for Luther. Wine and books, it seems, clung together with a constancy which would have gladdened the heart of Omar. To mention two further examples out of many: Norman Nelson, of Holborn, who published and sold law books, was described in a law-suit of 1680 as a vintner,[32] while Christopher Earl, printing in Birmingham between 1770 and 1778, was entered in Sketchley's *Birmingham Directory* for 1770 as a printer and publican.

In the seventeenth and eighteenth centuries, as at the present time, it was quite common for the small bookseller to run a general stationery business as a sideline. Christopher Coningsby, who kept a bookshop in London from 1687 to 1711, was typical of this class of tradesmen: he sold legal forms of all kinds, warrants for land-tax and licences for alehouses.[33] A Bristol printer, William Bonny, went farther than this: he regularly advertised in the *Bristol Post Boy*, which he published, that he was a buyer of old rope and paper; and he offered for sale Bibles, Welsh prayer books, paper hangings, music, maps, blank ale licences and blank commissions for private men-of-war; what is more, in May 1712 he had very good Bridgwater peas and excellent charcoal for sale.[34] An advertisement found in a book printed in Exeter in 1714 is worth quoting in this connection: "Sold by Thomas Butter, Bookseller near St. Martin's-lane in Exon, where (besides Books and Stationary Wares of all sorts) is sold the best of Mathematical and Sea Instruments, several sorts of Physical Medicines, as Dr. Daff's Elixir Salutis, Stoughton's Elixir Stomachicum, Spirit of Scurvy-Grass Golden and Plain, &c. Also the famous Cephalick or Liquid-snuff, prepar'd for the Queen. With Japan Ink, Indian-Ink, Cake-Ink, Ink-powder, Common Ink; Ink-Glasses, Pounce, shining sand; great variety of paper-hangings for rooms; the best of Stampt-Parchment and Paper, Bonds, &c., at reasonable rates, by Wholesale or Retail."[35] One cannot help suspecting that in this case it was bookselling which was the sideline.

Thomas Butter, we notice, included various medicines in his stock-in-trade. Strange though it seems, the sale of patent medicines was chosen more frequently than any other secondary occupation by the eighteenth-century publisher or bookseller. Perhaps he was better fitted than most tradesmen to assume the air of wisdom so essential to the sale of nasty liquids. The way had been prepared to some extent, it is true, by a few seventeenth-century booksellers: the lozenges mentioned in the *Mercurius Publicus* for April 1661 as being on sale in Joseph Bilcliffe's bookshop in Covent Garden

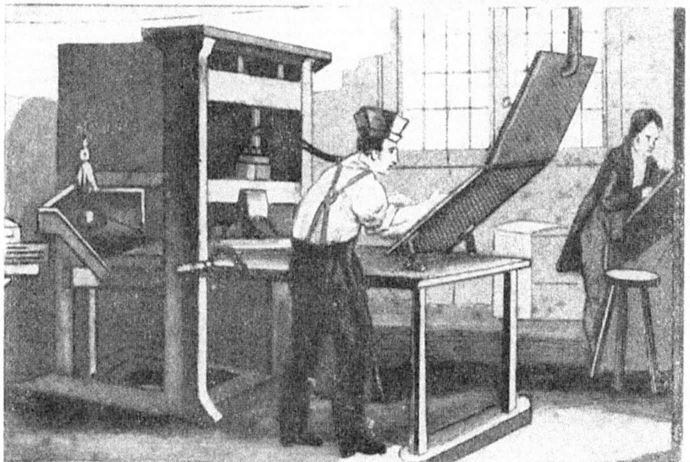

HAND-PRODUCTION
From Whittock (N.) and others, *The Complete Book of Trades*, 1842

may have been quite pleasant to the taste. The balsam, again, which was offered for sale on London Bridge among Tracy's collection of schoolbooks, and which was advertised as "lately brought from Chili, a Province of America," was presumably for external application only. It requires more confidence to buy a remedy which has actually to be drunk, but the seventeenth-century bookseller had a means of inspiring it: what he did was to publish a pseudo-medical work recommending certain remedies and then to advertise himself as an agent for these particular medicines. Salmon's *Select Physical and Chyrurgical Observations* (1685) was a case in point: it informed the reader that "Whereas, Dr. William Salmon, the author of this treatise, being some time gone beyond sea, These are to give notice that all persons that have an occasion for any of his medicines mentioned in his catalogues or books, may be supplied by John Hollier," to be found in the bookshop of Thomas Passinger on London Bridge. Bromfield's work on the scurvy, in the same year, gave a list of several booksellers from whom a certain medicine could be bought. Among them were William Bailey, of Burton-on-Trent, John Ball, of Banbury, Thomas Cadwell, of Derby and Richard Hunt, of Hereford.[36] It is clear that by the eighteenth century this had become quite a recognised proceeding. Newbery himself, the publisher of Goldsmith's works, and famous for his children's books, carried on a most flourishing trade in medicines. He had a monopoly of "that indispensable remedy," Dr. James's fever powder, and in 1760 he was advertising at least a dozen patent mixtures.[37]

All this seems to have been very successful, but the career of a certain Thomas Cottrell leaves one hoping that the remedies sold did at times bear some relation to the complaint. This gentleman was working between 1757 and 1785 as a letter-founder. He also served in His Majesty's Life Guards. He was also a Doctor for the Toothache, and this affliction he cured at once, so he claimed, by burning the ear.[38]

CHAPTER V

Copyright

For a full understanding of the rights of author and publisher in the sixteenth and seventeenth centuries account must be taken of certain aspects of mediaeval book production. The question of the right to copy, although it became more urgent with the introduction of printing, could not suddenly be introduced as a new legal problem merely because it was now possible to produce a thousand copies of a work in the same amount of time that had been taken to write twenty. If it had ever been lawful to make a laborious transcript of another man's work without his permission the same arguments must still apply.

As regards a large proportion of the works written in the Middle Ages the question of copyright would not arise. To be recognised as part of the common law, such a right must be shown to spring from the customary law of property. But, as we have seen, much of our mediaeval literature proceeded from the monasteries, and it was implicit in the nature of the monk's calling that he should renounce all forms of personal property. Monkish chronicles and works of piety were therefore freely reproduced not only in the writer's own monastery but also in any other to which the manuscripts might be lent; it was in this way that the monastic libraries were formed. Together with these books there were copied the classics and the works of the Fathers, but there was nobody to dispute the right of copying the works of authors long since dead.

Outside the monasteries matters were complicated by the existence of a market for manuscripts: the question of property has certainly arisen in the case of goods which are bought and sold. Yet here again many of the works involved, being copied for use in the monasteries, were those of Greek and Latin authors, and there were no original copies of them in existence. The question of publishers' copyright for these might well have arisen but for the impossibility of proving which was the first of a series of manuscripts. It was clearly just as impossible for an author to keep any check on the number of copies of his work which would get into circulation after he had once allowed a copy to be made. Copyright was unenforceable in the case of the hand-written book.

When we come to the era of printing we find a new reason for the publisher's wishing to safeguard his works against competition —the size of his initial expenditure. Manuscripts had as a rule been transcribed to the order of the individual customer; there was little risk that the bookseller would find himself burdened with a surplus stock. This was not true of the printed book. The printer-publisher, unless he resorted to the then very rare subscription-publication, had to bear the whole expense of providing type, paper and other materials as well as the cost of labour before he could be certain of the state of the market. Publishing risks were of so definite a nature that steps were taken to minimise them long before the vague claims of the author received any attention.

It would be difficult, indeed, to assess the rights of authorship, more especially in this early period. Was the commentator of a classical text entitled to privileges denied to the original writer himself? Moreover, when in a time of religious turmoil the greater number of original works were of a controversial nature, would there not have been something ludicrous in an author's attempt to restrict the rights of multiplying copies of a pamphlet whose great aim was propaganda? The printer, on the contrary, bore the risks of publication purely as a business venture, fired by none of that enthusiasm which kept the writer above all idea of monetary gain; to him it seemed vital to check the author's zeal so far as to keep him from passing on his manuscript to other publishers before the full profits of at least a first edition had been gathered in. The fact that so many early printed books consisted of classical works, mediaeval romance literature and theological pamphlets for which no reward was expected would have made it difficult for the author to substantiate his claim to property in his own works. Actually, it seldom seems to have occurred to him to do so. It seems to have been generally felt by those who wrote in the sixteenth century that the object of publication was to pass on ideas to as many other people as possible. Such an author may have regarded himself as comparable to a schoolmaster, able to spread knowledge and yet still to possess it himself in no way diminished; the fact that he could dispose of the physical text of his book certainly did not greatly worry him until nearer our own times. His attitude was due, no doubt, in part to the existence of literary patronage combined with the distaste (general at the time) for receiving payment from a publisher.

For the earlier period, then, we are concerned with publishers' copyright, and only in a small degree with the rights of the author. The position in England agreed with that in Germany: the possession of a manuscript carried with it the unquestioned right of reproducing it.[1] In Venice, too, grants of copyright were usually made to publishers, but the rights of the author received greater recognition there than anywhere at that time: a few authors, including Ariosto and Tasso, were given the whole rights in their own works, but far more striking than these grants was a decree of 1544 which forbade anyone to print a work without proving to the University Commissioners that the author or his representatives had consented to its publication, the penalty being a fine and a month's imprisonment.[2] Not until 1709 was there any such official safeguard of the claims of the English author.*

Patents

The neglect of the author's interests was specially easy in England from the nature of the first grants of copyright, which were made to the King's Printer. The printer appointed to that office, created in the late fifteenth century, had the sole right of printing any work issued by or belonging to the King. The King himself reaped no monetary benefit from these publications; how, then, could the ordinary author hope to press a successful claim? The works included in the King's Printer's monopoly at first were Acts of

* An order of the House of Commons of January 1642, "that the printers do neither print nor reprint anything without the name and consent of the author" was ineffectual.

Parliament, law books and year books, Bibles and service books, almanacks, and Latin grammars and other educational works. From 1547 onwards the royal printer was appointed by letters patent, and the same method came to be adopted in the case of other printing grants made by the Crown. Henry VIII had already, in 1534, issued letters patent granting to Cambridge University the right to appoint three printers who should be allowed to print any works approved by the Chancellor and three doctors and to sell them within the university, a right which was confirmed by statute in the reign of Elizabeth. The grant of this special privilege shows that there was already a groping towards the idea of copyright.

As distinct from these general privileges there were occasional grants of copyright in respect of particular works. Possibly the first grant of exclusive privilege for a single book was one to Richard Pynson in 1518: the colophon to the *Oratio Richardi Pacei, &c.*, states that the work was printed "cum privilegio a rege indulto, ne quis hanc orationem intra biennium in regno Angliae imprimat, aut alibi impressam et importatam in eodem regno Angliae vendat."[3] Another grant was obtained from the King for the second edition of Robert Witinton's *Treatise on Grammar.* Wynkyn de Worde, having perhaps in those early days too much trust in the good faith of his fellow-publishers, had issued the first edition in 1523 without special protection, only to find it followed by a reprint by Peter Treveris. In his second edition (1533) De Worde denounced the pirate in no uncertain terms.[4] A few other specific grants were made during the reign of Henry VIII, such as the one made in 1542 to Antony Morlar, giving him a four years' right to print the Bible in English,[5] and the one in the following year to Grafton and Whitchurch for the book of divine service.[6] In 1547 two important groups of books were assigned to individual printers: Reginald Wolff was appointed to the office of printer and seller of books in Latin, Greek and Hebrew,[7] and Richard Grafton was given the sole printing of the statute books.[8] A German, Laurentius Torrentinus, managed in 1551 to secure the sole printing for seven years of the digests of Roman Civil Law,[9] and two years later William Seres was given what were probably the most coveted rights of all—those for primers and for the catechism in English and the ABC.[10] In 1553 Richard Tottell obtained the privilege of printing common law books,[11] and John Cawood acquired a patent for Acts of Parliament and proclamations.[12]

Grants of monopoly, for such they really were, came increasingly to be made to individual publishers in respect of single books or whole classes of works from the middle of the sixteenth century onwards. It would perhaps be well to give a very brief sketch of the great problem of which book-patents formed part.

There were various reasons for the adoption of the patent system by Elizabeth. One was an attempt to foster industry by grants of mining rights and of privileges in respect of new inventions. The others were, in the main, ultimately based on the financial stringency of the time: the grant of a monopoly was an easy way of settling a debt, of rewarding a favourite, or of inspiring loyalty. It must be admitted that until about 1580 the system did little harm, the majority of the early patents being for new inventions. Between 1580 and 1600 abuses gradually crept in, and monopolies were granted in respect of salt, starch, train-oil, paper and other commodities to men who could not claim to be their first introducers, and who used their power in raising prices. By the end of the century public feeling was so outraged that the Queen had to submit to the appointment of a select committee to consider the question. In the course of the proceedings on a Bill designed to limit the Queen's prerogative (1601) a list of patents was read; of nearly fifty grants, six related to the printing of certain books. Elizabeth restored peace for a time by recalling the more objectionable grants and entrusting to the courts of common law the responsibility of deciding which of the remaining ones acted against the general welfare. James I began well by suspending all the existing grants except those to corporations, but in 1606 monopolies were the principal subjects discussed by the Committee of Grievances. On receiving further complaints in 1610 James published his *Book of Bounty*, in which he renounced all intention of making further grants. Yet they continued. In 1621 Parliament instituted an inquiry which led to the passing of the Statute of Monopolies in

1624. This declared monopolies to be illegal, except as regards those for new inventions and those held by companies, and provided that their validity should be settled according to the common law; but it is specially interesting from our point of view in that books were exempted from its provisions. But this Act by no means ended the problem; it arose again with renewed vigour under Charles I, who tried to augment his income by becoming a monopolist himself. Abuses grew to such an extent as to cause enormous rises in prices, so that in 1639 the Privy Council felt it advisable to revoke a long list of patents before Parliament should be called. In the following year the Long Parliament denounced the whole system, cancelled a large number of grants, and declared monopolists to be incapable of sitting in Parliament. The consequent decline in revenue was compensated by the introduction of the excise system in 1643.

As far as books were concerned the patent system began to be a specially important trade factor in 1559. In that year four grants were made: in January Richard Tottell obtained a licence to print *all* law books; in March Richard Jugge and John Cawood became monopolists on their appointment as joint printers to the Queen; William Seres was, in July, allowed a patent for primers and books of private prayers, and in November John Day was given a seven years' copyright for Dr. W. Cunningham's *Cosmographical Glass*.[13] During the next twenty years patents were granted to about ten people, covering a variety of publications. By the year 1582 certain individuals possessed the copyright of all Bibles, prayer books, psalms, catechisms, statutes, proclamations, law books, dictionaries, almanacks and music books, and for specified Latin textbooks. The period for which general industrial monopolies were granted was at first ten years. By 1580 it had grown to twenty or thirty, but the Statute of Monopolies of 1624 limited the grants to fourteen years. As regards book-patents long periods were allowed from the outset: three of the four licences issued in 1559 were for the lifetime of the patentee, while the patent granted in 1575 to Tallis and Byrd for music-books was for twenty-one years. Actually, of course, a monopoly might be brought to an abrupt end by the death of the patentee. Nicasius Yetsweirt was particularly unfortunate in this respect: in 1577 he was granted the reversion of Tottell's patent, for thirty years, but it so happened that Tottell outlived him.

These privileges could not long continue unchallenged. The first opposition to the system came from the stationers in their corporate capacity: in February 1576 the Company complained to Burghley that "some one person affectinge more his own private gaine then regardinge the ouerthrowe of a multitude of whole families, Dothe sue vnto the quenes maiestie for th[e] obteyninge of a priviledge for the sole imprintinge of all balades Damaske paper and bokes in prose or meetre from the quantitie of one sheete of paper to xxiiij tie. By th[e] imprintinge of which thinges the saide companie is chiefelie maineteigned, so as if the same be taken from them by waie of previledge they shalbe vtterlie undone."[14] This was no exaggeration: if the patent had been issued the monopoly of the greater part of the industry would have passed to one man. Fortunately, the Company's petition was successful. In the following year there was a combined appeal from printers, glass-sellers and cutlers against privileges to private persons, in the course of which it was complained that the patents held by Jugge, Tottell, Day and others were ruining all other printers and booksellers besides raising the prices of books so excessively that the student could ill afford them.[15]

By 1582 matters were ripe for civil war within the Stationers' Company. In the words of one of the patent-holders, William Seres the younger, "Certen yonge men of the said company beinge desirous for their owne pryvate comoditye and gayne to haue the said priviledge and all other the like priviledges taken awaye, Haue exhibyted a bill of compleynte to her maiesties most honorable privy counsell wherein they pretend that in Iustice yt standeth with the best pollicye of this realme that the printinge of all good and laufull bokes be at libertye for euery man to prynt without grauntinge or allowinge of any priviledge by the prynce to the contrary. And in dede they doe not onely go about to derogate the princes awthoritye aswell for grauntinge of suche like priuiledges as also of all lycences for the transportacon of clothe woole beare and suche like sayeng in expresse termes that the privilege for sole printinge of all bokes is agaynst the lawe But also they goe about to sett at libertye the feate of pryntinge both to all prynters and to all free men of the citye of London."[16]

The leader of this attack on monopoly was John Wolf, of the Fishmongers' Company, acting in association with Roger Ward, Francis Adams and others. Their method was the practical one of printing the most widely read books, complete with the name and trade-mark of the patentee, and selling them throughout the country. Ward, although he was at the time imprisoned in the Counter through representations made against him by various stationers, went so far as to infringe the most profitable patent of all, that held by John Day for the *ABC with the Little Catechism*, arranging for the printing and disposal of ten thousand copies of the work by his journeymen. Day was incensed, and brought the matter before the Court of Star Chamber as being in defiance of the royal prerogative. A commission was appointed to consider the whole problem, but the dispute dragged on for about four years. John Wolf sought to justify his breach of privilege by the argument, "I will live." The wardens of the Stationers' Company rebuked him for presuming to question the actions of Her Majesty's Government, but, "Tush," said he, "Luther was but one man, and reformed all ye world for religion, and I am that one man, yat must and will reforme the gouernement in this trade."[17]

According to Christopher Barker, Queen's Printer, who in December 1582 wrote a report on the printing-patents of 1558–82,[18] Wolf and his associates were "for the most part idle, vndiscrete, and vnthriftie persons, pretending suche skill in lawe, as to Discourse what the Prince by her highnes kingly office may Doe, what other magistrates ought to doe, and in the meane tyme forgett their owne Dutie toward God, toward their prince and their neighbour, Of which company being fyve in nomber, one John Wolfe nowe prysoner in the Clinck is the cheif, who after many loose pointes of behaviour, obtayned his freedome of the Fishmongers, by what meanes I knowe not." This criticism could hardly be called impartial: Barker was anxious to defend his own position as holder of one of the most coveted patents, that for the Bible and the Book of Common Prayer. In the course of his report he gives a very modest account of his personal benefits from the system: the Statutes of the Realm, he says, were printed by his predecessors in so great numbers that no more need be printed for twenty years; for the Abridgment of the Statutes he received only half the proceeds, owing to a contract with Tottell; proclamations had to be printed at such short notice that important works had often to be broken off in their favour, with the result that he lost more by one proclamation than he could gain by six; the *Paraphrases of Erasmus* and the Testaments were altogether unprofitable; as for the Bible, "The whole bible together requireth so great a somme of money to be employed, in the imprinting thereof; as Master Jugge kept the Realme twelve yere withoute, before he Durst adventure to print one impression; but I, considering the great somme I paide to Master Wilkes, Did (as some haue termed it since) gyve a Desperate adventure to imprint fower sundry impressions for all ages, wherein I employed to the value of three thowsande pounde in the terme of one yere and an halfe, or thereaboute: in which tyme if I had died, my wife and children had ben utterlie undone." What the actual financial result was he does not disclose. As regards the monopoly which the office of King's Printer gave to him for the Book of Common Prayer he was possibly right in denying its advantage to him. This was a curious case by which he held the patent for the work printed as a whole whereas individual parts of it, regarded as distinct items, were assigned to others. That is to say, Barker possessed the copyright of the complete Prayer Book, but the right of issuing separate copies of the morning and evening prayer, the psalms, the collects, the litany and the primer for children (consisting of the catechism and a few psalms) fell to Seres, while the catechism itself, and "the Psalmes in meeter, with notes to singe them in the Churches aswell in foure partes, as in playne songe," were the monopoly of John Day. Seres is reported as having sold a hundred copies of his psalter to one of Barker's complete prayer books. To add to Barker's annoyance, such men as Roger Ward had taken upon themselves to print their own combination of parts, such as the morning prayer together with the psalter, and were cutting prices.

With the exception of these grants to Day and Seres, which Barker condemned as being in direct conflict with his own, there was only one patent which he admitted to be profitable to its holder. That was the one held by Richard Watkins for almanacks and prognostications, "a pretty commoditie toward an honest mans lyving." As regards "the Grammar, and accidens for the instruction of youth," the five men to whom Flower had farmed out the patent had been heard to say that they would gladly give two or three hundred pounds to be rid of it. Tottell's benefit from law books had been great, but his privilege was now of less value, "and is like yet to be rather worse than better, except a man should with exceading charge take another course therein, then hetherto hath been observed." The patent for dictionaries, chronicles and histories placed Master Bynneman in a dilemma: "If the printer should print many of the said volumes, he must needes stande betwixt two extremes, that is, if he print competent nombers of each to mayntayne his charges, all England Scotland and much more, were not able to vtter [dispose of] them; and if he should print but a few of each volume, the prices should be exceading greate, and he in more Daunger to be vndone then likely to gayne, the provision of varietie of letter and other thinges, would be so chargeable." Thomas Marsh's right to print Latin textbooks should have been profitable but for his being "the vnfittest man in England, in deed neither profiting himself, nor the realme." Barker's report as a whole leaves one with the feeling that—if it were the whole truth—our sixteenth-century printers would have been hopelessly lacking in business acumen.

Having satisfactorily proved that the patent system was of no service to anybody Barker would next, one would suppose, go on to suggest its total abolition. But not at all. "I protest before God," he says, "that if I could see how it might tende to the honour of this Realm, or the credit of the professours of that science [printing], or might be any way beneficiall to the common wealth, that priviledges were dissolved, I would yeeld myne opinion so." He professes to have the interests of the working classes at heart: "there must nedes be Journemen, of whome the nomber is nowe aboute threescore, who Do both knowe and confesse that if priviledges were Disolved they were vtterlie undone, having no other qualitie to get their lyving." In his opinion what was required was more vigilant supervision by the officers of the Company of all printing, whether of the privileged or unprivileged.

John Wolf himself withdrew from the fray in the autumn of 1584, when he and Francis Adams were made two of the assigns of Richard Day's patent. Being now himself a monopolist he entirely changed his tactics, became an upholder of privilege, joined the Stationers' Company, and finished his career in the most respectable office of Printer to the City of London.

The position was still further eased in 1584 by the action of the patentees in giving up some of their privileges for the benefit of the poor of the Company. At the same time it was agreed that if a printer did not wish to reprint a work for which he had been granted a patent, or if a work had been out of print for a long time, one of the unprivileged might be granted permission to print it on paying sixpence in the pound on its cost to the Company's poor account.

The dispute was drawing to an end, but the patent-holders were loath to give up their privileges. In 1586 they wrote to the Privy Council professing altruistic motives which, really put into practice, would soon have found them in a debtors' prison: "priviledges are occasion, that many bookes are nowe prynted, which are more beneficial to the common welth, then proffitable to the prynter, for the Patentee beinge benefited otherwise by Bookes of profitable sale is content to bestowe part of his gayne in other bokes, which are within the compas of his patent, verie beneficiall for the common welth, and yet suche whereby the printer shall scarse reape the Tenth parte of his charge: which Bookes wolde neuer be prynted if privileges were revoked."[19] Another argument made at the same time was more plausible: the first printer of a work had commonly to make some payment to the author which later printers could avoid, with the result that the latter could sell more cheaply;

besides this the second printer could profit from the experience of the first, and could improve on the first edition by adding notes or using a different kind of paper. "These inconvenyences seen euery man will strayne curtesie who shall begynne, so farre that in the ende all prynting will decaie within the Realme." In answer to the criticism that monopolists raised prices unduly they pointed out that any such excess could be checked by the powers given in the statute 25 Henry VIII.

The author's point of view does not seem to have been expressed. The patent system must have drastically limited his choice of publisher. There is some truth in the claim that it merely gave official sanction to a natural specialisation, that Tottell, for instance, would in any case have chosen to print law-books. But, by the enforced absence of competition, there was no guarantee that a legal or any other writer could ever get his work published at all. If the monopolist did not want to work there was nobody to make him do so. Of Tottell himself it was reported in 1583 that he had "three presses and vseth but one,"[20] and he seems to have found it most profitable to use this one press for his own *Miscellany*, of which he issued seven editions between 1557 and 1600.

Any argument for monopoly was sure to be favourably received by the Government at this time. It was not long before further grants were made. The next one of importance was that of December 1588 by which Richard Watkin's patent for almanacks and prognostications was reassigned to Watkins and Roberts for twenty-one years. In 1589 there was a rare grant of authors' copyright: Dr. Bright was given a fifteen years' patent for works in shorthand and such other works as he might compile. Two years later Richard Wright of Oxford obtained the copyright for life of the English version of the *History* of Tacitus. In 1592 there was another grant to an author: John Norden was given a ten years' privilege in respect of his *Speculum Britanniae*. Grants continued at the rate of nearly one a year until the end of Elizabeth's reign.[21]

James I, as we have seen, abolished several patents on his accession. His most important action with regard to books was that of October 29, 1603, whereby he recalled the patents of John and

Richard Day for primers and psalters and of James Roberts and Richard Watkins for almanacks and prognostications, and granted them to the Stationers' Company for ever.[22] These works formed the English stock of the Company, shares in it being held by individual members according to their status. As in the case of monopolies in general, the King's good intentions were brought to nought by his financial difficulties. Within a short time he aroused popular resentment by new grants of privilege, some of them, such as the ones for the works of Hieronymus Xanthius in Latin and for the book entitled *Instructions for the planting and increasing of mulbery trees and breeding of Silkwormes*, being issued to men who were not members of the Stationers' Company. Of the forty-three book-patents granted by James and his successor only ten were allowed to members of the Company. One of the most important privileges lost in this way by the regular printer was that of printing grammar-books.

Although several of the new patents were unpopular they were not all wholly harmful. On the contrary, John Day rendered such useful service by one of his publications that it was pointed out to him as his duty to continue the good work. He had had the original idea of issuing weekly bills of the prices of foreign commodities, and the patent of November 1, 1634, which gave him the sole right of publishing them for fourteen years stated that the bills had been discontinued for nearly three years, "to the great hindrance of the merchants in their commerce and correspondence, to the disgrace of the city of London, and to the prejudice of the Customs."[23]

No monopoly ever caused greater fury than was aroused in 1623 by the grant to George Wither of a fifty years' patent for his *Hymns and Songs of the Church*.[24] To ensure this work a large sale it was prescribed in the grant that a copy should be inserted in every "Psalm book in meeter," for which the Company had the patent, and Wither was given the right of search of all printing-houses, bookshops and private dwellings of printers and stationers for the purpose of seizing any psalters sold without his hymns. The provision which specially incensed the members of the Stationers' Company was that Wither and his assigns should receive as much payment for each sheet of his *Hymns and Songs* as the Company took for a sheet of the Psalms. This would have been a far higher rate than Wither could hope to receive in the open market. It was in the course of the bitter dispute which followed that Wither printed his "Schollers Purgatory, Discouered in the Stationers' Commonwealth, And Discribed in a Discourse Apologeticall, aswell for the publike aduantage of the Church, the State, and whole Commonwealth of England as for the remedy of priuate iniuryes," whose sweeping denunciations of the bad stationer we have already noticed. For some years the stationers refused, not only to bind up his hymns with the authorised psalter, but even to publish any other work written by Wither. In January 1634 Wither summoned most of the London stationers before the Council to answer for "contempt of the great seal" with regard to his patent. The stationers won the case: that part of the grant which directed that the hymns and psalter should be bound together was recalled.

While this dispute with Wither was in progress the Stationers' Company was also engaged in an altercation with Legge, the Cambridge University printer, who had infringed the Company's copyright for psalms. In 1622 the Company referred the matter to the Privy Council, and obtained judgment that the Cambridge printer was not empowered by his charter to print any work already assigned to another. The chief London stationers, attacking from another point, boycotted the edition of Lyly's grammar printed by Legge; whereupon the university retaliated by a regulation of June 25th, "That no booksellers in the university should buy books from, or sell to, Bill, Norton, Barrett, and Knight, or any other Londoner who might join their society, without special permission." The order went still further: any present or future student of the university or any holder of a degree who should want a work printed, whether his own composition or that of another writer, should offer the copy in the first instance to the university printer. What was more, any graduate who became a schoolmaster was to promise faithfully to use only the publications of the Cambridge University Press in his school.[25] Meanwhile Legge, assisted by the Vice-Chancellor of the University and several doctors, proceeded with his unlawful occupation of printing the Psalms. Officially the Stationers' Company won. In November 1623 the Privy Council "ordered among other thinges that the vniversity should print all bookes except Primers, Psalters, or Psalmes, or anie part of them, and for the Almanacks they should not print anie whereof ye copies belong to the Staconers. Neuerthelesse the said Legge, since printed the Abcee, and hath this yeare printed Ponds Almanack. Wherevpon the companie Doe seaze all the said Almanacks that they can meet withall as they hope by a decree in Starchamber Concerning bookes and by their grant, they may lawfully Doe."[26]

The Cambridge Press next entered into competition with the King's Printer in the publication of Bibles. Some account of this was given in an anonymous tract of 1641 designed to show the effects of monopoly on the prices of books: "Scintilla, or A light broken into darke Warehouses. With observations vpon the Monopolists of Seaven severall Patents, and Two Charters. Practised and performed, by a Mistery of some Printers, Sleeping Stationers, and Combining Book-sellers. Anatomised and layd open in a Breviat, in which is only a touch of their forestalling and ingrossing of Books in Patents, and Raysing them to excessive prises."[27] The King's Printer, it appeared, had formerly issued small folio editions of the Bible at 12s. a copy, but in 1629 had stopped their publication in favour of a larger and more expensive edition. Thereupon the Cambridge printers produced an edition at 10s. a copy. The King's Printer straightway set six printing-houses to work on an edition of a thousand copies to be sold at 5s. each.

The next controversy, lasting from 1643 to 1645, had as its origin the publication of a new impression of the authorised version of the Bible "with Notes in the Margent, for the better exposition of hard places, and cleerer understanding of the Scriptures." In January 1643 the Stationers' Company sent a petition to Parliament complaining that eleven men had claimed the sole right of printing this impression, and asking for an order that it should be printed for the common benefit of the Company.[28] Three months later this petition was followed by another which most ingeniously set forth the case for the limitation of the number of printers and for the allowance of privilege. The Stationers' Company, it was argued, if allowed to increase its membership, "being like a feeld over-pestred with too much stock, must needs grow indigent, and indigence must needs make it run into trespasses, and break out into divers unlawfull shifts; as Cattle use to do, when their pasture begins wholly to fail." For the safety of the realm, then, it was essential to keep the industry small enough to be easily regulated. And, still purely for the good of the State, the individual printer must be allowed the privilege of copyright. In the absence of that right, any stationer who in the course of his duty to the Government complained of another's conduct was sure to find his copy reprinted out of spite. It was not to be thought that copyright was at all the same as monopoly. Monopoly consisted of the engrossing of necessary commodities into the hands of a few people, resulting in scarcity and high prices; books could not be considered necessary commodities, "many of them are rarities onely and usefull only to a very few, and of no necessity to any; few men bestow more in Books then what they can spare out of their superfluities." There were several reasons for the fear that community of copies would damage the State and the Stationers' Company alike. In the first place, it would cause wasteful printing of the same work by more than one printer, possibly resulting in discord, "whereby Christianity it self shall be scandalized." The risk of loss through the flooding of the market in this way was likely to prevent some men from printing at all, to the great obstruction of learning. Moreover, general freedom to print any copies would destroy the system of barter among stationers by which books were distributed without risk of monetary loss. Authors, too, would suffer; "Many mens studies carry no other profit or recompence with them, but the benefit of their copies; and if this be taken away, many Pieces of great worth and excellence will be strangled in the womb, or never conceived at all for the future." In some cases, again, widows and orphans had nothing to depend upon but their income from assignments of copies; "and there is no reason apparent why the production of the Brain should not be as assignable, and their interest and possession (being of more rare, sublime, and publike use, demeriting the highest encouragement) held as tender in Law, as the right of any Goods or Chattells whatsoever." The man who was sure of his copyright could afford to act as a public benefactor by selling his first impression at a loss, confident that he would gain on later issues. (Whether any printer adopted this policy we are not told.) "It is most humbly prayed," therefore, "that some speedy course may be taken for such a perfect regulation of the Presse, as may procure the publike good of the State, by the private prosperity of the Stationers' Company." Parliament responded to this petition by reviving the lapsed decrees of the Star Chamber with regard to licensing and entry in the Stationers' Register.

As well as licences for whole classes of books there were, as we have seen, royal patents for the publication of individual works. But the more usual way of obtaining the copyright of a single work was by entry in the Stationers' Register and payment of a minimum fee of 4d., raised to 6d. in 1588. Such entry could be obtained only by a member of the Company: this put authors' copyright out of the question. The author was, in fact, in an unfortunate position by this system. Any printer who came into possession of a manuscript, by whatever means, had it in his power to register it for publication; even though he should print an inaccurate version of it nobody could lawfully reprint it without his permission. He might never even print the book at all: the effect of an entry in the register was merely to prevent anybody else from doing so. In this respect the early Venetian copyright law was more satisfactory than our own custom: a decree was issued in Venice in 1533 ordering that if a work were not published within a year of its registration for copyright that right should lapse.[29] A somewhat similar ruling to this was made by the Stationers' Company in 1588 in an attempt to find work for the unemployed journeymen: it was ordered that if any copy was out of print and its owner did not begin to reprint it within six months of being warned, the journeymen should be allowed to print it for the use of the Company, the holder of the copyright being then charged a share of the expenses and being entitled to a proportionate part of the profits.[30]

Transfer of Copyright

The printer who did not wish to retain the copyright of a work was at liberty to transfer it to somebody else by means of a further entry in the register. The first mention of the sale of copyright is to be found in the entries for 1564, when Thomas Marsh is recorded as paying 1s. to the Company "for his lycense for pryntinge of Dygges *pronostication* and his tectonicon which he boughte of lucas haryson."[31] Two years later John Kingston is mentioned as having bought the copyright of Calvin's *Catechism* from William Copland for the sum of 5s.[32] Rights were not always sold as cheaply as this. In 1626 Mistress Hodgettes assigned four copies to Robert Allott with the provision that "if the said Robert Allott Doe pay or cause to be paid vnto Margaret Hodgettes her executours or assignes the some of fortye-five pounds of lawfull money of England vpon the second day of February 1626 [i.e. 1627] according as he hath giuen his bond that then the Copies to be absolutely to him but if he faile then the Copies to returne to Margarett Hodgettes againe."[33] The benefits arising from copyright were not transferable, in whole or in part, without this further registration. This was the subject of a further order in 1598: "Forasmuche as diuerse abuses, of late tyme haue been committed, by sundry persons of this Companye in procuringe of Copies and Bookes to be entred and alowed vnto them and then pryntinge the same for suche persons as be not of this Companye for Remedie thereof, yt is ordered that if any person or persons of this Company shall hereafter print or cause to be printed any copie or booke whiche shall not be proper to hym self and whereof he shall not reape the whole Benefit to his own vse by sellinge it in the Companye but shall suffer any other person or persons that shall not be of this companye to haue the benefit of the sale or disposition thereof. Then in euery suche case all and euery suche bookes and copies shall and may be disposed and printed againe accordinge to the discretion of the Master, Wardens, and Assistentes of this Companye for the tyme beinge or the moore parte of them. And the partie or parties offendinge herein shall ipso facto Lose and forfait all his and their Right and interest in all and euery suche booke and bookes."[34]

It was an easy matter to keep a check on the rights of publishing individual books during the earlier period of the Stationers' Company's existence, but after thirty years or so the search through the register to see whether any particular copy had already been entered had become an arduous task. From about 1595 the clerk frequently saved himself the bother of reading through previous entries by adding to the new grant of copyright the provision "vpon condicon that no man haue right vnto it by former entrance." This practice was hardly calculated to reduce publishing risks.

Piracy

Infringing of copyright was such a common offence that some of the most important editions of the works of Elizabethan writers were the products of piratical publishers. One particularly successful venture was the issue of an unauthorised edition of Sidney's *Arcadia* by Robert Waldegrave at the end of the sixteenth century; the work was produced in Edinburgh with the collusion of the Cambridge printer, and, as international copyright was as yet unthought of, the registered holder of the copy had to watch the sale of some hundreds of the volume before he managed to obtain an order forbidding their importation. Pirates were at great pains to hide their activities: of Roger Ward it was reported that he concealed "a presse and other printing stuff in a Taylors house neere adioyninge to his own howse and did hyde his letters in a henhouse neere St. Sepulchres churche."[35]

Where a printer was found to be infringing copyright he was fined by the Company, but the fines were so low that he must often have gained on the transaction and found it profitable to repeat the offence. Owen Rogers was one of the worst offenders: in the year 1559 he was fined 3s. 4d. for printing the Epistles and Gospels without licence and for keeping a foreign workman, also without licence; in the same year he was fined 20d. "for pryntinge of halfe a Reame of *ballettes* of a nother mans Copye by waye of Desceate"; and three years later he was found printing "*the booke of husboundry* beynge master Totteles," and was fined another 2s.[36] In some cases there was no monetary fine at all: William Copland was another printer tempted to issue the Epistles and Gospels without permission, and with regard to him it was ordered in 1560 that "for his fyne he shulde paye halfe an hundreth of ye same bokes to the vse of the howse."[37] In the following year Richard Harrison was fined 8s. for printing a Bible without licence, but there was no suggestion that he should discontinue the work; on the contrary, he was encouraged to go on with it by the order that "he shall brynge into the howse for a Copye whan yt is Donne one of the said Bybles."[38] Such copies were sold for the benefit of the Company; it was recorded in the register for 1562 that the sum of 20s. had been received for the sale of "bookes ballades and other papers brought in as copyes accordynge to our ordenaunces."

The Star Chamber decree of 1637 (renewed as an ordinance in 1643) and the Licensing Act of 1662[39] which was based upon it both recognised the existence of a property in copies which could be protected under the common law. It was none the less difficult to prevent piracy. A Stationers' Company ordinance of 1681[40] threatened a fine of 1s. upon any offender who was traced, but this order and its various successors seem to have been generally ignored. According to John Dunton a whole army of hackney authors were employed by the booksellers in adapting the works of others for republication; "these Gormandizers," he said, "will eat you the very life out of a copy so soon as ever it appears; for, as the times go, *Original* and *Abridgment* are almost reckoned as necessary as Man and Wife; so that I am really afraid that a *Bookseller* and a *good conscience* will shortly grow some strange thing in the earth."[41]

The Copyright Act of 1709

At the close of the seventeenth century it was still the bookseller whose rights of property were the subject of discussion. The author who wanted to sell his manuscript had as yet no reason to think that the sale of a literary work differed in any fundamental way from the sale of any other form of property. Entry in the Stationers' Register conferred a perpetual copyright on a particular member of the Company, who could seldom have been the author;

there was no reservation that after a certain period the copy should return to the original owner. Difficulty arose with the final lapse of the Licensing Act in 1694 and with the consequent loss to the Stationers' Company of the control of copyright. It was with the idea of regaining perpetual rights that the London booksellers petitioned in 1703 and 1706 for a Copyright Act. Their petition of 1709 was effectual so far as to produce an Act, but its provisions fell short of their hopes.

The preamble of "An Act for the Encouragement of Learning by vesting the Copies of printed Books in the Authors or Purchasers of such Copies during the Times therein mentioned" (1709)[42] confirmed the common complaint that printers, booksellers and other persons had been printing books without the consent of the "Authors or Proprietors of such Books." By the main provisions of the Act the copyright of works already published was secured to their present owners (whether authors or booksellers) for a further twenty-one years from April 1, 1710. The authors of books not yet printed were to have the sole printing rights (which they might assign to another) for fourteen years, but before publication all copies were to be entered in the Stationers' Register. After this period the copyright was to return to the author, if still living, for another fourteen years. It was, in fact, almost a return to the old patent system. Infringement of the Act was to involve forfeiture of the offending books and a fine of 1d. a sheet for all fraudulent copies found, half of the fine being payable to the Crown and the rest to the injured party.

The author was now in a better position than ever before. It appears to have been assumed until this time that if he were to sell his copy at all he must sell it outright. He had now no longer to lose the final control of his copy; he need not even sell it for the full period of fourteen years, but could offer it for a single edition and afterwards bargain upon the good name which it had won for him. That was what he *could* do if he could brave the booksellers—not an easy task for the more retiring writer. No less an author than David Hume has confessed to accepting poor terms rather than assert himself: "I concluded," he laments, "somewhat of a hasty bargain with my bookseller from indolence and an aversion to bargaining, as also because I was told that few or no bookseller would engage for one edition with a new author," so that he rashly agreed that he himself would buy any unsold copies of a second edition at the bookseller's price.[43] It seems to have been as an outcome of the 1709 Act, nevertheless, that the publisher was occasionally induced to pay £500 or more for the rights of a single edition.

When in 1724 and 1731 the two groups of copies under the Act of 1709 began to fall free there was a revival in the demand for perpetual copyright. A fourteen years' protection will cover the life of the ordinary book, but the copies falling free in 1731, those of Shakespeare, Milton and other great writers, were becoming ever more profitable. The London booksellers were anxious to ignore the Copyright Act where these volumes were concerned, and in 1735 presented a petition[44] to the House of Commons claiming the privilege to do so. A Bill which they were allowed to introduce led to their denunciation in *A Letter to a M.P. concerning the Bill now depending in the House of Commons*.[45] The renewal of copyright, which they wanted, for twenty-one years on each expiry would in effect, the writer pointed out, give a perpetual copyright, and permanent monopoly was a thing "deservedly odious in the Eye of the Law." The Bill was rejected by the Lords. A Bill introduced in 1737 was devoted to the author's interests, proposing that he and his assigns should have the copyright of his works for his lifetime and for eleven years after his death. This, too, was rejected by the Lords. Actually, before introducing new Bills it might have been logical to decide first on the meaning of the existing law. Although the Act of 1709 seems to read perfectly clearly there was still a genuine uncertainty as to its interpretation. *The Seasons* of James Thomson was destined to provide the test case. Andrew Millar, a London bookseller, had bought the copyright from the author in 1729. In 1763, fifteen years after the author's death, Robert Taylor published the work, to be involved three years later in an action against Millar in the Court of King's Bench. The Court found that perpetual copyright still existed at common law, in spite of the 1709 Act, and that in this case it belonged to Millar.[46] This decision was respected for five years. Then Donaldson, the Edinburgh bookseller, tried his fate: he republished *The Seasons*, whose copyright had been bought by Becket. Becket secured an injunction in Chancery against his rival, whereupon Donaldson in 1774 appealed to the House of Lords. Eleven judges were asked to give their interpretation of the Copyright Act, and it was by a majority of only one that they decided that perpetual rights were ruled out. Donaldson won the case by twenty-two votes to eleven.[47] The importance of this decision to the publisher of cheap reprints is too obvious to need stressing.

A matter which caused more vexation to the general publisher than these occasional disputes with regard to the length of copyright was the lack of any protection whatever for English books in Ireland. The Dublin booksellers managed somehow to issue their editions of copyright works shortly after their publication in England, and there was usually no legal redress. One author had the ingenuity to catch his pirate indirectly: Thomas Carte, who in 1736 found that his *Life of the Duke of Ormonde* was being printed in Dublin without his permission, had the good fortune to remember an order of the House of Lords, issued in 1721, to the effect that anybody presuming to print an account of the life of a deceased peer without the consent of his heirs or executors should be regarded as guilty of a breach of privilege. On the strength of this Lord Arran was able to put a stop to the proceedings.[48] Samuel Richardson was not so fortunate. While he was publishing *The History of Sir Charles Grandison* (1753) he took special precautions, by splitting up the work between his three printing-houses and among different workmen, to make it impossible for anybody to copy the work as a whole; yet by some means the work was published in Dublin by three different firms before his own main edition was out. How it was done is not known, but an Irish bookseller had boasted to him some years before that he could procure sheets of any book being printed in London before publication.[49]

For that matter piracy in England itself was little abated. "A work no sooner receives the Approbation of the Town," it was alleged in 1757, "but some trading miscreant prints it in a smaller Volume, and, as he is not at the Expence of Copy-Money, is able to undersell the original Proprietor, who ventur'd on the Work when there was not such a Certainty of the Sale."[50] Although any person pirating a book entered in Stationers' Hall was liable to be prosecuted, this was of little practical use; "for either the Piracy is done so private as not to be detected, or carried on in the Name of some Bankrupt, who has nothing to lose."[51] Dr. Johnson, finding that the essays in the *Universal Chronicle* were being reprinted in weekly and monthly periodicals without acknowledgment of their source, wrote a special advertisement threatening to make good his losses by returning the compliment and culling articles from other papers for his own.[52]

John Newbery, too, had occasion to write an advertisement.[53] "If Thomas Green, M.A.," it ran, "should exist in any region below the moon, and Thomas Green, M.A., be really the compiler of the Spelling Dictionary just published, it is a piece of work that Thomas Green, M.A., ought to be ashamed of, as the business was already done to his hands. The Bookseller, too, if he had not been a booby, or worse, would never have employed Thomas Green, M.A., to write a book which had been written and printed so many years before; and especially while the tenth edition of it was selling before his face with such rapidity."

CHAPTER VI

Early Trade and Labour Organisation

A PRINTING-PUBLISHING concern must always have given employment to a diversity of workers. Leaving out of consideration the author, who is not in general classed as a wage-earner, there is left a body of type-founders, ink-makers, compositors, press-men, press-correctors and binders, some of them to be found in even the smallest firm, some to be encountered only in the greater publishing-houses. Of these the press-corrector may be set apart as requiring a degree of knowledge akin to that of the author. He did, in fact, undertake a rôle that in the earlier years was normally carried on by the author himself, that of seeing a work through the press, attending daily for the editing of copy and correction of proofs. For this work he had usually to be well versed in foreign languages. His appointment was generally for a long period, if not permanent, and his maintenance was one of the heavier expenses in the printing industry.[1] In contrast to this essentially professional worker the rest of those mentioned above fall into the craftsman class, their working lives being ordered by the regulations of their respective gilds.

The earliest known book-producers' gild in Europe was that of St. John the Evangelist, founded at Bruges in the early fifteenth century.[2] Unlike the later Parisian gilds it was an organisation independent of political or university control. It was of far-reaching influence, including not only scriveners, illuminators, block-printers, booksellers and others concerned with the production and disposal of the actual book, but also the more distantly connected parchment and vellum makers, cloth shearers and curriers. The formation of gilds after the invention of printing was as a rule influenced by definitely political motives: new forces had been let loose which endangered the stability of State and Church; to keep them in check there was needed some central body which should enforce the will of authority. Italy, the headquarters of the Roman Church, had a number of organisations of a repressive type. The Council of Venice, for instance, decreed in 1549 that the city printers, publishers and booksellers should form a company, partly because every other trade was already organised, but mainly to promote the work of the Commissioners of Heresy in suppressing prohibited works.[3] Although the majority of the gilds springing up in the wake of the introduction of printing were founded on the initiative of outside authorities who wished to regulate the trade there were others, including some of the most prominent, which existed solely for joint commercial action. Such was the Milanese Gild of Printers, Publishers and Booksellers, founded in 1589; its membership was limited to citizens who had served an eight years' apprenticeship, and its avowed objects were to maintain the status of workers in the book industry and to guard against foreign competition.[4]

The beginnings of the English book industry were too tentative to be accompanied by any high degree of gild organisation. Such minor gilds as existed in various parts of the country were short-lived, and book-producers had to turn elsewhere for their corporate activities. At York, for example, the bookbinders formed a company of their own in 1476; twelve years later the whole of the book-producing crafts united, with the proviso that "no maner man religious or secular that is not fraunchesd nor abled by the said craft and sersours, take upon him to bring in or sett out any werke of this citie or fraunches," a ruling soon altered to allow priests with a salary of under seven marks to undertake text-writing;[5] but by the early sixteenth century this body had disappeared, and stationers were seeking admittance to that haven for workers in small crafts, the Gild of Corpus Christi. Chester had its Company of Stationers, chartered in 1534, but this, too, was of short duration.[6]

The London stationers until the second half of the sixteenth century kept the strangest of company. The most unaccountable of all in this respect was John Wolf, noteworthy as a stirrer-up of strife, who, although a fully-occupied printer running five presses, had allied himself to the fishmongers. Almost as curious is the case of John Day, acknowledged as the best English printer of the century: for about a dozen years he was a member of the Bowstringers' Company, possibly owing to some vague connection between the making of bowstrings and of the thongs by which the sections of a book were fastened together. The circumstances which brought printers and booksellers into the Drapers' and Grocers' Companies are easier to understand. It had long been customary for drapers to sell manuscripts with their other wares, and this practice spread for a time to the sale of printed books. Grocers were those who bought and sold "in gross," or in large quantities, and in a report made by Christopher Barker, the Queen's Printer, in 1582 on the early organisation of the book trade it is stated that besides printers there were writers "and other uses called Stacioners; which haue, and partly to this daye do vse to buy their bookes in grosse of the saide printers, to bynde them vp, and sell them in their shops."[7] From the year 1557 the Company of Stationers was all-powerful in the book world, but even in the second half of Elizabeth's reign there were still thirty-five out of about two hundred and seventy London printers and publishers who belonged, not to the Stationers', but to some other company, usually the Drapers' or Grocers'. By the beginning of the seventeenth century the proportion of those not belonging to the Stationers' Company had decreased as a result of transfers from other organisations; in one year alone thirteen members of the Drapers' Company were transferred to that of the Stationers'.

The Stationers' Company

The origins of the Stationers' Company are somewhat obscure. The body seems to have been the natural descendant of the Gild of Writers of the Court Hand and Text Letters, first recorded in 1357.[8] By the early fifteenth century, as is shown by a joint memorial from the Mayor and Aldermen of London in 1403, bookbinding had become associated with text-writing. But there was no complete continuity from this date to the sixteenth century: by 1422 text-writers and bookbinders were enrolled in separate gilds.[9] Judging from a list of gilds drawn up by the Pewterers' Company in 1488, both of these companies had since disappeared. This was doubtless due to the upheaval caused by the importation of printed books and by the influx of continental stationers. At some early date in the sixteenth century there was formed the Craft of Stationers. There is a lack of details with regard to its history, but occasionally in the wills of early printers there is a clause directing a sum of money to be paid to the brotherhood for the benefit of the poorer members, or towards the upkeep of the Stationers' Hall in Milk Street.[10] From the number of stationers who made no such provision, or who belonged to one of the greater companies, it can be deduced that membership of the gild was neither compulsory nor particularly attractive. Towards the middle of the century there was more sign of corporate life. In the account of the proceedings of the Convocation of Canterbury on March 17, 1542, it is stated that "the Prolocutor exhibited a book in parliament for the incorporation of the Stationers, to be referred to the King."[11] The charter of incorporation was not granted until May 4, 1557, but in the meantime the members showed sufficient interest in their society to subscribe for a second hall in St. Paul's Churchyard. The Company acquired further status on February 1, 1560, when the Lord Mayor formally created it one of the city livery companies.

Membership of the company thus incorporated was open to all those who took any part in the production and sale of books. There were included printers, booksellers, bookbinders, and their journeymen and apprentices, a few type-founders and paper-makers, and an occasional joiner. The total number of freemen in 1557, as stated in the charter, was ninety-seven.

Although the Stationers' Company was in a position to look after the general interests of the trade, it is obvious from the wording of the charter[12] that the motive behind the grant of incorporation was anything but anxiety for the success of the individual stationer. With the rise of nationalism as a vital force in the Tudor period there grew a desire on the part of the Government for the State control of industry, partly as a groping towards that elusive favourable trade balance which, it was thought, could be maintained only by the acceptance by each branch of industry of the dictates of a central council, partly as a means of suppressing the turbulence of the growing class of wage-earners. To this feeling was added, in the case of the book industry, a dread of sedition. The means to regulation lay conveniently at hand in the gild system. The sixteenth century therefore saw the incorporation of numerous companies; it also saw efforts, as, for instance, by the limitation of entrance fees, to overcome the growing exclusiveness of the gilds; but, lest the gild should acquire greater power than the State itself, there was passed in 1504 a Bill whereby the rules of each craft were to receive the sanction of the chief justices or other specified authorities. The Stationers' was one of many organisations to be brought under State supervision; but, as their trade involved the spread of ideas as distinct from mere commodities, control was specially rigid. The charter granted to the Company an almost complete monopoly of the printing industry, together with powers of national regulation rarely acquired by any gild: "no person within this our realm of England or the dominions of the same shall practise or exercise by himself, or by his ministers, his servants or by any other person the art or mistery of printing any book or any thing for sale or traffic within this our realm of England or the dominions of the same, unless the same person at the time of his foresaid printing is or shall be one of the community of the foresaid mistery or art of stationery of the foresaid City, or has therefore licence of us . . . the foresaid Queen by the letters patent." A later clause shows the purpose of this grant: the master and wardens were empowered to search at any time "in any place, shop, house, chamber, or building of any printer, binder or bookseller whatever . . . for any books or things printed, or to be printed, and to seize, take, hold, burn, or turn to the proper use of the foresaid community, all and several those books and things which are or shall be printed contrary to the form of any statute, act, or proclamation." The Company was, in fact, a detective agency intended to assist in the uprooting of heresy and sedition. One wonders whether it was purely by chance that the first master of the Company was Thomas Dockwray, one of the staunchest of Catholics.

In view of the amount of attention paid to the Stationers'

Company by the Government, it is rather surprising to note the comparative unimportance of that body in relation to other organisations. Far from ranking with the Grocers', the Mercers', the Goldsmiths', and the rest of the twelve great livery companies of London, the Stationers' occupied a humble position among some forty minor companies. The explanation is to be found not only in their small membership but also in their lack of wealth. At the time of the Company's incorporation there was developing one of the most conspicuous breaches from the traditional form of gild organisation: the company possessed of capital was emerging supreme; the trading company was rising above the gilds of craftsmen. The Stationers' was forbidden by law to have many dealings abroad, and the home market did not allow for any great accumulation of riches. In 1583, indeed, Christopher Barker reported to the Privy Council, "We Stationers are very poore and haue no land, but ye house we sit in, and our whole stock is under 100 li."[13] Prosperity increased by the end of the century, but as late as 1643 it was stated in an official remonstrance sent by the Company to Parliament on the question of monopolies that "since Propriety has been confounded, and their interest lost in those copies which anciently belonged to them, the whole Company (whose chief, and almost sole Revenues and support, was the annuall benefit accrewing from their Copies now printed from them) has drooped and grown poor. It has no common stock to provide Magazines of Corn, Arms, &c. for the States necessities, nor to pay Subsidies, or other frequent Assessments, charged by Parliament; nor to maintain their poor, being many, and requiring 200 *l. per annum*. And all the freehold they now have belonging to the Corporation, together with their Common-seal, lyes at this present engaged for 1,500 *l.*, borrowed lately at interest for the service of the Parliament."[14]

The actual civic position of the Company was settled on October 28, 1561, when it was decreed by the Corporation of London that the Stationers' should follow the Poulterers' in processions and in general precedence.[15] Some idea of the Company's standing may be gathered from the following statistics as to participation in public life. The letterbooks of the Corporation of London for 1574 show the numbers of men to be supplied for the navy: the Grocers' and Mercers' Companies were each to send forty, the Stationers' five, and the Curriers' one; fifteen companies were to provide more than the Stationers', twenty-one fewer, and seven the same. In the same year there was a compulsory loan for the provision of a stock of corn for the city: £62 10s. was demanded from the Stationers' as against £500 each from the Mercers' and Grocers', and £6 5s. from the Fletchers'. In 1591, again, the London companies were commanded by the Common Council to provide seven ships, the "London supplies" which formed the fleet of Lord Thomas Howard in his cruise to the Azores; for this purpose the Grocers' was assessed at £526, the Merchant Taylors' at £561 12s., the Stationers' at £80, the Fletchers' at £2 8s.; sixteen companies were rated higher than the Stationers', three the same, and thirty-five less. Civic duties seem to have been regarded seriously by the Stationers' Company, and failures of individual members to conform to city customs were punished by fine. Thus in 1579 nine masters were fined 1s. each for not attending the Lord Mayor on "Twelfe-daye"; ten years later, three were fined for the same offence on "Allhallowen Day."

Poor or not, the Company was called upon to share in smoothing the financial path of Charles I. The loan of £840 which it raised for him in 1627 involved pledging its plate. Two years later the Company had to find £60 4s. as its quota of the £4,300 spent on pageants and decorations for the Coronation. From 1640 the demands became more burdensome: in that year the Stationers' was required to lend the King £500; in 1642 another £1,000 were borrowed; while in 1643 the Company was told to pay £5 a week for three months, besides £32 for a royal subsidy. These heavy charges left the association with little money and with no plate.[16]

The Restoration provided the Company with a pleasanter task. A precept from the Lord Mayor, May 17, 1660, invited them to send representatives to attend him, with the Aldermen and other citizens, in welcoming the King.[17] Remembering that on ordinary weekdays the members of the Company were printers and book-sellers of the usual description, one feels rather curious to know

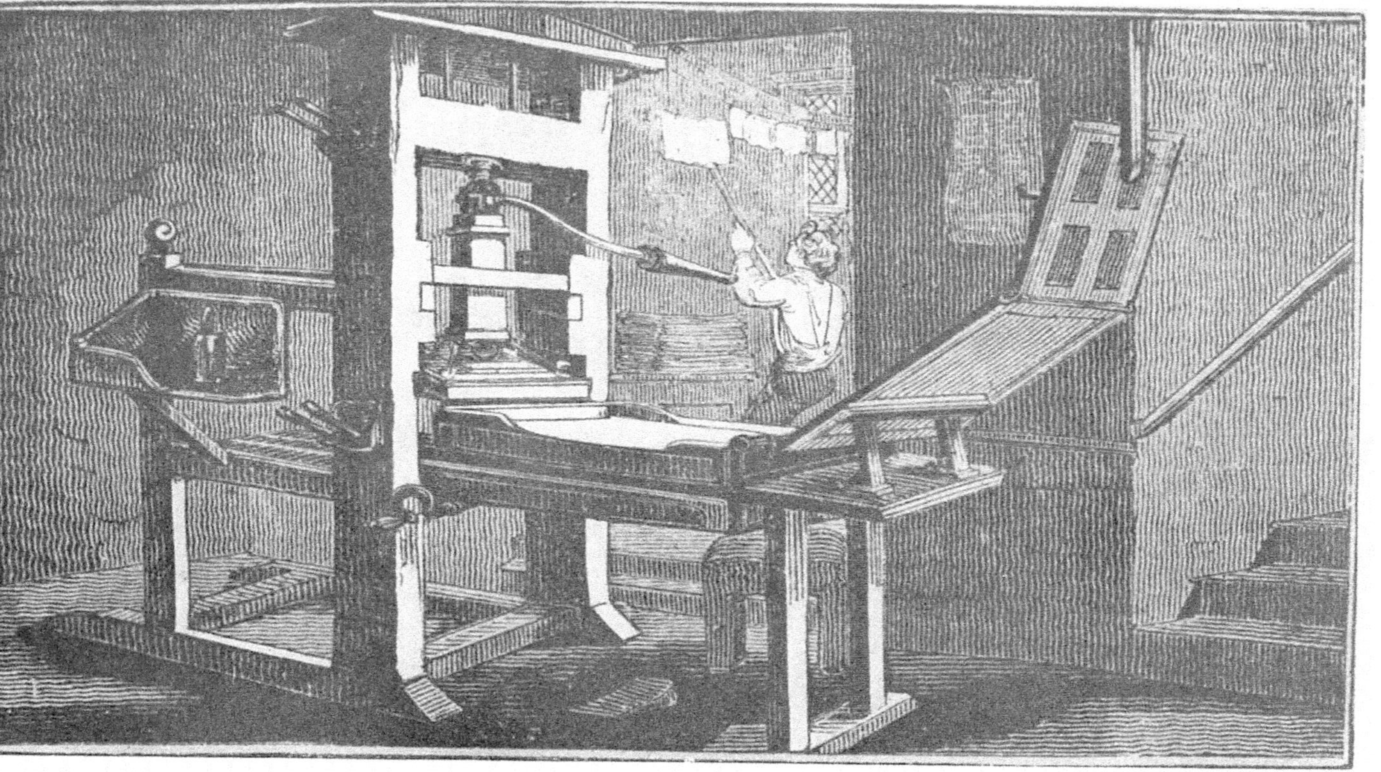

BLAEU'S PRESS
From Johnson's *Typographia*, 1824

how they set about selecting "ten of the most grave, tall, and comely personages of the Company, well horsed, and in their best array of furniture of velvet, plush, or sattin, with chains of gold"!

About this time the Company seems to have lost something of its prestige among the London livery companies. In 1665 its members were requested by the Lord Mayor to give up their pew in St. Paul's Church to the Company of Clothworkers, in exchange for another. On no account would they agree to this. The verger was given notice that they had no intention of relinquishing their ancient pew, and he was warned "to reserve it for the use of the Company, as he will expect their future favour and reward."[18] There need be no doubt that for the next few Sundays the members of the book trade were most punctilious in the matter of church attendance.

Throughout the eighteenth and early nineteenth centuries the Company's barge took a prominent part in ceremonial. In 1768, for example, the Company received a summons from the Lord Mayor to attend him on the river in their barge on the day when the King of Denmark was to dine in the City. Years later, on the death of Nelson in 1806, the master and wardens, with sixty members of the Company, took part in the funeral procession by water from Greenwich to Whitehall.[19] Even as late as 1827 it was customary, on issuing the Company's almanacs, for the master and high officials to go in their barge to Lambeth, to present copies to the Archbishop of Canterbury.[20]

The Constitution of the Stationers' Company

By the terms of the charter the government of the Stationers' Company was vested in a master, two wardens, and a court of assistants, as was typical of the Livery Company. It was further laid down, according to custom, that new officers should be elected by the present master and wardens and the whole community. But, in the general manner of sixteenth- and seventeenth-century livery companies, this democratic form of government gave way to an oligarchy. The master and wardens, having tasted power, were anxious for more. "If he [the mere stationer] once gett to be an officer in the society," complained George Wither in 1625, "he forgetts to speak in the first person for euer after; but (like a Prince) sayes, 'we will,' and 'we do this' &c. He thinks vpon nothing more then to keepe vnder the inferiors of the Corporation, and to draw the profitt of the King's Priveledges to his priuate vse."[21] A violent controversy raged on this constitutional point from 1577 onwards.[22] In 1582 the Queen was obliged to interfere by appointing Dr. John Hammond and Thomas Norton, the City Remembrancer, to inquire into the matter. In the following year three other London notabilities were added to the commission: Edwin Sandys, Bishop, Alexander Nowell, Dean, and Serjeant W. Fleetwood, Recorder. The issue was settled by a Star Chamber decree of June 23, 1586, which confirmed the power in the hands of the master, wardens and assistants and *those they should co-opt to succeed them*. The question came up again in 1645.[23] A committee of the Company demanded the resignation of the entire Court of Assistants on the ground that most of the Company's grievances proceeded from these officers, and immediately joined the master, wardens and two others in nominating thirty-one new assistants. Afterwards these five members altered the names without consulting the committee. On hearing of this the committee claimed that the assistants could not take office until their appointment had been confirmed at a common hall; to which the wardens retorted that the committee was no true committee, and that no general meeting of the Company was needed. The committee accordingly took matters into their own hands and distributed five hundred tickets calling a common hall to vote on the matter, but as a result of a petition from the masters, wardens and assistants to the Lord Mayor and Aldermen the members of the committee were summoned to appear before the Court of Aldermen to answer to the charge of threatening the peaceful government of the Company; the meeting was therefore not held.

The Company's original charter, as confirmed by Elizabeth, was confirmed again by Charles II in 1667. A second confirmation by Charles II, in 1684, contained certain new clauses legalising this growth of arbitrary power,[24] but these were soon afterwards declared null and void by the Act 2 William and Mary "for Reversing the Judgment in a Quo Warranto against the City of London and for restoring the City of London to its ancient Rights and Privileges." Legally, then, the election of officers was still vested in the whole body of freemen. By a by-law of the Company itself, dated 1678 and not repealed, quite the reverse was sanctioned: the election of master and wardens, "as usually heretofore hath been," was to remain the privilege of the existing master, wardens and Court of Assistants.[25] The abuse had thus become so well established that the virtue of custom could be called upon to uphold it. This does not mean that the ordinary members of the association accepted the new constitution without challenge: as late as 1741 the matter was still causing indignation, and was the leading theme of a protest entitled "The Charter and Grants of the Company of Stationers of the City of London, now in force, etc."

The Terms of Admission

The normal way of entering the Company was by apprenticeship to one of the freemen. From the pecuniary point of view this presented little difficulty. Gild fees in general had become so exorbitant in the first part of the sixteenth century as to call for Government interference. The Act of 22 Henry VIII "concernyng the avoydyng of Exaccyons levyd upon Prentyses" states that "dyvers Wardens and Felowshippes have made Actes and Ordenannces that every prentice shall pay, at his first entre in their comon halle, to the Wardens of the same fellowshipp, some of them 40s.; some 30s.; some 20s.; some 13s. 4d.; some 6s. 8d., after their own senester myndes and pleasure," and limits the entrance fees for the future to 2s. 6d. Yet for the first twenty years of the Stationers' Company's existence the fee was only 6d. When it did rise, in 1578, it increased immediately to the legal maximum of 2s. 6d., possibly owing to the Company's financial difficulties created by the general rise in prices.

By the custom of London the minimum period of apprenticeship was seven years, indentures being so arranged as to expire when the apprentice reached the age of twenty-four. This minimum was strictly adhered to by the stationers, who tended to bind their apprentices for much longer periods. During the year 1558–9 only three were bound for seven years as compared with two for eight years, three for nine, three for ten, one for eleven, and one for twelve. In 1584 a certain Abraham Sawyer was apprenticed for fourteen years, while fifteen others were bound for eight years, ten for nine years, and only eleven for seven years. In this respect conditions in France were less irksome: by a decree of 1541 apprentices to printers were to be bound for "a sufficient length of time," specified in an edict of 1571 as three years and in one of 1615 as four years.[26] A minimum of seven years was usual in England until late in the eighteenth century. Even in 1811 it could be enforced: in that year the London Consolidated Society of Bookbinders maintained an action against Mr. Fraser (Pratt *v.* Fraser), a prosecutor of that period, for infringing the Statute of Artificers. Lord Ellenborough enforced the Act in this case, but soon afterwards secured its repeal.[27]

These long terms of apprenticeship were all to the good of the masters: there were few processes on the mechanical side of book production which could not be learnt in a few months; the master could count on obtaining several years skilled work from each apprentice at a very low cost to himself. Edward Cave, indeed, who was apprenticed to Collins, the London printer, at the beginning of the eighteenth century, made so much progress in the first two years of his training that he was sent to Norwich to conduct a printing-house and publish a weekly paper, though still an apprentice. During this period he married a young widow (regardless of the custom which forbade an apprentice to marry) and was given an allowance to enable him to set up a home of his own.[28]

Even in the sixteenth century wage-payments to apprentices were not entirely eliminated, though according to the custom of London they should have been. When in 1583 John Shrobryche and William Bottomly were apprenticed to Mistress Jugge there was a special order from the Company that she should not allow them "to woorke for wages or to haue or take wages" during the eight years for which they were bound; this implies that apprentices did commonly receive wages for part of the period. There is very little clue in the registers of the Company as to the amount paid, but we find that when John Munnes, having served one master for ten years, is transferred in 1589 to Edward Alday for his final year, "yt is ordered: that the said Edward Alday shall gyve unto his mother weekly duringe the said Terme of one yere, xiiij.d. whiche shalbe quarterly paid." Yet in 1602 John Isham's enrolment as apprentice to James Roberts is crossed out, a marginal note explaining that "This prentise for disobedience and takinge wages within his prentiship is dismissed out of the company and neuer to be made free."

Mrs. Elianor James, who about 1720 wrote with much feeling her *Advice to all Printers in General*, had plenty to say on the subject of apprentices, being particularly averse to paying them anything at all. The boy who had served half his time and had therefore gained experience of the trade, she complained, too often tried to bargain with his master for better conditions and more freedom. On the least pretext he would run away, accusing his master of cruelty. In order to prevent this great evil, she urged, no man should employ another man's apprentice, "and then a master may (as he ought) have the benefit of the latter part of his time, to make him amends for his trouble and charge, which is according to the will of God and good men." Giving the apprentice money would in effect be making him a journeyman before his time.[29]

This cheap labour was felt to be a serious menace to the journeymen, and there were frequent petitions from the poorer freemen for the limitation of the number of apprentices. Such limitation had been common in other organisations since the fourteenth century, not, perhaps, for the sake of the journeymen so much as to keep down competition by limiting the number of potential masters. It was accordingly decreed by the Court of Star Chamber on June 23, 1586, that the Queen's Printer should keep no more than six apprentices, masters and upper wardens of the Company and their predecessors should have only three at a time, under-wardens and members of the livery two, and members of the yeomanry only one each. This was an even more drastic limitation than the French journeymen had secured after half a century of strikes: the Parisian regulation of 1572 allowed even the smaller master printers two apprentices for each press.[30] The printers of Oxford and Cambridge were limited by this decree of 1586 to one apprentice at a time, but were authorised to employ as many journeymen as they wished.[31] This order was supplemented in 1635 by a regulation of the Stationers' Company "that those, that are become partner or partners in anie printing house, shall not be suffered to take any Apprentice. Nor shall there be allowed by reason of anie Copartnership anie more Apprentices, than the Master or Owner of such Printing house shalbe capable to haue by his Ranke and degree in this Company. . . .; Where a Jorneyman and Apprentice worke togeather, they shall both take their worke as it falles out and not otherwise, the one the First part, and the other the Last, as at first they agree."[32] The Star Chamber decree of 1586 was confirmed by another of July 11, 1637, which further ordered that no master founder should keep more than two apprentices, although he might keep one extra boy, not an apprentice, for pulling off the knots of metal hanging at the ends of the type when first cast.[33]

These orders account for a remarkable series of entries in the Stationers' Register by which various master printers were allowed to take apprentices on condition that they refrained from teaching them anything of the trade. Thus when Christofer Hall was bound to John Wolf in 1595 it was ordered by the Company that "this apprentise of John Wolf shall not at any time during his said terme be putt to the trade of printinge nor bookselling nor bookbinding, but be brought vp in the trade which the wife of the seid John vseth viz. distillacon or any thinge not perteyning to this company." Four years later Henry Dunne was made to promise that he would bring up his two apprentices "to the art of Musick and not to the Stationars trade or any faculty of this Companye." There were numerous cases in which no special instructions were laid down beyond the ruling that "this apprentise shall not be trayned in printinge nor any thing els perteyning to ye Staconers mystery." Anything more remote from the traditional view of the duty of the master to his apprentice would be difficult to imagine. The natural conclusion to be drawn from these arrangements would be that the masters in question had some secondary occupation for which they required these boys and into the mysteries of which they would initiate them. In some cases this was definitely not so, and the apprentice, having spent seven or eight years in making himself generally useful, must have found himself at the end of his period of service untrained for any calling.

There were, as we have seen, a number of printers who were not freemen of the Stationers' Company and were therefore held incapable of binding apprentices. A system of apprenticeship by proxy developed whereby the member of another company or one of the mere "brethren" of the Stationers' Company in fact suffered no disability in this respect. In 1576, for instance, a certain Hugh Astley was apprenticed to William Seres, stationer, for seven years; "it is agreed that the said Hughe Astley shall serue the said terme of seven yeres with Abraham Veale Draper beinge a brother of this cumpany." Two years later, John Wynnington was apprenticed to Richard Watkins, stationer, for eight years, and "yt is ordered and Agreed that this Apprentyce abouenamed shall serue his wholle apprentiship with Andrew Manssell Draper exercysinge the Art of a stationer." It is difficult to reconcile these entries with those quoted above. In these transfers of apprentices the object is sometimes clearly stated: the apprentice is to learn the art of bookbinding, of typefounding, or of printing. Yet the apprentices of ordinary freemen were, on occasion, definitely discouraged from learning any branch of the trade. Nor did the transfers prevent the registered master from keeping another apprentice for his own convenience: thus when Henry Conway passed on an apprentice in this way in 1594 the proviso was made: "the same Apprentise not to be accoumpted for any of Master Connewaies apprentises which he may kepe by th[e] ordonances." There seems to have been no general regulation on this question, but policy seems to have been based on the understanding that every stationer, member of the Company or not, was entitled to at least one apprentice.

It may have occurred to some busy printer that, though he was not entitled to any more apprentices, he could obtain just as great advantages by employing boy labour and ignoring the matter of formal enrolment. If so, the Stationers' Company spoilt his plans. In 1678 the ruling was made that no master printer should teach the art of printing to anybody (except his own son) who was not actually bound as an apprentice to some authorised printer.[34]

The statistics of apprentices enrolled annually do not, as one would expect, show a decline following the decree of 1586. Between 1565 and 1585 the average number of new indentures was thirty-six, the highest number in any year being sixty-six, in 1576–7, and the lowest being seventeen, in 1582–3. For nineteen years after 1586 the average was thirty-seven, the highest number being seventy-nine, in 1604–5, and the lowest being nineteen, in 1587–8. In the light of these figures alone one would conclude that the effect of the decree was negligible; that either it was not enforced or some similar regulation had been in force before 1586. But there is no doubt about the first point. One of the duties of the official searchers appointed in 1576 was to find out "howe many prentizes every printer kepithe, and whether they be his owne or any other mans, and whether any be kept in woorke that is neither prentis, Journeyman, nor a brother admitted"; and it is evident from the fines imposed by the Company that this part of their work was zealously performed, both before and after the Star Chamber decree. It is equally certain that there was no limitation of the number of apprentices before 1586. In fact, we find Richard Tottel presenting three on one day in 1556, while Thomas Marsh had two enrolled in June and three more in December of that year. The effect of the regulation must, then, have been to slow down the natural growth of the Company.

By the eighteenth century the routine of enrolling apprentices had evidently become rather a tiresome business to the Court of Assistants. At a meeting of the Court in 1728 complaints were made that some members of the Company who had apprentices to bind did not attend until eleven o'clock or later, "tho' this Court is always sitting at Ten for the doing thereof," and the Assistants were therefore kept sitting longer than was needed, and other business was often interrupted. As a remedy it was ordered that for the future anybody attending later than half-past ten should pay double fees.[35]

It was towards the close of the eighteenth century that the system of out-door apprenticeship became common, foreshadowing the final overthrow of the strict conditions of former days and the introduction of child-labour pure and simple. As the apprentice was not to be provided by his master with food and lodging he had necessarily to be given a small wage. In the case of one boy of the age of twelve, who appears to have been representative of his class, this was 8s. a week, increasing to a maximum of 12s.[36] In the early nineteenth century it was estimated that nearly half the boys employed in trade were out-door apprentices.[37] Richard Taylor, a printer, told the Select Committee on Artizans and Machinery in 1824 that in years gone by some masters, in a fit of irritation, had taken a large number of these apprentices in order to show the journeymen that they were not indispensable; the by-law of the Stationers' Company limiting their number had been given up for some time.

Freemen

Having served his master for the specified number of years the apprentice could be admitted to the freedom of the Company. From this time he was entitled to print or publish in his own name, but the normal procedure was for him to spend some years, if not the rest of his career, as a journeyman. The process of "making free" involved the provision of a banquet, in the earlier years described as a "brakefaste" and later as a dinner; for this the charge to the new freeman was 3s. 4d., this being the maximum sum allowed by the Act of 1531. In spite of the absence of prohibitive fees, by no means every apprentice rose to be a freeman. The average number made free between 1565 and 1600 was only sixteen (ranging from nine in 1565 to thirty in 1599) as compared with the average of thirty-six apprentices. For 1601 to 1640 the average rose to thirty-two. From this it would seem that a large proportion of apprentices had now satisfactorily completed their eight or nine years of service and were desirous of becoming full members of the Company; but an examination of the accounts of freemen admitted causes one to modify this view. In 1599–1600, for instance, thirteen of the thirty new freemen had never been apprenticed to stationers at all, but were transferred from the Drapers' Company. Between 1576 and 1605 fifty-two were made free by patrimony; these again had served no apprenticeship. There were other more irregular cases, as when in 1601 Thomas Jones was admitted "althoughe he was bound by Indenture in the Countrey all his terme, And was neither presented, inroled, nor bound by indenture here in London." Various marginal notes in the registers of the Company explain the falling-off of some members: a number of apprentices, perhaps fired by stories of the new discoveries, had run away; others were "putt away for vntruth and mysbehavior and neuer to be made free." A number of the rest had probably died; it must be remembered that of a London population of somewhere about 130,000, over 11,000 died of plague in 1592, over 10,000 in 1593, and over 30,000 in 1603, to mention only three of the plague years.[38]

It is doubtful whether the transfer of members from other companies was ever strictly legal. There had certainly been a tendency in London for freemen to abandon their own trades in order to adopt others to which they had not been apprenticed, and in 1614 a decision was given that this was agreeable to the custom of London. As a reason it was pointed out that some consideration must be shown to those tradesmen who, from one misfortune or another, could no longer carry on their former occupations. Some years later the decision was reversed by Recorder Littleton. He argued that there had never been a general custom to this effect; the custom was not that one who had been apprenticed as, say, a goldsmith, might turn to any other manual trade, but that a tradesman whose business consisted of buying and selling, such as a mercer or grocer, might exercise any other trade of buying or selling.[39] From this reasoning it would have been in order for a mercer to take up bookselling but not to undertake practical work as a printer.

It was one of the conditions for obtaining freedom that the candidate should not have married during his apprenticeship. Thomas Gent, in 1717, narrowly escaped rejection on this account, being accused by a certain Cornish of having married; "but my master, Midwinter," he records, "proved him a notorious liar, and he was reprehended by the warden and others. We dined at a tavern that day, and my part of the treat, with other expenses came to about three pounds."[40]

The Livery

The next stage of advancement was to the livery, or "clothing," of the Company, the body from which was appointed the Court of Assistants. The trade benefit to be derived from membership of the livery was the power to keep a second apprentice; but, even so, there was some unwillingness among the freemen to leave the yeomanry and join this higher branch of the Company. The higher entrance fees may have been a deterrent in some cases; until 1570 the fee was 15s.; it was then raised to 20s., and in 1598 to 40s.; in addition, each member of the livery had to provide himself with a gown "decently faced with fur." In order to keep up membership it had to be made compulsory, and from 1578 several freemen were fined 40s. for refusing to join after having been elected, the alternative being a term of imprisonment. Nor did the payment of one fine exempt the culprit for ever; Jonas Willing and Ephraim Dawson were fined in July 1624 and both joined the livery in June 1625. It seems likely that the objection to joining was due to fear of further promotion to the Court of Assistants, with its added expenses and responsibilities. The number admitted annually was seldom above six; more often there were only two or three, sometimes none at all. As late as 1619 the livery consisted of only forty-nine members.

The ceremonial on admission to the livery was specified in the orders of 1678 as follows: "After election of any person into the Livery or Cloathing aforesaid, the Master of the said society shall cause the Beadle of the said Society to put upon him so elected a Livery Gown . . .; and then the said Master shall put upon his shoulder a party-coloured Hood made after the usual manner"; after which, "according to the ancient usage of the said Society," the victim was to pay an admission fee of £20, the "usual fee" of 10s. to the Clerk, and to the Beadle his "usual fee" of 5s. The "usual" fees had somehow increased to ten times what they had been fifty years before. The way of escape, too, was more expensive to tread: the fine of 40s. had grown to £40.[41]

It was now necessarily the Company's policy that membership of the livery should be open only to men of property. None others could pay the entry fines. Accordingly, we find John Dunton writing of the year 1692, "About this time I was put in possession of a considerable Estate, upon the decease of my Cousin Carter. And now the Master and Assistants of the Company of Stationers began to think me sufficient to wear a Livery."[42] He therefore paid his entry fee of £20, and soon afterwards, with about fifty other members of the livery, formed a friendly society to bear the expense of the annual entertainment which they were expected to provide for the whole Company. Towards this each member of the society contributed 20s. a year. It speaks well for the general prosperity of the book trade that in 1724 there were two hundred and fourteen members of the Stationers' Company sufficiently wealthy to have joined the livery.[43]

Reluctance to bear office increased as the duties became more exacting. Heavy fines were preferred to the loss of time involved in acting as master or warden or even as one of the assistants. Full advantage of this feeling was taken by the Company to improve its financial position: from 1579 it was possible to buy exemption from office. Thus in 1579 Christopher Barker compounded for the rentership for a payment of £3, and in 1604 he paid a further £20 rather than serve as second upper-warden. It appears rather as if the policy were to choose the person who was least likely to want to take office, for the sake of the addition to the Company's revenue which would necessarily accompany his refusal; in 1604, for example, Master Leake, Master Standish and Master Field were in turn chosen to be renter, but were excused on the payment of £10 each.

The fines for refusing office according to the orders of 1678 were as heavily increased as those for refusing the livery, but provisions were made in each case for the fine to be reduced at the discretion of the Court of Assistants. Thus, whereas the fine for refusing the office of master was fixed at £20, it could be moderated to any sum not under £10.[44] To decline the upper-wardenship cost £24, or a minimum of £12, unless the member had served the preceding year, when he need pay only £6. The fine for escaping the position of under-warden was £20, or a minimum of £10.[45] The office of all others which it was costly to avoid was that of renter-warden: the fine was £50, or, at the discretion of the Court, any smaller sum down to £24. One can well see why. His was the thankless task of collecting the rents and the "quarteridge-money," a quarterly subscription (ranging from 4d. to 8d.) exacted from 1678 onwards from each member of the Company towards its upkeep. What is more, it was ordered that each year on Lord Mayor's Day he should provide "one competent and sufficient dinner" for the whole assembly of officers and all the members of the livery, "and if default shall be made hereof, that then every such person shall forfeit . . . fifty pounds."[46] Whether the dinner was found to be incompetent or merely insufficient is not known, but it was ordered in 1681 that *two* renter-wardens should be elected, and that both should be responsible for the dinner.[47]

In spite of the increased cost of refusing office it still happened occasionally that, through stress of work or for some other reason, promotion in the Company was declined. Miles Fletcher, having been fined for Alderman of London in 1662, and wishing to avoid further expense, asked to be excused from election as Master of the Company, but without success.[48] In the early nineteenth century T. N. Longman paid the fines rather than become warden or master, but in his case the refusal to bear office has been ascribed to the characteristic modesty of his disposition.[49]

There were others, on the other hand, who were anxious for promotion, and yet, by the general perversity of life, could not secure it. One of them, Giles Sussex by name, took his complaint as far as the Court of Aldermen. In his petition to the Lord Mayor, on June 16, 1691, he stated that although he had been a member of the livery for twenty years, and had served as renter-warden, he had never been admitted to the Court of Assistants; any vacancy had been filled by electing a junior member of the livery. The Court of Aldermen, having listened to him and also to the master and wardens of the Company, "who being asked what Objection they had against the Petitioner, now declared they had no exception to him," ordered that Sussex should be admitted as an assistant within the next week or ten days. The order was defied. Over a year later, on July 12, 1692, a summons was issued to the master and wardens to appear before the Court and explain their negligence, bringing the Company's charter with them. This order was likewise ignored. They were given another seven days in which to admit Sussex to the Court of Assistants, and were further ordered to "appear before this Court on Thursday next come seven-night, and between this and then take out their Charter, which (as they now alledge) is locked up in a Chest under Keys kept by the late Master and Wardens, and bring the same then unto this Court." The story had a sad ending: Edward Brewster, John Symms and William Phillips, master and wardens of the Company, appeared before the Court as commanded and, without giving any satisfactory reason, "peremptorily and contumaciously" refused to admit the said Giles Sussex. "Whereupon the said Edward Brewster, John Symms and William Phillips, and every of them, for their said several Contempt and Disobedience are by this Court committed to the Gaol of Newgate, according to the Custom and Usage of this City, there to remain until they shall yield Obedience to the Orders, or be otherwise discharged by due Course of Law."[50]

The Rise in Admission Fees

By the middle of the eighteenth century the entry fines to the Company had escaped from legal bounds. The Acts of Henry VIII regulating such charges were still in force, but they were now quite ineffectual. The table of fees hanging in the Stationers' Hall in 1741 included a list of twenty payable to the clerk, amounting to £10 14s. It was noticed that this list was pasted over an earlier one, and an inquisitive member discovered, "by looking thro' the Paper with the Light of a Candle," that by this former schedule, dated 1714, only five fees had been exacted, amounting in all to £1 11s.[51] The new apprenticeship fees were 5s. payable to the warden, 7s. 6d. to the clerk and 1s. to the beadle. The candidate for freedom had now to pay 8s. 6d. to the warden, a sum ranging from 2s. 6d. to £1 1s. to the clerk, according to circumstances, and 2s. 6d. to the beadle. These fees scarcely seem high enough to have raised an outcry, but one member, at least, declared his annoyance in no uncertain terms. "Never before, sure," he wrote, "did any Corporation, who were not under an actual Rebellion, ever dare to commit such breaches upon the Government, or fly in the Face of Authority at this Rate. For a few unskilful, and, in Affairs of this kind, very ignorant or very wicked Men, to assume to themselves a Power superior to any the King himself hath in like Cases, in order to lay heavy burdens upon the People, and to levy Money upon their Fellow Subjects in so unmerciful a manner, is quite astonishing!"[52]

The Position of Aliens

As aliens were incapable of being apprenticed they could not become freemen of the Company, but as it was found convenient occasionally to employ foreigners for the more skilled work a special class of brethren was formed for them. For some years the entrance fee was only 1s.; in 1561 it rose to 2s. 6d. Later on the fee became more prohibitive: in 1577 a certain Salomon Kyrkner was admitted as a brother, "for whiche his admission it is ordered that he shall paie Tenne shillinges by Twelve pence a weeke vntill it be payde and master Bynneman muste staie the same xij d weekelie out of his wages." The greatest number of brethren admitted in any one year was thirteen, in 1567–8. Only eleven were enrolled after that date, probably owing to representations made by English unemployed journeymen. In any case, the brother could not hope to rise far in the profession; a decree of the Stationers' Company of November 24, 1578, is proof of this: "At a court holden this daie Richard Skilders Dutchman brother admitted to worke in this Cumpanie: havinge presse and letters

[type] with other fourniture for the Art of printinge being him self a compositor and havinge a booke in woork for hans steele conteyning XX shetes of paper or thereabout and having printed vj sheetes thereof: was by authority of the charter of this cumpanie enjoyned to cease and procede no further therein for that no person that is not of the comminalty of this companie may not vse the art of printinge in this realme otherwise then in the servyce of the freemen of this mistery. As by the said charter appeareth. Wherevpon the said Richard was appointed to Deliuer the said booke to Thomas Da[w]son a printer of this cumpanye to be finished by him and the said Richard was assigned to serue the said Da[w]son as a Journeman to compose the formes for the Rest of the said booke for weekely wages till it be finished."[53]

Censorship

It has already been mentioned that the primary duty of the Stationers' Company was to aid the Government in stamping out sedition, and that the Company was given a general right of search for this purpose. The search was by no means merely nominal: twenty-four searchers were appointed in 1576 to make a weekly inspection of printing-houses and to note what every printer was printing, and for whom; how many apprentices and journeymen he kept; whether he employed any journeymen who were not freemen or brethren; and how many presses he had. Failure to search was punishable by a fine of 6s. 8d. Where any infringement of the rules was found the officers of the Company were authorised to inflict fines and even to seize and destroy type. Twenty-four searchers must have been quite enough to maintain order when the total number of printing-houses did not exceed twenty-three!

As a result of the allegations of Sir Roger l'Estrange that the Company was failing in its duties of censorship that body in 1662 lost much of its power to control the Press. The Licensing Act of that year provided that no book should for the future be printed unless it had first been duly licensed by the appropriate authority. Law books were to be licensed by the Lord Chancellor, the Lord

Keeper or the Lord Chief Justice, history by the Secretary of State, heraldry by the Earl Marshal or King of Arms, and all others by the Archbishop of Canterbury and the Bishop of London, except that the chancellors and vice-chancellors of the universities were allowed to be responsible for the publications of their own presses. The Company was still further slighted by the appointment of Sir Roger l'Estrange as Censor of the Press. Owing to the ill-feeling aroused by the Act it was allowed to lapse after three years, but it was renewed by James II in 1685 for a period of seven years, after which it was extended for one year more. This was the end of the attempt at complete State control.

Conflict within the Company

At the time of the Restoration the Company's position was also jeopardised by internal dissent. The rise of the publisher to ascendancy in the book trade was reflected in the Company itself: very seldom did a printer attain high rank. About 1660, therefore, eleven of the leading London printers combined in a Company of Printers. This new body issued a pamphlet in 1663, entitled *A Brief Discourse concerning Printers and Printing*, setting forth the printers' grievances. The main complaint was that the Stationers' Company had become mainly a company of booksellers, bent on reducing the cost of printing, and to this end admitting far more printers than were really required. There may have been some truth in this, but the Company of Printers was too small and weak a body to do more than protest, and seems to have broken up after a very short existence. Obviously, the total number of printers would have been not at all reduced by limiting the number of members of this new company while the Stationers' Company remained open to all who came. The Parisian Company of Printer-Publishers, incidentally, was faced with similar problems: from the early seventeenth century there had been discord between the three main bodies in the association—printers, publishers and binders. Here, too, the printers felt themselves exploited by the publishers. Their principal grievance was ended in 1686, with the limitation of their number to thirty-six. From this time until the dissolution of the association in 1791 printing was closed to publishers, though publishing was still open to printers.[54]

The Maintenance of Order

Apart from the fines imposed by the Stationers' Company in connection with the search for seditious books there were others which seem to have been exacted for trivial reasons, as when Henry Conway was fined 1s. "for yat he cam to the hall in his cloke" and Edmond Bolifant 6d. "for Departinge on the Quarter Daye without Lycence before the ordinaunces were Read"; but others were imposed, in accordance with tradition, for bad workmanship, or for using unsuitable binding materials. The gild spirit had survived in other directions. It was the Company's practice to relieve members in distress, giving them annual grants of 6s. 8d. or thereabouts in the sixteenth century, rising to more considerable sums as various new bequests raised the capital available for this purpose.

A not insignificant part of the work of the master and wardens was to maintain peace. The accounts for 1561–2 show the receipt of 1s. from John Harrison "for his fyne for that he Revyled Gregory Brodehed with vnsemely Wordes"; the said Brodehed, presumably more fluent, was fined 3s. for his retort. Within the printing-house, too, abusive language was punishable by a "solace," or fine, but by the end of the seventeenth century a way had been found of avoiding expense and yet obtaining the same satisfaction: "I told you before," says Joseph Moxon, "that abusive Language or giving the Lye was a Solace: But if in discourse, when any of the Workmen affirm anything that is not believed, the compositer knocks with the back corner of his composing-stick against the lower Ledge of his Lower Case, and the Pressman knocks the Handles of his Ball-stocks together: Thereby signifying the discredit they give to his story."[55]

CHAPTER VII

Labour Supply and Conditions of Employment

THE printing industry has always required, and afforded scope for, workers of special aptitudes and proficiency. The specialisation which became an early feature of the trade accentuated this need. To appreciate the situation in the labour market at the various stages of development it is necessary to know the various kinds of work to be performed in a hand-printing works, and the special qualities desirable in each class of worker.

To begin with the compositor: his is the task of setting up the type, with due regard to accuracy and artistry. His work requires no great amount of physical strength; rather must he be set on "minding his p's and q's"—by no means an empty phrase in arranging type. His most obvious need is a good knowledge of at least the English language. In addition he requires a quick eye and nimble fingers, for, as Moxon laboriously puts it, "as his eyes are very quick in reading his Copy, and in shifting its Visual Ray to the several Boxes he is to have a Letter out of, so is his choice what Letter to take up very sudden; for though the Box be full of letters, yet in an instant he resolves and pitches his Fingers upon that one, which for its posture and position his Fancy reckons lyes most commodious for his immediate seizing."[1]

The pressman, to whom the compositor passes on the formes of type, has work demanding far greater physical strength. It consists of inking the type and "pulling off" the required number of copies. Beyond the reasonable amount of care needed to avoid spoiling the sheets it calls for no special skill. The pressman is sometimes helped in lifting off the finished sheets by young boys, who, because they "commonly black and daub themselves,"[2] are familiarly known as devils.

The finished sheets are passed on to the corrector, or reader, whose duty it is to look out for any mistakes made by the compositor. Incidentally, it may also fall to his lot to put the ignorant author to rights. In the early years of printing it was usual to hand over the correction of classical works to scholars otherwise unconnected with the printing trade, but by the time the industry was well established the position of corrector was the next stage in the compositor's progress to the management of the works.[3] The modern printing-works would probably employ as many correctors as there were foreign languages to be read. This was not always so. It is therefore instructive to note the modest qualifications required of the seventeenth-century corrector: he should be "well skilled in Languages, especially in those that are used to be Printed with us, *viz.* the Latin, Greek, Hebrew, Syriack, Caldae, French, Spanish, Italian, High Dutch, Saxon, Low Dutch, Welch, &c.; neither ought my innumerating only these be a stint to his skill in the number of them, for many times several other languages may happen to be printed, of which the Author has perhaps no more skill than the bare knowledge of the Words and their Pronunciations, so that the Orthography (if the Corrector have no knowledge of the Language) may not only be false to its native Pronunciation, but the Words altered into other Words by a little wrong Spelling, and consequently the Sense made ridiculous, the purpose of it controvertible, and the meaning of the Author irretrievably lost to all that shall read it in After times. He ought to be very knowing in Derivations and Etymologies of Words, very sagacious in Pointing, skilful in the Compositors whole Task and Obligation, and endowed with a quick Eye to espy the smallest Fault."[4]

The folding of the printed sheets and arranging them in order requires neatness and care, but no particular skill or bodily strength. By the nineteenth century the work was frequently given to women.[5]

The next process, binding, requires in its early stages of sewing, beating and pressing no great mental ability; but the finishing processes in the case of leather-bound books offer unlimited possibilities for artistic hand-tooling.

The final stages of all are publishing and bookselling, for a long period normally undertaken by the same person. The publisher in particular needs, besides a keen business sense, a fair share of learning and culture; if he is also a bookseller he needs all those qualities of tact and persuasiveness which make up good salesmanship.

Considered independently of one another, all these necessary qualifications (except, perhaps, those demanded of the corrector) fall within the bounds of human possibility. The great difficulty is that it is not appropriate to consider them independently. For the first century of printing at least, as we have seen, all the stages of printing and publishing were normally carried on by the same firm, and this firm might consist of a master, a single journeyman and one apprentice. That being so, the master and journeyman needed to possess between them all the above qualities: a good general education, including a knowledge of every dead and living language, perfect accuracy, neatness, quickness of movement, a keen artistic sense, tact and physical strength. And some of the early printers also cast their own type.

Actually, for the whole of this period of small-scale production there were few who could be regarded as scholar-printers. In England there has never been an educational test such as formerly existed in France and Italy for aspirants to the higher positions in the trade. As late as 1618 it was impossible for anyone to become a master printer in France who did not hold a university certificate testifying to his skill in the art of printing and to his knowledge of Latin and Greek.[6] The Gild of Printers and Booksellers of Venice held a formal examination for those wishing to become booksellers;[7] an examination paper of 1667 required proficiency in Italian, French and Latin, together with a knowledge of the principal editions of the Bible, the names of the principal theologians, philosophers, artists, historians, Greek and Latin poets, lawyers and geographers, numismatists, mathematicians, physicians and botanists. These regulations tended to confine the trade to the wealthier classes. In England, too, the early printer-publisher was usually a man of social standing, as in the case of Caxton, John

Day, Richard Grafton and Richard Tottel; but by the end of the sixteenth century there were a number of poor men in the trade, such as John Wayland, who could leave nothing in his will but "desperate debts."[8] The man of enterprise was now turning to foreign trade, which offered a far greater return on his capital than was possible in so over-regulated an industry as this. Book production offered attractions of another kind to the studious type of man, but learning and wealth seem seldom to have gone together in the sixteenth century. So it happened that by the early seventeenth century the English stationer held an unfavourable position in comparison with that occupied by his foreign competitor, as was pointed out in 1643 in the *Humble Remonstrance of the Company of Stationers*:[9] "France especially is famous for the value she sets upon that Profession and Trade of Men (whom we in England incorporate by the name of Stationers) for there they are priviledged above meer Mechanicks, and honoured with a habitation, as it were, in the Suburbs of Literature it self." For the physically unfit the book industry did offer opportunities which were to be found in few other occupations. In 1586 a certain John Gylpin was admitted as a freeman "but not sworne, *quia surdus et mutus est* [because he is deaf and dumb]." We even find that one of the twenty master printers approved by the Star Chamber decree of 1637 was "John Beale: he is blinde, and Rich";[10] it would be interesting to know his system of maintaining the quality of work turned out by his journeymen.

Social Conditions

New entrants to the trade in the sixteenth century were drawn largely from the ranks of yeomen and husbandmen. In the year 1576–7, for instance, fifteen of the apprentices enrolled were sons of yeomen and ten were sons of husbandmen, as compared with eight whose fathers were tailors; of the rest, the father was in three cases a mercer, in two a tanner, baker, stationer or shearman, while the others represent nineteen different occupations, one of which was bookselling. In 1596–7 there were still eleven sons of yeomen presented out of a total of twenty-two. There was probably some truth in Latimer's statement that until well in the sixteenth century the yeomanry had supplied the greater number of university students; some of the most eminent clergy, including Latimer himself, had proceeded from among them. It seems natural, then, that as the fortunes of the yeoman declined with the progress of the agrarian revolution, and he could no longer afford an expensive education for his children, he would try to apprentice them to the trade which approached most nearly to the learned professions. A significant fact to be noted from the registers of the Stationers' Company is the very small number of merchants who wished their sons to become printers or booksellers; in not more than a dozen cases between 1560 and 1590 was the father's occupation given as mercer, goldsmith, haberdasher or merchant tailor. Throughout this period an almost constant proportion of one in three of the new apprentices were orphans, but this probably testifies to the generally unhealthy state of the population at that time rather than being peculiar to the book industry. It may have been due to the high rate of mortality in London that four out of five of the apprentices came from other parts of the country, from places as far afield as Yorkshire, Lancashire, Cumberland, Flintshire and Worcestershire.

By the eighteenth century it had become customary to demand a premium on the enrolment of apprentices. William Bowyer, for instance, in the middle of the century advertised for an apprentice with "some share of learning, the more the better," and stipulated that £50 should be paid down, of which sum £30 should be returned at the end of the seven years if the apprentice had behaved well for the whole time. When John Nichols was bound to him it was agreed in the same way that half the apprentice-fee should be given back, and Nichols records that this was honourably carried out.[11] Between this time and the early nineteenth century apprenticeship became more specialised and the premiums rather higher in some branches of the trade. For printing and for bookbinding the premium was still about £50; for retail bookselling it varied from £50 to £100; for publishing it ranged between £200 and £500; while the apprentice to an engraver would have to pay up to £500 according to the talent of his master.[12]

In returning part of the premium the master's intention was, perhaps, to give the newly promoted journeyman a sense of financial security. However that may be, it is not the nature of every youth who suddenly receives a windfall of £20 or £30 to keep it intact. John Dunton's first act on breaking loose from his apprenticeship (1681) was to invite a hundred apprentices to celebrate a funeral for it—a proceeding which he describes as a youthful piece of vanity, very expensive and soon forgotten.[13]

The premium system necessarily barred some of the poorer members of society from the book trade, but it did not on that account raise the general educational standard of the employees. Bowyer mentioned in his will that he had long been concerned at the number of printers' apprentices who had no school-learning whatever; he therefore bequeathed to the Stationers' Company (1777) a sum of money sufficient to buy £1,000 3 per cent bank annuities, to be held for life by a journeyman compositor with the following qualifications: he was to be a man of good life and conversation, a regular attender at church, and one who had not worked on a newspaper or a magazine for at least four years; in addition, he must be able to read and construe Latin and Greek, bringing a testimonial to this effect from the Rector of St. Martin's, Ludgate; if possible, he should have attended Merchant Taylors', or some other public school for at least ten years.[14] He was not to receive the annuity until the age of thirty-one, so it was not unduly difficult to reach the required educational standard in time.

A man thus qualified might bear some faint resemblance to Moxon's ideal press-corrector. His ability would far exceed that of the typical translator, if one may believe Pope's famous letter to the Earl of Burlington (1714) describing a conversation with Lintot: Lintot, speaking of translators, says, "Those are the saddest pack of rogues in the world; in a hungry fit, they'll swear they understand all the languages in the universe; I have known one of them take down a Greek book upon my counter and cry, 'Ah, this is Hebrew. I must read it from the latter end.' "

Unemployment

The prospects of the new entrant to the book trade in the sixteenth and seventeenth centuries were not good. He had a very small chance of ever becoming a master printer, on account of the drastic limitation of numbers authorised by the Government. If he possessed capital he might become a publisher, but there was little chance of success in this field when it was still usual for the printer himself to act as publisher. A great number could never rise above the journeyman class, and, as time went on, it became increasingly difficult to obtain employment of any kind. The restrictions regarding apprenticeship were imposed partly for the sake of the journeymen, as we have seen, but these were not enough to stem unemployment, and the Company received one petition after another calling attention to the desperate state of affairs. "The peticons of the poore men of this Companie for their Relief," 1578, begin with the simple request, "That they maie haue woorke," to which the Company replied by an ineffectual order that "the bookesellers of this companie shall deliver sufficient worke to the poore bretheren of this companie that can and will well and honestlie doe and bringe home their woorke," concluding with the promise that "If anie of the poore bretheren of this companie shall for his benefyte praie to haue allowance to him of anie laufull copie wherevnto noe other man hath righte or whereof there is noe number remayninge by the fourmer printer vnsold or yf he shall make anie other reasoning request for his relief suche poore brother shalbe favourablie and lovinglie heard and holpen."[15] Ten years later, in answer to further petitions, an order was issued by which the welfare of the individual worker was placed above the efficiency of the industry as a whole: no type was to be kept standing "to the preiudice of woorkemen at any tyme," and, except in certain cases, no impression of any book was to exceed 1,250 or 1,500 copies;[16] in other words, the journeyman was periodically to distribute the type in order that he might be paid for putting it together again. Following further concessions at this same time restricting the employment of apprentices it is ordered that if the journeymen are still not content, "but shall move or begyn any newe sute peticon or complaint to or against the Mayster Wardens and Gouernors or any other of the Society," these orders shall be void. In 1637 the Court of Star Chamber tackled the problem. It was felt that the unemployment among journeymen-printers was endangering the security of the State by giving rise to secret printing. The master and wardens were therefore enjoined to take any unemployed journeyman-printer to the master under whom he served his apprenticeship or to any other master printer, "and euery Master Printer shall be bound to imploy one Iourneyman, being so offered to him, and more, if need shall so require, and it shall be so adiudged to come to his share, according to the proportion of his Apprentices and imployments . . . although he the said Master Printer with his Apprentice or Apprentices be able without the helpe of the said Iourneyman or Iourneymen to discharge his owne worke";[17] any journeyman refusing to take such work was to be imprisoned. (This order was afterwards incorporated in the Licensing Act of 1662.) When the Corporation of London had introduced measures for the relief of the poor towards the end of the sixteenth century matters had been complicated by the immediate immigration of beggars from other parts of England. Lest similar difficulties should arise in this case it was decreed that the printers of Oxford and Cambridge should keep their own journeymen employed, and not allow them to wander to London.

By the eighteenth century the journeyman found it more easy to obtain casual employment, or "smouting" work as it was called. Thomas Gent, indeed, on giving up a regular appointment in 1714, accepted several of these temporary positions, and found it more profitable to be a "smouter" than a "cuz" (a full-time journeyman).[18] The independence of the journeyman was by now becoming well pronounced. Horace Walpole's *Journal* for 1759–61 contains some illuminating entries on this point: "1759. March 5th: Robinson the Printer went away. March 29th: My new Printer,

Benjamin Williams, came. May 25th: He went away. June 19th: James Lister, a new Printer, came; staid but a week. July 16th: The fourth Printer, Thomas Farmer, came. 1761. Dec. 2nd: Thomas Farmer ran away for debt. . . . Took one Pratt to finish the work." There were still occasional clashes between masters and men on the subject of apprenticeship, but these were now caused not so much by unemployment as by the newer struggles of the workers to raise wages. The great essential to raise the price of labour is to keep down the supply and eliminate competition. Masters and men both realised this. Towards the end of the century, therefore, strikes frequently occurred among the journeymen for the renewal of the old restrictions on the number of apprentices. The reply of the master printers was either to prosecute the men for illegal combination or else to employ outdoor apprentices.[19] These were regarded by the working printers as a class of indentured journeymen, and were specially resented for their low social standing: being taken without premium they were of poor parentage and therefore of little education, and it was argued that their advent would drive away the regular employees.[20] Their function was similar to that of the French *alloués*, who were employed in large numbers from 1724 onwards: these were bound for a period of two to four years, but, being exempt from the regulations regarding religion, education and nationality, were incapable of becoming masters; they were useful as pressmen, but by the journeymen they were regarded as a menace.[21]

Wages

We have little information as to the wages paid to the various workers in the book industry in the early days. The average wages of an artisan between 1401 and 1540, according to Thorold Rogers, were 3s. a week; between 1583 and 1612 a carpenter earned about 6s. a week, and from 1633 to 1642 7s. a week, or 1s. 2d. a day. A Winchester stationer who was employed for several months of 1520–1 at binding books in Eton College library received 4d. a day in wages and 1s. a day in commons, his materials being supplied to him. In 1597 and 1598 All Souls

College, Oxford, employed a bookbinder and man jointly for 2s. 2d. a day in the first year and 2s. 4d. in the second. The piece-work rate for bookbinding ranged in 1614 from 10d. to 5s., according to the size of the book, but the binder had to provide his own vellum. Clasp-makers were paid 2s. a week in 1576; each man had to make five dozen clasps a day, but the cutting-out was done for him.[22] For printers there is little definite evidence. At a court held by the Stationers' Company in November 1577, it was agreed that a certain John Moore should serve Thomas Dawson "for the wage of iij li. by the yere, and meate drink lodginge and wasshinge of his lynen as the other servaunts of the said Thomas Dason shall haue. And that the said Ihon shall finde him selfe apparell withe his wages."[23] In 1581 wages were a little higher: Christopher Hackford was ordered to work "for meate Drinck wasshinge lodginge and xviijd. weekelie wage."[24] According to Joseph Moxon, printers seem to have been paid at much higher rates by the middle of the seventeenth century: "It is now customary that Journey-men are paid for all Church Holy days that fall not on a Sunday, whether they work or no: And they are by contract with the Master Printer paid proportionably for what they undertake to earn every Working day, be it half a Crown, two shillings, three shillings, four shillings, &c." Payment for holidays was an old custom which had been confirmed by the Stationers' Company in 1653, as was the other custom mentioned by Moxon, that "if the Compositor or Press-man make either the other stand still through the neglect of their contracted Task, that then he who neglected, shall pay him that stands still as much as if he had Wrought." To this extent it was the journeyman and not the master printer who was the risk-bearer. It had been usual for the journeymen to be given a copy of every book on which they had worked, but in 1635 it was decided to give them three-pence a week instead; but, at the same time, it was ordered that if any compositor should fail to keep his cases of type in good order a deduction should be made from his wages sufficient to pay somebody else to clear up, while if any journeyman spoilt a piece of work he was to bear the cost of paper and printing.[25]

For the eighteenth century there is more definite information. Before 1765 the wages paid to an ordinary labourer varied from 9s. to 10s. a week, while a journeyman in the less well-paid trades received from 12s. to 15s. At the other end of the scale were the skilled workers such as jewellers and makers of optical instruments: such men as these would earn anything between £1 and £4 on piecework.[26] Printers fell into the class of better-paid journeymen. Although Gent in 1714 was receiving a money wage of only £18 a year from a York printer, his employer supplied board and lodging and paid for his washing. Five years later a former employer offered him £1 a week to return to him, but Gent was already receiving this in another printing-office.[27] William Strahan, a London printer, was in 1739 paying journeymen's wages amounting to £4 10s. a week; he employed either four or five men.[28] It is interesting to note the wording of an agreement made twenty years later between Horace Walpole and one of his printers: "Hond. Sir, Having now managed your Press for Six weeks, and thereby become acquainted with your Business of this Sort, I hereby offer to engage myself faithfully and diligently to work your Press for Two Years more certain from the Date hereof, upon your agreeing to pay me one Guinea per week, as my Wages for such Service. And for your Satisfaction that I am fully resolved to be steady in your Service, and not to be corrupted, or tempted from it in that Time, I do agree, That you shall retain my First Three Months Wages in your own Hands 'till the End of the said Two Years; And that such retained Wages shall be forfeited to you, in case before the End of the said Two Years I desert your Service. I do further agree to instruct in the Art of Printing, during the said Two Years, any young Man you shall appoint to attend upon me, upon your agreeing to pay me, as a gratuity for the same, Two Guineas at the End of the first Year, and Three Guineas more at the End of the Second Year. . . . Thomas Farmer."[29]

In 1774 there was adopted the system of paying compositors at piece-work rates. From that year until 1785 the rate was 4d. for a thousand letters. It was then raised to 4½d., and two further increases brought it up to 5¼d. by the year 1800. In 1793, too, the

London book-compositors successfully claimed payment for "head and direction lines of pages, and the en and em quadrats at the sides,"[30] a point which illustrates the difficulty of measuring the exact amount of work performed. Although this was now the general method of calculating wages it was still necessary at times to engage day-labour. The payment for this was based on the average earnings of a good workman on piece-work: it worked out at 20s. a week in 1774, 21s. to 27s. in 1785, 30s. in 1793 and 33s. in 1805.[31]

Bookbinders were rather less well paid. In the last quarter of the eighteenth century their wages were from 15s. to 18s. a week; a few men received a guinea.[32]

Printing-House Customs

From early times the journeyman had to be prepared not only for the demands upon his income for bad workmanship but also for arbitrary fines imposed by the general vote of the printing-house, or "chapel."[33] It was a recognised custom that every new workman should pay half a crown, known as his "Benvenue," to the chapel. Every apprentice paid half a crown to the chapel on being bound and another half a crown on becoming a freeman; if he continued to work as a journeyman in the same printing-house he was expected to pay still another. If he married, he again paid half a crown. If his wife came to the chapel she paid 6d., and the journeymen subscribed 2d. each to welcome her. On the birth of a son the journeyman paid 1s., but for a daughter 6d. was considered enough. The money thus collected was spent on drink. The oldest freeman, or Father of the Chapel, was allowed to drink first, unless one of the journeymen produced a token-coin proving that if the last chapel-drink had held out his turn would have been next. As these payments were not sufficient to provide a steady revenue to the chapel there were a number of more general penalties ("solaces"), to be bought off at rates varying from a halfpenny to a shilling. In case of dispute as to the justice of these fines the matter was put to the vote of the members, "It being asserted as a maxim, *That the Chappel cannot Err.* But when any Controversie is thus decided, it always ends in the good of the *Chappel*!" Solaces were demanded for offences ranging from swearing, fighting and drunkenness to leaving a candle burning at night. Where the workmen were conscientious the income was still too low, and fines were levied for more trivial offences, such as singing at work, or suggesting spending the chapel-money before Saturday night. Even visitors to the printing-house were fined if opportunity could be found; a favourite trick was to send some unsuspecting stranger to the King's printing-house to ask for a ballad, or to a compositor to inquire whether he had received news of a certain galley at sea; the chapel could then claim to have been affronted, and would demand a solace from the inquirer. This method of collecting money was not peculiar to England. French printing-houses, too, levied fines ranging from 5 sols to 3 livres for similar offences. Forgetting to snuff a candle, for instance, cost 5 sols.[34]

When the journeymen were not trying to levy fines from one another they seem to have been playing quadrats. These are the rules of the game, as given by Moxon: "They take fiue or seuen more m *Quadrats* (generally of the *English body*) and holding their Hand below the Surface of the *Correcting Stone*, shake them in their Hand, and toss them up upon the *Stone*, and then count how many *Nicks* upwards each man throws in three times, or any other number of times agreed on: And he that throws most Wins the Bett of all the rest, and stands out free, till the rest have try'd who throws fewest *Nicks* upwards in so many throws; for all the rest are free: and he pays the Bett." Unfortunately, the master printer was apt to object to this pastime on the ground that, besides hindering the work, it battered his type.

It is curious to find how the ecclesiastical tradition has lingered through the centuries. The group of men in each department still forms the chapel. Even the names of some of the types are a constant reminder that these letters were originally designed for use in service books. Canon, for instance, was the specially large type in which was printed the Canon of the Mass; Great Primer and Long Primer were used for the Primers of the early Church, and so on. We have already noticed the title of "devil" given to the printer's boy: in harmony with this is the epithet "friars and monks" given to the white and black blotches caused by uneven printing; while, not to be outdone, the pot into which waste type is thrown is called "hell."[35]

The ceremonial within the printers' chapel of the seventeenth and eighteenth centuries was undoubtedly a travesty of Church ritual, with its consecration ceremonies, its ordinations and excommunications. Here we have a detailed and almost incredible account of their proceedings: "When a printer first sets up, if it is an House that was never used for Printing before, the Part designed for that Purpose is consecrated, which is performed by the senior Freeman the Master employs, who is the Father or Dean of the Chapel; and the chief Ceremony is drinking Success to the Master, sprinkling the Walls with strong Beer, and singing the Cuz's Anthem, at the Conclusion of which there is a supper given by the Master. All the workmen are called Chappellonians, who are obliged to submit to certain Laws, all of which are calculated for the Good of the whole Body, and for the well-carrying on of the Master's Business. To the Breach of these Laws is annex'd a Penalty, which an obstinate Member sometimes refuses to pay; upon which it is left to the Majority of the Chapel, in Convocation assembled, whether he shall be continued any longer a Chappellonian; and if his Sentence is to be discontinued, he is then declared a Brimstone; that is an excommunicated person, and deprived of all Share of the Money given by Gentlemen, Authors, Booksellers and others, to make them drink, especially that great annual Solemnity, commonly call'd the Way-Goose Feast. Whilst he continues in this State, he can have no Redress for any Mischief that is done him; so that, in a short Time, he is glad to pay the Penalty, which he had incurr'd, and a discretionary Fine besides to reconcile himself to the Chapel.

"When a Boy is to be bound Apprentice, before he is admitted a Chappellonian, it is necessary for him to be made a Cuz, or Deacon; in the Performance of which there are a great many Ceremonies. The Chappellonians walk three Times round the

BENJAMIN FRANKLIN IN A LONDON PRINTING OFFICE
After Eyre Crow, R.A.

Room, their right Arms being put thro' the Lappets of their Coats; the Boy who is to be made a Cuz carrying a wooden Sword before them. Then the Boy kneels, and the Father of the Chapel, after exhorting him to be observant of his Business, and not to betray the Secrets of the Workmen, squeezes a Spunge of strong Beer over his Head, and gives him a Title, which is generally that of Duke of some Place of the least Reputation near which he lives, or did live before. . . . Whilst the Boy is upon his Knees, all the Chappellonians, with their right Arms put through the Lappets of their Coats, as before, walk round him, singing the Cuz's Anthem, which is done by adding all the Vowels to the Consonants in the following Manner.

B a ba; B e be; B i bi; Ba-be-bi;
B o bo; Ba-be-bi-bo; B u bu; Ba-be-bi-bo-bu—

and so through the rest of the Consonants.

"There are several other Solemnities, of the same Kind, belonging to a Printing-Chapel; but these are sufficient to shew the sacred Institution of it, and the Reverence that is due to it."[36]

It may well be believed that the new workman was not too willing to submit to his initiation ceremony. Thomas Gent, on entering a printing-office in Blackfriars (1714), paid his "Ben-Money" without protest, but objected strongly to the proceedings by which he was dubbed a "cuz." The master himself insisted that he must submit to this immemorial custom, and Gent accordingly went through all the game of walking round the chapel, singing the alphabetical anthem, and having his head first struck with a sword and then drenched with ale. Yet it was all in vain. "After all this work," he laments, "I began to see the vanity of human grandeur; for, as I was not yet a freeman, I was discharged as a foreigner in about a fortnight or three weeks' time."[37]

It will have been noticed that the customs of the printing-house were not wholly unconnected with beer. Births, funerals, initiations and all other social events were made the occasions for drink. When John Johnson, a compositor of the Cambridge University Press, died in 1679, leaving only 9s. 6d. in money, his funeral expenses included 12s. for a coffin and 13s. 4d. "for beare and sugar."[38] It was alleged of Mark Baskett's printing-house in the mid-eighteenth century that it was more like an ale-house, and that his servants were a set of idle and drunken men.[39] Benjamin Franklin found it impossible to reconcile himself to these habits. Many years later he had a vivid recollection of his feelings of disgust while employed at Palmer's printing-house in Bartholomew Close (1725): there was an ale-house boy in constant attendance, and Franklin's companion at the press drank each day "a pint before breakfast, a pint at breakfast with his bread and cheese, a pint between breakfast and dinner, a pint at dinner, a pint in the afternoon about six o'clock, and another when he had done his day's work . . . and had four or five shillings to pay out of his wages every Saturday night for that vile liquor." Franklin was at first none too popular among his fellows, owing to his refusal to hand over 5s. for drink on his promotion from the press to the composing-room; for a time everything went wrong for him—his founts of type became mixed and the matter which he had set up fell out of order whenever he went out of the room, and all on account of the chapel ghost, which was said to haunt all those who were not regularly admitted. Franklin soon deemed it wiser to pay. But he had the satisfaction, before he left, of converting his fellow-workers to his own preference for bread and milk. Or so he believed![40]

These habits were by no means confined to the lower grades of workmen. The booksellers of Paternoster Row had their own society, founded in the early eighteenth century, known as the Cauliflower Club. This was no meeting of amateur gardeners. The "free and easy counsellors under the cauliflower" were so called because they held their meetings under a ceiling decorated with a large cauliflower. This represented the head on the gallon of porter for which every new member had to pay.[41]

For all that, where drink was concerned the English printer was no more depraved than his continental colleagues. The French, too, paid their *bienvenues* for the same purpose and, according to eighteenth-century writers, kept up their celebrations for days at a time. Dolet wrote of them, in despair, "Quelle négligence, quel manque de soin montrent les imprimeurs! Combien de fois ils sont aveuglés et mis hors d'état de travailler par la boisson! Quels ivrognes! Avec quelle hardiesse, quelle témérité, quelle absence de raison ne font-ils pas de changements dans les textes si, chose qui se présente souvent, ils ont quelque teinture littéraire!"[42]

More prosaic times were to come. When in 1824 a London printer was asked by the Select Committee on Artizans and Machinery for his opinion on the general state of morals among his workmen he replied, "I think it is very much improved; a printing-office was like a public-house on a Monday, when I was apprentice, and now we have no drinking at all." This he attributed partly to the improvement in working-class education and partly to the breakdown of apprenticeship restrictions, giving a better choice of workmen. Pressmen, in fact, were "becoming as respectable and as intelligent a class of operatives as they were within recollection, degraded and sottish."[43]

CHAPTER VIII

Premises and Equipment

THE technique of book production, so far as hand-printing and the manufacture of hand-made paper are concerned, has remained almost unchanged since the earliest days of the industry. Nevertheless, for the first century or more the scarcity of certain necessary commodities raised difficulties which, now they have been surmounted, are not easily realised.

The first process in the actual hand-printing of a book is the composition of the type.[1] The compositor stands before his case of type holding in his left hand a "stick," a shallow tray capable of holding about twelve lines of type. He fills the stick with the required type and transfers the text thus set up to a long tray, called a galley, repeating the process until the galley is full, and adding the headlines and pagination as they are required. After the "make-up" has been checked, the pages are slid on to the stone for imposition. The "stone" is a large table which in the early years of the industry was actually made of stone, but which has of more recent times been built with a metal top. (In the sixteenth century it was quite usual to print one page at a time rather than a whole sheet, or section, of the book.) The forme thus set up, consisting of the whole matter to be taken off at a single impression, is secured in an iron frame called a "chase," and is then ready for the press. It is laid on the bed of the press and is inked, this process being carried on until the eighteenth century by means of balls consisting usually of wool covered with leather, attached to handles. Meanwhile another pressman is fixing the paper into a double-hinged frame, known as the tympan, so arranged that the outer half of the frame, the "frisket," which is fitted with a piece of paper or parchment cut into windows of the exact size of the type-page, shall protect the margins from the ink. The impression is made by means of the platen, a flat weight which, on the turning of the screw above it, presses the tympan on to the inked forme. The sheets thus printed are piled up ready for the printing of the second forme on the other side of the paper. An illustrated edition may add to the press-work: in the case of a woodcut no extra work is involved, as the part of the block to be printed stands out in relief at the same height as the general body of the type, and can be inked with it; but as regards intaglio illustrations, such as copper engravings, the design is to be printed from the hollows in the plate, not from the surface, so that the paper has first to be damped and then pressed into the furrows by a special press. The work of producing a book may end with gathering the sections into order and stitching them into a paper jacket, the usual method adopted for pamphlets in the sixteenth century; or the book may be given an elaborate binding to the order of the publisher or the individual customer.

The minimum requirements for book production were, therefore, a workroom, a press and its accessories, a quantity of type sufficient for at least one page of a book, and a supply of ink and of paper. Secondary needs were ornaments and devices for use on the title-page, woodcuts or engravings, and binding-materials.

Premises

As far as premises were concerned expenses were not high. Rents naturally differed according to locality, being highest in the vicinity of St. Paul's Cathedral, the main bookselling quarter. For this reason a great number of printer-publishers rented only a small shop or stall in the Churchyard and had their printing-house in some less expensive district, such as Fleet Street. A position in the Churchyard could not be secured merely for the payment of a rent: the new applicant was eyed with jealousy and suspicion by those already established, who would do all in their power to prevent the rise of further competition in the district. Day, indeed, would never have obtained a footing at all but for the intervention of Archbishop Parker, who in December 1572 wrote to Burghley on his behalf. "Dayė hath complained to me," wrote Parker, "that dwellinge in a corner, and his brotherne envienge him, he cannot vtter his bookes which lie in his hande[s] ij or iij thousand powndes worthe, his frendes haue procured of Powles a lease of a little shop to be sett vp in the Church yearde, and it is confermed, And what [that?] by the instant request of sum enviouse booksellers, the maior and Aldermen will not suffer him to sett it vp in the Church yearde. . . . This shop is but little and lowe and leaded flatt, and is made at his greate cost to the sum of xl. or l.*li*, and is made like the terris, faier vailed and posted fitt for men to stande vppon in any triumphe or shewe."[2] To judge from the wills of various early printers leasehold tenure seems to have been general in the Churchyard. Thus the will of Johanne Woolfe, which was proved in 1574, contains a clause bequeathing to John Hun "all that shoppe in Pawles churche yarde aforesaide being parcell of the said Chappell [a disused chapel converted into warehouses] and now being in the teanure and occupation of the same John Hun . . . unto the ende and terme of fortie yeres . . . paying therefore yerelie . . . fortie shillings."[3]

Rents in Fleet Street seem ridiculously low when judged by modern standards. Wynkyn de Worde, for instance, who in 1500 moved from Caxton's house in Westminster to a dwelling-house and printing-house near St. Bride's Church, paid a rent of only £3. 6s. 8d. for these two buildings.[4] In the inquiry held in March 1594 into the estate of the late Richard Tottell it was recorded that his "messuages in Fleet Street were held of the Queen for a part of a knights fee and were valued at four pounds per annum."[5] The bookseller who wanted merely a warehouse for his books could rent one for a few shillings a year; the Stationers' Company owned property in various parts of the city, and in the year 1559 were letting off one tenement at an annual rent of 7s., while charging only 4s. for "a seller which ys in the occupynge of master Doctour May Deane of powlys."[6] Thirty years later a twenty-one years' lease of a house in Salutation Alley, Thames Street, was sold for £30, while "certen Rowmes" in the Alley were leased for the same period for £20.[7]

Among the most conveniently situated business premises were rooms in the Stationers' Hall itself. There was a large demand for these, so that the rents were rather higher than the usual charges for single rooms. Cawood and Jugge, joint royal-printers to Queen Elizabeth, paid £1 a year for an office in the hall, and a half-year's rent of 10s. was paid for "a chambre which the *premer* masters hath for thayre bokes."[8] John Wolf, the fishmonger-printer, for a time occupied the rooms over the great parlour, but it was agreed at a court held in 1594 that these, together with the ones over the little parlour, should be let to a barber-surgeon for £6 a year.[9] They were officially described as "One chamber openinge Estward lyinge ouer the great parlour of the hall. An entry and buttry at the west ende of the same chamber. One chamber openinge southward and westward into Mr. Deane of Paules garden Lyinge ouer the little parlour of the hall. In yche chamber is a chymney. And in the Est chamber a glasse wyndowe with ij clere storyes. And in the west chamber ij glasse windowes and a coumpting house. And betwene the ij chambers are the entry and buttry parted and divided. Twoo garretes ouer the said ij chambers. beinge nowe devided into iij partes. one Estward. one toward mr deanes garden and one betwene them bothe."[10] A curious method of rent-fixing was adopted: on June 6, 1597, it was recorded that "Concerninge the grauntinge of a warehouse in the hall late in the occupacion of the parteners of the grammar. Mr. Warden dawson and Mr. Bonham norton were in election for yt And thelection by most voyces fell vppon Mr. norton. But he must give asmuche for yt as any other will."[11] Presumably the officers of the Company spent the next few days in securing high bids from people who were in no danger of having to pay, for three weeks later a note was added stating that £3 a year had been offered for the room. It must be remembered that these rents were by no means so low as they seem: the whole yearly salary of a professional worker in the sixteenth century was quite commonly in the neighbourhood of £10.

While the printer was limited to the use of one press he could manage quite well with one workroom. Joseph Moxon, in the technical manual which he issued in 1683, gave the necessary floor-space as 7 feet square for each press and 5½ feet by 4½ for each frame of type-cases. Although he points out that the presses and cases could stand in the same room he remarks that in England it is not customary. What was of the first importance was that the flooring should be strong enough to stand the weight of the press; "and as the Foundation ought to be very firm, so ought also the Roof and Sides of the *Press Room* to be, that the *Press* may be fastned with Braces overhead and on its sides, as well and steddy as under foot. He is also to take care that the Room have a clear, free and pretty lofty Light not impeded with the shadow of other Houses, or with Trees; nor so low that the Skylight will not reach into every part of the Room: But yet not too high, lest the violence of *Winter* (*Printers* using generally but Paper-windows) gain too great advantage of Freesing the Paper and Letter, and so both Work and Workman stand still."[12]

John Dunton, a contemporary of Moxon, made it his first care in setting up his publishing business to take "a convenient shop in a convenient place." Not wishing to commit himself to the payment of a high rent until his business seemed likely to prosper he took to begin with only half a shop, and a warehouse, together with a "fashionable chamber."[13] William Hutton was another who had to be content at first with half a shop. In 1750 he paid 1s. a week for half a shop in Birmingham. In the same year he took a shop at Southwell, paying an annual rent of 20s. By 1751 he had become prosperous, and began business on a larger scale, paying £8 a year for a house in Birmingham.[14] Where a room was hired for short periods, as for auction-sales, the rent was higher. Dunton paid 10s. a week for the use of the back room of Dick's Coffee-house, Dublin, in 1698; nor was he compensated by security of tenure. It so happened that a certain Patrick Campbell also wanted to auction some books, "and thinking," so Dunton alleges, "that the Room where Gentlemen had found such fair usage in my Auction would give a reputation to his, takes it over my head . . .; pressing Dick to the bargain by those moving arguments of 'a double price,' or 'going to another place'; and easy Dick (though otherwise, I hope, honest) finding that it was the Law of Auctions that he who bids most is the buyer, even lets the room to Patrick, at the time when it was actually mine, without being so fair as to cry 'Ten shillings Once, Ten Shillings Twice,' either to myself, or to Mr. Wilde, to whom he promised the refusal."[15]

On the whole, rents during this period probably formed so small a proportion of the cost of production that they had little effect on the price of the individual book. The Clarendon Press paid no rent at all, according to Samuel Johnson's letter on its management (1766), yet in spite of this, and although workmanship should have been cheaper in Oxford than in London, its publications were particularly dear.

Equipment

Once a workroom had been obtained, the setting-up of a printing-press and its accessories was a fairly simple matter. Some of the minor requirements, indeed, it was customary for the compositor to provide for himself. In the eighteenth century this obligation appears still to have obtained. When Thomas Gent obtained his first appointment, in 1714, anxious to make a good impression, he laid in a stock of materials: "I furnished myself," he records, "with a new composing iron, called a stick, because anciently that useful material was made of wood; a pair of scissors, to cut scale-boards; a sharp bodkin, to correct the letter; and a pretty sliding box, to contain them, and preserve all from rustiness; I bought also a galley, for the pages I was to compose, with other appurtenances that might be of service to me when occasion should require."[16] The galleys he need not have bought for himself. Moxon includes them (1683) in his list of materials to be provided by the master printer, comprising type-cases, oak frames to put them on, a correcting-stone, a shooting-stick, a dressing-block of pear-wood for use in levelling the type-faces, and such supplies as shears, sponges, and fine packthread for use in tying up pages.[17] He accepts the tradition that the compositor should bring his own composing-stick, but holds that the master printer must in any case provide a certain number of them; his apprentices, "unless by contract or courtesie," were not bound by the obligation; moreover, when several compositors were working on the same book it was essential to have one composing-stick for common use, set to a definite measure for titles.[18] As for incidental needs, "for *Pelts*, or *Leather*, *Ball-Nails* or *Pumping-Nails*, *Wool* or *Hair*, *Vellom* or *Parchment* or *Forrel*, the *Pressman* generally eases the *Master-Printer* of the trouble of choosing, though not the charge of paying for them: And for *Paste*, *Sallad Oyl*, and such accidental Requisites as the *Press-man* in his work may want, the *Devil* commonly fetches for him."[19]

The Printing Press

The main material required for the press was wood, of which there was a growing shortage in Elizabeth's reign. Burghley, in his anxiety to preserve timber for the navy, made stringent regulations for its conservation on episcopal and other lands, and in 1586 even ordered that no barrels should be exported from London, so that no wood should be wasted.[20] It is fortunate, considering the attitude of the Government towards printing, that the opportunity was not taken of prohibiting the waste of timber on the building of printing-presses! The press in its earliest form was merely a slight adaptation of the familiar wine- or cheese-press, consisting of a wooden frame with a vertical screw which raised or lowered the platen, and its construction required no greater skill than was possessed by the general carpenter. The printing-press in this primitive form, as used by Gutenberg, was capable of producing three hundred impressions a day.[21] In the early years of the sixteenth century several improvements were made on the press in Germany, the chief of them being the adoption of a copper screw in place of the wooden one and the introduction of the sliding bed, the tympan and the frisket. These alterations increased the rate of printing to two hundred impressions an hour.[22] By the middle of the century the newer form of press seems to have been generally established in England: Thomas Vautrollier, who had been appointed a brother of the Stationers' Company in 1564, and who printed in Blackfriars and also in Scotland, bequeathed to his son Manasse the printing-press which he brought back from Scotland "furnished with all her appurtenaunces that is to saye with fower Chassis, and three Frisketts, two timpanes and a copper plate. With a copper marbell and other smale tooles and instrumentes. All my ensamples in woode the which I have printed and also others that were not as yet printed together also two bookes of pictures or figures . . . for the sum of thirty pounds."[23]

Some further improvement of the press was introduced in Amsterdam in 1620 by William Janzoon Blaeu: by adding an iron lever for turning the screw and also a new device for running the bed in and out by means of a crank and strap he increased the production of one press to two hundred and fifty impressions an hour.[24] No notable amendment on this Dutch press was made until 1798. But, in any case, it was difficult for the English printer to adopt a new form of press in the first half of the seventeenth century: on May 9, 1615, the Star Chamber had decreed that of the nineteen printers mentioned (including all except Robert Barker, the King's Printer) fourteen should be limited to the possession of two presses and the other five to one each; any printer noticed to be building a new one would, therefore, have been regarded with suspicion. On July 11, 1637, it was further decreed that no carpenter or joiner should make a printing-press, and no smith should forge any iron for a press, without first telling the Master and Wardens of the Stationers' Company for whom it was to be made.

Looking back over the centuries this Government attitude to the printing trade seems sufficient excuse for the general failure to instal Blaeu's press. Moxon, some sixty years after its invention, was more condemnatory. "There are two sorts of *Presses* in use," he wrote, "*viz.* the old fashion and the new fashion. The old fashion is generally used here in *England*; but I think for no other reason, than because many *Press-men* have scarce reason enough to distinguish between an excellently improved Invention, and a make-shift slovenly contrivance, practiced in the minority of this Art. The New-fashion'd *Presses* are used generally throughout all the *Low-Countries*."[25] Matters seem to have been very much the same a hundred years later. A sentence from Luckombe's *History and Art of Printing* (1771) might well have been Moxon's: "There are two sorts of presses in use, the old and the new-fashioned; the old sort till of late years were the only presses used in England." Actually, a comparison of these two books shows that the later one *was* Moxon's, for the most part. Luckombe certainly acknowledges in his preface that he has occasionally quoted other writers without specifying which are quotations. What he does not say is that the second part of his work, dealing with technology, is an almost word-for-word reprint of the second volume of Moxon's *Mechanick Exercises*. We are not here concerned with the ethics of authorship. Assuming that Luckombe had at least checked the accuracy of the statements he copied he has really done us a service by proving, conclusively though unintentionally, that for a hundred years or more the technology of printing had stood still.

It was part of the pressman's duty to learn the construction of the press and to explain it, if required, to the joiner. By the seventeenth century this was seldom necessary except in the surreptitiously rising provincial trade; in London there had arisen a special class of printers' joiners who, through being constantly in touch with printers, knew as much about setting up a press as the pressman himself.[26] It was not an expensive item. "One presse with the furneture" was valued in an inventory of 1558 at £3 6s. 8d.[27] Another, in 1625, was put down at £4.[28] These presses were, of course, no longer new, and on account of this and the general rise in prices the cost of a press in 1775 appears much higher: George Allan wrote to a friend in that year, "I have lately got a complete screw-press from London, made by the best hand there, which cost me 16 guineas."[29] As it happens, Allan was a private printer; if he had been the owner of a large printing-house he would probably have saved much of this expense by making his own. Baskerville boasted to Horace Walpole, in 1762, "The Ink, Presses, Chases, Moulds for casting, and all the apparatus for printing, were made in my own Shops."[30]

Type

Besides a press, the printer needed a supply of type, and the provision of this was to cause him greater difficulty. The method of type-making is as follows: the design of each letter is transferred to a "punch" of hard metal, usually steel, on which it is cut in relief (the cutting of two letters being a full day's work);[31] the punch is then driven into a block of copper or some other soft metal to form the "matrix," or mould; the type is cast by pouring molten metal into the matrix. To judge from some specimens of fifteenth-century type which were dug from the bed of the River Saône the metal used in the earliest times was lead, slightly alloyed with iron to give greater hardness. By the end of the century antimony was coming into use as the alloy, giving extra toughness and sharpness to the type.[32] Joseph Moxon gives the necessary proportions of the type-metals as 3 lb. each of iron and antimony to 25 lb. of lead. These, he says, are boiled in brick furnaces in the open air, the iron and antimony being in one furnace and the lead in another. To find out when the metal is boiling the men "lay their Ears near the Ground and listen to hear a Bubling in the Pots; and this they do so often till they do hear it." When all are melted they are mixed and allowed to cool. At this stage, while the metal is cooling, "now (according to Custom) is Half a Pint of Sack mingled with Sallad Oyl provided for each Workman to Drink; intended for an Antidote against the Poysonous Fumes of the Antimony, and to restore the Spirits that so Violent a Fire and Hard Labour may have exhausted."[33]

The next process is the actual casting. Deft movements are required for this. The caster "takes up the Ladle full of Mettal, and having his Mold as aforesaid in his left hand, he a little twists the left-side of his Body from the Furnace, and brings the Geat of his Ladle (full of Mettal) to the Mouth of the Mold, and twists the upper part of his right-hand towards him to turn the Mettal into it, while at the same moment of Time he Jilts the Mold in his left hand forwards to receive the Mettal with a strong Shake (as it is call'd) not only into the Bodies of the Mold, but while the Mettal is yet hot, running swift and strongly into the very Face of the Matrice to receive its perfect Form there, as well as in the Shanck. Then he takes the upper half of the Mold off the under half . . . and . . . throws or tosses the Letter Break and all upon a Sheet of Waste Paper laid for that purpose on the Bench just a little beyond his left-hand, and is then ready to cast another Letter as before, and also the whole number that is to be Cast with that Matrice."[34] Moxon states that a workman will ordinarily cast four thousand letters a day, which is an even higher estimate than one given a hundred and fifty years later,[35] but according to the complaint of Arthur Nicholls, one of the four men authorised by the decree of 1637 to carry on the work of type-founding, the process as a whole was slow: "the complainant being the cutter and founder of Letters for Printers is 3 quarter of a yeares time cuttinge the Punches and Matrices belonginge to the castinge of one sorte of letters, which are some 200 of a sorte, after which they are 6 weekes a castinge, that done some 2 monthes tyme is required of triall of every sorte, and then the Printers pay him what they themselves list; thus he is necessitated to lay out much money and forebeare a long tyme to little or noe benefitt."[36]

Our English printers of the fifteenth century and first half of the sixteenth were not at all well stocked with type. William Caxton had in all eight founts, some of which he had brought with him from Bruges. These served him well for his ordinary requirements, but in one work they failed him: in his edition of the *Mirror of the World* (1480) there is a series of diagrams; the explanatory notes accompanying them are not printed, as none of his type was small enough, but in each copy they are written by hand.[37] His apprentice, Wynkyn de Worde, continued to use the battered founts left to him by his master, this being one reason for his reputation as a careless printer. One of Caxton's sorts he handed on to Hugo Goes of York, who used it in the York *Directorium Sacerdotum* of 1509.[38] Three more founts he passed on to John Scolar, the second printer at Oxford, who had begun work by 1517.[39] Richard Faques, who succeeded William Faques, the King's Printer, in 1508, used his predecessor's types, and by the time he stopped printing, in 1530, these were badly worn.[40] It is, indeed, the gradual deterioration in the type used in the early presses which provides the bibliographer with one of his most valuable clues for the dating of individual works.

Type was so scarce that there is evidence of its being lent by one printer to another. In one work it was felt necessary to apologise to the reader for this scarcity: in Pynson's issue of Linacre's *De Emendata Structura* (1524) is the note, "Lectori. S. Pro tuo candore optime lector aequo animo feras, si quae literae in exemplis Hellenissimi vel tonis vel spiritibus vel affectionibus careant. Iis enim non satis erat instructus typographus videlicet recens ab eo fusis characteribus graecis, nec parata ea copia, quod ad hoc agendum opus est" [i.e. Greeting to the reader: Of thy candour, reader, excuse it if any of the letters in the Greek quotations are lacking either in accents, breathings or proper marks. The printer was not sufficiently furnished with them, since Greek types have been but lately cast by him; nor had he the supply prepared necessary for the completion of this work].[41] Similarly, in the advertisement to *Roberti Wakefeldi oratio de utilitate ling. Arabicae et Hebraicae*, printed by De Worde (1524), is the apology: "The author excuses himself to the king [Henry VIII] to whom he dedicates this speech, that he is forced to omit one third part of it for want of Hebrew types, which he says his printer had none of." William Blades shows, from instances of the type-pages being out of parallel, that it was quite common for early books to be printed one page at a time.[42] This may, as he suggests, have been due to the influence of the scribe, or, more probably, to a shortage of type. When it is remembered that between three and five thousand letters might be required for a single page of a folio volume it is easy to realise that a printer might have only enough for two pages, one of which would be composed while impressions were being taken from the other forme.

Shortage of type was to cause difficulties for many years to come. To a certain extent it made for specialisation in the publishing-trade: the house of Thomas Brudenell, for instance, is specially noted for its printing of astrological works (1621–60), this being one of the few firms to possess astrological signs at that time.[43] For Walton's *London Polyglott* (1657) it was found possible to obtain sufficient types in Hebrew, Latin, Greek, Chaldaean, Syriac, Arabic, Samaritan, Persian and Ethiopic; but this was an effort which could draw on the resources of the whole book trade. Over twenty years later Moxon was instructing compositors to set foreign languages as written, if the master printer had the type; if not, the author must translate these passages into English.[44]

Matrices and type were sought with all the zeal of the modern collector. Here is an extract from a letter written in 1697 by Dr. Tanner, from All Souls College: "Mr. Thwaites [afterwards Regius Professor of Greek] and John Hall took the courage last week to go to Dr. Hyde about Junius's matrices and punchions, which he gave with his books to the University. These nobody knew where they were, till Mr. Wanley discovered some of them in a hole in Dr. Hyde's study. But, upon Mr. Hall's asking, Dr. Hyde knew nothing of them; but at last told them he thought he had some punchions about his study, but he did not know how they came there; and presently produces a small box-full, and taking out one he pores upon it, and at last wisely tells them that these could not be what they looked after, for they were Ethiopic: but Mr. Thwaites, desiring a sight of them, found that which he looked on to be Gothic and Runic punchions, which they took away with them, and a whole oyster-barrel full of old Greek letter, which was discovered in another hole."[45]

The Cambridge University Press itself was still short of type in the middle of the eighteenth century. The Rev. William Ludlam complained to William Bowyer that the appearance of his early tracts had been ruined because the university printers, having no plus signs, had been forced to use daggers turned sideways.[46] Even Bowyer, a printer of great repute, wrote to the secretary of the Society of Antiquaries in 1763 to explain that he could not print two sheets at a time of Folkes's *Tables of English Silver and Gold Coins* because he had not enough small capitals. True, he partly justified himself by reckoning that more small capitals were required for this work than for the whole Bible![47]

For the first hundred years of printing there was little inducement for the English printer to set up a type-foundry of his own. If, as in so many cases, he was to print only five or six books in his whole career it would have added considerably to his costs to design and cut his own punches and form his own matrices for the one or two founts which were all he needed. It is probable that several printers followed the example of Pynson and Faques and imported their type from Normandy: Rouen was the great market from which type was sold to other towns in France and also to Switzerland and England. There is no evidence that any of the early sixteenth-century types were cut in England, and there is no doubt that similar faces were in use in France at this time.[48] Moreover, it is evident from the works issued during this period that the founts were primarily cut for some language other than English: the letter "w," not required in Latin or French, appears very often to have been cut independently of the rest.[49]

Bearing in mind the fact that a single square inch of type weighs about four ounces it is obvious that transportation charges must have been considerable, and that the printer would be chary of importing more than he actually needed. Most probably he would import the actual matrices rather than the finished type, and make his own arrangements for founding. Sometimes it is quite clear that this was done: although the same fount might be in use for fifteen years or more, certain letters liable to become worn before the rest, notably the "m," will on investigation appear to have been recast from time to time. By the Elizabethan age a number of type-founders had arrived in England among other refugees from the Continent, and these no doubt contributed to the greatly improved appearance of English typography at this time. Even so, there is still no evidence that the Elizabethan roman and italic letters were designed or cut in England. It would appear, on the contrary, from Plantin's *Index Characterum* of 1567 and from the Berner type-specimen sheet of 1592, that nearly all of these were already in use on the Continent.[50] The secrecy maintained in the English trade was probably a main cause of its slow development: Moxon comments in 1683 that "Letter-Cutting is a Handy-Work hitherto kept so conceal'd among the Artificers of it, that I cannot learn any one that hath taught it any other; But every one that has used it, Learnt it of his own Genuine Inclination."[51] One's genuine inclination may lead to strange expedients: round about the year 1750 it led Caslon's apprentice, Joseph Jackson, to bore a hole through the wainscot so that he could watch his master's method of cutting punches, and, having learnt the secret, to bring his knowledge to perfection by practising at home.[52]

By the end of the sixteenth century Holland was the source of our most artistic type, and the use of Dutch founts was common among English printers until their importation was forbidden, in the year 1720. Thomas Guy was one of those who obtained type from Holland, using it for the Bibles which the University of Oxford allowed him to print during the sixteen-seventies.[53] Between 1670 and 1672, too, the Oxford University Press itself was acquiring Dutch type through the agency of Marshall, afterwards Dean of Gloucester, who remarks in one of his letters, "I se in this Printing-designe, we English must learn to use o^{r} own hands at last to cut Letters as well as print wth them. For ye Founders here being reasonably furnished wth Matrices from Franckfort, ye old van Dijke, &c. have no regard to cutting & justifying, unles perhaps to supply a Defect or two. So that some famous cutters, they say, are gone, to other Countries for want of Imployment. And now not one here to be found."[54] Perhaps it was owing to the general use of these foreign supplies that Arthur Nicholls, as he stated in the petition mentioned above, made only £48 by four years' work in his foundry, and that there were in London between the years 1650 and 1700 only three foundries of note—those of Joseph Moxon, Joseph and Robert Andrews, and James and Thomas Grover. It was a different story by the time that William Caslon's foundry, set up in 1720, had become well established. His letters, though modelled on the Dutch, had in them an artistry which brought about a minor revolution: England became an exporter of type.

One of the influences which kept the English industry for so long in this backward condition may have been the difficulty of obtaining copper for the matrices. The actual founding was a fairly cheap process. John Day, for instance, was enabled in 1570 by Archbishop Parker's support to cast a fount of Italian letter for 40 marks[55] (approximately £26). Of all the necessary materials used towards the production of type the copper required for the matrices was the most expensive. Lead was cheap, its price between 1545 and 1560 varying between £4 and £12 a fother (19½ cwt.); but a hundredweight of copper cost over £5.[56] The scarcity of copper was so acute that in the year 1529 a Bill was passed forbidding its export, and in 1574 a patent was granted to Sir Thomas Smith, Cecil, Leicester and Sir Humphry Gilbert, for "changing iron into copper" by heating it with blue vitriol. It was no wonder that the printer was glad of the opportunity of hiring type seized by the Stationers' Company from clandestine presses, as when in 1575 Bynneman was charged fifteen pence "for wearinge the lettre that came from Hempsted."[57]

Granted that the well-equipped printing-house would be provided with stocks of all the English and foreign founts in general use, together with such mathematical and other signs as were likely to be called for by the nature of the firm's business, there remains the problem of how big these stocks should be. The quantities which Moxon gives as essential for the small printing-house would have been beyond the reach of many of the earlier printers. He suggests that the minimum quantity of Long Primer should be 500 lb. There should be between 800 and 1,000 lb. of both Pica and English, and 300 or 400 lb. of every other fount.[58] These are certainly very small amounts, considering that about 180 lb. of Pica were required for four quarto pages,[59] but such inventories as exist for the sixteenth and seventeenth centuries give the impression that smaller quantities had often to suffice. The inventory of Thomas Thomas's Cambridge printing-house (1588) shows his stock of type to have amounted to 1,445 lb., valued at 3½d. a pound; of these about 500 lb. were Long Primer, but of Pica there were only about 450, while the only foreign alphabet included was Greek.[60] Cantrell Legge, Cambridge University printer, has in his inventory (1625) only a vague note of "one thousand waigh of letter at iijd. per lb."[61] It is less surprising that Horace Walpole, much later on, should want only a small quantity of type for his private press at Strawberry Hill. His account with William Caslon shows that on August 13, 1768, he bought 282 lb. of "English" and 10 lb. of "two-line letters," and during the following year 51 lb. 9 oz. of "English" and 9 lb. 14 oz. of "Double Pica," costing altogether £17 13s. 5¼d.[62] His business must have been planned throughout on a diminutive scale: in 1785 he paid 6d. "to the letter founder for 100 acute é," together with 1s. 4d. for 2 lb. of pearl ashes, used for cleaning type.[63]

The stocks of type in the possession of the more important printers of the eighteenth century were on an altogether different scale. John Baskett, the royal printer at Oxford, mortgaged his materials in 1718 for £4,000. These included large founts of Pearl, Nonpareil, Brevier, Long Primer, Great Primer, English and Double Pica, several of them "new cast in Holland," and a set of silver initial letters.[64] Some of these varieties it would have been uneconomic for the small printer to buy at all. What he needed, according to Luckombe (1771), was type "cast of good metal, fit to wear well, at least so long as till it has paid for itself, besides good interest for its long credit; thereby to ease the charges of such other sorts of letter that never make a return either of the principal nor interest."[65] On consideration, there was much to be said for the old practice of sharing these unprofitable types between several printing-houses. In Luckombe's view it was not advisable to have large founts at all: "Sometimes a very large fount has the effect to make negligent Correctors, when they know how far a fount goes, and therefore give themselves no concern about returning proofs, till they find that the whole fount is set up, and that the Workman can go no farther. In such case the intention of having large Founts is frustrated, and the Compositor as well as Pressman are prejudiced in their endeavours; whereas a tolerable large Fount of Letter, and a regular dispatch of proofs, is beneficial to Master and Men."[66] Can it be that the typical printing-house was still setting up only one work at a time?

Illustrations

After the choice of type comes the question of illustrations. The high price of copper may have added to the early printer's inducements to illustrate his books by means of woodcuts rather than copperplates, but in view of the small quantity of copper required for an engraving it can hardly have been the main reason for his choice. It was probably owing to the extra presswork involved in the printing of engravings that very few of them are to be found in books published before 1600, although their use had been known throughout the century. As we have seen, an extra press was needed for printing this form of illustration, and matters were complicated when no allowance was made for this fact in the regulations as to the number of presses to be maintained by each printer. The time and expense involved in the extra printing-process might not have been grudged if we had had any noted artists whose work would have added to the value of a book; but, with the exception of Thomas Geminus, an immigrant from the Netherlands who was employed as surgeon at the Court of Henry VIII, we had no skilled engravers until about 1590, when William Rogers was beginning work in London.[67]

As regards woodcuts, the necessary materials consisted merely of a block of fairly soft wood, such as beech or apple, and a sharp knife. The finished design stood up at the same height as the type with which it was to be printed; there was, therefore, no difficulty in passing the work through the press. Yet our fifteenth- and sixteenth-century printers were surprisingly poorly provided with even this form of illustration. Until Caxton published his *Mirror of the World*, in 1480, no woodcuts had appeared in any English book. His *Game of Chesse*, 1481, and his *Canterbury Tales* and *Aesop*, both issued about 1484, were also illustrated in this way. While the *Golden Legend*, which appeared next, contains some of his most ambitious woodcuts, it also happens to include some very crude work, and the same cuts are used over and over again to represent different saints.[68] Lettou and Machlinia, Caxton's contemporaries, produced over thirty books, but none were illustrated. The St. Albans press owned a very few woodcuts.[69] The scarcity was not to be imputed to the lack of artists; it is true that until Hans Holbein came to England we had no great woodcut-designers of our own, but in Basel, where Holbein lived until 1526, he had a large school of Formschneiders working for export to England and other countries, and it was also possible to buy illustrations second-hand from Germany and the Netherlands. Wynkyn de Worde was one of those who took advantage of this: when, about 1492, he bought some type initial letters from Godfried van Os, of the Netherlands, he bought in addition at least one woodcut. Early in the sixteenth century Pynson, too, obtained cuts from abroad, buying from Vérard the ones which he used in his edition of the *Kalendar of Shepherdes* (1506).[70] Even so, such dealings were rare.

Despite the miserable show of illustrations, there was no lack of woodcut borders and printers' devices in early sixteenth-century books; it seems, then, that the printer was willing to buy ornaments which could be used, in the same way as his type, in every book which he produced, but hesitated before he went to the expense of purchasing illustrations for specific works. Nevertheless, he was not at all nonplussed by his shortage of illustrations: if none of his pictures were appropriate to the work in hand he was quite content to use one which had no bearing at all upon the subject of the book. Caxton's contemporary at Oxford was in proud possession of two sets of woodcuts, but neither was intended for the book in which it actually appeared; one cut, really representing Jacobus de Voragine writing the *Golden Legend*, is made to serve for Lyndewode writing his *Constitutions*. As for Wynkyn de Worde, he "minded as little about using the same illustrations over and over again as some of our modern publishers."[71] When producing theological works, for instance, he made indiscriminate use of Caxton's woodcuts for the Sarum Horae, the Crucifixion, the tree of Jesse, the rich man and Lazarus, and David and Bathsheba, and the same cuts were afterwards used with equal indifference by Julian Notary.[72] At times a single illustration was made to serve more than once in the same book: in Pynson's edition of Chaucer's *Canterbury Tales* the picture of the serjeaunt was slightly altered in order to represent the doctor of physick; that of the squire was used later on to portray the manciple.[73]

The early printer-publisher seems to have been as happy to lend his illustrations and his ornamental borders as his type. In the seventeenth century, by which time the principle seems to have evolved that the picture should bear at least some relation to the text of the book, this generosity is not so evident. One even finds illustrations—woodcuts and copperplate engravings alike—entered specifically in the Stationers' Register, for such copyright protection as this would give. Francis Leach, for instance, on March 12, 1655, entered forty "portractures or pictures hereafter mentioned cutt in wood," illustrating such subjects as the Last Supper and the parable of Dives and Lazarus. A few days later Nicholas Bourne entered eight "mapps, pictures and cutts cutt in copper." Maybe there was still good reason for this caution. It was only about fifteen years since there had appeared the ballad entitled "Doctor Do-Good's directions to cure many diseases both in body and minde," with its much-travelled illustration: the right-hand section of the woodcut had first appeared in 1492 in Vérard's *Art de Bien Vivre et de Bien Mourir*; in 1503 it was used in the same printer's *Kalendar of Schyppars*, and next wandered into Pynson's translation of this same work, in 1506. Whereas the original picture represents Aaron and the Israelites going out to meet Moses, the balladmonger has so adjusted matters that they are meeting two Elizabethan gentlemen.[74] One would have thought that by the eighteenth century the integrity of the printer in this respect would have been an accepted fact, yet here is the Rev. Michael Tyson writing to R. Gough in 1777: ". . . I will send you what impressions of my Plates I have, for Forster and Mr. Tutet—and will send you also the Plates themselves of those I have not, and will beg you to get me about 40 impressions from each. Of these take what you please—but employ an honest Printer, who will not take off more than are ordered. Many of my Prints have got into the *Magazin des Estampes* in Cockspur-street—this robs them of their only value, *scarcity*."[75]

Between 1600 and 1660 woodcuts were ousted to a great extent by copperplate engravings, but from the Restoration to about 1780 illustrated books of any kind were very few, being confined almost entirely to county histories and books of antiquities with large plates.[76] The English engraver, possibly finding the book trade unprofitable, had turned his attention to the newer art of mezzotint, which was not so well suited to book illustration. It was not that there was any alteration in the public preference for illustrated books: Thomas Edwards, who in 1751 was preparing an edition of the *Faerie Queene* to compete with that of John Brindley, wrote in bitterness to Samuel Richardson of people who "come in shoals to subscribe" whenever "a bookseller can but get a few paltry cuts to raise the price of a book" in "this picture-loving age."[77] Copper cuts certainly did raise prices. The works advertised by the firm of Newbery between 1750 and 1780 as "adorned with copperplate cuts" cost from 1s. upwards; books of a similar nature but illustrated by woodcuts were only 4d. and 6d.[78] Although woodcuts had a charm of their own for these children's books, causing Malcolm to say, in his *Londinium Redivivum*, "I date my first partiality for literature to have arisen from the splendid bindings and beautiful wooden engravings of Newbery," the adult reader probably by now wanted something more sophisticated. The copperplate was still the main alternative.

Thomas Edwards's comment, quoted above, implies that there was a real difficulty in obtaining copperplate engravings. The copperplate was, at all events, not the means of illustration for the publisher who wanted his work quickly through the press. This was the complaint made by James Bentham with regard to his *History and Antiquities of the Conventual and Cathedral Church at Ely* (1759). In a letter to Dr. Ducarel he wrote, "I have but one engraver employed on my plates; so that I find it very tedious in getting them forward; which necessarily delays my publication; for I would not even publish proposals, till the plates are near finishing. I have about fifty plates in the whole; and I think about 31 are now finished, besides that of Bp. Gray's monument; and the rest are going on as fast as my engraver can work. He lives at Cambridge at present, on purpose to engrave my plates; and tells me he has tried to get another hand from London to assist him in the work, but has been unsuccessful in it, they are all so full of work at London."[79]

Quite apart from the delay, the expense of the engravings was a formidable proposition. George Vertue's charge to the Society of Antiquaries in 1718 for his picture of Richard II in Westminster Abbey was £21, including the copperplate; three years later he charged 15 guineas for his engraving of the Shrine of Edward the Confessor, and this time the Society provided the plate.[80] Dr. Grey wrote to him in 1737 asking his price for portraits. His reply was, "What you propose to have done I can't justly be certain as to the expence of engraving; because for octavo plates, the head only of any person, I have had different prices, as the difficulty or labour is more or less. The general prices I have had for such works, has been 10 guineas, 8 guineas, and 6 the lowest."[81] The 50 plates in Cheselden's *Anatomy of the Bones* cost over 600 guineas, and yet, according to the proposals,[82] only 300 copies were to be printed, the price to subscribers being 4 guineas.

Some of the so-called copperplate engravings were partly etched. This process, too, requires copper as its foundation, but, whereas in engraving the design is cut out by hand by means of a burin, in etching it is eaten out by acid, varying intensity being given to the lines by stopping them with varnish as soon as the acid has bitten to a sufficient depth. The Rev. Michael Tyson described this in 1779 as a cheap enough process. "For a plate of the size of the Wooden Knight of Southwark," he told Richard Gough, "the *pertinentia* required are, *Imprimis*, a bottle of aquafortis, being the only kind of spiritous liquor not drunk and sold at Abridge. 2dly, a *burnisher*. 3dly, some soft varnish for stopping up. 4thly, and lastly, a *hand-vice*, to melt off the varnish, when the Knight is dead drunk with aquafortis.—All these materials ought honestly not to cost you more than 10s. 6d."[83]

Ink

Copperplate printing demanded a special kind of ink. It was described in the early nineteenth century as "a composition made of stones of peaches and apricots, the bones of sheep, and ivory, all well burnt, and, as the best which is used in this business comes from Frankfort on the Main, it is known by the name of Frankfort black. It comes over in cakes, and being mixed with nut-oil, that has been well boiled, it is ground by the printer on a marble, after the same manner as painters do their colours."[84]

One is apt to assume without further worry that when the art of typography was invented, in the fifteenth century, printers' ink was there to hand. This was true, but only because the older block-book had borne the brunt of the necessary experiments. Some of the block-books in the British Museum show clearly how vitally important to the appearance of the book is the quality of the ink. Although in most of the examples it is of a full black, there are several Italian books issued between 1465 and 1472 in which it is very brown, probably because an impure carbon was used. From some early German books, again, it is evident that the ink-maker had not yet managed to prevent its "setting-off" on the opposite page. The early efforts at ink-manufacture must be left to the imagination. There seems to have been no printed account of the process until the seventeenth century. According to the recipe given by the Venetian Canneparius in his *De Atramentis* (1660), his ink consisted of 1 lb. of a varnish of linseed oil and juniper gum mixed with 1 oz. of smoke-black, boiled over a slow fire.[85]

In England during the fifteenth and sixteenth centuries printers' ink does not seem to have been an item of home or foreign trade. The making of ordinary writing-ink was one of the regular duties of the housewife, judging by recipe-books of the period, but there was also scope for the pedlar, who roamed the streets crying, "Buy any Ink, will ye buy any Ink, buy any very fine writing Ink, will ye buy any Ink and pens."[86] There is no evidence that pedlars added printing-ink to their stock-in-trade, but the fundamental difference between the two kinds of ink is a sufficient explanation of this: while writing-ink is a liquid consisting mainly of oak-gall, printers' ink is a paint made from linseed oil and lamp-black.

It is probable that printers here, in common with those on the Continent, made their own.

By the seventeenth century ink had become an article of commerce, greatly to Moxon's disapproval. "The providing of good *Inck*," he ruled, "or rather good *Varnish* for *Inck*, is none of the least incumbent cares upon our *Master-Printer*, though Custom has almost made it so here in England; for the process of making *Inck* being as well laborious to the Body, as noysom and ungrateful to the Sence, and by several odd accidents dangerous of Firing the Place it is made in, Our *English Master Printers* do generally discharge themselves of that trouble; and instead of having good *Inck*, content themselves that they pay an *Inck-Maker* for good *Inck*, which may yet be better or worse according to the Conscience of the *Inck-Maker*."[87] Dutch ink, in his opinion, was much better than ours, for various reasons. In the first place, the Dutch used only the best linseed-oil, whereas the English ink-maker substituted train-oil and a great deal of resin; train-oil made the ink dull and smeary, while the resin made it turn yellow. Secondly, ink here was insufficiently boiled, partly to save labour and fuel, and partly to obtain more ink from the same quantity of oil; here again the effect was that the ink turned yellow and would not dry. Finally, because lamp-black was dear and added scarcely at all to the weight of the ink there was a temptation to stint it, "so that sometimes the *Inck* proves so unsufferable *Pale*, that the *Press-man* is forc'd to Rub in more *Blacking* upon the *Block*; yet this he is often so loth to do, that he will rather hazard the content the Colour shall give, than take the pains to amend it; satisfying himself that he can lay the blame upon the *Inck-maker*."

Having thus relieved his feelings, Moxon proceeds to tell us how ink ought to be made. The Dutch method, which alone should be followed, was to procure the oldest linseed-oil that was to be had and to boil it in a cauldron until pieces of onion dropped into it would cause a scum to rise. While the oil was boiling, powdered resin was strewn in a handful at a time, in the proportion of one pound to every gallon of oil. The next process was to set fire to the oil by dipping a piece of lighted paper into the cauldron.

To tell when the mixture was hard enough a few drops were put on an oyster shell to cool, and it was then tested with thumb and finger. Next it was clarified by throwing in an ounce of "Letharge of Silver" to every four gallons of oil and boiling it again. When it had been allowed to cool, the ink-maker strained it through a linen cloth into a stone pot, in which it was allowed to stand as long as possible. Finally it had to be coloured by adding lamp-black, a substance consisting of incompletely carbonised oil. This could be bought ready-made; there is evidence that as early as 1549 it was on sale in Oxford, half a pound of it costing two shillings.[88]

The Cost of Equipment

The total cost of the permanent equipment of a printing-house, consisting of the items with which we have dealt so far, was, for the ordinary small firm of the sixteenth and seventeenth centuries, in the neighbourhood of £150. In 1624, for example, the widow of Thomas East sold his printing materials to William Lee for £165; they consisted of presses, woodcut letters, ornaments and several founts of type.[89] The really well-stocked printing-works cost far more than this: the cost of setting up the Oxford University Press with materials from Germany, France and Holland in the year 1672 was, according to Dr. John Fell, Vice-Chancellor of the University, over £4,000. This printing-house was certainly exceptionally well equipped: besides seven printing-presses and stocks of the usual roman type it contained matrices for Greek, Coptic, Syriac, Hebrew, Armenian, Arabic and other letters and also music-type.[90] Roger Ward's "printinge stuffe" was very humble in comparison. In 1595 he pawned it to the Stationers' Company for £7 10s.; it consisted of "4 forme of the *Catechisme* in 8[vo] 4 paire of Chases 3 of them of wood, and th[e] other of yron One paire of newe cases with somme Englishe letter in them and iij ymposinge boardes."[91]

The printing trade, as we have seen, remained at the end of the eighteenth century almost untouched by the industrial revolution. The equipment which had been in use for a hundred years or more would still serve. Even stagnation can have its advantages: ownership of a printing-house was still possible to the man of humble origin. As late as 1826 Jacob Unwin, founder of the Gresham Press, had to pay only £200 for the small printing business of Mr. Robins, consisting of one hand-press and a few accessories. Very pleased he was to get it, too. On June 26th he proudly wrote in his diary: "I rose this morning in a new character —Master of an establishment."[92]

CHAPTER IX

The Supply of Paper

ALTHOUGH it seems somewhat freakish nowadays to print a book, other than the child's rag-book, on any material besides paper, this was not the only possible substance at the time of the invention of printing.

In the Middle Ages the manuscript book was almost invariably composed of parchment. As literary output increased parchment became scarce, and the same piece was commonly used more than once, giving us that interesting collection of documents known as palimpsests. Even so, this shortage did not lead to a rapid growth in the paper-making industry; although paper had been manufactured in China in the second century A.D. and was used among the Arabs in the eighth century it does not seem to have been known in Europe until the Spanish production began in the twelfth century.[1] Its manufacture spread slowly to Italy, France and Germany, and by the fourteenth century it was in occasional use in England, being used for a few gild returns and for the accounts of Bridport, Southampton, Hythe and other boroughs.[2] But tradition was powerful, and parchment continued in competition with paper for a time even after the invention of printing. Of Johann Gutenberg's 42-line Bible, for instance, printed in 1485, 180 copies were on paper and 30 on parchment. For each parchment copy, consisting of 641 leaves, there were required the skins of more than 300 sheep.[3] Clearly, for the printed book whose edition was to run to a thousand or more copies paper was the only possible material; parchment and vellum had to be reserved for the type of work valued rather for its artistry than for its literary content.

The materials required for paper-making are of the simplest. For the very best paper as regards both appearance and durability nothing is superior to linen rag, cotton rag being next best, and it was from these that paper was regularly manufactured until the use of esparto and wood-pulp was discovered in the nineteenth century. Flax and cotton are used in the form of rags rather than in the raw state because in the process of manufacture the unwanted cellular matter has been removed. For the production of paper it is necessary simply to disintegrate these vegetable fibres and to reintegrate them in water. John Evelyn gives a general account of the method in an entry in his Diary for the year 1678 which describes his visit to the paper-mills at Byfleet: "They cull the rags which are linen for white paper, woollen for brown; then they stamp them in troughs to a pap, with pestles, or hammers, like the powder-mills, then put it into a vessel of water, in which they dip a frame closely wired with wire as small as a hair and as close as a weaver's reed; on this they take up the pap, the superfluous water draining through the wire, this they dexterously turning, shake out like a pancake on a smooth board between two pieces of flannel, then press it between a great press, the flannel sucking out the moisture; then taking it out, they ply and dry it on strings, as they dry linen in the laundry; then dip it in alum-water, lastly, polish and make it up in quires."

The Origins of Paper-Making in England

Materials and processes alike being so simple it is surprising that the paper-making industry was so long in becoming established in England. It had been set up in various places on the Continent by the fourteenth century, as we have seen, but there is no direct evidence of any paper manufacture in England until the close of the fifteenth century, when John Tate, a London mercer, owned a mill at Hertford which produced some of the paper used by Wynkyn de Worde between 1495 and 1498.[4] Yet the identity of prices of paper in inland and coastal towns during the later Middle Ages (as shown by Professor Thorold Rogers's tables) rather suggests the existence of paper-mills at that time; it would be difficult otherwise to explain the absence of price-variations due to transportation charges. If any such early mills did exist it is doubtful whether they were working for long. Tate's mill was certainly not a success: by his will, proved in 1507, he left most of his property to his eldest son, but directed that the mill should be sold.

There seems to have been no further attempt at paper-making in England until after 1550. About that time Thomas Thirlby, Bishop of Ely, visited the court of the Emperor Charles V and brought back with him Remigius, with whose help he founded a paper-mill at Fenditton, near Cambridge. This water-mill was still described as "the Paper Mill" in a survey of the temporalities of the Bishopric of Ely, 1599, but in 1559, when it was leased to Corpus Christi College, Cambridge, it was probably converted into a corn-mill.[5] Some time in the third quarter of the century there was founded the mill at Bemerton, Wiltshire,[6] which was to continue in occasional use until the nineteenth century. The next venture was that of Sir Thomas Gresham. He built a mill at Osterley, Middlesex, in about the year 1575; but, partly no doubt on account of Gresham's more public interests, it had decayed by the last decade of the century.[7]

In 1585 Richard Tottell, lawyer and printer, lodged an unsuccessful petition with the Government for a grant of land on which to establish a mill, for the prohibition of the export of rags, and for the sole privilege of making paper for thirty-one years.[8] The concession which was refused to him was granted four years later to John Spilman, the German goldsmith to Queen Elizabeth. He was given the exclusive right for ten years to "gather provide and buye all and all manner of lynnen ragges Scrolles or Scrappes of parchment peeces of lyme leather shreddes and clyppinges of Cardes and old fyshing nettes fytt and necessarye for the making of all or anye sorte or sortes of whyte wryting paper," and nobody else was to bargain for this remarkable collection of pieces or to export them.[9] The grant was to cease if Spilman or his assigns used the scraps for any other purpose or gave up the making of paper for six months without just cause, but for the first time in the history of the English paper manufacture there was no fear of this sudden collapse: the letters patent refer to Spilman as being already established in the royal mills at Dartford, Kent, at the

A TYPE FOUNDER
From Moxon's *Mechanick Exercises*, 1683

time of the grant, in 1589; when he died, in 1626, the firm was still in existence, and seems not to have left the family's control until the death of his son John in 1641. The mill was a success from the outset. Thomas Churchyard, the sixteenth-century poet, was so impressed by Spilman's work as to make it the subject of a special poem, "A Description and playne Discourse of Paper, and the whole benefitts that Paper brings, with rehearsall, and setting forth in verse a Paper-Myll built near Darthford, by an High Germaine, called Master Spilman, Jeweller to the Queen's Majestie."[10] If Churchyard's description is reliable, Spilman maintained an exceptionally large number of employees for this period:

> . . . Then, he that made for us a paper-mill,
> Is worthy well of love and worldes good will,
> And though his name be *Spill*-man by degree,
> Yet *Help*-man now, he shall be calde by me.
> Six hundred men are set at work by him,
> That else might starve, or seek abroad their bread;
> Who nowe live well, and go full braw and trim,
> And who may boast they are with paper fed.

It seems incredible that Spilman should have had such immediate success in an industry hitherto incapable of being established that he was able to employ six hundred people within his mills. We may assume, perhaps, that Churchyard included in his reckoning the more distant employees, the rag-gatherers. Regarding these there was a complaint in 1601 from the Lord Mayor and Aldermen of London that Spilman "began to offer wrong to the charters of the city by authorising great numbers of poor people, especially girls and vagrant women, to collect rags, etc., within the city and liberties, who under pretence of that service, ranged abroad in every street, begging at men's doors, whereby the discipline of the city was weakened (the said poor people sometimes assaying to steal small things from houses and stalls), and thinking it more convenient for the city in the gathering of such refuse stuff, to employ rather our own poor, otherwise idle; it was thought by a Common Council to take order that none should be suffered to walk abroad for collecting such stuff unless licensed by the

Governors of Bridewell, for the benefit of that house, the charge whereof is greater than the revenue that belongs to it."

Spilman was soon impatient to extend his efforts beyond the production of white writing-paper. In 1597 he gave up his first patent in order to receive another, for fourteen years, applying to paper of every description, and in 1617 he acquired one for the making of "a new and more pleasant kind of playing cards." By this time he was not alone in the field. At the end of the sixteenth century he was petitioning the Privy Council to uphold his rights: John Turner, Edward Marshall and George Frend had set up a mill in Buckinghamshire and were procuring the best rags in defiance of the patent. In 1601, as a result of a suit in Chancery, a certain Robert Style was ordered to give up the making of paper, but Marshall was allowed to continue on condition that he bought his materials from Spilman. In 1612 paper was being manufactured at Cannock Chase, Staffordshire,[11] but as one of those interested in this mill, Robert Heyricke of Leicester, was the brother of Spilman's partner in the office of royal jeweller, it is probable that Spilman had given his consent to the undertaking. By 1635 there were two or three paper-makers at work at Hounslow and High Wycombe. In 1640 a fourteen-years' patent for making white writing-paper was granted to Endymion Porter, John and Edward Reade and John Wakeman, but the onset of the Civil War, together with Porter's well-known Royalist sympathies, effectually prevented the venture from making much progress. Of what little significance these early attempts really were, even including Spilman's own, is shown with startling clearness by the wording of the next grant: in 1675 Eustace Burneby was given a patent for the making of white paper, "being a new manufacture never practised in any our kingdomes or dominions."

There was certainly some dire influence at work against this particular trade. The revocation of the Edict of Nantes in 1685 was followed by an influx of French refugees, who were successful in setting up several of their native industries in Great Britain. Paper-making was one of their activities, and the first paper-mill in Glasgow was established by a refugee who had painstakingly gathered up rags in the street until he had enough to begin work.[12] Yet even these skilled French workmen found it difficult to make a success of the industry away from their own land: Alexander Daes, one of the chief proprietors of a French mill erected at Dalry, on the water of Leith, very soon gave up this occupation in favour of the more lucrative one of showing an elephant about the country.[13]

As regards the reason for our poor achievements in paper-making we may accept the contemporary statements of John Hales, an astute reasoner on many sixteenth-century economic problems. Speaking of foreign trade he says, "As for sume thinges, they [foreigners] make it of oure owne commodities and send it vs againe . . .; as of oure woll they make clothe. . .; of oure broken linnen cloth and ragges, paper both whit and browne. . . . A booke-binder . . ., when I asked him why we had no white and browne paper made within the Realme, as well as they had made beyonde the Sea, Thanne he aunsweryd me that there was paper made a whyle within the Realme. At the last, said he, the man perceaued that made it that he could not fourd his paper as good cheape as that came from beyonde the Seaze, and so he was forced to lay downe makinge of paper."[14] Richard Tottell, too, was of the opinion that we could not compete with the foreigner. In his petition to Burghley he imputed the failure of former projects to the policy of the French, who "were ever castinge blockes in the waie for the overthrowe therof, as by procuringe all our ragges (beinge the chief substance that paper is made of) to be brought over to them, by bringinge in greate aboundaunce of paper at that tyme and sellinge it (although to losse) better chepe then they were hable to doe, therby to bring the doers therof in this Realme out of credit, and so to beggerye, and lastlye by practisinge the destruccion of the workmen, and by writinge and callinge them Traytours to theire Contrey, and sendinge men of purpose to slaye them, as it hathe byn credeably declared vnto me."[15]

The cheap production of paper in France as compared with England was probably to be attributed in part to the lower level of wages paid on the Continent. In a petition to the House of Commons in 1700 for a higher duty on foreign paper it was claimed that English paper-manufacturers had to pay their servants eight or nine shillings a week, whereas foreigners paid only three or four, and it is possible that a similar discrepancy had existed before this time. This would be a handicap, but not the chief one. The main difficulty with which our manufacturers had to contend must have been the shortage of materials. Cotton was not manufactured in England until the seventeenth century, and before that time was imported only in insignificant amounts. In any case, it would have been but a poor substitute for linen in the making of paper. Attempts were made to establish the linen manufacture in England, notably by the Act 24 Hen. VIII. c. 4, "An Act concernyng sowing of Flaxe and Hempe;" "considering the evil results of the importation of linen cloth upon the industrial occupation of this country" it was ordered that every person occupying land fit for tillage should sow yearly a quarter of an acre of flax or hempseed for every sixty acres. It was, nevertheless, one thing to legislate and quite another to enforce the ruling, and the industry was never established. Linen was imported in small quantities, mainly for use in the larger households and in the gild halls, but the ordinary material from which clothing was made was wool. The rubbish heaps were therefore far more likely to yield scraps of wool than of the materials wanted by the paper-manufacturer.

Vigorous as were the attempts of Burghley and others to foster home industries in the sixteenth century, little encouragement was given by the Government to this branch of manufacture. One reason for the official attitude to the trade has been shown above in the complaint of the Lord Mayor and Aldermen of London: poor relief was a problem of such dimensions that the danger of filling the town with a body of potential beggars in the guise of rag-gatherers was fearfully to be avoided. Graver still was the risk that this unwholesome trade in street-refuse would spread the plague, whose ravages caused a setback to economic development on many occasions in the sixteenth and seventeenth centuries. The plague of 1636–7 led to a mass of official correspondence on the subject of rag-gathering for the making of paper.[16] On September 12, 1636, the Privy Council ordered the Justices of Middlesex to search the twenty or more rag-shops on the outskirts of the city and to burn their contents.[17] About a week later an order was issued for the closing-down of paper-mills. Consequently the Privy Council had shortly afterwards to recommend that local measures should be taken for the relief of those thrown out of work from this cause. The inhabitants of Buckingham and Middlesex did not take kindly to this idea, but sent in a wordy protest under cover of a letter from their respective Justices of the Peace: ". . . The petitioners offer various considerations against the allowance of this charge. They allege that the landlords by converting their corn mills into paper mills have advanced their rents from 10*l.* and 15*l.* to 100*l.* and 150*l.* per annum; that the paper-makers have brought many poor and indigent persons into their parishes, whom they ought to maintain; that their workmen have double wages in comparison with other labourers and may well save; that the paper-makers brought the plague into the country places where they work by means of their rags, as into Horton where sixteen or seventeen persons died, and also into Colnbrook; that they have flooded the country by penning up the water and have killed the fish by their double wheels; that the noisome smells of the rags spread an infection . . . dangerous to His Majesty; that the paper made is so unuseful that it will bear no ink on one side, and is sold at dearer rates than formerly. Upon these grounds the writers are so far from consenting to the relief of the paper-makers, that if it may stand with the law they desire their mills may be suppressed or removed further off." It was probably as a preventive measure against plague that the "grant for gathering of rags" was among those recalled on April 15, 1639. For social and hygienic reasons, therefore, the Government was unable to help the book producer by assuring him a steady supply of home-made paper. There still remained one service which it could render him, and that was to remove the barriers against the importation of foreign paper. Yet it was not until the middle of the seventeenth century that the duty on paper was remitted, and even then the concession applied only to the paper to be used for Brian Walton's Polyglott Bible of 1657.

Foreign Supplies

The classification of paper as a "necessary" as distinct from a "superfluous" import from the Low Countries and from France as given in lists drawn up in about the year 1563 can thus be accepted without question.[18] The quantity imported in 1570 was 1,728 reams, valued at £403 4s. and liable to a customs duty of £10 6s. 2d.[19] In 1662–3 the import from France amounted to 116,074 reams, costing £38,691.[20] France was the main source of supply throughout the sixteenth and seventeenth centuries: there were more than 600 paper-mills in the Angoumois alone.[21]

"Necessary" import or not, paper was one of the first commodities to be cut off by a shortsighted Government on any breakdown in diplomatic relations. In 1678 "An Act for raising money by a poll and otherwise to enable His Majestie to enter into an actuall warr against the French King and for prohibiting severall French commodities" prohibited the import of paper and various other commodities. Its repeal, in 1685, was followed by buying on a scale which well shows the extent to which the book trade had been inconvenienced by the ban: during the next year 90,652 reams were imported from France. The respite from economic war was short-lived: in 1688 there came the Revolution and renewed hostility with France, leading to the royal proclamation of 1689 suspending all trade whatever with that country. According to Edward Bohun paper then became so dear as to stop all printing.[22]

As might be expected, the ban on importation set wits to work to fill the gap. By 1682 two inventions were ready for registration: George Hagar's, for making paper and pasteboard by sizing it in the mortar, and Nathaniel Bladen's, for "an engine, method, and mill, whereby hemp, flax, lynnen, cotton, . . . are prepared and wrought into paper." Hagar's energies were, perhaps, misplaced, for in 1691 it was reported in the course of legal proceedings against the Company of White Paper Makers that although he had set up mills at Eynsham and Stanwell he was now bankrupt.[23] Further patents were granted in 1684 to Robert Fuller and Christopher Jackson and in 1685 to John Briscoe for various technical processes, followed during the next few years by other grants.[24] Meanwhile, in 1686 the Company of White Paper Makers was incorporated, with "the sole power, privilege and authority of makeing, sizing and compleately finishing all sorts of writing and printing paper" for fourteen years.[25] An Act of 1690 "for Encouraging and better Establishing the Manufacture of White Paper in this Kingdom" confirmed the Company's charter but limited its activities to the making of paper valued at more than 4s. a ream, leaving the manufacture of cheaper paper open to the rest of the trade. The Bill did not pass without opposition, notably from the "ancient paper-makers of this kingdom," who argued plausibly but in vain that they themselves employed skilled workmen and regularly made paper of up to 20s. a ream in value.

As a result of all these endeavours it was possible to say, in 1713,[26] that whereas before the Revolution England had produced little paper other than brown, by now most of our paper-makers were producing quite good paper for writing and printing. Nearly two-thirds of the 400,000 reams consumed annually in this country, it was claimed, were now made in England. As for the remaining one-third, that could well be produced at home if a little encouragement were given by taking off the 12 per cent excise duty and increasing the tax on "outlandish" paper. There were, after all, more than 120 vats working within sixty miles of London and several more in Yorkshire and Scotland; and these were all capable of increasing their output so long as high duties were imposed on French paper, "being that which they dread most, by reason of its extraordinary cheapness."

The advantages which accrue to one small body of producers from taxing imports do not extend to the community as a whole. The taxation of paper was not in the best interests either of the publisher or of the reading public. The publisher of the eighteenth century, no less than of our own day, could further his own welfare and serve his readers by using paper of good quality and pleasant appearance, buying it in the cheapest market. Before the invention of intricate machinery able to offset local handicaps, the cheapest market was decided very largely by geographical factors. France, with her abundant water-power, was in an ideal position for supplying good, cheap paper. The English Government, nevertheless, thought fit to divert the trade to less obvious channels; whether with the effect of attracting to paper-making men who might have been more usefully occupied, who shall say?

The Paper Duties

Until 1696 paper was included for tax purposes in the general import lists. The *Book of Rates* of 1660 had fixed the duty on imported commodities at a shilling in the pound on their value, assessing printing paper at from 4s. 6d. a ream upwards, according to size. The Act 8 and 9 Will. III. c. 7, "for granting to His Majesty several duties upon paper, vellum and parchment, *etc.*," raised the tax to 25 per cent of the value of all paper and books imported. There was as yet little attempt to foster the home manufacture by discriminating duties, for the same Act imposed a duty of 20 per cent on paper or parchment made in England, while all stock-in-trade was to pay 17½ per cent. The new regulations were not at all well received by the paper dealers. Their argument was that the tax would not raise £18,000 a year, judging by the consumption of paper in recent years; while, as for the tax on stock-in-hand, it was entirely without precedent, and would not in any case bring in more than £2,800.[27] Fortunately, the Act expired after two years. The paper-makers, glad enough to be freed from their exorbitant excise duty, were well in favour of a heavy duty on imported paper, and petitioned the House of Commons for its renewal. This time the printers and booksellers were able to show their own case clearly enough for the matter to be dropped. There was, accordingly, no further change until 1712.

In 1712 there came into force "An Act for laying severall duties upon all sope and paper. . . ." Now for the first time the English paper-mills were given a clear advantage: the tax on imported paper now varied between 1s. and 16s. a ream, whereas that on

English paper ranged only from 4d. to 1s. 6d. a ream. At the same time an *ad valorem* duty of 30 per cent was imposed on imported books, prints and maps. Owing, possibly, to some vague sense of duty to the cause of education, a concession was made to the universities: the paper made or imported for printing books in Latin, Greek, or Oriental or northern languages at Oxford or Cambridge or at one of the Scottish universities was to be given a complete remission of duty. The general publisher might well resent this discrimination. Why, it was asked, should one man at Oxford be allowed to gain a monopoly of the greatest part of the printing trade in Britain?[28] And why, demanded the London printers, should they, too, not be given a drawback on paper?[29] Even apart from this point the new Act was seriously against the interests of the English book trade. After it had been in operation for a year a petition was sent to the House of Commons complaining that since the duty of 30 per cent was imposed on books only about one-fourth of the number formerly imported had been brought into the country. The intention of the duty was to secure the revenue from paper by preventing books being printed abroad for the English market, but this could better be ensured by a duty regulated by weight. As it was, the duty was hindering the sale of our books in the learned languages in foreign markets, "for if we cannot buy theirs, they will not Buy ours."[30] The tax was abolished by resolution of the House of Commons on May 25, 1714.[31] Even so, the publishers were not satisfied. The duties now acted in such a way that English books could be printed in Holland and Ireland and imported to England more cheaply than they could be produced here. As Buckley, afterwards Master of the Stationers' Company, expostulated in an address to Parliament (1733), "As the duty now stands, the blank paper to be used by our own printers at home, pays a great deal more than what is already printed by workmen abroad, the first paying by the ream, the latter by the hundred weight."[32] Meanwhile, in 1714, the Act 13 Anne c. 18 had raised the duties on home and foreign paper by 50 per cent. Protests came this time from all quarters: printers and publishers complained of increased costs, while paper-makers forecast that a most certain fall in demand would ruin them. None the less, the additional duties, which by the Act were to be imposed for thirty-two years, were in the time of George I made perpetual.

Whether on account of oppressive taxation or for some other reason, there was at this time a distinct lack of interest in paper-making in England. Not a single patent for its manufacture was granted between 1695 and 1747. There were, it is true, 278 paper-mills with 338 vats at work in England and Wales in the year 1739, but the Commissioners of Excise reported that three out of four of these were making coarse paper, worth only 2d. to 9d. a ream to the revenue.[33] Judging from a letter which Conyers Middleton wrote to Lord Hervey on April 6, 1740, publishers at this time were again dependent on foreign supplies: "As to Tully, I am ashamed almost to mention it on account of a total cessation of the press, occasioned by the uncertain return of ships from Genoa since the commencement of the war, during which our large paper is exhausted and not a sheet of it to be had in London till a fresh cargo arrives, which is expected, however, every day."[34]

Although the printing-paper produced in England during this period was thus quite insufficient for the needs of the book trade, the mills were not incapable of producing good paper. The Wolvercote Mill, encouraged by Dr. Fell, had achieved such a high standard of work as to win the admiration of Hearne, the antiquary. Round about 1750, too, Baskerville was experimenting to find a paper which would show off his type to the best advantage, finally hitting on the idea of treating the sheets with thin varnish and pressing them between heated metal plates, thus producing his famous "hot-pressed" paper. Nevertheless, for special purposes foreign-made paper was still essential. Ralph Bigland pointed this out in 1769 in a letter to a friend: "The paper I had for our Plate I buy of one Mr. Boydell, one of the first if not only importer of the proper paper for the copper-plate work in London. It comes chiefly from France; the English made is too smooth or fine for it."[35]

In order to realise the extent to which an individual publisher would be affected by the various taxes one needs some idea of the quantity of paper which he would require for a whole edition of a book. The number of reams required obviously depends upon the size of the individual sheet of paper. By the end of the sixteenth century there were two sizes which were specially common, the sheet in one case measuring about 15 in. × 20 in. and in the other 12 in. × 16 in. The former corresponds to the modern "crown" sheet, but the paper used in present-day book production is more commonly of the size known as "quad" crown, being four times as large. Dr. McKerrow shows the number of reams required for a thousand copies of an octavo book on this "quad" paper to be equal to the number of pages in the book divided by 32.[36] An edition of a 160-page octavo work would thus take 5 reams of modern paper or 20 reams of the size used before the nineteenth century; for a quarto work of the same number of pages twice this quantity would be required, and for a folio four times as much.

The Cost of Paper

We have seen that quite frequently in the early period no money passed between the printer and his paper dealer, but that the payment for paper consisted of a number of copies of the finished book. Those printers who bought their supplies in the open market would find considerable variation in price from time to time. The decennial average prices rose steadily from 2s. 4d. a ream in 1511–20 to 6s. 5d. in 1571–82, fell to 4s. 9¼d. in 1583–92 and then rose again to 6s. 7d. in 1643–52 (the sudden fall after 1582 being partly due to the fact that the ream, which had formerly consisted of 20 quires, for a time contained only a little over 12).[37] These averages conceal wide disparities. In London, for instance, a ream measuring 15½ in. × 11 in. was sold in 1532 for 3s. 4d.; four years later a much smaller-sized paper, 12¼ in. × 8½ in., cost 6s. 8d. a ream. Between 1564 and 1566 paper was sold in Oxford at 3s. 4d., 6s. 8d., 3s. 7½d., 5s. 4d. and 6s. a ream. In the Star Chamber case of Day *v.* Ward and Holmes, 1582, Thomas Man gave evidence that he had sold paper to Ward at the rate of 2s. 10d. a ream, "and he also denieth that he Dyd after the imprynting of the said bokes take any of them in parte of payment for his paper."[38] As a contrast to this, when the Stationers' Company gave permission to Peter Short to finish Denham's impression of *The Book of Martyrs*, in 1595, it was ordered that the paper should be rated at 7s. a ream.[39] The paper which Thomas Thomas, printer to Cambridge University, had in stock on his death in 1588 was variously valued: the 39 reams of "pott paper in the garret" were valued at £8; 3 reams of "hand paper" were put down at only 8s.; while 5 reams of demy accounted for 30s. of the total.[40] It is, therefore, impossible to give a general estimate of the cost of the paper for an edition of a medium-sized work during the first century or more of printing; one can only suggest that it would be somewhere between £10 and £20. Matters were further complicated in that, although paper was generally dearer by the quire than by the ream, quite often the reverse was true: in 1503, for example, a ream cost 4s. 4d., whereas half a ream (presumably of the same kind of paper) was only 1s. 8d.[41] It seems in such cases as if the dealer was willing to sell off odd quires cheaply, and it may be for this reason that so many sixteenth-century books contain a number of different watermarks.

Prices of paper during the eighteenth century were very much higher, even allowing for the rise in the general price-levels. Eleven shillings a ream seems for many years the lowest possible price. In 1704, indeed, somebody was induced to pay £6 for a single ream of superfine imperial paper,[42] but more probably for elegant correspondence than for a mere printed book. By this time paper was quite definitely the most expensive item in book production, leaving apart any specially fine binding provided for the connoisseur. For Samuel Johnson's *The Idler* (1761) the paper cost £52 3s. as compared with £41 13s. for printing.[43] The 96 reams of paper for the second edition of *Humphry Clinker* (1771) cost £72; printing cost only £41 2s.[44] Other publishing accounts of the period show similar proportions.

Paper might be a heavy expense to the printer, but, after all, the appearance of a book depended quite as much upon the quality of this as upon the excellence of the type. In Venice the aims of the Government towards perfection in book production had led to strict supervision of the printers' choice of paper. In 1537 a law had been enacted to the effect that all copyright books were to be printed on paper which could be written upon without blotting; if any five copies of an edition were found to blot the printer was liable to a fine of a hundred ducats and to the forfeiture of his copyright.[45] There was no such compulsion in England, but, to judge from the sixteenth- and seventeenth-century books which are known to us, there was no need for it. The pressman was trained to reject any paper which fell below the desired standard; "if he meets with naughty Sheets in his Work; as torn, or stain'd, &c. he Prints them not, but throws them under the *Paper-bench*."[46] Normally two of the twenty quires in each ream had already been removed by the warehouseman before the pressman received his supplies: these were the two outside or "cording" quires, so called because the whole ream was corded or tied up between them, and they consisted quite often of torn, wrinkled, stained, or otherwise "naughty" sheets. Good paper could sometimes be gathered from these cording quires, but the careful warehouseman would so arrange it in the various heaps that it would be used somewhere near the middle of the book, so that it would escape notice if it were at all inferior to the rest of the ream.[47] Attempts were made, too, to suit the quality of paper to the kind of work to be produced. Dr. Brian Walton, writing about the arrangements for publishing the *London Polyglot* of 1657, says, "We have resolved to have a better paper than that of 11s. a ream, viz., of 15s. a ream."[48] Surprising forethought was exercised in the case of the "Bishop's Bible" of 1568: Archbishop Parker, on sending the first copy to the Queen, wrote that "The printer hath bestowed his thickest Paper in the Newe Testament bicause yt shalbe most occupied."[49] One ought not, perhaps, to compare this announcement with the complaint of Prynne in 1633 that "Shackspeers Plaies are printed in the best Crowne paper, far better than most Bibles."[50]

CHAPTER X

Binding Materials

THE materials and equipment which we have considered so far have all, with the exception of illustrations, been indispensable to the production of a printed book. Take from a printer his printing-press, his type, his ink or his paper, and he must straightway stop work. Take from him his binding materials, on the other hand, and he may merely feel relieved that he need no longer pander to the wants of that too exacting customer who likes his book to be handsome as well as legible. For all that, it sometimes pays to pander to the idiosyncrasies of particular customers. It may, on the whole, be worth while for the producer of a book to arrange for some sort of a binding to be worked upon it—unless he can hoodwink the innocent purchaser by pasting on it a publisher's casing. This has never been a generally accepted idea, it is true. In the sixteenth century it seems very often to have been left to the customer to suggest the kind of binding he would prefer. The modern French novel, again, is more often than not issued unbound. The same result arose from two quite opposite causes: in the sixteenth century the buying of a book was something of an event in a man's life, calling for as much forethought as the buying of a piece of furniture for his house; in the twentieth century books may be cast aside after a single reading or bound uniformly with the buyers' permanent library. Whether or not, then, the cost of binding should be budgeted among the expenses of publication has always been left to the discretion of the individual publisher.

Materials Available in the Sixteenth Century

For the first century or more of the printed book the materials used for binding varied according to the kind of book to be covered. The illuminated service book might, perhaps, be given elaborately carved covers of ivory. The book of private prayer or the collection of verse belonging to one of the ladies of the Court was almost certain to have a silk or velvet binding embroidered by its owner. But velvet, costing up to 30s. a yard, was far too expensive for the ordinary commercial binding. The thin pamphlet was seldom given a binding of any description, but was only stitched. The cheap cover given to the rather thicker work was generally of parchment, but the Stationers' Company would not allow this material to be used indiscriminately: in 1561 William Hill was fined 1s. "for that he bounde *premers* in parchement contrary to the orders of this howse," and four years later Frances Godlyf was fined 4s. for a similar offence.[1] The regulation applied not only to parchment but to sheepskin in general; thus in 1557 Richard Tottell was fined "for byndynge of bokes in shepes lether, contrary to our ordenaunces the xvij Daye of Decembre," while two years later Richard Harvey was in trouble "for byndynge of greate bokes in shepes lether" and Randall Tyerer for using the same leather for "mediante books."[2] The Company was acting for the good reputation of the trade, for sheepskin is one of the least durable of leathers. Chief among the remaining materials in general use were calf, vellum and goatskin.

There was no difficulty in procuring leather at this time. Towards the end of the sixteenth century it was stated that "in most villages of the realm there is some one dresser or worker of leather, and . . . in most of the market towns three, four, or five, and many great towns 10 or 20, and in London and the suburbs . . . to the number of 200 or very near."[3] This large body of workers was forced by gild regulations to specialise; from the Middle Ages the tanners, who dressed ox, cow and calf hides by immersing them in a decoction of oak bark, were forbidden to work the skins appropriated to the tawyers, who prepared the skins of deer, sheep and horses with alum and oil. Parchment-making was a distinct occupation. It is interesting to find that Andrew Day, who was apprenticed as a stationer in 1593, is described as being "son of William Day of Kynbern in the county of Berk[s] parchement maker."[4]

In 1530 complaints that butchers were setting up tanneries led to the Act 22 Hen. VIII. c. 6, "for Bochers not to kepe Tan-houses," in which the accusation is made that butchers "dayly make moche false untrue and deceyvable Lether . . .; And also by meane that they do occupie aswell the said crafte of Tanners as of Bochers, they do many tymes bye stolen oxen kyne steres calves and shepe . . . conveyenge the hides skinnes and felles of such stolne cattall unto their tanne houses, causynge the same to be tanned and transposed into tanned lether." Two years later it was enacted that "For asmuche as great multitude of Hydes and tanned Lether is untruely insufficiently and deceyvably tanned coried and wrought" no tanned leather should from henceforth be sold except in Leadenhall Market or some other public market or fair.[5] Tanned leather had long been subject to examination by searchers, but until the end of the sixteenth century tawed leathers escaped supervision. It was the growing practice of selling tawed leathers in packets of a dozen, containing three or four worthless skins, which led to a demand for the regulation of the trade, and to the appointment in 1593 of Edmund Darcy as official searcher.

The cheapest material in general use was parchment, consisting of sheepskin specially dressed with alum. The mediaeval scarcity of parchment had been brought to an end by the spread of the enclosure movement and the conversion of land to pasture. In discussing the rapid growth of sheep-farming in England in the sixteenth century one is apt to think chiefly of its benefits to the woollen industry and of its less desirable social effects. Actually, of course, it gave in addition a considerable impetus to the skin trade, large numbers of skins now being available for export; in the year 1570, for instance, 18,400 lambskins were exported and 57,800 sheepskins.[6] Except in a few minor industries, such as the making of common gloves, there was little demand for these skins in England other than for the manufacture of parchment.[7] A dozen skins of parchment could therefore be bought between 1520 and 1540 for as little as 2s. 6d., the price rising gradually to about 7s. in 1600 and 8s. in 1650. After this time the rise was considerable: in 1785 Horace Walpole had to pay 2s. 6d. for a single skin.[8]

Vellum, consisting of calfskin, is prepared in the same way as parchment, but is superior as regards both appearance and durability. Its supply was limited owing to the scarcity of cattle. In 1529 a Bill was passed "for the bringinge up and rearing of Calves to encres the multitude of Cattell,"[9] providing that for three years no calf should be killed that was born between January and May 1st; the reason given was that oxen had been abundant and cheap "untyll nowe of late yeres passed that the breders of such calves of their covetous myndes have used to selle their Calves young suckyng to Bouchers, waynyng rearyng bryngyng up fewe or none." Taking into consideration the Act of the following year,[10] "for Bochers not to kepe Tanhouses," and bearing in mind that the vellum of the highest quality is made from the skin of the newly-born calf, it seems possible that butchers occasionally occupied themselves in making vellum. A skin of vellum in 1540 cost about 1s., or over four times as much as a skin of parchment, and by 1660 the price had risen to 2s. 4d. and by the early eighteenth century to over 4s.;[11] the binder therefore often used the vellum leaves of large service books rather than buy new and expensive skins.[12] The tanned calfskin cost rather less than a skin of vellum. In Oxford in the year 1592 calfskins were sold at 1s. 4d. each, while in the following year a skin of vellum cost 1s. 8d.

A costly skin which was coming into use in the sixteenth century for binding the more valuable works was that of the goat. It is thought that Jean Grolier (1479–1565), of Lyons, was the first to use this "morocco" leather, so called from its country of origin. Goatskins were among the goods imported into England by the Levant Company in the seventeenth century,[13] a fact which gives point to the name of the most beautiful of moroccos—crushed levant.

The Equipment of the Binder's Shop

In reading the inventories of sixteenth-century bookbinders one is struck by the very small quantities of leather which were habitually kept in stock, a fact which confirms the view that supplies were always easily obtainable. All the leather to be found in Nicholas Pilgrim's Cambridge workshop in 1545 consisted of three calfskins, valued at 1s.[14] John Denys had, in or about 1578, only one dozen "shepe forells."[15] In 1588 Humfrey Archer, the Oxford bookbinder, had in stock just three of these forels.[16] Nicholas Smith, working in Oxford early in the next century, carried a much larger stock: he had seven dozen skins of white leather, worth 7s., eighteen skins of fine vellum, worth 15s., and twenty-three of coarse vellum, valued at 16s., what is more, he had a "quartern of Glwe" with which to fasten them to the boards.[17] Even so, the day of large-scale commercial book-binding had evidently not arrived.

These small stocks of material might give the impression that binders' workshops at this time were primitive concerns incapable of producing artistic work. This was not so. The very same inventories which mention such scanty supplies of leather give lists of tools ample for forming the most intricate of designs. The Nicholas Smith just mentioned had permanent equipment valued at over £30. The whole of the goods belonging to John Denys were worth only £4 9s. 6½d., but even they comprised, besides his dozen sheepskins and seven planing and sewing presses, "an alphabet of Roman letters; 2 printes for the cover of books; a gilding coushin with the kniffe to cut gold; 4 payer of compasses; 2 pay^{r} of pinsers; a preser with oute a podd; a gymlot to bore a hole; 2 greate bodkyns; 2 small bodkyns; a greate cheesyll & a riping cheesyll; a little cheesyll; a gowge; a scraping iron; 2 cutting irons for the backe of a booke; a riglet for the backe; a riglet of three for the side; a fylletting iron; 2 polishing irons for the backe; 1 polishing iron for the side; 3 burnishing teethe; 2 workyng hamers small; a beating stone with a great hamer; a fylle; a paste bolle with 2 paste brushes; 2 greate grynding stones for knyvis; 2 little whetstones; a stone with the millet to grynde colors; 2 stones to pare leather; a payer of sheres; whip corde to corde bookes; a great corner flower; a little corner flower deluced; a rose for the backe of a booke; a little pincke; a greate pott to make inck; a greate pott to make blacke in; 3 color dishes; 4 color potts; boards."[18]

Taxation of Binding Materials

The leather covers were originally stretched over wooden boards, which in the fifteenth century were quite often left only half covered. By the eighteenth century these had given way to millboards, which on the imposition of the heavy paper duties in 1712 became a matter of disagreement between paper-makers and binders. The paper-makers argued that pasteboards, consisting of compressed paper, were put at an unfair disadvantage to millboards, which were made of old ropes and waste; they demanded, therefore, that a duty of 60 per cent *ad valorem* should be laid on millboards. (Although the Act of 1712 had laid a duty of 3s. a hundredweight on pasteboards and millboards alike, the term "millboard" in this case seems to have been reserved for boards made in the paper-mills from paper.) The bookbinders replied that it was quite untrue that pasteboards and millboards served the same purposes. Books had been bound in millboards for over a century, and great improvements had been made in them in the last twenty years, since a way had been found of making them from old cables and other ropes used in shipping; the boards had certainly been made at one time of shavings of books, but these were now being used for making white paper.[19] Although the paper-makers alleged that the importation of millboards had stopped the consumption of at least 30,000 reams of paper a year,[20] the binders denied that pasteboards had ever been used for binding books; they were, in fact, utterly unfit for the purpose. If a tax were imposed it would be a serious hardship to the bookbinders, who by hard work had become superior in their art to the binders of any other nation. It would not, in fact, help even the revenue; there was only one mill employed in making the boards, and the owners of that never "did Return above Six hundred Pound per Annum in that Commodity."[21]

Millboards might escape the demands of the Treasury; leather did not. In 1710[22] a duty of a penny a pound was laid on all hides and skins tanned, tawed, or dressed in Great Britain. A year later it was increased by a halfpenny.[23] The prices of leather in Leadenhall Market were still, as a rule, quoted as so much for a skin, or for a dozen skins (sheepskins, for instance, worked out at from 6d. to 1s. 6d. each, calfskins at up to 10s.). From such sales by weight as were recorded raw hides seem to have cost between 2d. and 5d. a pound,[24] prices which would certainly justify the complaints that a tax of 1½d. a pound was exorbitant.[25] For rough-tanned calfskins the Act allowed a drawback of duty, but this did not apply to skins which had been dressed or curried. This, again, aroused ill feeling: the curriers accused the Government of acting against their interests, prophesying that they would be ruined by the export of undressed skins.[26]

Eighteenth-Century Developments

For one reason or another, then, it is hardly surprising that until about 1770 the bookseller-publisher chose to issue many of his books in loose sheets, or perhaps in a paper wrapper, leaving their final owners to grapple with the problem of giving them a permanent cover. It is to be hoped that the final owner understood what was awaiting him when he gave the binder a free hand. Was it, one wonders, a great shock to Earl Spencer in 1795 to receive Roger Payne's bill for £16 7s. for binding a copy of the Glasgow *Aeschylus*? Or perhaps the wording of the bill (or was it an apology?) set his mind at rest, reassuring him that this was indeed a worthy addition to his library: "Aeschylus . . . Bound in the very best manner, sew'd with strong Silk, every Sheet round every Band, not false Bands; the Back lined with Russia Leather, Cutt Exceeding Large; finished in the most Magnificent Manner Em-border'd with Ermine expressive of the High Rank of the Noble Patroness of the Designs, the other Parts Finished in the most elegant Taste with small Tool Gold Borders Studded with Gold; and small Tool Panes of the most exact Work. Measured with the Compasses. It takes a great deal of Time, making out the different Measurements; preparing the Tools; and making out New Patterns. The Back Finished in Compartments with parts of Gold studded Work, and open Work to Relieve the Rich close studded Work. All the Tools except studded points, are obliged to be worked off plain first.—and afterwards the Gold laid on and

Worked off again, And this Gold Work requires Double Gold being on Rough Grain'd Morocco, The Impressions of the Tools must be fitted & cover'd at the bottom with Gold to prevent flaws & cracks."[27]

The more humble booklover would not in any case have employed Roger Payne to do his binding, for at the end of the eighteenth century Payne was the acknowledged master of the art. Even so, the general public would probably have preferred to be relieved of all bother in the matter, and therefore welcomed advertisements such as those of the Newberys, which gave alternative prices for the same works according as they were sewed or bound. William Dodd's poems, for instance, were issued in 1767 at 4s. 3d. sewed or 5s. bound; *The Bible in Miniature* was published in 1780 at 1s. in calf or 2s. in morocco.[28]

So far there had been little variation in binding materials since the very earliest times. Leather was still the obvious choice, although the popularity of particular skins had waned. The deerskin so largely used in the Middle Ages had for some reason fallen entirely out of favour. Sheepskin, on the contrary, whose use in the sixteenth century had been barely tolerated by the Stationers' Company, had now come into its own as a highly suitable material for binding schoolbooks and other cheap volumes for which a long existence was not to be expected. Morocco was by now regarded as unequalled for really fine binding. As for calf, it was losing its good name. Sixteenth- and seventeenth-century calfskins were thick, and had proved serviceable in use. Nevertheless, fashions change, and this same thickness appeared as a disadvantage in the eighteenth-century search for elegance; binders therefore chose a thinner calf from younger animals,with fatal consequences.

If sheepskin is undurable, what can be said for skiver, which is merely the outer half of a split sheepskin? It had not yet begun to play its shameful part in English bookbinding, but it appears that we must trace its origin to the eighteenth century, and in particular to William Powers, a leather dresser of Coventry: in 1768 he was granted a patent for "his new invented method of splitting and dividing sheeps pelts, lambs pelts, and other skins, and rendering the grain and upper part thereof more useful for binding of books and other purposes of trade, and the under part thereof to be wrought into leather."

Other inventions connected with bookbinding had more to commend them. There was in 1785 a grant to James Edwards, a bookseller of Pall Mall, "of his new invented method of embellishing books bound in vellum, by making drawings on the vellum which are not liable to be defaced but by destroying the vellum itself." There was another grant, in the next year, for a special machine to be used in preparing leather for bookbinding and other purposes, "and for embellishing the same with ornaments in gold, silver, and colours." Here is the most attractive of all: in 1771 Sam Samuel, a leather dresser of Walworth, was given a patent for his new method of dyeing goatskins, kid, calfskins, sheepskins, lambskins and hides of all sorts, "in the following colours; (to wit), in lobster red, rose red, scarlett, crimson, and morocco; in light green, gay green, laurell green, molequin green, deep green, caladon green, parrot green, duckwing green, saxon green, sea green, pea green, cabbage green, and grass green; in milk blue, pearl blue, pale blue, flat blue, midling blue, sky blue, king's blue, queen's blue, turkish blue, and purple blue; in straw yellow, pale yellow, lemon yellow, and orange yellow, and in chocolate colour and coffee colour." So much for the poetic instincts of Walworth!

Leather bindings were expensive, there was no doubt. It was perhaps owing to the still comparatively small volume of publications that the search for a substitute was so late. The credit for the first successful attempt at commercial bookbinding seems to be due to the firm of Newbery, who in the middle of the eighteenth century introduced their method of binding "in the vellum manner." The volumes so turned out were half bound in green vellum and green paper, and inside the cover was pasted this notice: "The Purchasers of Books bound in the Vellum Manner are desired to observe that they are sewed much better than the Books which are bound in Leather; open easier at the Back, and are not so liable to warp in being read. If by any accident the covers should be stained or rubbed they may be new covered for a Penny, an advantage that cannot be remedied in Leather; so that this method of binding is not only cheaper, but it is presumed will be found more useful. The only Motive for trying this Experiment was to adopt a Substitute for Leather which was greatly enhanced in its price, either by an increased Consumption, or of Monopoly; how far that purpose will be answered, must be submitted to the Determination of the Reader."[29] A circular which the firm issued in 1774 pointed out that during the last five years over fourteen thousand volumes had been sold bound in this way, and less than a hundred had been returned to be re-covered, "a sufficient Proof of its Utility and the Approbation of the Public."[30] This claim was probably well-founded, although it might have been that the public was too indifferent to send back the volumes as they wore out. However that may be, there can be no doubt that binding in "the vellum manner" was cheaper than any yet in regular use. The Newberys did not force the new binding on their customers; their books could be had either in this new type of cover or in the old. *The World Displayed*, for example, was advertised at £2 for the twenty bound volumes or £1 12s. for the same number of volumes bound in ten in the vellum manner. Samuel Ward's *A Modern System of Natural History* was issued in 1775 at "4s. elegantly bound, or, 1s. bound in the vellum manner."[31]

For all that, the Newberys were before their time. In the second half of the eighteenth century leather was still the usual binding material. The mass-produced commercial binding, when it did really come to stay in the nineteenth century, was after all not made of paper, as in the Newberys' efforts, but of cloth.

CHAPTER XI

Financial Organisation and Terms of Publication

The financial beginnings of any industry which dates from the fifteenth century or earlier are inevitably somewhat obscure. Monetary values as recorded are unreliable, partly because of the circulation of debased coinage and partly because the use of money had not yet penetrated as the customary means of payment throughout all branches of industry. The lateness in the development of monetary transactions is shown remarkably well in the English book industry.

The equipment of the early printing office, we have seen, was commonly of the humblest description, demanding little outlay of capital. But for this the book industry in England must have been of even slower growth. The printer-publisher was not as a rule a great capitalist. Caxton himself, as a mercer with influential friends, had acquired sufficient means to allow him to toy with this new pastime, to pay to the full, if need be, for his adventures as a pioneer. His immediate successors were not so well endowed. The sixteenth-century printer was poorly placed, especially in comparison with his continental rivals. One has only to glance at a few inventories of the property of our early stationers to realise how very low was their estate. There was John Denys, of Cambridge, who about 1578 left property to the value of £69 8s. 0½d., including over £8 in "desperate" debts.[1] There was his neighbour, John Sheres, who a few years later left goods and money valued at £893, of which £300 consisted of "detes in his dett booke."[2] These are typical of the trade as a whole.

The circumstances of those engaged in the book industry abroad were very different. Several foreign publishers, including Henry Estienne of Paris, Koberger of Nuremberg and Froben of Basel, were supported by members of the Fugger family, the chief financiers of the age. Robert Estienne enjoyed the patronage of King Francis I, who paid amongst other things for his founts of Greek type. No such help was forthcoming in England: the English Crown was itself in the position of needing financial assistance rather than having resources with which to subsidise the very industry which threatened to undermine the stability of the State. Such loans as could be made by goldsmiths and scriveners, our earliest bankers, were made largely to the Government. The small funds on which the poorer printer or bookseller could draw were mostly in the nature of charities provided by past members of the Stationers' Company. There were several bequests similar to that of Robert Dexter, who in 1603 left to the Company "twentye poundes to be lente foorthe by them vppon securitye for three yeares vnto poore yong men freeborne of the same companye gratis, and so from time to time for three yeares gratis unto two others of the same company beinge poor yong men as aforesaid."[3] There was also a limited amount of financial assistance from the universities to their own printers: in 1520 the University of Cambridge lent £20 to John Siberch, and in 1584 the University of Oxford lent £100 to Joseph Barnes to start a press.[4] These sums must have been quite inadequate for printing on any but a very small scale. Christopher Barker, in his report on the printing patents of 1558–82, declared that "Even my poore printing howse which is but onlye for the Englishe, and som Hebrew, Greeke and Latin letter if any suche work happen, hath cost me with in these few yeres twelve hundred pound."[5] John Day was fortunate in securing assistance and general encouragement from Archbishop Parker, but such cases were far more rare in England than on the Continent. There were certain expenses, such as the purchase of materials and the payment of wages, for which the publisher needed a supply of cash, but there were various transactions which could be carried on on a credit basis.

Payment in Kind

By fair means or foul it was quite easy, we have seen, for the sixteenth-century printer to obtain sufficient copy without any cost to himself. His method of paying such authors as refused to have their claims entirely over-ridden provides the clue to his general financial dealings: he paid, as far as possible, by handing over a certain number of copies of the finished work, thereby transferring the risk of selling them. Payment in kind, such as this, had been usual at home and abroad from the early days of printing. In Germany during the first half of the sixteenth century the author rarely received any money payment: he was given instead a number of books, sometimes consisting entirely of his own works and occasionally of copies of the works for which his own had been exchanged.[6] Christophe Plantin of Antwerp seems from his account books always to have paid partly or wholly in kind: when he published Jean Isaac's Hebrew Grammar in 1554 the full payment was 100 copies of the book; in 1567 he gave Pierre de Savonne 45 florins and 100 copies for a treatise on book-keeping.[7] Such a system was entirely to the benefit of the publisher. The author had seldom the necessary facilities for making a good bargain from his copies, but had rather to rely on his patron's help in their disposal. This payment in kind was customary in all branches of the English book industry for at least the first century of printing.

The Star Chamber case of John Day *v.* R. Ward and W. Holmes with regard to the infringing of Day's patent for the "A B C" incidentally illustrates this avoidance of the handing over of money in connection with the purchase of paper. Roger Ward stated in his evidence that he had bought part of his paper from Master Eckhard and some from Thomas Man, "and the paper he had of the same Echard and Man he had the same vpon trust and not for Redye money."[8] (John Dunton refers as late as 1705 to the six months' credit commonly given in the trade.)[9] Perhaps more usual than this simple credit system was that whereby the printer and the paper dealer shared the risk on the venture. In this same lawsuit, for instance, Abraham Newman, a London draper, gave evidence that he "solde not any paper to the said Warde to imprynt the said bokes with all . . . the bargayne betwene them was to Delyuer him so many Reames of paper as this Deponent should have Reames of bokes and so to paye but for the pryntyng of the same and thereupon the said Warde had ten Reames of paper of this Deponent for ten Reames of the said bokes."

Royalties, too, could be paid in copies. When the right of publication of Pagett's *History of the Bible* was transferred in 1615 from Waterson and Welby to John Legate it was recorded in the register of the Stationers' Company that Legate had agreed to give 75 copies of the work at each impression to both of the former publishers.[10] This was not a universal practice. The assignment of John Sprint's *Propositions tending to prove the necessary Use of the Christian Sabaoth or Lords Day* by Jonah Man to John Grismand in 1622 was accompanied by the provision that for every new impression of the work Grismand should pay Man at the rate of 2s. a ream.[11] Similarly, Thomas Jones, on taking over from John Marriot the publishing rights of the 10 books of Lucan, in 1630, undertook to give Marriot 200 copies of the work within six days of the next impression and 25 after every following impression.[12]

Payment in copies resulted in the accumulation by various people of stocks of books for which they had no personal use. The more obvious way of disposing of them would be to sell them to a bookseller, but it happened quite frequently that the possessor of a number of copies of a work would use them towards the formation of a bookshop of his own.[13] By exchanging a number of volumes for copies of other works he was able to build up a varied stock, the nucleus of a flourishing business. So recognised a proceeding did this become that in 1620 it was made a condition of the grant of copyright to George Latham for several works, including *The Plain Man's Pathway*, "that he shall not refuse to exchange *the plaine mans pathwaye* with the company for other good wares."[14] This somewhat primitive system died a natural death as money flowed more freely, yet even in the early nineteenth century a faint memory of it lingered. At the meeting of the Select Committee on the Copyright Acts, in 1818, a publisher was asked, "Are copies of the works given to other persons, such as printers or other persons, in part or in lieu of payment in money?" "Never by us," was the answer. On being pressed, the witness denied that this was the practice of any reputable publishers, though he admitted that it might be resorted to by those in difficulties.[15]

The Cost of Production

On account of these methods of barter it is difficult to estimate the monetary cost of producing a work in the sixteenth and seventeenth centuries. Such details as we are given are rather scanty. The *Matthew's Bible* of Tyndale and Coverdale, published in 1537 by Grafton and Whitchurch, cost its producers over £500 for an edition of 1,500 copies. This seems a reasonable sum for a work on this scale, which was to be sold at about 10s. a copy, although in a letter to Thomas Cromwell Grafton stated that the Bible had been "brought forth to our most great and costly labours and charges."[16] The cost really compared favourably with the charges made by Thomas Berthelet, printer to King Henry VIII: his account for printing the 1,600 copies of the proclamation of 1530 "for ordring and punishing of sundry beggers and vacabundes" was at the rate of 1d. a leaf.[17] In 1542 he was still charging 1d. each for proclamations on "bastard" paper and ½d. for those on "iene."*

By the end of the sixteenth century printing was remarkably cheap, especially in view of the fact that between 1550 and 1600 general prices doubled. In 1598 the Stationers' Company issued an order limiting the price of work: "No new copies without pictures to be printed at more than the following rates: those in Pica Roman and Italic and in English [i.e. black letter] with Roman and Italic, at a penny for two sheets; those in Brevier and Long Primer letters at a Penny for One Sheet and a Half."[18] The "sheet," of course, constitutes one section of a book, being 8 pages of a quarto volume, 16 of an octavo, and so on. An octavo work of 160 pages would therefore cost about 5d. a copy to print. The usual selling price of a book of that size seems to have been 1s., but in the case of plays, on account of their quick

* Presumably a size.

sale, the price was only 6d. even for a work of this length. In practice, printing was performed at much lower rates than the maximum allowed by the Company. In 1607, for instance, it was provided that Adam Islip was "to have 6s. a reame [500 sheets] for an impression of 1,500 of the book of *presidentes*,"[19] being approximately 1d. for 7 sheets. Twenty years later John Norton and Augustine Matthews obtained a contract for printing "the whole Ten books of Lucans Pharsalia" at the rate of 1,500 sheets for 15s.—more than 8 sheets for 1d.[20] By 1640 the cost was still lower: it was agreed that Mrs. Griffen and her son should print Lambard's *Perambulation of Kent* for 4s. 6d. a ream.[21] These charges would have to cover the cost of wages, rent of premises and wear of type, but not the cost of paper. If the printer was expected to provide the paper this was made clear in the agreement, as when in 1599 James Roberts agreed to deliver to William Wood a whole impression of Markham's *Horsemanship*, at the rate of 8 . a ream for paper and printing.

By the end of the seventeenth century the price of printing had risen to a figure more in accordance with modern charges. In 1699 Edmund Jeffery paid at the rate of 16s. a sheet for printing 1,000 copies of a sermon by John Leng.[22] We must beware of too hasty a comparison between this price and the 8 sheets for 1d. of earlier years. Whereas this charge had covered 8 sheets of only one copy of a work, the 16s. obviously referred, in agreement with present-day practice, to the printing of one sheet for the whole impression, in this case of 1,000 copies. On the old basis of reckoning this works out at 8s. a ream, or about 5 sheets for 1d. So, in spite of a rise in the general price-level uncounteracted by any notable improvement in printing technique, the charges were still well below the maximum allowed by the order issued a century before.

It was probably at about this time that the printing trade instituted a system of charging which was to prevail as long as the hand printing-press remained in general use, that is, well into the nineteenth century. This was the practice of quoting the rates for press-work at so much for 250 copies, charging this full amount for any smaller number. A bookseller, in his evidence before the Select Committee on the Copyright Acts, 1818, said, "It has been the regulation of the trade time immemorial to print and pay for tokens of 250, which is an hour's work for two men; 250 forms half a ream of paper, and it is the custom of paper-makers and stationers to sell their paper in reams. . . . Were a smaller number printed, there would be necessarily a considerable waste of paper from the negligence of the printers, warehousemen, pressmen, &c." Why this negligence should have been beyond control seemed no less of a problem to the committee than it does to-day, but when the witness was asked, "Is it not in the power of the publisher to prevent that portion of the ream not used in the edition from being embezzled, and to preserve it for the next work in hand?" he declared, "I conceive it to be totally out of his power."[23] The system of reckoning press-work by tokens, "accounting every Token to an Hour's work," was already established when Moxon wrote in 1683, but he speaks of the token as being equivalent to 10 quires.[24]

The Rise of Publishing Societies

The printer was not always his own financier even in the earliest period. *The History of Kyng Boccus and Sydracke*, published in 1510, has as its colophon a note stating that the work was printed in London by Thomas Godfray at the cost of Robert Saltwode, monk of Saint Austen's at Canterbury. Exactly a hundred years later the works of St. Chrysostom were published by John Norton and printed by Melchisidec Bradwood, its cost, said to be £8,000, being borne by the editor, Sir Henry Savile. From about that time the individual printer, master of his own business, came more and more to relinquish its management to a capitalist who took no active part in printing. In 1611 the Authorised Version of the Bible was printed by Robert Barker at the expense of Bonham Norton, John Norton and John Bill; these were to be recompensed by a share in the profits. The chief capitalists in the trade by 1635 were John Haviland, Robert Young and Miles Flesher. These had businesses of their own and also a share in the King's printing-house; besides this they had jointly taken over the concerns of William Stansby, George Purslowe and Edward Griffin. Publishing syndicates such as this were of late development in England. A highly organised association had been formed in Milan as early as 1472: it was composed of the printer (Antonio Zarotus), a priest, a schoolteacher, a professor of Latin, a lawyer and a physician; the books to be printed were selected and their prices fixed by the whole board; the printer himself invested no capital but received one-third of the net proceeds, the remainder being divided among the other members, who were the financiers.[25] Similar associations were common in France in the early seventeenth century. The Grand Navire (1610), the Source (1622), and the Soleil (1629) are perhaps the best known. They differed from the Milanese association in that the individual members, while combining for expensive publications, reserved the right to publish other works independently.[26]

Permanent associations for the publication of expensive works were in England an eighteenth-century development. The Printing Conger, formed about 1719, consisting of seven booksellers, and the New Conger of 1736 gave way to a bigger organisation, the Chapter, so called from the Chapter Coffee House, in which meetings were held. The list of members of the Chapter includes several familiar names—Thomas Longman, John Murray, John Rivington and James Dodson, to mention a few of them. The "Chapter Books" resulting from their endeavours included such notable publications as Johnson's *English Poets*. Towards the close of the century a new association arose, known from the beehive used as its vignette as the Associated Busy Bees. Among the members were Thomas Hood (father of the poet), James Nunn and James Lackington.[27]

The growth of powerful organisations caused a certain apprehension among those who regarded themselves as the objects of attack. The author who thought himself ill-used by his private publisher could not cope with a whole association of publishers. In 1736, therefore, there was formed the Society for the Encouragement of Learning, its object being to enable authors to publish independently of the professional booksellers. It was a co-operative venture with a managing committee of over a hundred. The society was to bear the expense of printing the works of individual authors, taking a share of the profits but allowing each author to retain his own copyrights. Although the society was formed as a direct attack on the booksellers three of their number were called in to help. During 1742 the society did try to undertake its own publishing, but soon had recourse to the booksellers again.[28] In all, nine works were published by the society by 1748, but in that year, according to *A Memorial of the present State of Affairs of the Society*, the whole project had to be abandoned through debt. "Their Plan was too narrow,—They also forgot, that the Booksellers were Masters of all Avenues to every Market, and, by the Practice of one Night's Postage, could make any Work resemble Jonah's Gourd after the Worm had smote it."[29]

Partnership

The place of these permanent publishing syndicates was to some extent taken in England by simple partnerships, whose formation did not always have happy results. There was, for instance, the case of John Beale and Thomas Brudenell, of whom it is recorded in 1634 that "They are now parted. Beale tooke 140 li. of Brudenell: and after wrangled with him and ou[s]ted him and made him take his 140 li. againe after he had spent in Chauncery as much."[30]

Complete fusion of two or more businesses was not so usual in this period as temporary partnership for the publication of single works. Co-operation of this kind seems to have begun as early as 1514. In that year Wynkyn de Worde printed a treatise entitled *The Dying Creature*. Two copies of this, one from the British Museum Library and the other from Cambridge University, have been compared: while both have De Worde's colophon, the Cambridge copy bears his device and the British Museum copy that of Robert Copland,[31] from which it would seem that the printing was undertaken jointly, probably on a profit-sharing basis. Probably no individual publisher contracted more of these

PAPERMAKER
From *The Young Tradesman*, 1839

temporary partnerships than did John Dunton during the second half of the seventeenth century. His reminiscences are full of such comments as, "Mr. John Laurence, an upright honest Bookseller. We were neighbours some years, and Partners in printing the late 'Lord Delamere's Works,' 'Mackenzie's Narrative of the Siege of Londonderry,' and 'Mr. Baxter's Life' in folio; . . . Mr. Thomas Bennet . . . I was Partner with him in 'Mr. Lecrose's Works of the Learned'; and, I must say, he acted like a man of conscience and honesty." He seems to have entered into these agreements in any but a cautious manner, judging by his remark on one of these casual associates: "I was Partner with him in Keith's 'Narrative of the Proceedings at Turners' Hall'; and so had an opportunity to know him."[32]

It is frequently found in the Stationers' Register that a work whose publishing rights were originally granted to one man has afterwards been reassigned to several publishers. The moral works of Plutarch, for instance, were entered in 1600 as the copy of Master Ponsonby. It may be that he found his resources insufficient for the undertaking, for two years later the publishing rights were granted to Bishop, Ponsonby, Waterson, John Norton and Adams, on condition that "Arnalt Hatfeild and Melchisedeck Bradwood printers shall haue the workmanship of the printing of the said book for the said parteners at all Impressions thereof hereafter."[33] The copyright of Camden's *Britannia* was granted in 1610 to six partners, their shares in the venture being recorded by the Stationers' Company: "Master George Byshopp is to enioy one Third parte and of that Third parte master Banckworth and William Aspley are to haue and enioy the one moity or half parte, And master John Norton is to haue one other Third parte, And master Adames and master Edward Byshopp are to haue the other Third parte betweene them."[34] Most important of all the works published in England by a temporary syndicate was Shakespeare's First Folio (1623); it was produced by two printers (William and Isaac Jaggard) and three publishers (Smethwicke, Aspley and Blount) working in co-operation with representatives of the acting company which owned Shakespeare's manuscripts. This share system was at its height in the eighteenth century. It was then so general that in the records of the Stationers' Company a column was ruled off and headed "Shares," being divided into halves, quarters, sixteenths, twenty-fourths, and so on. This led to some complication in the dealings of publishers. Here, for instance, is an extract from Lintot's Memorandum-book: "Mr. Thomas Ballard, Little Britain. 1718–19. Bought of him a Fourth of a Half of the several shares of all the Copies formerly belonging to Mr. Thomas Basset, deceased (except his Law Copies); *viz.* Heylin's Help to History, &c. &c. in all 133 books: among which, Miege's Dictionary, 4to and 8vo; on every impression of which, the Author to have 10s. a sheet on each book for revising, and 100 books."[35] Much of Thomas Longman's business centred on the buying of shares. In 1724 he bought one-third of the Delphin *Virgil* from Jacob Tonson; four years later he invested £40 in one-twentieth of Ainsworth's *Latin Dictionary*; later on he bought one-quarter of the *Arabian Nights' Entertainments* for £12.[36]

In the case of transfer of publishing rights it was a common practice to safeguard the former publisher from loss by forbidding the issue of a new impression while there remained a large number of copies unsold. Thus in 1622 a book entitled *The Godly Mans Assurance* was assigned to Timothy Barlowe by the former holders of the copyright, Richard Woodrofe and Master Budge, with the proviso that "because Master Budge hath manie of them left, the said Timothy Barlowe shall not print nor cause to be printed the said booke till the last of Aprill. 1624. And if the said Master Barlowe shall print or cause the same to be printed before the time prefixed Then to paie for all the Bookes that Master Budge shall haue aboue the number of fiftie bookes then left after the rate of Eleauen shillings the Reame."[37] Ten years later John Rothwell took over the publishing rights of *Thesaurus Poeticus* on the understanding that he should not reprint the work while two hundred copies remained unsold.

In spite of these elaborate precautions against loss, the publisher was in constant danger of heavy fine by the Government for anything which could be regarded as blasphemy or sedition. The classic example of this was the arraignment of the King's Printers, Robert Barker and Martin Lucas, before the Court of High Commission, and their fine of £200 and £100 respectively, for the omission of one word in one of their publications: the occasion was the printing of the "Wicked" Bible of 1631, in which the Seventh Commandment was made to read "Thou shalt commit adultery," incidentally giving the publication a higher market value than many a more accurate version.

Subscription Publication

The share system was a useful method of spreading risks, but, even so, no publisher would willingly share in a certain loss. If a work was shunned by the trade the author's only chance of publication, if he could not defray the cost himself, was by subscription. John Foxe, for instance, was enabled to publish his *Tables of Grammar* (1552) by subscriptions from eight Lords of the Privy Council. John Taylor, "the Water Poet," collected subscriptions for nearly every pamphlet which he published, obtaining 1,600 names for one of them.[38] John Minsheu was driven to sell his *Guide into Tongues* (1617) by subscription owing to the refusal of the booksellers to stock the work.[39] The daughter of Doctor Fulkes adopted similar measures for the printing of her father's *Answer to the Rhemish Testament* (1620); this treatise was not one with a popular appeal, so "Mistris Ogden hath gotten by begging from ye clergie and others diuers great somes of money towards ye printing of her fathers workes."[40] Other works published by subscription were Walton's *London Polyglott*, in 1657, and Tonson's folio edition of *Paradise Lost*, in 1688, but it was not until the eighteenth century that this became the recognised form of issuing the more expensive works.

Subscriptions were commonly invited through the medium of the daily and weekly newspapers. *The Postboy* of August 14, 1716, for instance, announces the forthcoming publication of John Le Neve's *Monumenta Anglicana*, and continues with the words "All gentlemen and others who shall think fit to encourage this undertaking by subscription are desired so to do before Christmas next, after which no subscription will be taken in, nor any more printed than shall be subscribed for. The terms are 2d. per sheet, for so many sheets as the book shall amount to; and no money will be required till the book be in the press." Robert Dodsley inserted an advertisement in the *London Evening Post*, March 24, 1743, reading: "As all our Old Plays, except Shakespeare's, Jonson's, and Beaumont and Fletcher's, are become exceeding scarce and extravagantly dear, I propose, if I can procure 200 Subscribers, to select from such of our Dramatic writers, as are of any considerable Repute, about Forty or Fifty Plays. . . . I desire no Money but upon the Delivery of the Books." This was a most successful enterprise. Within a week Dodsley had secured the required number of promises, and by the time the 10 volumes had appeared, in 1746, there were nearly 800 subscribers.[41] Usually part of the subscription was to be paid immediately and the remainder on delivery of the book, as in the case of Christopher Smart's poems, price half a guinea, of which half was to be paid on subscription and the rest later.[42]

Although there was as a rule no place for the wholesaler in these transactions it was stipulated in the proposal for printing John Free's *Controversy with the Methodists*, 1759, that each subscriber should pay one guinea, for which he should receive six sewed or five bound copies. For the benefit of the slow-witted it was pointed out that "Those, who are inclined to have single Books, may easily join, five or six together, and make the full Subscription in the name of one of the Company, afterwards dividing the Books among them as they please."[43]

The practice of demanding part payment before publication was undoubtedly necessary to all but the wealthier authors. Sir Joseph Ayloffe pointed out in the proposals for a *History of Suffolk* (1764) that the preliminary subscriptions, being intended solely to defray working expenses, would be paid into Messrs. Hoare's bank; only at the completion of the work would the profit, if any, be paid to the author.[44] This particular work received so little support that it was never published. Presumably such subscriptions as had been paid were returned, but it was not always so. It was the temptation to defer repayment, speaking vaguely of publication at some future time, that helped to discredit the whole system. Surely the worst possible aspects of it are shown in this letter written by the Rev. Tobias Heyrick in 1774: "I have sent you the First Volume of 'Bridge's History of Northamptonshire,' which is brought down no lower than the year 1720. The Editor has had the manuscript 20 years in his own hands; has not given a line of his own; and cannot be explicit when the remainder will be published, though he promised a friend of mine five years ago it would be finished and delivered to the Subscribers at Christmas 1769. His Bookseller got the last Subscription (two guineas) *nine years ago.* John Bridges, Esq., the original Author, was a gentleman of £1,000 a year, near Kettering in Northamptonshire: and unfortunately died (March 16, 1723–4) after he had finished a rude draught of it, to the irreparable loss of the County. His Brother sold the Manuscript to a Bookseller, who got Subscriptions from the Gentlemen of the County, and ran off with them. After this, Sir Thomas Cave got the copy; and put it into Whalley's hands, who promised to bring it down to the present times, and has only given us Three Parts of Bridges's History, without an additional line of his own; and can't promise when the remainder shall be published. Another fellow, *an historical cheat*, has played the same trick with regard to the 'Antiquities of Leicester'; has pocketed the money, turned Critic, and writes Notes on Shakespeare."[45]

We must beware of condemning the whole subscription business on the evidence of occasional roguery. There is no doubt that the system had served a useful purpose—as it still does where the extent of the market is difficult to forecast. The publisher was safeguarded from loss, and the author sometimes managed to make a profit. Fanny Burney, indeed, gained about £3,000 from the subscriptions for her *Camilla.*[46] Robert Dodsley collected over two hundred names, many of them belonging to the peerage, for *A Muse in Livery; or, The Footman's Miscellany*, written while he was still a footman (1732), and it was his success in this and similar undertakings which enabled him to turn publisher.[47]

Generally speaking, perhaps too much depended on the business sense of the author for his success to be a foregone conclusion, even given a satisfactory subscription-list. Leonard Twells had no lack of subscribers for his edition of Pocock's *Theological Works* (1740), but he admitted to Dr. Zachary Grey that he had made £50 at the most from the transactions; "I am ashamed," he added, "to own my weakness in the contract to any but such a friend as you."[48]

There was another serious drawback to subscription-publication: the author placed himself in the importunate position which he had occupied in the old days of patronage. His demands must indeed have taxed the patience of his friends. Here is Twells writing to Dr. Grey in 1734, reminding him of their long friendship: "This emboldens me to desire your assistance in promoting the subscription mentioned in the Proposals herewith transmitted to you, both in Cambridge, and among your neighbours in Bedfordshire. I have made the same request to our worthy Master, Dr. Ashton; and Dr. Waterland has likewise recommended it to some of his friends. With this you will receive 18 Proposals; 12 of which have indorsed receipts, signed and numbered, for the use of those who shall please to subscribe; and six more unsigned, for those whom you may think useful in promoting the design. I must farther beg that you would take account not only of the name of each Subscriber, but also of the number of his receipt."[49] It is little wonder that the system, so useful in many ways, fell into disrepute, and that a friend of Cowper's who tried to obtain subscriptions for his *Homer* was told at Oxford that they subscribed to nothing there.[50] By the middle of the eighteenth century it was even regarded as a special point in a book's favour for it to have been published by some other means, to judge from Warburton's advertisement to Pope's collected works (1751): "The Editor hath not, for the sake of profit, suffered the Author's name to be made cheap by a *subscription*."

The various proposals inviting subscriptions give some clue to the financial position of the industry in the eighteenth century. Edward Cave's "Proposals for printing Du Halde's *History of*

China" (1736) as given in the *Gentleman's Magazine*, set out the charges in full: the edition was estimated to take up about 300 sheets besides plates; the price to subscribers was to be 1½d. a sheet, with three guineas as the maximum; maps were to be reckoned as 4 sheets of letterpress; the work would be put to press as soon as enough subscribers had come forward to cover the cost, "which, in such Works as this, is never calculated under 1,000"; any profits were to be divided among the first 1,000 subscribers, "only deducting 50 *l.* to be given to such of His Majesty's British Subjects, as shall in the Opinion of the Royal Society, make (from the Hints given in this Description of China) the best and most useful improvement in any beneficial Branch of Art, and exhibit the same to the said Society within 3 Months after this Work is finished." It seems that the rewards of merit were not so attractive as chance gains, for in a subsequent advertisement Cave saw fit to change his offer: instead of the scheme for the £50 he offered "to give *ten five pounds* to such subscribers as they shall by lot fall to. But he is willing to do more: he will be ready to give the whole profits of the undertaking to fall by lot among the first 1,000 subscribers, which profits, if encouragements offer, may produce *fifty* or *a hundred five pounds*; or, if it be thought proper to make only a few lots of five pounds, and divide the rest into lots of two and three pounds, there may be a fortunate lot to every five or six subscribers."

The charge of 1½d. a sheet was unusually low for this period: Wm. Bowyer's standard price for works delivered in sheet-form was 2d., or 3d. for large-paper editions.[51] On the whole, the alternative system of charging, at a guinea or so for the book, was likely to cause less argumentation. In a complete volume a certain amount of blank paper is an asset, but the man who is paying 2d. for a single sheet is apt to prefer it well covered with ink. Judicious advertising will overcome even this difficulty. What did it matter that there was very little news for the *Flying Post* of November 26–28, 1695? This was all to the good of the purchaser: "If any gentleman has a mind to oblige his country friend or correspondent with this account of publick affairs," ran the advertisement, "he may have it for 2d. of J. Salusbury, at the Rising Sun in Cornhill, on a sheet of fine paper; half of which being blank, he may thereon write his own private business, or the material news of the day." This may be so, but Bowyer, the publisher, had hard work to convince one of his authors on a similar point. John Jackson wrote to him in 1752 complaining of various details in his printing account, giving his chief grievance last. "You have reckoned mere blank paper as if printed. . . . I had no meaning but to pay for so many pages as should be actually printed, and wonder you should reckon a sheet and more of mere blank paper, that has not a letter upon it."[52] Bowyer, in a patient if specious reply, showed the other side of the question: authors of a lower class were commonly paid by the sheet, and would certainly not welcome deductions for blank pages or for titles or dedications in larger type; moreover, the printer himself contracted with the workman at so much a sheet, so that any advantage arising from blank pages would be divided between the author and the journeyman. "But what a world should we have," he remonstrated, "if every thing was brought to such mathematical nicety; if every subscriber was to cavil at a blank page, and complain he had paper imposed on him instead of print!"[53]

Number-publication

There was still another method of testing the state of the market besides that of inviting subscriptions. That was to issue a work in weekly or monthly parts. It may well be that the originators of the scheme of number-publishing had no idea of sending out the earlier parts in a purely tentative way to see how many would sell; it is more likely that they were envious of the greater prosperity of the periodical Press, and wanted to see what disguising their products as magazines would do. Even so, one may be sure that if the first two or three numbers of a work did not attract customers the rest would not be forthcoming. In one instance at least this was so: William Harrod's continuation of Wright's *History and*

Antiquities of Rutland (1788) was discontinued after the second number for this very reason.[54]

The success of the early number-publishers created something of a mania in the rest of the trade for a share in this system of quick returns. As it happened, not every publisher could lay hands on suitable material. According to a pamphlet by the Rev. Thomas Stackhouse, a curate of Finchley, two booksellers wrote to him in 1732, "when the success of some certain things published weekly set every little bookseller's wits to work," proposing that he should "write something which might be published weekly, but what it was they knew not."[55] It is not altogether to be wondered at that in this case no agreement was reached as to what should be published.

Number-publication never became so usual a practice during the eighteenth century as did sale by subscription. It is a system which one associates rather with the nineteenth-century novel writers, particularly with Charles Dickens. It must be admitted that the type of work chosen for weekly sale before that time appears totally unfitting. William Dodd's *Commentary on the Bible* (1765), issued weekly in sixpenny parts, was, no doubt, an estimable work; but can one imagine any great outcry should one part have come from the press a day late?

In spite of the highly respectable nature of these weekly publications, there was no lack of criticism from those who objected to all and every means of making education available to the working man. One writer in the *Gentleman's Magazine* held forth in high dudgeon: "Amongst several *Monstrosities* I take notice of that strange Madness of publishing books by piece-meal, at 6 or 12 Pennyworth a week. You have *Bayle's Dictionary*, and *Rapin's History* from two places. The *Bible* can't escape. I bought, the other Day, three Pennyworth of the Gospel, made easy and familiar to Porters, Carmen, and Chimney-sweepers: But how? Why, by scraps taken out of *Grotius*, *Hammond*, &c. What an Age of Wit and Learning is this! In which so many Persons in the lowest Stations of Life, are more intent upon cultivating their Minds, than upon feeding and cloathing their Bodies. You shall see a

Fellow spend Six-pence upon a Number of *Rapin*, or Three-pence upon a bit of *St. Matthew's Gospel*, when perhaps his Wife and Children want a Bit of Bread, and himself a pair of Breeches. I used to think, that 19 in 20 of the Species were designed by Nature for Trade, and Manufactures; and that to take them off to read Books, was not the Way to make them wiser or better, but impertinent, troublesome, and factious."[56] Well, well! Yet the sale of weekly parts went on.

Eighteenth-century Finance

By the eighteenth century financial transactions had lost the last remnants of their mediaeval nature. The Bank of England had been founded in 1694, and the great family banks were arriving one by one. Printers and booksellers, in common with men of other trades, became accustomed to monetary dealings, and abandoned the old system of semi-barter. This is the century to which one can trace the origins of some of the great publishing-houses of to-day—the Longmans, the Murrays, the Lanes. The financial keynote of the sixteenth-century printing-publishing business had been one of "desperate debts"; that of the eighteenth was of stability and modest prosperity. There were still few prospects of rising to fabulous wealth. The Royal Printing House itself still offered so little attraction that John Barber relinquished the reversion of it for £1,500 on the death of Baskett in 1742.[57] Thomas Longman in 1724 paid only £2,282 9s. 6d. for the publishing business of Wm. Taylor in Paternoster Row,[58] one of the most substantial properties of the day. Even in the middle of the century the £1,300 cleared annually by the Cambridge University Press seemed sufficiently attractive to John Nicholls for him to urge Wm. Bowyer to take over the management of the press.[59] True, there was at this time one bookseller, Knapton by name, who was reputed to be of considerable means, with stock valued at £30,000; but even he failed very shortly afterwards, unable to meet his debts of over £20,000.[60] There were still to be found a few men who had hard work to pay their way, men like James Lackington, who in 1774 was thankful to borrow the £5 allowed him as a good Wesleyan,[61] and who on two occasions pawned books to obtain the money to buy others,[62] but in course of time some of these fought their way to the most eminent positions. The typical printer-bookseller now was able to deal generously with his authors: Richard Gough, for one, bears witness in his *Memoirs* to the help given him by Richardson, who printed for him on credit, refusing all offers of interest.

For this period there is no lack of information regarding publishing costs. Henry Woodfall's ledgers[63] show that in the seventeen-thirties his price for printing 1,000 copies of a single sheet was normally about 14s., as compared with the 16s. paid by Edmund Jeffery in 1699. Woodfall's charge to Bernard Lintot in 1735 for the first volume of Pope's *Works* (3,000 copies) was £34 6s. 3d., comprising £30 9s. for printing, £1 1s. for the title in red and black, and £2 16s. 3d. for 2¼ reams of paper. In the year 1770 Benjamin Collins of Salisbury, according to his publishing-book, was charging about 17s. 6d. for printing 1,000 copies of a sheet.[64] Gibbon's *Roman Empire*, published seven years later by Cadell and Strahan, cost 26s. the sheet for printing (still for 1,000 copies),[65] but the clue to the increased price is contained, no doubt, in the words "with notes at the bottom of the page." The paper normally cost rather more than the printing, as we have seen, and advertising had now become an item of importance, amounting to anything between £5 and £20.

Here, for instance, is the account, from John Newbery's papers, of the publication of Samuel Johnson's *The Idler*, in two volumes, 1761, sold at 5s. sewed or 6s. bound. The total expenses for the 1,500 copies were £113 16s. 6d., of which advertising accounted for £20 0s. 6d., printing £41 13s. and paper £52 3s. The sets were sold at £16 a hundred, thus bringing in £240 and giving a total profit of £126 3s. 6d. Dr. Johnson was paid two-thirds of this, and Newbery kept the rest.[66]

In 1770 there appeared *Humphry Clinker*, published in three volumes by Benjamin Collins and William Johnston. For this Smollett was paid £210 "copy money"; printing and paper for 2,000 copies cost £155 15s. 6d., the nine sets for the Stationers'

Company and ten for the author cost £6 1s. 10d. and the advertisements £15 10s. After selling the entire edition at £24 a hundred the publishers had made only £46 6s. 4d. each.[67] The demand for a second edition in the following year gave them a better return. A second edition called for no extra payment to the author and for a much smaller expenditure on advertising. Hence the total profits this time were £240 12s.; "my Moiety of Profits," enters Collins, "£120 6s., for which I have drawn on him at 6 wks. and 2 months, Oct. 27, 1774, for £60 3s. each."[68]

It would be tedious to quote further. For ordinary printing these accounts may be taken as representative. "Fine" printing was, as nowadays, a different proposition, an extreme case of this arising when, in 1769, it was suggested that the Government should issue a facsimile edition of Domesday Book in the form of copperplate engravings. The estimate procured by the Society of Antiquaries put a definite stop to any further proposals which might have been forthcoming : the 1,664 pages, it was reported, would cost 4 guineas each ; the copper for these could not be procured for less than £582 8s.; the charge for rolling off would be £2,560, and the paper would cost £2,550. The Government decided, without much trouble, that £12,681 4s. was rather more than it wished to pay.[69]

The little note above by Benjamin Collins reminds us how cumbrous were the methods of payment in this era before the rise of modern banking. Until well in the nineteenth century the bill of exchange was in regular use for the settlement of the larger debts. This did not make for simplicity in publishers' contracts. John Wilkes, for instance, in arranging for the publication of his *History of England* by John Almon, in the July of 1767, included in the conditions : "Mr. Almon shall accept and pay my bill of this day's date, drawn in favour of Mr. Heaton Wilkes, due on the first day of next September."[70] As the scale of business grew the failure of the financial organisation to keep pace caused many an irritating experience. John Murray on one occasion (1807) wrote in annoyance to Constable, his associate, "A bill of yours for £200 was due yesterday, and I have been obliged to supply the means for paying it, without any notice for preparation; and on Wednesday, the first of your bills to Longman for £333 6s. 8d. is due, and I am to remain until that day under apprehensions, lest it should be forgotten to be remitted, as it is not stated in your cash account.... The best bills in the world I cannot get discounted at a moment's notice."[71] Lackington tells how difficult it was in the late eighteenth century for the country customer to get the books he wanted, and part of the trouble was that "many in the country found it difficult to remit small sums that were under bankers' notes (which difficulty is now done away, as all post-masters receive small sums of money, and give drafts for the same on the post-office in London)."[72]

It was not only in long-distance payments that difficulty arose: there was also an inconvenient shortage of small change. In this case numerous traders throughout the country took matters into their own hands. Tired of waiting for the Mint to coin pennies and halfpennies in sufficient quantities they issued token coins of their own, and thus eased an awkward situation. It has been estimated that between 1787 and 1797 about three million tokens were issued by the bookselling and allied trades alone.[73] William Clachar, a Chelmsford bookseller, issued a ton of them in over a hundred thousand pieces. As for James Lackington, who by dint of pawning his watch, his clothing and his stock had risen to be the largest second-hand bookseller of the century, he struck over seven tons of them, in halfpenny pieces.

CHAPTER XII

The Sale of Books

THE conviction that the success of any one publication must necessarily destroy part of the demand for every similar work led in the early years to a keenness on the part of both author and publisher to be first in the field with a topical subject. The registers of the Stationers' Company afford plentiful examples of this. John Wolf, as ever, proved himself more alert than his law-abiding contemporaries: he had the temerity to enter a description of the Queen's state entry into London in November, 1588, before the event. On November 6, 1612, the Prince of Wales died, and by the next day Henry Gosson was able to obtain the copyright of a poem called "Great Britaynes greatest woe or an Elegiacall lamentinge Poem for the Incomparable losse of losses of Henry our late hopefull Prince," by John Taylor. The funeral provided material for seventeen different works; one of them, a full account of the ceremony, was registered by John Budge on the day before it took place.[1]

The Prices of Books

In view of the limited size of the market at that time in relation to the possible output of the printing-press it was to the interest of the individual publisher to fix a price within the range of the purses of most potential buyers. Parliament was prepared to enforce the sale of books at reasonable prices if there were signs of profiteering. By an Act of 1533[2] it was ordered that if in the opinion of twelve honest and discreet persons any printer or bookseller should charge "too high and unreasonable prices" for books or the binding of them the Lord Chancellor, Lord Treasurer and two chief Justices, or any two of them, should have power to fix maximum prices and to fine the offender 3s. 4d. No action appears to have been taken on this clause, but the prices of new books were occasionally fixed by authority. Thus in the quarto edition of a work entitled "A necessary Doctrine and Erudition for any Christen Man, set furthe by the kynges maiestie of Englande," issued by the King's Printer, Thomas Berthelet, in 1543, is the note, "This boke in paper boordes or claspes, not to be solde aboue xvi d." The octavo edition, published on the same day, contained a similar order, limiting the price to xiii d.[3] Edward VI's Prayer Book (1549) has on the last page a royal edict giving full instructions as to the selling-price: "No maner of persone shall sell the present Booke vnbounde aboue the price of two shillynges and two pence. And bound in Forell for iis. xd., and not aboue. And the same bound in Shepes Lether for iiis. iiid., and not aboue. And the same bounde in paste or in boordes, in Calues Lether, not aboue the price of iiijs. the pece."

This method of price-fixing was seldom adopted. There seems, indeed, to have been little occasion for it. Actual prices of books appear quite low even when multiplied by six to give some approximation to present-day prices. The work which was probably in greatest demand in the sixteenth century, the children's book known as *The ABC and Little Catechism*, was in 1520 sold for as little as 1d. a copy in paper and 2d. in vellum.[4] Ballads at this time cost only ½d. each, with curious reductions in price for a quantity. John Dorne of Oxford sold them at the rate of two a penny, but frequently gave in an odd one without extra charge: for four ballads he charged 2d., for six 3d., for eight 4d., and so on, but the customer who wanted five obtained them for 2d., while he who required seven, nine, eleven or thirteen paid 3d., 4d. 5d. or 6d. respectively for them. The purchaser wanting ten ballads was thus well advised to make two journeys: by buying two batches of five he saved 1d. Dorne had also a good sale for "Kesmes corals" (Christmas carols), for which he charged 1d. each, and for such manuals as a "bocke of kokery," costing 4d. (His sales were not confined to this popular type of work; his day-book frequently records the sale of a Latin theological work whose price was in the neighbourhood of a pound.) Other books which had to be sold cheaply in order to attract custom were those from which the old women obtained their nostrums. These, such as "The Antidotharius, in the whiche thou mayst lerne howe thou shalt make many and dyuers noble playsters, salues, oyntmentes, powders, bawmes oyles, etc." (*c.* 1535) sold at ½d. or 1d. each.[5]

Apart from this lighter type of work, whose main appeal was to the uneducated classes, the steadiest demand was for religious works. Some light is thrown on the prices of these by the accounts of the royal printers and those of the churchwardens of various parishes. Of the fifteen copies of *The Golden Legend* which Caxton bequeathed to St. Margaret's Church, Westminster, two were sold by the churchwardens in 1496 for 6s. 8d. each while another was sold for 6s. 4d.; by 1512 the rest had been sold at prices averaging 5s. 8d.[6] Coverdale's Great Bible (1539), printed by Grafton, was sold at 10s. a copy unbound or 12s. bound. In 1542 Berthelet sent in an account to Henry VIII for several books, including "a newe Testament in Englisshe and Latyn of the largest volume, price ijs.," and for "a booke of the psalter in Englisshe and Latyne the price viijd. and a booke entiteled Enarracones Evangeliorum Dominicalium the price xijd." The prices quoted were normally for unbound books, so that in this case a further sum of 3s. 4d. was demanded "for the gorgious byndyng of them backe to backe."[7]

The churchwardens of St. Michael's, Cornhill, were frequent buyers of books, but at times they seemed rather uncertain as to what they had bought. For the year 1555–6 the entries in their account-book included, "Paide to the Curat for ij bookes called the homiles xvjd.; Paide for a booke for the Curat bought in Lombard Streate ijs.; Paide for ij bookes for the Preste ijs."[8] In 1563 "a little booke set forthe by the Bysshoppe" and "a little booke of Prayers sent from the Bysshoppe for the Curate to rede" both cost 2d., while in 1595 11s. 6d. was paid for "a gilte booke."[9] Fortunately, some of the information supplied is more definite. The prices of books of prayers for special occasions ranged from 2d. to 6d. Psalters cost 10d. each in 1548, 2s. 4d. in 1563 and 3s. 8d. in 1578. The new service book of 1560 together with the Ten Commandments cost 5s. 1d., but another service book was bought in 1565 for 18s. The sum of 27s. was paid for a Bible in 1569, and in 1573 the vestry ordered Foxe's *Book of Martyrs* together with a lock and chain and four keys, at a cost of 42s. 6d. How much of this latter amount was for the binding we are not told, but in 1595 it was arranged by the Stationers' Company "that peter Short shall finishe the Impression of the book of martyrs from the place where Mr. Denham left . . . For the Whiche he is to haue after the rate of xvijs. vid. for a booke."[10]

Plays were cheap in comparison with other books. The usual price for them at the end of the sixteenth century, even for the quarto running into 10 sheets, was only 6d. Yet a book of this size, consisting of 80 quarto pages or 160 in octavo, normally cost 1s., while one of 20 sheets cost 2s.[11] Shakespeare's First Folio (1623) is said to have been sold at the high price of 20s., but this is explainable by the fact that the work ran into nearly 1,000 pages, as well as by the general rise in the price-level.

Some idea of the fall in the value of money as shown in the prices of books can be gathered from the increasing expense of providing psalters for St. Michael's, Cornhill, as shown above. The evidence here is sufficient only to show the general tendency; we cannot be sure that the volumes were uniform as regards production. The *Paraphrases of Erasmus*, a work directed to be placed in every parish church, will provide a safer example. The copy of it bought by St. Michael's in 1548 cost 5s. Five years later the churchwardens of Marston, Oxfordshire, paid 6s. 8d. for their copy.[12] In the St. Michael's accounts for 1587 is the entry "Paide unto Mr. Sadler for avoidinge of an excomunicacion for not having in our Churche a paraphrasis of Erasmus iijs. viijd."; followed by, "Paide for a booke called the paraphrasis of Erasmus xiijs."[13] In the circumstances it is likely that the churchwardens bought the cheapest edition which they could find. Thus in less than forty years the price of this work had more than doubled, even allowing for possible variations in binding.

As usual, the rise in prices was ascribed to any reason but the right one, which was the fall in general purchasing-power brought about by the influx of silver from America and by the debasing of the coinage. As in the case of so many other commodities, the blame for the high prices of books was laid upon the holders of the most coveted monopolies. The writer of the anonymous tract *Scintilla* (1641)[14] was specially severe in his denunciation of the King's Printer, whom he accused of raising the price of the Authorised Version of the Bible by £1,500 on an impression of three thousand. *The London Bible Quarto English Letter* again, "with the Notes and Concordance of the old Translation in times past was sold at 7sh. in quires, and then it was 139 sheets, and now but 116 and no Notes, and sold at 9sh. 2d. with Concordance." The holder of the patent for Greek works also came in for criticism: "Camdens Greek Grammar sold at 8d. a Book in quires alwayes, now sold at 1sh. 2d. Raysed 6d. on a Book." As a remedy the writer suggested that the Statute 25 Henry VIII. c. 15 concerning the prices of books should be put into operation, but times were too troubled for any such regulation. In any case, the Government by now had begun to realise the futility of such an action.

The prices quoted for books were usually for the unbound sheets. Binding, at least in the sixteenth century, normally required a separate order to the bookseller, and might more than double the original cost of the book. Berthelet undertook the binding of the volumes which he sold to Henry VIII, and in 1542 rendered an account "for a little psalter, takyng out of one booke and settyng in an other in the same place, and for gorgious byndyng of the same booke xijd. and to the Goldesmythe for taking of [f] the claspes and corners and for settyng on the same ageyne xvjd." For a New Testament and psalter, bound together, "the bookes came to ijs., the byndyng and arabaske drawyng in golde on the transfile iiijs."[15] These royal bindings were specially elaborate, and not for general use. This appears from a later item in Berthelet's bill: "V Tullius de officijs bounde in paper bourdes at xvjd. the pece and one gorgiously gilted for the kinges highnes price iijs. iiijd." Charges varied with the choice of materials, and seem to have formed about the same proportion of the total cost of the book as at the present day. In 1581 parchment bindings for volumes belonging to James VI of Scotland cost 3s. each; vellum bindings were 5s., and "gylt" (probably morocco) cost 10s. "A generall note of the prises for binding of all sorts of bookes," issued in 1619, quotes prices ranging from 15s. for a church Bible in folio gilt to 2d. for octavo grammars in sheep's leather.

It would be interesting to know what was the effect of the invention of printing upon the prices of books, but for various reasons it is impossible to form any true estimate. Where printing was a substitute for hand-lettering it was presumably cheaper, but the work in manuscript and the early printed book were not really comparable. The value of the printed book depended upon its power to instruct or to amuse; the manuscript, on the other hand, might be of considerable value for its artistic production even though its text were worthless. Printing, again, had created its own market. There was no manuscript work with which one could compare the halfpenny ballad of the sixteenth century: such tales had been spread hitherto by word of mouth. Pamphlet-literature was also a product of the printing age. In the case of classical works matters were rather different: there had been a demand for them throughout the Middle Ages; but how is one to assess the monetary cost of a book produced by the joint labours of several monks in the course of their religious duties? Even where the various items of expenditure are known, there are difficulties of interpretation. Here, for instance, is an entry from the account book of the Church of St. Ewen, Bristol, for 1468, showing the cost of a manuscript lesson-book, called a "Legend":

i. doss [dozen] and v. quayers [quires] to perform ye Legend		xs.	vid.
Item for wrytyng of ye same		xxvs.	
Item for ix. skynns and i. quayer of vellom to same Legend		vs.	vid.
Item wrytyng ye foreseyd Legend		iiis.	ivd.
Also for a red skynne to kever the Legend			vd.
Item for binding and correcting of the said boke		vs.	
Also for guming of the said Legend		xiiis.	vid.
Also for clensyng of the same boke			xiid.
Total	iii*l*.	ivs.	iiid.

This total would be about equal to £30 in modern money. The two separate entries for "wrytyng" the Legend are puzzling; it may be that the first refers to authorship and the second to copying; or the first amount may have been paid to the man who wrote on the seventeen quires and the second to a different person who wrote on the vellum.

The most satisfactory means of comparing the prices of manuscripts and printed books is to find what the scriveners were actually charging during the first century of printing. In 1548 the churchwardens of St. Michael's, Cornhill, paid 5s. "to the scolle Mr of Polles for wrytyng of the masse in Englysh and ye benedicites."[16] A printed "communion booke" bought a few years later cost only 4d. In 1562 the Stationers' Company paid 26s. 8d. to Edward Cater for copying the Constitutions of the Company, having provided him with vellum and a shilling's worth of red ink for the purpose.[17] The charge for writing a letter in 1570 was 8d., while twenty-five years later the Stationers' Company had to pay 5s. for a copy of a will.[18] At this same time the clerk to the Company was given 10s. for writing two copies of the Star Chamber decrees, with a further 1s. 6d. for a copy of a *Commission to Suppresse Disorders*. Most of these charges seem at least ten times as high as for a printed work of the same length.

To be comprehensible the prices of books need to be related to those of other commodities: it is of little use to say that the prices of the late sixteenth century should be multiplied by six to give an approximation to prices in 1914 unless we know the individual items which made up the general price-level; many commodities included in a twentieth-century price-index were unknown in the sixteenth. On investigation, then, we find that the man who in 1520 spent 1d. on two ballads might be denying himself two pounds of cheese or a pound of butter. For 2d. he could buy a hen, or for 6d. a pair of shoes. A sheep in 1595 cost about 9s., or rather less than the price of an unbound copy of the Bible. A pig could be bought at that time for 1s. 2d., while beef was 2d. a pound. Soap cost 4d. a pound in 1590, and starch was 6d.[19] The Stationers' Company in 1559 spent 6d. on "flowers for the pottes in ye wyndowyes" in preparation for the annual banquet and paid 2s. 2d. to the cook "for bakynge of vij pastyes of venyson and vij tartes at his howse"; a few years later 6d. was paid "for a newe bottom to the buckett" and 6d. more "for sweepinge of Twoo chymneyes in ye kitchin."[20]

For some time after the Great Fire of 1666, which played such havoc with booksellers' stocks, there was inevitably a rise in the prices of those books already published which had more than an ephemeral interest. Pepys was well aware of the increase, but could not quite understand it. In his diary under March 20, 1666–67, he wrote, "It is strange how Rycaut's 'Discourse of Turky,' which before the fire I was asked but 8s. for, there being all but twenty-two or thereabouts burned, I did now offer 20s., and he demands 50s., and I think I shall give it him, though it be only as a monument of the fire." The prices of new publications, too, may have been indirectly affected by the fire through the destruction of part of the supply of paper. Milton's *Paradise Lost*, for instance, in the small quarto edition of 1667, cost 3s. in a plain binding, whereas Ponder's bound edition of *Pilgrim's Progress*, eleven years later, was only 1s. 6d. This is only conjecture. The system of fixing published prices of books had not become general; until the end of the seventeenth century the retailer was free to sell at the prices he thought fit, in spite of the Act of Henry VIII. There may well, therefore, have been wide variations in the prices charged for copies of the same work.

By the beginning of the eighteenth century booksellers' catalogues were more regularly being issued with the price marked against each item. The normal price for an ordinary octavo volume was 5s. or 6s.; a duodecimo cost from 2s. 6d. to 3s., and a folio or quarto 10s. to 12s.[21] The specially well-produced book might cost far more. The third volume of Clarendon's *History*, in 1704, was sold at 30s., and Hickes's *Thesaurus* at £5.[22] Earhard's *History of England* (1718) was £3 15s. A Bible on elephant paper, two years later, cost £3 5s., and the two silk strings to it were another 25s. One on royal paper cost £5. In the meantime further legal restrictions had been imposed. The fourth clause of the Copyright Act of 1709[23] provided that on any complaint of unreasonable prices the Archbishop of Canterbury or some other "discreet" person should settle the matter; in that case a fine of £5 should be levied for any book sold at too high a price. The clause in question was repealed by an Act of George II, probably owing to a belated understanding that the bookseller might know his own business.

It is unlikely, as things happened, that the official ban on high prices had attracted much attention. For one thing, publication by subscription was coming to the fore; if the proposals sent out to possible subscribers fixed too high a price the project merely collapsed for want of support. Then again, the eighteenth-century bookseller seems to have developed a long view of his own interest, none more so than Mr. C——. One of his customers asked him for "the works of a writer, whose sentiments are generally supposed to be unfavourable to the cause of Christianity. On being asked the price, Mr. C—— took occasion to express his abhorrence of the sentiments imputed to the writer, and declared with much earnestness 'that he would not read them himself for all the wealth in the world.' The purchaser urged Mr. C——'s opinion of the book as an argument to obtain an abatement in the price. Of this plea Mr. C—— admitted the force; and, to prove his sincerity, astonished the purchaser by a *voluntary* deduction of two-thirds of the price he had fixed, observing that 'he thought the book *dear at any price*'."[24] That being so, it would perhaps have been better to burn his copies rather than facilitate their circulation.

The fixing of prices, where the publisher had omitted them, called for careful judgment on the part of the retailer. The wholesale cost to him was a clear enough guide as to the lowest charge which he could afford to make, but how high a price was in the end to be most profitable? James Lackington confessed that for several years he had been charging far too much; as he gathered experience he found that he gained more by selling at less than a half of his former prices.[25] As far as one can tell there certainly seems to have been a good margin of profit on sales. There was one work, the *Historical Register*, whose quarterly numbers were in 1740 being sold at 1s. each; but if the prospective buyer happened to hold a policy in the Sun Fire Office he could for some reason get them for 6d.[26] For second-hand volumes price-fixing was easy enough: the bookseller had merely to arrange for an auction sale; the judgment was then left to his customers, who, knowing the reputation of the various items, outbid one another for the more famous works and left the rest. It was in this way that a Virgil incunabulum in 1721 fetched what one librarian considered the "unaccountably high" price of £46. The man who bought it knew better, for "he huzza'd out aloud, and threw up his hat for joy that he had bought it so cheap."[27] The customer could not be called upon so directly to fix the prices of new publications, even though the bookseller were willing to make a new bargain for every volume he sold. Where the bookseller did fix a uniform price for a whole edition he was liable to be accused of overcharging, but, after all, the remedy was in the customer's hands. As Dr. Johnson replied in the name of one so accused, "If, therefore, I have set a high value upon books—if I have vainly imagined literature to be more fashionable than it really is, or idly hoped to revive a taste well nigh extinguished, I know not why I should be persecuted with clamour and invective, since I shall only suffer by my mistake, and be obliged to keep those books which I was in hopes of selling."[28]

Advertising

With many alternative methods of spending money and no system of compulsory education what was the inducement to buy books? Clearly, at a time when those most anxious to read were so often least able to buy, some system of advertising was urgently needed to arouse the interest of the moneyed classes. Advertising was actually almost neglected throughout the first century or more. Even the booksellers' catalogue was unknown until the year 1595. The title-page, with its possibilities of advertising by making known the author's qualifications and his works previously published, in the earlier years of printing gave only the name of the book, without reference even to the author's name. It was many years before publishers began to realise the value of a short, pithy title as a means of popularising a work. Here, for instance, is a typical title of a late sixteenth-century ballad: "Trewe and Dreadfull new tydinges of bloode and Brymston which God hathe caused to Rayne from heaven within and without the cytie Strale Sonet, with a wonderfull apparition seene by a citizen of the same Cytie named Hans Germer whiche mett him in the feild as he was travaylinge on the waie." There was little hope that the reader to whom this ballad had been recommended would remember its name by the time he reached the bookshop! And here is the sixteenth-century title in spite of which the story of *The Babes in the Wood* has won popularity: "The Norfolk gent his will and testament and howe he commytted the keepinge of his Children to his owne brother whoe delte moste wickedly with them and howe God plagued him for it."

By the Elizabethan period there was some attempt to advertise new publications: the title-page came to be nailed up on the whipping-posts in the streets, on the pillars in St. Paul's, and on the walls of the Inns of Court. An account of an assault made on two of Richard Baldwin's apprentices some years later mentions that it was an established custom for bookbinders' servants every Saturday night to post up the titles of those works which were to be bound during the coming week.[29] (The posting up of titles was, incidentally, a return to the advertising methods of the Roman Empire.) The growing practice, too, of reading in the booksellers' shops as a fashionable pastime, although exasperating enough to the bookseller, may also at times have recompensed him by the publicity which it afforded to his stock. Nevertheless, it can scarcely be said that there was much deliberate advertising before the middle of the seventeenth century. Considering the scant regard which seems in other respects to have been paid to the wishes of the author it is perhaps assuming too much to say that in this the publisher did give way to him. At all events, it was true enough that many authors shunned publicity. The fear of appearing vulgar led to several expressions such as this:

> I have common made my book; 'tis very true;
> But I'd not have thee prostitute it too;
> Nor show it barefaced on the open stall
> To tempt the buyer; nor poast it on each wall
> And corner poast, close underneath the Play
> That must be acted at *Black-Friers* to-day;
> Nor see some Herring-cryer for a groat
> To voice it up and down with tearing throat;
> Nor bid thy 'prentice read it and admire,
> That all i' the shop may what he reads inquire;
> No: profer'd wares do smel: I'd have thee know
> Pride scorns to beg: modestie fears to wooe.[30]

That was all very well. The bookseller could not afford to subscribe to the modesty of a mere author.

By the second half of the seventeenth century an advertising medium had arisen which could scarcely offend the most retiring of authors. The journals then coming into being had space, after discussing the more arresting news of the day, to give in dignified form a note of newly published books, pamphlets or plays. Some of the new periodicals, it is true, appeared only for one or two issues, but others speedily arose in their place; after about 1660 there was always some journal open to receive Press notices. It must be admitted that the general tone of the notices was strikingly unlike that of present-day announcements. Here is one blunt statement from the *Mercurius Publicus*, No. 1 (1661): "There is stolen abroad a most false and imperfect copy of a poem, called *Hudibras*, without name either of printer or bookseller, as fit for so lame and spurious an impression. The true and perfect edition, printed by the author's original, is sold by Richard Marriott, under St. Dunstan's Church in Fleet-Street; that other nameless impression is a cheat, and will but abuse the Buyer as well as the Author, whose Poem deserves to have fallen into better hands."

In 1680 there appeared a journal similar to the *Publishers' Circular* of modern times: the *Mercurius Librarius*, designed to appear weekly, or at least once a fortnight. In the second number (April 16–22) booksellers were invited to send in books or pamphlets which they wished to have included in the list. The charge for insertion was 6d. for each item. Any other advertisement relating to the trade would be accepted for 1s., "unless it be excessive long." Very few numbers seem to have been issued. In October of the same year there appeared another paper on the same lines, the *Weekly Advertisement of Books*, printed by R. Everingham and annexed to the *City Mercury*. The sixth number, of November 11th, advertised itself in subtle terms: "It is not unknown to Booksellers, that there are two papers of this nature weekly published; which, for general satisfaction, we shall distinguish. That printed by Thomas James is published by Mr. Vile, only for the lucre of 12d. per Book. This printed by Robert Everingham is published by several Booksellers, who do more eye the Service of the Trade, in making all Books as public as may be, than the profit of Insertions. All men are, therefore, left to judge who is most likely to prosecute these ends effectually; whether a person that is no Bookseller, nor hath any relation to that trade, or those who have equal ends with all others of the trade, in dispersing the said papers both in city and country." One feels tempted to give the answer which was not expected: for "the lucre of 12d. per book," presumably, any book would be advertised; a clique of booksellers, on the other hand, might find it expedient to overlook the publications of the rival bookseller who threatened to attract too much of their own trade. As it happened, neither journal continued for long. There seem to have been no further efforts on the same lines until the eighteenth century, with "The Gentleman's Journal, and Tradesman's Companion: containing the News Foreign and Domestick . . . and a Catalogue of the Books and Pamphlets published in the Week" (1721) and "The Monthly Catalogue; being a general Register of Books, Sermons, Plays, and Pamphlets, printed and published in London or the Universities" (1725). In the meantime book announcements could be inserted in the more general periodicals, such as *The Protestant Mercury* (1699) and *The Observator*

Reformed (1704), at a charge of 1s. for an advertisement of eight lines or thereabouts.

Booksellers' catalogues gradually became fairly common. In 1698 John Dunton was issuing separate catalogues for each of his auctions, and was having them distributed free at various coffee-houses.[31] Half a century later the coffee-house was still being used in this way as a repository for reference-catalogues. A note on the back of the title-page of Osborne and Shipton's catalogue of 1754 implies that it was the normal procedure: "Notwithstanding these Two large Volumes of the Catalogue are attended with a great Expence, they are, as usual, sent to the most eminent Coffee-houses in and near Town, for Gentlemen's Perusal, who are earnestly desired not to take them away; and if taken away, a Fine laid upon the Landlord or Landlady of the House; for, as this Sale will continue for Two Years, they will always be an Amusement to Gentlemen."[32] Apparently the landlord, far from rendering a service to the bookseller, was held to be under an obligation to him for attracting extra custom to the coffee-house!

It was not every bookseller who could afford to issue special catalogues. He might instead introduce into each of his books a leaf giving the names of other works printed for or sold by him. That was the practice, for instance, of Thomas Warren, a well-known Birmingham bookseller of the early eighteenth century.[33] Although the underlying intention of these lists may have been to give the impression that no books of any other publisher could be as good, one does not often find a deliberate statement to that effect. One is certainly known to us. In 1734–5 Jacob Tonson was publishing an edition of the six plays attributed to Shakespeare, and seems to have worried lest a rival publisher should spoil the market for him. He therefore inserted a warning note in one of his volumes, *The History of Sir John Oldcastle*: "N.B.—Whereas one R. Walker has proposed to pirate all Shakespear's plays, but through ignorance of what plays are Shakespear's, did in several advertisements propose to print 'Oedipus King of Thebes' as one of Shakespear's plays; and has since printed Tate's 'King Lear' instead of Shakespear's, and in that and Hamlet has omitted one half of the genuine edition printed by J. Tonson and the other proprietors; the world will therefore judge how likely they are to have a complete collection of Shakespear's plays from the said R. Walker."

John Newbery seems to have been particularly happy in his drafting of advertisements. He had the knack of addressing himself directly to the children for whom he was publishing, and making them want more. Those of us who remember *Goody Two Shoes* possibly recall a passage which did not strike us at the time as the advertisement it really was: "She then sung the 'Cuzz's Chorus' (which may be found in the 'Little Pretty Plaything' published by Mr. Newbery)." Several of his publications were linked up in the same way. With some of his books he offered small presents, such as balls and pincushions.[34] Some of his newspaper announcements make delightful reading. Here is one from the *London Chronicle* of December 19, 1765: "The Philosophers, Politicians, Necromancers, and the learned in every faculty are desired to observe that on the 1st of January, being New Year's Day (oh, that we all may lead new lives!), Mr. Newbery intends to publish the following important volumes, bound and gilt, and hereby invites all his little friends who are good to call for them at the Bible and Sun in St. Paul's Churchyard, but those who are naughty to have none."

The eighteenth century was the age of subscription-publication. Subscriptions might be invited through the medium of the newspapers, but usually a number of prospectuses were sent to likely purchasers. It was not often that so many were sent out as John Bridges circulated for his *History and Antiquities of the County of Northampton*: the 7,000 proposals of 1735 were followed 10 years later by 1,650 more.[35] But surely it was seldom that a publisher resorted to the methods adopted for advertising Smollett's *History*: packets of prospectuses were sent, with half a crown enclosed, to every parish clerk in the kingdom for distribution through the pews of the church.[36]

By the middle of the eighteenth century authors had lost their one-time aversion to advertising, and were inclined to blame their failures on the negligence of their publishers. For all that, advertising was still inadequate, and seems scarcely to have reached the general public at all. James Lackington recalls that he and his friends had for many years been ashamed to go into booksellers' shops, having no idea at all as to what they wanted. "I assure you, my friend," he says, "that there are thousands now in England in the very same situation: many, very many, have come to my shop, who have discovered an enquiring mind, but were totally at a loss what to ask for, and who had no friend to direct them."[37]

Bookshops

Lackington's youthful diffidence in entering bookshops was not due to any novelty in them. They were to be found in many towns from quite early times. The wardens' accounts of the Church of St. Nicholas, Hull, for instance, record the purchase of a (manuscript) missal from a local bookseller in the year 1469.[38] There was a bookseller living in Lichfield in 1576, for in that year his son, John Martin, was apprenticed to Robert Walley of London.[39] In the Star Chamber case of John Day *v.* Ward and Holmes, 1582, it was stated that a number of copies of the *ABC* had been sent to a bookshop in Shrewsbury. Four years later "Richard Snape son of Henry Snape of the parish of Asbery in the countie of Chester bookeseller" became an apprentice.[40] The trade of the provincial booksellers could scarcely have been very extensive. Even at the beginning of the eighteenth century, although Michael Johnson had bookshops in Lichfield, Uttoxeter, Ashby-de-la-Zouche and Birmingham, it seems that the shop at Birmingham, and probably the ones at Uttoxeter and Ashby, were open only on market days.[41]

In London St. Paul's Churchyard had become established as the main bookselling quarter by 1500, and there were few printer-publishers of note who did not maintain a shop or at least a stall there. These stalls opened very early in the morning: in a deposition before the Coroner of London in December 1514, Thomas Symonds, stationer, stated that a certain Charles Joseph came to him at his stall "within a quarter of an hower after vii. a clock in the morning"[42]—a decidedly chilly hour for bookselling in December! In the course of the next century the stalls were cleared away from the Churchyard to other parts of the city; by about 1750 they seem to have congregated especially in Moorfields.[43] But not all of the trade in books in the eighteenth century was carried on in regular bookshops or stalls. When publication by subscription was at its height it was quite usual for the author himself to supply the customers. For example, when the second edition of Tomlinson's *The Art of Dancing* appeared in 1744, it was advertised as being on sale by the author, "at the Red and Gold Flower Pot, next door to the Widow Edwards's Coffee-house, over-against the Bull and Gate in Holborn."[44] Charles Jennens, the editor of Shakespeare's works, was more original in his choice of a bookseller: he had had a period of bad fortune which he blamed on the machinations of publishers and booksellers; determined to be freed from their ill practices, "the important sinecure of vending his Works he at last conferred on the truly honest Master Owen of the Mineral Water Warehouse at Temple Bar."[45] It was the pawnbrokers who, in Lackington's opinion, had the most profitable book trade at that time. He himself sold large numbers of books to them, and the volumes were soon resold at much higher prices to purchasers who, assuming them to have been pawned, thought that they were securing bargains. Some of the so-called pawnbrokers, it seems, managed to carry on a profitable business without ever actually taking in any pawns at all![46]

An even more unexpected bookselling establishment was Vere Street Theatre. It was here that Ogilby, the writer on English roads, ran the book-lotteries advertised in the *Gazette* for May 1668. He charged an entrance-fee of 5s. and awarded thirty-six prizes of books worth from £51 down to £4. Lotteries were a sure way of attracting money, as the Government itself was finding. Swift tried his fortune on one occasion, but complained that he had lost £4 7s. to the bookseller and obtained only half a dozen books.[47]

Trade in the London bookshops seems at one time to have been so brisk that the proprietors were with difficulty restrained from selling books during the prohibited hours. In 1558 the Stationers' Company fined Master Walley and Master Smythe 5s. 8d. "for that they ded kepe thayre shoppes open festivall daye and solde bokes."[48] In the following year Richard Waterson was fined 1s. 8d. for opening his shop on a Sunday, while in 1564 nineteen people were fined for selling books on St. Luke's Day. There were a number of similar instances during the next few years. The most incorrigible offender was Arthur Pepwell: in 1560 he was fined 6d. for opening his shop on Sundays; shortly afterwards he had to pay 1s. for repeating the offence; apparently he found that even this left him with a good margin of profit on his Sunday sales, for in 1562 he was fined a further 3s. 4d., a sum which appears to have been big enough to check his enterprise.

These fines were small compared with those which the Company levied in attempting to obtain the complete monopoly of the trade. Hitherto books were frequently to be found among the other wares on the counters of drapers' and haberdashers' shops, or as part of the stock-in-trade of the pedlar. Sale by pedlars was made illegal in London by the middle of the sixteenth century, and the Company took advantage of its right to confiscate books offered for sale in this way; thus in 1561 the Register records the receipt of 4s. 4d. from the sale of "serten bokes in frynshe and Englesshe which was taken goynge hawkynge aboute the stretes which ys contrary to the orders of the Cytie of London."[49] Sale to members of other companies was forbidden by the Stationers, and occasioned some of the heaviest fines ever exacted by the Company. Thomas Purfoot had to pay £6 13s. 4d. on the charge that in 1565 he had sold primers [prayer books] to the haberdashers, and had to bring in a surety for £100 against a repetition of the offence. Strangely enough, two years later he was fined only £2 for having sold both primers and catechisms to the haberdashers.[50] The problem had not been solved to the Company's satisfaction even at the end of the century, and for a time it had become the practice to grant the copyright of ballads only "provided that noe Drapers name be set to them."[51] The Star Chamber decree of July 11, 1637, should have settled the matter: the tenth clause runs, "*Item*, that no Haberdasher of small wares, Ironmonger, Chandler, Shop-keeper, or any other person or persons whatsoeuer, not hauing beene seuen yeeres apprentice to the trade of a Book-seller, Printer, or Book-binder, shall within the citie or suburbs of London, or in any other Corporation, Market-towne, or elswhere, receive, take or buy, to barter, sell againe, change or do away any Bibles, Testaments, Psalm-books, Primers, Abcees, Almanackes, or other booke or books whatsoeuer, vpon pain of forfeiture of all such books so receiued, bought or taken as aforesaid. . . . " The political upheaval of the following years caused the decree to remain ineffectual. In any case, it is doubtful whether its enforcement would have been in the interests of the customer. Until late in the eighteenth century there were many small towns and villages with no shops at all, and the population had to rely on the visits of pedlars, or "chapmen," for anything they wanted to buy, from haberdashery to "chap-books."[52] Moreover, the individual members of the Stationers' Company were in any case not all above fraudulent dealing. In 1558, for example, William Jones was fined "for that he solde a Communion boke of kynge Edwardes for one of the newe."[53]

Wholesale Prices

We have little information regarding the profits from bookselling in the earlier period. The English publisher was often his own retailer, while until quite late in the sixteenth century the contents of a bookshop were frequently acquired by a system of exchange rather than by purchase. One entry in the Stationers' Register for 1577 does give some idea of the usual rate of profit: this was an agreement that Mr. Watkins should pay Dunstan Whapland either thirty shillings' worth of books or 26s. 8d. in ready money.[54] (Christophe Plantin of Antwerp allowed his bookselling customers an average discount of 15 per cent. In the case of the "Bible Royale," included in his catalogue of 1576, the price to the public was 70 florins and to dealers 60 florins.)[55] There are one or two instances of sale on credit and of reduction of price on the sale of a quantity. Thus in July 1592 it was agreed that Edward

JOHN DUNTON

From his *Life and Errors*

From Lackington's *Memoirs*

White should buy up John Legatt's stock of *The Golden Chain* at the rate of £4 16s. a hundred, the sum to be paid in three instalments in May, August and November, of the following year.[56] About this time it was ordered that *Bullinger's Decades* should be sold to all freemen of the Stationers' Company "at the rate of Fyve shillinges the peece [and not aboue], and shall allowe to euerie one of them that buyethe a quarterne of the same together, one Booke freelye and without demaundinge anythinge for the same one booke";[57] that is, twenty-six were to be sold for the price of twenty-five. Similar arrangements were at times made by the individual publisher. In 1578 Christopher Barker issued a circular offering his large Bible to the London companies on advantageous terms. He arranged to send out copies of the Bible on approval, and suggested that the clerk of each company should send him a list of the members wishing to buy one. Barker would then deliver the volumes at the price of 24s. bound or 20s. unbound (although "if it were prised at XXXs. it were scarce sufficient"), and would allow the clerk of the company 4d. commission on each copy sold; and to any company whose members bought forty pounds' worth he would give one Bible for use in the common hall. "Further if there be anie that is not willing to disburse present money, may haue time till Candlemas next, so that the Master and wardens be then answerable for so many bookes as shall be so deliuered . . . and although here can rise no great gaine to me in this bargaine, yet must I needs thinke my selfe bounden to this most honourable citie."[58]

Even in the eighteenth century wholesale prices were sometimes regarded as a special inducement. The notice of William Loughton's *A Practical Grammar of the English Tongue* (1737) gives the price as 1s. 6d., "with allowances to school-masters, and those who buy a number."[59] Newbery, in the list of books for children which he issued in March, 1759, vaguely draws attention to his policy of making "great allowances" to those who buy quantities to sell again. Some of his advertisements show the actual reduction which he was prepared to make. The *Colloquia Selecta* of Corderius, for example, was 1s. 6d. a copy or 15s. a dozen.[60]

The Organisation of the Book Trade

Perhaps we may assume that by the middle of the eighteenth century the trade was becoming organised somewhat on the lines described by Samuel Johnson. In 1766, writing a letter on the management of the Clarendon Press, he took as an illustration the case of an imaginary agent in London, "Mr. Cadell," who was selling to "Mr. Dilly," a wholesale bookseller, who again sold to a country bookseller. " . . . We must allow, for profit," he maintained, "between thirty and thirty-five *per cent.*, between six and seven shillings in the pound; that is, for every book which costs the last buyer twenty shillings, we must charge Mr. Cadell with something less than fourteen. We must set the copies at fourteen shillings each, and superadd what is called the quarterly-book, or for every hundred books so charged we must deliver a hundred and four. The profits will then stand thus: Mr. Cadell, who runs no hazard, and gives no credit, will be paid for warehouse room and attendance by a shilling profit on each book, and his chance of the quarterly-book. Mr. Dilly, who buys the book for fifteen shillings, and who will expect the quarterly-book if he takes five-and-twenty, will send it to his country customer at sixteen and sixpence, by which, at the hazard of less, and the certainty of long credit, he gains the regular profit of ten *per cent.* which is expected in the wholesale trade. The country bookseller, buying at sixteen and sixpence, and commonly trusting a considerable time, gains but three and sixpence, and if he trusts a year, not much more than two and sixpence; otherwise than as he may, perhaps, take as long credit as he gives. With less profit than this, and more you see he cannot have, the country bookseller cannot live; for his receipts are small, and his debts sometimes bad."

Lackington would have said that the difficulties which beset the bookseller who granted long credit were entirely his own fault. He himself had begun by allowing credit to his customers, but soon found that he was making a mistake. He found that most of his bills were not paid for six months and some of them not for two years. Many tradesmen of his acquaintance had accounts of seven years' standing, and were in consequence handicapped for lack of ready money. The whole position seemed so unsatisfactory that he resolved to give up the practice. His porters were from henceforth given a strict order to bring back all books for which the money was not forthcoming on delivery. The result, he found, was that he could sell more cheaply than before and thereby attract an ever growing body of customers.[61] By 1791 he was able to record an annual profit of £4,000.

Before Lackington made his name there were few big undertakings in the bookselling world. In the sixteenth century the business on the largest scale was probably that of John Day, whose stock was at one time stated to be worth £3,000.[62] One of the most notable booksellers of the first half of the seventeenth century was George Thomason, of St. Paul's Churchyard, famous for his collection of Civil War tracts. Some idea of the size of his business may be gathered from his catalogue of works imported from Italy in the year 1647: the list includes 1,970 books and manuscripts, 1,302 being in Latin, 294 in Italian, 36 in Spanish, 6 in Scandinavian languages, 300 in Hebrew and 32 in Arabic, Coptic, Persian, Syriac and Turkish.[63] Parliament ordered the Hebrew works for Cambridge University, and agreed to pay Thomason £500 for them. Eight months later he was still unpaid and, such was the financial stringency of the time, he had then to be content with receiving interest of 8 per cent on the unpaid capital.[64]

The Importation of Books

Thomason stated in the preface to his catalogue that no books from Italy had been brought to this country for nine years, nor were any likely to come in the future. There had, in fact, for over a century been obstacles in the way of importing books. The Act for Printers and Binders of Books, 1533, had repealed the Act 1 Ric. III. c. 9, which had encouraged importation of books; it was now ordered that "noo person or persones recyant or inhabytaunt within this Realme . . . shall bye to sell agayn any prynted bokes brought frome any partes out of the Kynges obeysaunce redy bounden in bourdes lether or perchement . . . No person

. . . shall by within this Realme of any Stranger borne out of the Kynges obedyence other then of denyzens, any maner of prynted bokes brought frome any the parties behonde the See, except only by engrose and not by retayle." The intention of the latter clause was doubtless to prevent the sale of seditious literature. (The regulation was similar to the one enforced by the University and Booksellers' Gild of Paris in the sixteenth and seventeenth centuries: foreigners were forbidden to buy or sell at the fairs of St. Germain and St. Laurent; and they were forbidden to go to Paris for more than three weeks in the year, or to accept orders from any but the booksellers of the Gild.)[65] Further restrictions had been imposed in 1539. Injunctions were set forth in that year by the King's authority against persons who imported and sold *English* books without special licence.[66] A proclamation of 1555 was specially designed to repress heresy: it forbade, under cover of a Statute 2 Henry IV, the importation of "the bokes, writinges, or workes" of Luther, Calvin, Melancthon, Erasmus, Latimer, Coverdale, Tyndale, Cranmer and others, "and the booke commonly called 'Halle's Cronycles' . . . or any other lyke booke . . . conteyning false doctryne contrarye to the and agaynste the Catholyque faythe and the doctryne of the Catholyque churche."[67] This order was destined to lapse after three years with the re-establishment of the Church of England. None of the regulations had excluded foreign-printed books altogether. That would have been intellectual suicide, for our own Press was not yet capable of satisfying the needs of the scholar. As late as the year 1563, in classifying French imports as "necessary" and "superfluous," it was thought advisable to include "books (unbound)" in the first group.[68] In the following year Cecil sent a memorandum to the Lord Treasurer arranging that Arnold Birckman and Conrad Mollar of Cologne should be allowed to land five tubs and two baskets full of books, together with some boxes of green ginger, which they had already shipped from Antwerp.[69]

By the end of the sixteenth century several booksellers were paying regular visits to the continental book fairs; John Bill, for instance, spent much time abroad between 1596 and 1603 in buying books for Sir Thomas Bodley; but the Thirty Years' War (1618-48) almost suspended the trade with Frankfurt, Leipzig and Cologne, the chief centres of the book trade. In the meantime an effort was made to protect the university presses: a proclamation of April 1, 1625, forbade the sale of Latin works reprinted abroad "havinge been first printed in Oxford or Cambridge."[70] The second Star Chamber decree concerning printing, 1637, imposed new restrictions, ordering that no foreigner not a freeman of the Stationers' Company should bring in any book printed abroad, and also that no books should be imported to any place other than the port of London, "to the end the said Bookes may there be viewed."

Later policy was closely connected with the question of the paper-duties. The Copyright Act of 1709 made it an offence to import English books, but that did not satisfy the booksellers. They argued, as we have seen, that by the current rates of taxation it was far cheaper to import books than paper, and demanded a complete embargo on books. Buckley, afterwards Master of the Stationers' Company, did obtain a special Act of Parliament in 1733 to prohibit the importation of one work, Thuanus's *History* in Latin, on the plea that an imported copy could be sold here at a lower price than the work cost him to produce.[71] Fortunately, this was not taken as a precedent.

There is no doubt that during all this time prohibited books did find their way to England. It was, indeed, the practice of printing the more unorthodox theological works in Antwerp or some other continental centre which kept alive the religious controversies of the sixteenth century. Once the books had been smuggled into this country their sale must have been a fairly easy matter. As at the present day, the surest result of condemning a book was a rapid growth in the demand for it. Raleigh's *History of the World*, for example, had a better sale after its attempted suppression than before, although, as a precaution, it was now sold without a title-page. It is probable that, as Professor Thorold Rogers suggested, prohibited and unlicensed works were sold at fairs, places which were "at once so open and so secret."[72]

Fairs

The fairs had not lost their mediaeval importance as trading-centres. We had here no fair so noteworthy as the great book marts of Frankfurt and Leipzig, to which the chief European publishers regularly sent large consignments of books, but attendance at the principal English fairs, including those of Oxford, Stourbridge, Coventry, Bristol and Ely, was customary for the London stationers until the end of the seventeenth century. There seems to have been a special art in buying at the fairs. John Dunton speaks of a Mr. Shrowsbury as being a frequenter of Stourbridge Fair, and says of him that perhaps he is "the only Bookseller that understands *Fair-keeping* to any advantage."[73] (Three of the booths at Stourbridge were at one time owned by a local printer, Robert Leete, who on his death in 1663 left them to his wife.)[74]

Many a bookseller found the fair more profitable than his own shop; in a controversy over the rights of the Cambridge University printer mention was made of "Sturbridge faier now drawinge neere, beinge the chiefest time, wherein he hopeth to reape greatest fruite of this his travaile."[75] But there was another side to the question. In 1583 the wardens of the Stationers' Company, appealing to the Privy Council against John Wolf and his associates, accused them of pirating copyright works, after which they "runne vp or downe to all ye faires and markets through a great part of ye Realme, and make sale of them; whose charges in cariage with their expences in Innes and Alehouses and other places considered . . . they returne home more poore then they went out, and so spoile ye whole trade of ye Company."[76]

The works sold at fairs were not all, as one might imagine, of an ephemeral nature. The day-book of John Dorne, which includes the accounts of his sales at St. Frideswide's Fair and the Austin Fair in the year 1520, although recording the sale of a number of ballads, shows that he also disposed of several copies of the

Colloquia Erasmi and similar works. The most expensive work which he sold at the Austin Fair was a *Corpus canonicum magnum*, for which he obtained 26s., and the next highest amount, 15s. 8d., was paid for a *Corpus canonicum parvum*. Dorne's total receipts at St. Frideswide's Fair that year were £7 2s. 8d. At the Austin Fair, lasting from May 7th–17th, he sold 293 volumes, for which he received £14 4s. 10d.[77] Over two hundred years later James Lackington, then a journeyman shoemaker, was walking with a friend through the Bristol Fair. "We saw a stall of books," he records, "and in looking over the title-pages, I met with Hobbs's Translation of Homer's Iliad and Odyssey. . . . At this stall I also purchased Walker's Poetical Pharaphrase [*sic*] of Epictetus's Morals."[78]

Libraries

The average reader of the present day owns only a very small proportion of the books which he reads, but in the sixteenth and seventeenth centuries there were few facilities for borrowing books. There was no great library until 1597, when Sir Thomas Bodley offered to Oxford University the large collection which he had imported from the Continent, estimated to be worth over £10,000. It had been customary for the religious houses to lend volumes to one another, but the dissolution of the monasteries was accompanied by the ruthless destruction of their literary treasures. Very infrequently in local records for later years one reads of books being hired, as when in 1606 4d. was paid by the Barnstaple authorities "for a loan of the book of the new Canons."[79] As a general rule, then, the reader had to rely on his own private library and those of his friends.

It is difficult to estimate the size of the private libraries of the sixteenth century, for, although a large proportion of the annual literary output consisted of ballads and romances, the few collections of which there is any record were almost entirely composed of works of a serious nature. Presumably the lighter type of book was thumbed out of existence too quickly to allow for its entry in a catalogue. To judge from Henry VIII's accounts with his printer, that monarch bought no frivolous works whatever; the £117 which he spent on books between December 1541 and June 1543 paid mainly for religious or classical works.[80] The Earl of Warwick had in 1551 only about forty works, and of these only ten were English.[81] William Rastell, an eminent lawyer and printer whom one would have expected to possess a large private library, forfeited his books to the Crown when he left the country in 1561; the inventory of them lists only forty-one works, consisting mainly of law books, such as the *Year-books*, Lyttelton's *Tenures* and *The Great Abridgement of the Statutes.*[82] It is pleasant to contrast with this the list of books owned by a mason in the year 1575: these consisted of illustrated romances such as *Kyng Arthurz Book*, *The foour suns of Aymion*, *Bevis of Hampton*, *Lucres and Eurialus* and *Huon of Burdeaus.*[83]

The rise of a new class of readers on the introduction of the novel in the eighteenth century opened a way to the profitable lending of books. From about 1740 private individuals began to lay in stocks of literature and to charge annual subscriptions of a guinea or thereabouts for the use of it. By 1761 it was thought worthy of mention in *The Annual Register* that "the reading female hires her novels from some country Circulating Library, which consists of about a hundred volumes."[84] These libraries seem, as in our own day, to have attracted more especially the fiction-reading public, and on that account an author had more hope of success with a serious work if he could cast it in the form of a novel. That was the reason which William Hutchinson gave for the apparent lightness of a moral essay of his, *The Doubtful Marriage*, which he published in 1775.[85] However, in London there were enough readers of a serious turn of mind to justify the stocking of more general literature, as Dr. Thomas Campbell found to his satisfaction: he records in his diary for March 21, 1775: "Strolled into the Chapter Coffee-house, Ave Mary Lane, which I had heard was remarkable for a large collection of books, and a reading society. I subscribed a shilling for the right of a year's reading, and found all the new publications I sought."[86]

Booksellers at first took alarm at the new developments, foreseeing a fall in sales. They were soon reassured. "Experience has proved," says Lackington, "that the sale of books, so far from being diminished by them, has been greatly promoted, as from those repositories, many thousand families have been cheaply supplied with books, by which the taste for reading has become much more general, and thousands are purchased every year, by such as have first borrowed them at those libraries."[87]

PART TWO

THE APPLICATION OF MECHANICAL POWER

CHAPTER XIII

The Application of Mechanical Power to Printing

Whatever bewilderment might have been felt by a fifteenth-century cloth-maker transported by some means to a cotton mill of the late eighteenth century, whatever might have been his reaction to the network of canals and the other evidences of industrial revolution which he saw about him, his contemporary, Caxton, would have found little to surprise him in his own trade. The screw press was still turning out its few hundred sheets a day. Although Blaew had given enough elasticity to some parts of it to save the type from injury and to allow for a rather bigger output the old principle still remained—as many screwings and unscrewings were required as there were copies to be printed.

There had really been very little incentive to improve the old methods. The general interest in reading cannot be said to have grown in any spectacular way since the earliest times. A steady demand was certainly being created for a new form of literature, the novel, but popular works of this kind were still comparatively few and far between; their production seems to have thrown no excessive work upon the printing-house. After all, if the old type of press were already inadequate, would not eighteenth-century wits have already devised some machine able to keep pace with growing needs? One might argue that the Government attitude was unsympathetic to any such change; as late as 1798 a ruling was made that all persons keeping presses or type should notify the Clerk of the Peace;[1] but, as hitherto, it was the fear of sedition which lay behind this Act, and any reputable printer seeking to modernise his works would have found little to prevent him. The inventor would probably have arisen with the need.

Even before such need arose there were a few attempts at

improving the press. It is significant that the first to be patented had been designed with an eye to the new developments in the textile industries rather than to any burst of enthusiasm among the reading public. The grant, in 1771, was to Isaac Moore and William Pine, letter founders and printers, for a method of casting metal cases to hold types for printing on silk, muslin, linen, wool, leather, paper, parchment and vellum; "and also new invented printing presses, the plattens whereof are made of iron and other metals, as well as wood, and are suspended and counteracted by a ballance or weight." The invention is interesting for its introduction of iron into the building of printing-presses; otherwise it is of little importance to the book industry. The printing of books and that of textiles were very soon to part company, and it was the textile industry which held most attraction for the inventive mind.

In 1790 there came an idea which a few years later might have won fame for its originator, but the world was not yet ready for it. This again was intended as much for textile fabrics as for letter-press printing, though the designer, William Nicholson of Red Lion Square, seems never to have made one of the machines for either purpose. His idea was to fix types to a cylinder and, after inking them, to cause the paper to pass between this cylinder and another faced with cloth, in this way taking off the impression. Nicholson was the first to suggest the use of cylinders for printing. What is more, he foresaw the use of steam-power as a substitute for the laborious duties of the pressman: "Lastly," he announces in his specification, "I must take notice that in these and every other of my machines, as well as in every machine whatever, the power may be wind, water, steam, animal strength, or any other natural change capable of producing motion."[2] A later inventor, Edward Cowper, said of him rather slightingly, "Had Mr. Nicholson paid the same attention to any one part of his invention which he fruitlessly devoted to attempting to fix types on a cylinder, or had he known how to curve stereotype plates, he would, in all probability, have been the first *maker* of a printing machine, instead of merely suggesting the principles on which they might be constructed."[3] That may be so, but one would imagine that if any real interest had been shown by the printing world Nicholson would have found the means of perfecting his machine. Twenty years later, when speed in printing had become a more urgent problem, experiments were made on the very lines which he had planned.

The *Repertory of Arts and Manufactures* for 1796 records the grant of a bounty of 40 guineas to Joseph Ridley for his improved printing-press.[4] The notable point was the substitution of a perpendicular steel bar for the screw hitherto in general use. A spindle passed through each side of the press, being attached to the bar by three chains, whose function was to raise and lower the bar and platen. The force required for taking the impression was applied by a lever fixed to one end of the spindle. In principle the press is similar to the Apollo, imported about that time from France.[5] It too was furnished with a lever and spindle, the pressman working the lever up and down like a pump handle. It required so much force that it soon fell into disuse. Roworth's press, the next, showed some improvement: in its head there were fixed two solid steel rollers which brought the platen down with constantly decreasing velocity and increasing force until it reached the type.[6]

The first real improvement on the press was made, strangely enough, not by a working printer but by a disinterested inventor, Charles Mahon, third Earl Stanhope. The outstanding feature of his press (patented in 1798) was that it was made entirely of iron. In common with the Apollo and Roworth's it had a specially large platen, allowing a bigger sheet to be printed, and it further embodied a neat system of levers in place of the cumbrous handle-bar and screw.[7] "The press which is said to be best adapted for any kind of printing," it was stated in 1809,[8] "is that lately invented by Earl Stanhope, and originally made by Mr. Walker. This gives a vast accession of power with a very considerable diminution of labour. It is to be regretted, however, that the expence of the purchase is so great as to preclude its general use. Mr. Brooke, a printer's joiner, has, however, improved the common press on the principle of the Stanhope one."

The experiments were not long confined to England. In 1816 George Clymer of Philadelphia designed an iron machine without a screw, and shortly afterwards it was in use in England under the name of the Columbian press.[9] It is interesting to find from the autobiography of a journeyman compositor who was working during 1826 in France that in one Parisian printing-house, while in one room a pressman was working at a "super-royal stanhope," in another there stood "arranged in precise line a whole regiment of Columbian presses, of London manufacture, the number of which," he writes, "as the crowning eagles rose and fell with rapid irregularity, I in vain essayed to count."[10] The London press manufacturer had been quick to adopt the American idea. This was not the end of American activity, even so; in 1827 Samuel Rust of New York gave extra strength to the press by providing it with uprights of wrought instead of cast iron.[11] Meanwhile, in 1817 T. C. Hansard, the London printer, had invented a press which printed paper of double the ordinary size; but it was used solely in his own works.[12] The Albion press, designed by R. W. Cope of London, was shortly afterwards competing with the Columbian and the Stanhope. In spite of all these efforts, Edward Cowper was to point out, in 1828, that although as a press Earl Stanhope's had never been superseded, as regards the possible speed of output it was in no way better than the old wooden press; the rate of impression was still only 250 an hour.[13] But it is surprising to find how quickly a book could be produced by the old presses. The production by Messrs. Cadell and Davies of Charles Patton's *The Effects of Property upon Society and Government Investigated* is a good example. The preliminary inquiry was sent from Portsmouth on October 7, 1796. The manuscript was forwarded by mail coach a week later and on February 8, 1797, the author wrote to acknowledge the receipt of 2 copies of the finished book of 470 pages.[14]

A witness before the Select Committee on the Copyright Acts (1818) was asked whether printing had not been very much accelerated by the recent improvements in the printing-press. He replied that this was so in only two or three printing-houses; "if the question refers to Lord Stanhope's press, the art of printing is not made more rapid by these presses being used than by the presses before in use; but if it refers to the press of Messrs. Bensley and Taylor, printing is certainly performed with greater rapidity by the steam engine."[15] It was on the use of steam-power and of the printing machine as distinct from the printing-press that the rapid developments of the future were to depend.

Early Printing Machines

There had been few attempts at constructing a machine since Nicholson had procured his patent. The first successful one was the invention of Frederick Koenig,[16] a native of Saxony, who brought his project to England in 1806. With the financial assistance of Thomas Bensley of Bolt Court Koenig took out five separate patents between 1810 and 1816. The first machine, which took three years to build, was set up in Bensley's office, and it has been said that part of the *Annual Register* for 1811 was printed on it.[17] Various other patents for improvements in printing, including one granted to Joseph Bramah of Pimlico "for his invented certain machine, whereby valuable improvements in the art of printing will be obtained," appear to have disappointed the hopes bound up in them.

In November 1813 two further inventions were patented. The first was a grant to John Ruthven, an Edinburgh printer, "for his invented machine or press for printing from types, blocks, or other surfaces." The other, granted jointly to Richard Mackenzie Bacon, a Norwich printer, and Bryan Donkin, a Bermondsey engineer, was the more successful. The patent[18] was for a machine in which the types were placed on a revolving prism; the ink was applied by a roller, and the sheet of paper was wrapped on another prism built to meet the type prism. One of these machines was set up for the Cambridge University Press, but although it was credited with being a beautiful piece of workmanship it was found too complicated for general use; the inking, moreover, was defective. Within a few years it was described as obsolete.[19] Nevertheless, even though it was a failure when brought to the practical test, the machine incorporated a useful improvement: the inking rollers were covered with a composition of treacle and glue, which worked more successfully than the leather used by Koenig.[20]

The printing machine which has won fame as the first to be run by steam was the one patented by Koenig in 1814.[21] It had as its main feature a double cylinder. The type was made to pass under a cylinder to which the paper was held by means of tapes. The ink was placed in a cylindrical box, from which it fell between 2 iron rollers; below these there were a number of other rollers, the whole system terminating in 2 which applied the ink to the type. After minor alterations had been made the machine was capable of making 1,800 impressions an hour. Another machine which Koenig built in the same year was designed to print both sides of a sheet in the same operation. It resembled 2 single machines placed with their cylinders towards each other, at a distance of 2 or 3 feet. The track of the paper between the 2 cylinders resembled the letter **S** turned horizontally, so that at the first cylinder the paper received the impression from the first forme and at the second the reverse side of the paper received the impression from the other forme. In this way the machine could print 750 sheets on both sides in an hour. Koenig made only one of these, for Thomas Bensley.[22]

Koenig's improvements could not have come at a more favourable time. The one form of literature which had never from the time of its origin failed to attract a wide public was the daily newspaper. The unprecedented growth in population since the middle of the eighteenth century was in itself enough to impose a still heavier demand upon the newspaper press. Added to this, the newspaper, which in former years had served as a basis of gossip or as a means of literary intercourse, had come to be an essential source of commercial information. There was a new urgency in newspaper publication which did more than anything else to show up the shortcomings of the old, leisurely hand-printing.

It was not long before the proprietor of one paper took advantage of the new means of increasing output. John Walter, of *The Times*, went into consultation with Koenig, and the edition of that paper for November 28, 1814, bears the proud announcement that this was the first number to be printed by steam. That was almost as much of a revelation to the employees of *The Times* as it was to the general public. In an age of machine-breaking any innovation which might threaten the security of the workers had to be made by stealth. The Koenig machine, therefore, was secretly set up in a building adjoining *The Times*' works; although the pressmen heard rumours which gave them some uneasiness they had no definite knowledge as to what was happening. What did happen may be read in John Walter's obituary notice:[23] "The night on which this curious machine was first brought into use was one of great anxiety and even alarm. The suspicious pressmen . . . were directed to wait for expected news from the Continent. It was about six o'clock in the morning when Mr. Walter went into the press-room and astonished its occupants by telling them that '*The Times* was already printed by steam; that if they attempted violence there was a force ready to suppress it; but that if they were peaceable, their wages should be continued to every one of them till similar employment could be procured'; a promise which was no doubt faithfully performed; and having so said, he distributed several copies amongst them. Thus was this most hazardous enterprise undertaken and successfully carried through, and printing by steam on an almost gigantic scale given to the world." Nevertheless, in a history of the book industry Koenig's machines are of little direct interest. They were cumbersome affairs, expensive, and soon put out of order. If one may accept the possibly biassed opinion of Edward Cowper the system of inking was "extremely complicated, and very difficult to manage, so much so as sometimes to require two hours to get it in order; it has been completely superseded," he claimed, "by my invention."[24] Although no immediate benefit had been conferred on the general book-printer by Koenig's inventions, they did at least point the way to more practical developments.

In 1815 Cowper patented one of the inventions which were to be held in such high esteem. It was for curving stereotype plates in order to fix them to a cylinder.[25] He stated in 1828 that several of the machines incorporating this idea, capable of printing

1,000 sheets an hour on both sides, were still in use.[26] The invention which he patented in 1818[27] was a definite advance on Koenig's work, giving better distribution of the ink. About that time he joined forces with his brother-in-law, Augustus Applegath, in an attempt to obtain speed with simplicity. Together they secured several patents, and by 1828 had constructed more than 70 machines modified in 25 different ways according as they were to be used for books, newspapers, bank-notes, or some other form of printing. The Applegath-Cowper machines certainly show a simplicity never attained in Koenig's inventions. One of the first undertakings of the joint experimenters was to improve the Koenig machine in Bensley's office, and that was done by removing 40 superfluous wheels and by simplifying the inking arrangements. By 1828 Cowper could claim to have installed one of the new machines in place of every one set up by Koenig,[28] and 50 years later Messrs. Clowes still had 25 of them at work.[29] The one which the two partners erected for *The Times* in 1827 was a four-cylinder machine able to print both sides of a sheet at once at the rate of 5,000 copies an hour. It was used by many newspaper offices in London and the provinces for the remainder of the century. Even then the resources of Applegath and Cowper were not fully spent: the eight-cylinder machine which they devised in 1848 was one of the marvels of the Great Exhibition of 1851.

It may be helpful to describe the working of a printing-machine as it was round about 1840. The whole process was superintended by a "laying-on" boy, who had only to lay the sheet of paper on a flat table before him, with its edge ready to be seized by the apparatus for conveying it upon the drum. At the first movement of the great wheel the inking apparatus was set in motion. A steel cylinder attached to the reservoir of ink began to move slowly, the "doctor" (a technical name for a roller originally called a "conductor") rose to touch the cylinder for an instant and thus receive a supply of ink, the inking-table passed under the "doctor" and carried off that supply, and the distributing-rollers spread it equally over the surface of the table. This surface then passed under the inking-rollers, transferring the ink to them, and they in turn passed it to the forme which was to be printed. At the moment when the forme was passing under the inking-roller the sheet which the boy laid upon the table was caught in the web-roller and carried to the endless bands which passed it over the first impression cylinder. The moment after the sheet was seized upon the first cylinder the forme passed under it, and the paper received an impression on one side. The sheet was then reversed by means of two drums and an impression taken from the second forme.[30]

The various improvements in mechanism could not be without their reactions, both on master printers and employees. The dread of unemployment which in other trades had brought rioting and machine-breaking in the wake of the most ingenious inventions was not entirely wanting here, although it led to no violent demonstrations. It may be that the reasoned tactics which were so typical of printers in the first stormy years of trade unionism led them to seek a remedy for loss of work rather than to indulge in useless threats of vengeance. The formation of the Printers' Pension Society was one means to this end. "Detector," writing to *The Times* in 1828, gave it as his opinion that the Society was not worthy of encouragement, but a letter in the *Morning Herald* of June 13th answered him indignantly: ". . . of the pressmen, *The Times* itself can answer its correspondent how far he is correct, and can inform him, likewise, that they have alone given, by the introduction of machinery, a death-blow to eighteen or twenty men and their families." It is difficult to estimate how much of the distress among journeymen printers was really due to the introduction of machinery and how much to general economic depression. The total number of printing machines was still very small, but so, for that matter, was the industry as a whole. On the newspaper side at least it is probable that the rate of growth was soon sufficient to reabsorb those workers who had been thrown idle.

The master printer had his own reason for welcoming or disapproving of the rise of the machine, according to his temperament and the state of his finances. A distinction had arisen between the up-to-date printing works and the rest. In the old days of the wooden press, with its slow, steady output and its lack of variation, one printing works differed from another only in size. A printer could go to an auction sale and furnish his office completely for a few pounds. There is in existence a catalogue for one of Paterson's sales in 1781, with the prices of the various articles entered in manuscript by John Nichols.[31] A small press, "compleat and good," was sold for £4 10s.; a bellows-press fetched only 5s. 6d., and a "new and compleat rolling-press" 5s. By 1860 the printer was offered an embarrassing selection. He could choose between a simple cylinder gripper machine for newspapers and bookwork, costing £130 for the double-crown size, a two-colour printing machine, which in the same size cost £170, a perfecting machine for bookwork at from £335 to £410, or an improved double-platen machine for bookwork, "used in most large offices," which cost £390. Or, if he had more humble tastes, there were improved Albion, Columbian, Imperial and Stanhope presses to be had at prices ranging from £30 to £85.[32] All traces of the old-time equality had disappeared.

The printer and his men were not the only people affected by the installation of a printing machine. Their neighbours complained repeatedly of the noise and vibration. When Clowes installed his steam-press on his premises at Charing Cross the Duke of Northumberland, whose garden adjoined, brought an action against him for damages. The case was heard in the Court of Common Pleas in June 1824. Charles Knight, publisher-to-be, who was there, was disgusted with the proceedings: "Ludicrous it was to hear the extravagant terms in which the counsel for the plaintiff and his witnesses described the alleged nuisance—the noise made by this engine, quite horrid, sometimes resembling thunder, at other times like a threshing machine, and then again like the rumbling of carts and waggons."[33] The judgment was something of a compromise: the steam-press was to be removed to other premises, but the Duke was to pay compensation. Clowes obligingly moved in the following year. In the words of a mock drama based upon the action:

> . . . Surely so small an inconvenience as
> The Chimney furnace of a ten-horse engine
> Vomiting by day and night its eatable smoke
> Into his Grace's lungs and chamber—stifling his wife,
> And servants, male and female—could not excuse this
> Terrible infliction.[34]

The firm of Clowes was not the only one to meet with opposition on introducing machinery. The Unwins were to suffer repeated attacks. The works in which the firm introduced steam-power in 1847 adjoined an insurance office in the Poultry, and the secretary of that company soon complained of the noise. Fortunately, in this case the printing firm was the older occupier and could not be driven out. In 1864, by which time premises had been acquired in Oxford Street and Cannon Street, private residents were complaining of the vibration, and Edward Unwin himself, as a conciliatory gesture, took rooms in one of the houses. This was by no means the end of the trouble. Ten years later a Cannon Street firm of wine merchants sought an injunction for injury through machine vibration, and mercurial tests had to be applied before Unwins won the case. When the Salters' Company, with premises next door, shortly afterwards threatened legal proceedings the firm decided that it was high time to move. A new site was chosen in Southwark Street, only to cause a further exasperating hindrance: Sir James Whitehead, an important customer, announced that he would never cross the bridge to deal with the firm. At last the press did find unoffending quarters in Pilgrim Street off Ludgate Hill.[35]

It is strange that the opposition had not died out long before. A witness told the Children's Employment Commission of 1862 that the bulk of the printed matter was being produced by steam-power, and it was with rather an air of apology that he admitted that there were still some firms employing as many as eight or ten men without any steam-power on the premises.[36]

The steam-presses in use were not all of British manufacture. America had up to this time been occupied with her own experiments. Until the middle of the century the bed and platen system was the favourite for fine books, and the first American steam-press was designed on this principle in 1822 by Daniel Treadwell of Boston. Although it was modern in mechanism the machine was doomed to failure by having wooden frames, and only three or four were ever constructed. Later Boston inventions, those of Isaac Adams, 1830 and 1836, and of Otis Tufts, 1834, were successful enough to be sent abroad. By 1850 the search for a perfect machine was international. The British eight-cylinder machine which was the pride of the Great Exhibition of 1851 was soon afterwards improved by Messrs. Hoe of New York, who raised the output to a scale hitherto unheard of, twenty thousand impressions an hour. French activity during this period culminated in the stop-cylinder press of Dutartre (1852); but it was not long before this press, too, achieved greater things in the hands of Messrs. Hoe.[37]

The American firm of Hoe was destined to play an important part in our printing developments. In 1848 Colonel Hoe erected a multiple-cylinder machine for the Parisian daily paper *La Patrie* which, although in general principle similar to Cowper and Applegath's, was more compact and less complicated. It was soon popular with newspaper proprietors. The one which was erected in London for *Lloyd's Weekly Newspaper* was obviously such an advance on the Applegath that the proprietors of *The Times* straightway ordered two ten-cylinder Hoe machines on condition that they were manufactured in England. Sir Joseph Whitworth undertook the work, and his firm erected the first machines; but the inventors soon thought fit to set up their own establishment in London.[38] Here they flourished almost unworried by competition until in 1866 *The Times* abandoned the Hoe machine in favour of its own new invention, the Walter rotary press. Subsequent developments in the newspaper machine have been based on the Hoe or on the rotary, but the book-printer is not concerned with these higher intricacies.

Where a large number of copies of the same work are wanted in a short time the printing machine is invaluable. As Edward Cowper told a committee of the House of Commons in 1836, such works as the *Penny Magazine* could not have existed without it. How much more, then, did the daily newspaper owe to it! It was now possible to fulfil the demand of thousands of readers that nobody should be before them with the news of the day. Nevertheless, on consideration, apart from journals of this kind there were probably not a great number of publications which were wanted in such large editions. A more numerous reading public would demand variety; it could not be altogether satisfied by extra copies of the same books. The difficulty was that, quite apart from any question of obtaining extra copy, the type could scarcely be set up fast enough to keep the press fully occupied. It was the old trouble of one process outstripping another in efficiency. The cotton industry had encountered very much the same problem in its early days of expansion: whereas it had once been hard work for seven or eight spinners to supply enough material to keep one weaver occupied, after the inventions of Hargreaves, Arkwright and Crompton between 1764 and 1775 the weaver was overwhelmed with work, and Cartwright's power loom came as an attempt to restore the balance. In the same way the printing machine gave a one-sided impetus to press work; unless it could be used to profit in turning out more and more copies of the same work it had either to be fed by far more compositors than before or, during long periods, to stand idle. What was needed to re-establish equilibrium in book-printing was some kind of machine to supersede hand-composition.

Composing Machines

The first attempt to find a solution was made by William Church. In 1822 he was granted a patent[39] for a composing machine and printing machine combined. It was an ingenious contraption, to judge by the specification. The types were arranged in "files" in a case at the top of the machine, each file being directly over a slit in a horizontal frame. One of a number of jacks protruded through each of these slits, each jack being connected with a key "in a manner somewhat similar to the jacks and keys of an harpsichord." On the depression of any particular key its jack pushed a type forward into a "race," and a lever pushed it down an aperture answering the purpose of a composing stick. The invention does not appear to have been successful.

Young and Delcambre were the joint inventors of the next machine. Their patent,[40] obtained in 1840, was followed almost immediately by a grant to Clay and Rosenborg[41] for a very similar device. Both of these rival machines were worked by means of a keyboard. In the first the key moved a lever, which pushed a type out of a small receptacle; the types slid down an inclined plane by way of a funnel into a box; the compositor then had to lift them up and arrange them in his composing stick. In Clay and Rosenborg's machine the keys set free the types from a vertical rack and dropped them on an endless belt which carried them to a receiver. When a whole line of type had been set up a bell rang as a signal for the compositor to remove this line to make room for another. This machine was accompanied by another intended for the reverse process, the distributing of the type. Yet again an invention which had seemed full of promise fell short of expectations. After ten years it had to be confessed that the hopes had not materialised. Critics complained that men were still required to attend to the machines and to do part of the work. Worse than that, according to one expression, the machines could not *think* sufficiently, so that by the time all the necessary corrections and adjustments had been made nothing was saved.[42]

As far as thinking went the later inventions could scarcely have been any more helpful. The patents granted to Joseph Mazzini in 1843 for his "uniplane machine for composing"[43] and to W. H. Mitchel in 1853 and 1857 for distributing and composing machines[44] seem to have been unsuccessful from the outset. The machine of Boule and Caillaud (1853),[45] though as much of a failure as the rest, had some claim to originality: in composing the finger keys acted on a series of forceps which picked the type from the case; in distributing the letters were picked up one at a time by a pair of forceps and dropped into the end of a series of grooved channels, the direction which they took being governed by finger keys. We are not told the working-speed of this contrivance. One suspects that the forceps acted rather more slowly than the fingers of a skilful compositor.

Up to the middle of the nineteenth century the best substitute for hand composition seems to have been produced by M. Sörensen, of Denmark, whose type machine was on show at the Great Exhibition of 1851. In general appearance it was like a bird-cage. A top circular cage was for distributing type and a lower one for composing. In the distributing process the compositor placed the type between the brass bars of the upper cage so that they slid on to a plate separating the two cages. This plate was perforated in such a way that each hole would admit only one kind of type-letter. If the upper cage was slowly turned round, therefore, the types dropped one by one through their proper holes. The lower cage had as many vertical brass bars as there were letters of type, and by degrees the space between any two bars became filled with type all of one letter. The process of composition began, as usual, with playing on keys. They acted on strings which themselves worked upon springs; the springs let out the type on to a sloping plate from which they passed by a spiral tube into a receiver, where they ranged themselves side by side. The receiver was moved along slowly by means of a foot-pedal until a whole line was set up. The line was then removed and the receiver adjusted for another. The machine cost £100, and was easier to learn, so the inventor claimed, than hand composing.[46]

Sörensen's invention was not accepted in England as the final solution. Between 1854 and 1857 seven more designs for composing-machines were patented, and more were to come. In 1868 Charles Kastenbein, of *The Times* office, began work on a typesetting machine which was to prove of real practical use. It was perfected in 1879. The machine could set up 298 lines of *The Times*, amounting to nearly 17,000 separate types, in an hour. In principle it was a magazine of separate types, each type being released and set in line by means of a finger-key. Several attempts were made to build a machine for distributing the type after use, by means of a special nick in each; but in the end common sense prevailed over ingenuity and the melting-pot was agreed to be quicker and cheaper.[47]

The use of composing machines caused as much opposition on the part of the men as the printing machine itself had done. There was the same dread that skilled labour would be ousted by the cheaper women and boys. Most of the dispute was centred round the Hattersley, a composing machine which is thought to have been first introduced into the *Bradford Times*' office in 1868 and which by the 'nineties was in fairly general use.[48] A strike had been declared at the Bradford works on the firm's refusing to promise that the machine should be worked only by journeymen or by bound apprentices, and the office remained "closed," to use the trade-union expression, for 25 years or more. The union attitude changed slightly during this time. When, in 1875, the *Southport Daily News* office installed a Hattersley the men agreed that girls should be allowed to work the *distributing* machine. This was not a particularly generous act, for distributing was a slow and tedious business. It was carried on by means of an instrument rather like a revolver in appearance, capable of picking up a whole line of type at once. Then, with an effect of firing a toy pistol, the individual types were ejected one at a time into their own special grooves.[49] The members of the Typographical Association in 1878 voted in favour of allowing boys and girls to do this mechanical work. At the same time they voted, by 2,291 votes against 40, that no opposition should be offered to the introduction of composing machines so long as they were worked by journeymen or by duly bound apprentices.[50] Fifteen years later, when the machines were introduced into the *Manchester Courier* office, there began a lengthy correspondence in the *Typographical Circular* as to the wisdom of allowing even distributing to be done by boys not regularly apprenticed.[51] A new fear had arisen with the unexpected success of the machines.

The Hattersley had been prophesied an early end. It struck one visitor to the Caxton Exhibition of 1877 that the machine showed "such a predetermination to get out of order, to fall more or less to pieces at a critical moment," that no employer with the slightest amount of common sense would give it a trial.[52] Time showed this judgment to be wrong, but the Hattersley never achieved perfect smoothness of working. To use it satisfactorily, it was once claimed, the machinist needed two qualifications:

he "must be endowed with a good patience, and also be a downright honest swearer. Without these finishing touches he has no chance of success. The first named is difficult to acquire, but the latter is easily managed. Contact with the machines teaches it. . . . A bit of dust in the tubes down which the type runs will cause stoppage and irritation to the worker, although a second previous he may have been spending a lot of time in finding out some other cause of delay—a bit of broken type, a twisted letter in the charge, a slack string or a worn-out spring; in fact, there are a million-and-one causes to produce vexation in working the 'king of type-setters.' "[53]

As far as newspaper printing was concerned the solution was to be found in the linotype machine designed by Ottmar Mergenthaler, which was already being produced by the Mergenthaler Linotype Company of New York. For book work another American invention, the monotype machine, was soon found to surpass all former efforts. This machine, which at the present time is used for most of the fine printing of England and America,[54] consists of two separate parts, the composing machine and the casting machine. In the composing machine the keyboard acts on a paper ribbon: as each key is touched compressed air rushes in and perforates the roll. When the ribbon is taken from the composing machine it is ready to be fed into the casting machine, which delivers the type as separate entities set up in line. Hand-composition is still preferred for the best work, but the monotype machine frequently provides the type for it, which can be stored in cases ready to be picked up one at a time by the compositor and set in his stick. There is another advantage: the monotype ribbon can be used a number of times, and can be stored far more easily and cheaply than either type or stereotype moulds.

The immediate effect of introducing these American machines was to endow the Hattersley with virtues never before discovered in it. Although the automatic distributor which was one of the greatest points of the linotype machine was welcomed by the officials of the Typographical Association because it did away with the need for unskilled labour, there were critics who deprecated the displacement of any workers whatever.[55] A correspondent in *The Times*[56] alleged that the men tried to nullify the advantages of the new machinery by never working it to its top capacity—a charge which was indignantly denied by the general secretary of the London Printing Machine Managers' Trade Society.

Modern Printing Machinery

The same complaint of deliberately slow working was made in connection with the flat-bed printing machines at that time being introduced from America, which were really capable of greater speed than the English machines for which they were substituted; but the newer models had not as great advantages over other presses as the monotype machines had over the Hattersley. Printing-machine design had been making steady progress. By the 'eighties there were two distinct types of bookwork machine in use, the platen and the cylindrical. Owing, perhaps, to the power of tradition it was still felt by some printers that a flat impression, as given by the hand-press, must be better than one obtained from a cylinder. For fine bookwork, therefore, they used the platen machine, a steam-press in which the pressure was given by a platen in a similar way to the hand-press. The platen was placed in the centre of the machine, with the inking-tables and the coffins at the ends, and the whole was set in motion by means of a large iron drum lying under one of the tables.[57] The Napier double platen press, the most successful of its kind, was as expensive as the cylindrical form, and even it had limitations which led more and more printers to give it up in favour of the cylinder. For one thing, it required four boys to mind it—two at each end. The Wharfedale cylinder, in comparison with the platen machine, could turn out twice the amount of work with half the number of boys; it could print a sheet twice the size of any capable of being taken under a platen. Added to that, it took only one-third of the driving power needed for the other.

The Tumbler, with the Wharfedale and other constructions which superseded it, were single-cylinder machines consisting of an impression cylinder mounted on parallel side-frames over a moving table or "coffin." They could be made of any size, from demy to quadruple royal, and would give from 800 to 1,200 impressions an hour. The best of them were fitted with contrivances for double inking, giving a clearer impression than could be obtained from a platen machine.[58]

There was still another alternative, the perfecting machine, made up of two large impression cylinders with two intermediate drums designed to turn the paper from one side to the other on its way between the two cylinders. Various adaptations of the machine had been made, but all were capable of running simply and at a good speed. That is not to say that they were necessarily economical to use. Unless the impression was to run into at least 5,000 it was much cheaper to use a Wharfedale; the formes for the perfecting machines took longer to make ready, and some of the machines needed four boys to attend to them. Their chief value was for magazine work.[59]

To some printers the cost of any of these machines was prohibitive. It was not that their prices were increasing; by 1913, in fact, the cost of some of the more intricate models was well below the prices of 1860. Nevertheless, some small printers had to think twice before spending £200 or more on one machine. It is an encouraging thought that the Albion, Columbian and Stanhope presses are still available, capable of giving good service to the printer of smaller means. They could be bought in 1913 for from £15 to £68 as compared with £30 to £85 in 1860.[60] The hand-press can turn out quite as attractive printing as the most elaborate piece of mechanism. "Many a young Printer," we are reminded in 1878, "may be so fond of his trade as to entertain the idea of becoming his own master in it; and he might, to our way of thinking, do much worse, now that there are so many small cheap hand-presses in the trade, to be had for a small sum, which can be worked when screwed down on to a table or a bench. For £20 a capital little office can now be started, capable of turning out cards, billheads, and circulars."[61] The book-printer of repute, for all that, although he might not need a mammoth newspaper machine of many cylinders, did not base his hopes on a small jobbing-press. The normal printing-office cost far more than £20 to equip. Lest one should be left with a wrong impression it would be as well to quote a broad financial statement of one firm: "In January, 1828, Jacob Unwin estimated his plant value at only £240! It has to be remembered that he acquired a good deal of this at a sale. He afterwards bought type from Caslon and Figgins, Thorogood and also from Dorrington, as well as some odd letter from Mr. Pewtress, presumably connected with the firm later known as Messrs. Marlborough and Pewtress. About 1829, 579 lb. of Pica came from Mr. Pewtress for just under £30. In 1831 a copperplate press was bought for £8 12s. In December, 1831, the plant was deemed to be worth £578. But considering the manner in which the greater part of the plant was originally acquired, and his general shrewdness in business dealings, it is very doubtful whether he would have replaced it in 1831, even allowing fully for depreciation, for less than £1,500 to £2,000. When in 1860 a valuation of the business was necessary to determine for what sum Mr. George Unwin should become responsible, the goodwill, plant and stocks were valued by Messrs. Harrild at £4,214."[62]

At the end of the nineteenth century most of the machines were still being run by steam-power. The steam engine itself was simple in construction and was rarely out of order, but a complete standstill seems sometimes to have been caused by faulty boilers. A number of printing works took the precaution of insuring their steam-boilers in a reputable company; it was worth while for the sake of the examination made periodically by the company's inspector, who would give a timely warning of any repairs to be undertaken.[63] For all its efficiency, steam-power was a costly item of printing-house expenditure. Several experiments were made with a view to economising in its use, but the most hopeful developments were expected from a new motive power, gas. By about 1875 the gas engine was well on its way to supplanting steam-power, and before 1880 Messrs. Nelson, of Edinburgh, had changed to gas engines for the whole of their printing machinery. It was claimed that the new engines were economical; what is more, they were seldom out of repair.[64] A one-man power engine capable of working a demy or double-

THE STANHOPE PRESS
From Johnson's *Typographia*, 1824

crown Wharfedale cost only £25, and the expense of working was only ½d. an hour.[65] It had a rival in the water-motor, another new invention. Water-power proved to be rather more expensive than gas, but it had advantages of its own; not the least was the absence of heat, allowing the motor to be fixed in any part of the building. The first printing-house to use water-power seems to have been that of the firm of Unwin, which in 1871 opened the St. Martha Printing Works at Chilworth, Surrey, on the River Tillingbourne.[66] Perhaps on account of their expense water-motors were not generally adopted. In 1907 only 227 horse-power was being obtained from water for the printing and book-binding trades of the whole of the United Kingdom as compared with 15,257 from steam engines and 23,127 from gas, oil and other internal combustion engines.[67]

Before the end of the nineteenth century it had been discovered in America that electricity would provide a more successful motive force than either gas or water. In 1897 the *Daily Mail* office imported electric motors from the United States for use with the rotary press, and in the same year Messrs. Hazell, Watson and Viney began to use the new power for flat-bed machines.[68] By 1924[69] printing machines were being generally run by electricity: 54,400 of a total of 57,500 horse-power in the book industries was being applied electrically, a proportion which by 1930[70] had risen to 94,300 out of 96,300.

As compared with the 250 impressions an hour of the hand-press about 1,000 are given by the modern heavy platen machine and between 1,000 and 2,000 by the Wharfedale. The cost of press-work round about 1930 was in consequence considerably lower than that of a century earlier in spite of the increased cost of labour. The machining of 3,000 copies now cost roughly 17s. for a 16-page sheet. For Babbage's *On the Economy of Machinery and Manufactures* (1832) the charge for press-work for the same number of copies of a sheet was £3 10s.

CHAPTER XIV

The Accessories of Modern Printing: Type, Illustrations, Ink

Type

THE printing machine, to be run economically, needed to be fed with a constant supply of material. The whole of its advantages could be frustrated by a shortage either of type or of ink. The few hundred pounds of type which were enough for the early printer were hopelessly inadequate for the growing output of the nineteenth century. Whereas John Nichols and his contemporaries had bought a dozen pounds or so at a time, by 1830 printers were ordering their founts either by the hundredweight or by the sheet. "If they order a fount of five hundred, they mean that the whole shall weigh about five hundred pounds. But if they require a fount of ten sheets, it is understood, that with this fount they shall be able to compose ten sheets, or twenty forms, without being obliged to distribute. The founder reckons one hundred and twenty pounds to a sheet; but this varies with the nature of the letter."[1] These were small enough quantities by modern standards. Babbage, on advising authors to leave their proof-correcting until the whole work was in galley-proof, pointed out that this was on the assumption that the printer had enough type for the whole work.[2] It was evidently still a matter of doubt. Even the Spottiswoodes had not very large stocks. In 1825 Thomas Cadell, the publisher, had to remind one author of that. "I have enquired," he said, "at Messrs. Spottiswoode's respecting their progress in the printing of Tytler Vol. 1 and 2, and am sorry to find that is [*sic*] is stopped for want of a return of the proofs, of which you have five at present in your possession, a number occupying such a large portion of Types as to render it very inconvenient for more sheets to be set up until those already sent to you, or a part of them, have been returned."[3]

While the old system of type-founding prevailed it was impossible to bring about a phenomenal increase in output. Some growth there might be; we have seen that the old type-founders had had to fill up their time with unrelated occupations. There was now, moreover, no longer a shortage of metal. While the printing and composing machines were still in the experimental stage it is probable that the founder, by some small increase in the number of his employees, could keep pace with the demand without much difficulty, but it was not long before the inventor thought this a profitable field for experiment.

The earlier patents for type-founding, granted in 1767 and 1784, related only to the printing of music. Others, such as those of Robert Barclay in 1790 and William Caslon the younger in 1811, were directed to the improvement of the individual types, not to any scheme for mass production. All the same, the necessity had already been foreseen. William Nicholson's invention of 1790,[4] so surprising in its failure, had been concerned not only with the introduction of mechanism but also with a quicker means of casting type. Instead of leaving a space in the mould for the stem of only one letter he proposed to cast several at a time by using ordinary moulds communicating "by a common groove at top." He went on, it is true, to suggest that the tails of the letters should be tapered off to allow the type to fit into a cylinder, but his idea would have applied just as well to ordinary flat work.

The first patent relating specifically to type-founding by machinery was obtained by A. F. Berte in 1806.[5] His method was to apply the mould to one of several apertures in the side of the metal-pot, "which at that instant, by means of a lock or valve or any other well-known similar contrivance," is opened, so that the metal flows into the mould. Elihu White, in the same year, suggested casting by means of a sliding plate.[6] In 1809 John Peek had another idea:[7] by adding a bolt and a spiral spring to the mould in common use he thought he could save three motions out of five made in the ordinary method of casting types.

When William Church designed his composing machine, in 1822, he realised that it was useless without an unlimited supply of letter, and his patent[8] covered yet another attempt at type-casting. Roughly, his scheme was to have a series of matrices, in a matrix bar, applied to a mould bar with a corresponding number of moulds, and to fill them with metal from a series of jets. It was followed, in the next year, by a patent[9] to L. J. Pouchée for an invention communicated by Didot, of Paris. This was the most ambitious scheme so far put forward: up to two hundred types were to be cast at each operation, and there were to be two or more operations a minute. The moulds this time were to be made up of four steel bars, one for each side of the type, placed so as to form a trough for the molten metal. One of the bars was to be grooved to form the type-body. Henfrey and Applegath, the same year, had their own idea: they proposed to cast type in a space between two flanges set at right angles on a spindle, and pressed to and drawn from one another alternately by a spring.[10] There was a most bewildering choice of processes. The next was different again. In Thomas Aspinwall's mechanical type-caster (1828)[11] the working parts of the machine were to be mounted on a table suspended so as to move to and from the melting-pot. A cylinder communicating with the pot was to cause some of the metal to be dropped into the mould; the table would then swing back from the pot, the parts of the mould would separate and the matrix would be withdrawn from the cast type by a lever. James Thomson's device, three years later, was more rough and ready: "My improvements," he announces in his specification,[12] "consist in making printing types by casting or forming a cake of metal having letters formed and protruding on one side of it, and in afterwards sawing this cake directly or transversely, so as to divide it into single types."

It would be wearisome to describe them all. By 1850 there were eleven more inventions, all fundamentally different. One of them, Henry Bessemer's (1838), had a counting machine attached, to count the number of letters cast.[13] Joseph Mazzini (1843) had thought out a pneumatic machine;[14] and in the same year John Duncan, keeping as close as possible to the old methods, found a way "to perform by means of a machine the motions required in casting type" by a series of arms radiating between the nozzle of the jet pipe and the mould.[15]

Perhaps owing to the embarrassing number of ideas in the air, one of the chief London printing works was in 1840 still following the old methods; but those methods seem to have been wonderfully efficient. The type was cast in the traditional way and was then passed on to "breaking-off" boys, who had the task of breaking off the surplus metal. The average speed in breaking off was two thousand an hour, but some boys had been known to deal with five thousand in the time. That was remarkably rapid considering that the boys had to pick up the type by its edges, to avoid damaging it. Next the type was sent on to other boys, the "rubbers," who had to rub each piece on a circular piece of grit-stone to remove any roughness. Two thousand types were rubbed on both sides in an hour, on an average. The type had lastly to go to "dressers," whose duty it was to bring it all to an equal height. That was done by forming it into a compact mass, with the bottom ends upwards, and running a plane along to give a level surface. The dresser had also to examine the face of every type through a magnifying glass, and to throw aside any which were defective.[16] The cost of type at this time ranged from 6d. a thousand for great and long primer, pica and English to 8d. for pearl and 10d. for the smallest of all, diamond.[17]

A firm of the public importance of Messrs. Clowes would, one would have thought, have been eager to adopt any mechanical device which offered increased speed and cheapness. It may be that the specialist type-founders were strong enough to prejudice them against the new processes. Although there were still only about half a dozen type-foundries in the whole of Great Britain they were so far well able to defy competition;[18] and, as commonly happens where there is freedom from conflict, there was no desire to change the traditional methods. It was not for lack of inventions. One has only to read the reports of the juries for the Great Exhibition of 1851 to be told of the success of, for instance, Pouchée's type-casting machine, which would cast about two hundred types at one operation, to be repeated twice in a minute. Pouchée's experience may explain the fate of other equally sound devices. Finding himself in difficulties he had to dispose of his machine, and was relieved to find a Covent Garden printer who was more than anxious to obtain possession of it. What Pouchée did not know was that the printer in question was acting for a syndicate of type-founders who thought the machine cheap at £100—not to use, but to destroy. That was done quite efficiently, according to the report of Pouchée's son to a technical journal, by taking it out to sea and throwing it overboard.

It was impossible for the founders to maintain this attitude beyond the middle of the century. Printers were not to be handicapped indefinitely by the obtuseness of a small section of the trade. American experience showed that hand casting was no longer either necessary or economical. Since January 1831, the date of the first American patent for a type-founding machine, there had been a series of inventions, and one in particular, that of David Bruce of New York (1838), embodied a process which was to be widely adopted. It was a pumping device which filled the moulds with metal and ejected type at the rate of about 6,000 an hour. During the next 10 years Bruce's machine was brought into use in several American and Continental foundries and was at last introduced into England. Here it was not adopted in its original form so much as modified for a further series of patents, more numerous than ever now that the founders had withdrawn their opposition.

The demand for type was now enormous as compared with earlier years. To realise this one has only to be told that the British and Foreign Bible Society had already printed the whole or parts of the Bible in 170 different languages. For an idea of the amount of type which this must have involved we may remind ourselves that when Messrs. Clowes printed the official catalogues of the Great Exhibition of 1851 they had first to cast 58,520 pounds of letter.

The patents of the second half of the century are too numerous to describe one by one. The pumping system is found in almost all of them, whether they belong to the class known as pivotal type-casting machines, in which a pivoted frame rocks so as to move the mould to and from the nozzle of the melting-pot, or to those described as rapid type-casters, whose main principle is that the hot nozzle is held against a cold mould, a system of water circulation making it possible to turn out over 10,000 types an hour. A third group, formed by means of multiple moulds, was already a source of interest in 1852. "M. Le Grand, of Paris," it was recorded, "has devised an ingenious mode of casting many types at once, by ranging the matrices side by side in a mould which will contain them all. He casts from 100 to 150 at once, and claims to have the power of producing 30,000 to 50,000 per hour by the aid of two men only."[19] In the hands of Frederick Wicks, of *The Times*, this form of machine was to produce type at still greater speed. His contrivance has 100 moulds mounted in a wheel revolving continuously before a stream of metal, giving an output of from 35,000 to 70,000 letters an hour, according to size.[20]

Punch-cutting, a more difficult operation, was later in becoming mechanised. The earliest known machine was of American origin. It was patented in Great Britain in 1885 by Linn Boyd Benton, of Milwaukee, but was very expensive. Benton's patent of two years before, for "self-spacing" types, was of far greater practical importance as leading the way to the modern "point" system of measuring and describing type. The need for standard type-measurements had been realised as long ago as 1737 by a French printer, Fournier, who published an account of his system in his *Manuel Typographique* (Paris, 1764). In England the problem seems to have escaped attention until 1841, when a pamphlet was published in Sheffield setting forth a reasoned argument for a common standard.[21] There could be no doubt as to the value of the point system once it had become established. Hitherto all uniformity of type-sizes was confined within the walls of individual foundries. The pica or the long primer of a single firm, provided that it was cast from moulds produced by the same punches, would be of uniform size. What likelihood was there that the pica or long primer to be obtained from a second foundry would approach so nearly to the same measurements that a printer could appropriately use the products of the two foundries in different parts of the same work? The standardisation of weights and measures had long been regarded as a matter of State concern, but type measurements were of too little interest to the general public to demand regulation. Even the Stationers' Company in the days of its greatest industrial power had ignored the problem. The pains of producing type at all, it may be, had rendered absolute uniformity of size a refinement not to be considered. While the printer was content to cast his own type or to buy it from a single foundry this was a matter of no moment, but by the time that type had become a regular article of trade there was every need for an accurate description of it. The point system provided the solution. In future the printer could rest assured that "10-point," no matter where he bought it, measured exactly ten seventy-seconds of an inch.

If another idea of the mid-nineteenth century had proved as practicable as it sounded there would have been an end of the tiresome process of pulling and reading proofs. Major Beniowski had produced type which he described as exactly the same as the usual kind except that it had on its other side a similar letter to the one on the face.[22] Whereas ordinary type when set up could only be read in reverse this could be read in the direct form, so that a whole page could be corrected without taking proofs. The printer had then only to reverse the type into another galley and lock it up. What was more, according to the inventor, composition would be so simple that apprenticeship would no longer be necessary: even beginners could set up 5,000 or 6,000 of these letters in an hour, whereas with ordinary type even a good compositor could do only about 1,000. A further improvement, he claimed, was in his methods of spacing. He had two sets of every letter, the second set having a space attached for use at the ends of words. For example, in setting up the word "London" the first "n" would be an ordinary one and the second would be "n+space." In offering his services for the Government printing contract Beniowski claimed that if he had sufficient capital he could obtain all the composition in London by reducing its price by 1d. or 1½d. a thousand. His invention was not accepted by the printing trade, he alleged, because it would render their equipment useless; the publishers in their turn were against it, according to him, because new books would be so much cheaper that their large stocks would depreciate in value. What the representatives of the printing trade actually said in Parliament when asked for their opinion was that the reversing of type from one galley to another would soon damage its face and render it unfit for use. The specimen of Beniowski's printing which is attached to the report leaves one with the feeling that his type had long since reached this stage. His system of spacing, moreover, is reminiscent of the product of the typewriter at its worst.

A plentiful supply of type, although an essential factor in any large-scale printing developments, did not in itself confer any extra speed. After a point, type-casting might become more and more swift without any effect at all on the rate of printing. For the extra type to be brought into use there had to be either more compositors or a workable composing machine. It was at one time thought possible to overcome these drawbacks by casting, instead of innumerable copies of the same letter, combinations of letters based upon their frequency of use together. This was the art of logography.

Logography

The first attempt to introduce this idea may be attributed to Henry Johnson, of Saint Marylebone. In 1780 he registered "his new method of casting and moulding types, for the purposes of composing and printing by or with entire words, with several words combined, with sentences and syllables, and with figures combined, instead of the usual method of composing and printing with single letters, and of rendering the use of the said types, and printing with the same, easy and familiar to the most ordinary capacity, whereby every species of printing may be executed in one fourth part of the time in which they have been usually executed, and consequently at much less expense."[23] Johnson admitted that his invention was not entirely original: "by an old Magazine," he wrote, in explaining the system, "it appears, that about sixty or seventy years ago, a Gentleman had received encouragement from one of the Universities to form something upon this principle, but the reason of his not carrying it into execution is not declared."[24]

It was not in connection with books at all that Johnson first thought out his plan, but in relation to a lottery. It was his intention to publish a daily list of the prizes and blanks, in numerical order. This had never been attempted before, probably because it was realised, as Johnson himself found, that by the usual methods of printing the list could not be ready on the evening of the same day as the draw; delayed any longer it was useless. He got over his difficulty by having types of two, three, four or five figures composed in one body, instead of having them separate; "as by this means any entire number may be taken up ready composed, with exactly the same Dispatch that every single Figure required; consequently the work is performed in one sixth part of the usual time, with the additional advantage of there being no possibility of misplacing, inverting, or substituting one Figure for another."[25]

Just as the printing machine itself had been called into being as an adjunct to the textile industry, logography too was turned to the printing of text as an afterthought. Its success in turning out lottery results gave Johnson the idea of adapting it to this other use. It was a tremendous task which he had set himself. He set about collecting words from twenty newspapers, the *Spectator* and the Book of Common Prayer, cutting them out and sorting them to see how many times each word occurred in each sheet; that told him which words it would be most profitable to cast whole. Next he made a collection of endings such as -ed, -ing, -ly, -ment, -ness and -ify, which could be added to various roots. By the time he had finished he had a fount of about 3,500 words and syllables. He was well satisfied with the result. "As a proof of the expedition in composing by this arrangement," he says, "a section of the present treatise was indiscriminately taken, containing two thousand two hundred letters, and was composed in thirty-four minutes, and it is allowed by all the Trade, that it requires a good Compositor to do one thousand with correction in an hour; consequently this was performing the work of four hours in one."[26] It is certainly impossible to tell by looking at the treatise which pages were set up by logography and which were composed in the ordinary way.

There is no knowing how the use of logography might have extended if it had been given a fair test. As it was it was abandoned owing to opposition from the journeymen. John Walter used the method between 1785 and 1789 in printing *The Times* and was able to reduce the price of the newspaper from 3d. to 2½d.; but the compositors soon frustrated his scheme by demanding to be paid as if each combination was taken from the case in separate letters.[27]

Stereotype

There was a still earlier invention than logography which bears some superficial resemblance to it—the art of stereotype. Although solid blocks of type are used in both processes there is, for all that, no real connection between them. In logography the text is actually set up in solid pieces intermingled with individual types; in stereotype the letters are set up singly, and not until a whole sheet is set up is the cast taken from it which is to form the mould for a solid plate of metal. At the outset, therefore, this process saves no type at all. The economy arises when a later edition of a work is called for: rather than keep the whole of the type standing, moulds can be taken from it in readiness; the type can then safely be distributed and used for another book.

In Holland stereotype moulds seem to have been taken as early as the sixteenth century by J. Vander Mey, of Leyden. Little is known of his invention, and it appears to have died with him.[28] About a hundred years later stereotype was in limited use in Paris: plates were used for printing the calendars prefaced to prayer books. In the eighteenth century the same plates were being used by Valleyre, a Parisian printer.[29] It was not until 1727 that any attempt was made to introduce the art in Great Britain.

One cannot but feel that any criticism of our printers' lack of enterprise in making use of stereotype may justly be levelled against the policy of the Stationers' Company. As long as there was a rule that not more than a limited number of copies should be taken from any standing type there was no incentive for the printer to try to reduce his costs in this way. It was the set intention of the Company that printers should not cut down expenses by any means that might lessen the amount of work available for the compositor; it was not realised that cheaper production might work to the good of all. It was not that there was any lack of suitable material. There could have been no work more profitable to stereotype than Lily's *Grammar*, or the *ABC and Little Catechism.* The block-books of the fifteenth century had been school textbooks very similar to these; and what, after all, is a work in stereotype but a block-book whose blocks consist of moulded metal instead of hand-carved wood?

William Ged, a goldsmith of Edinburgh, was the first to try to break down the opposition. In 1727 he entered into partnership with an Edinburgh printer in order to carry out his ideas, but after two years his partner repented of his decision, seeing what it was likely to cost him, and withdrew. Ged did not wait many months before forming a company with William Fenner, a London stationer, and Thomas James, the founder. He would have been well advised to go for help to a general iron-founder rather than to a type-founder. It was not to James's interest that the experiment should succeed: he was afraid that in the long run it might lower the demand for his type. Instead of co-operating, therefore, he allowed his workmen wilfully to damage the plates; and a plate once damaged was most difficult to mend. Ged did manage to produce two prayer books, but such ill-feeling was aroused that they were suppressed by authority and the plates were destroyed. From this time on Ged could not persuade a single compositor to set up type for him, and the few theological works which by 1740 he did manage to finish were printed in Newcastle by his son.[30]

Henry Johnson was very sceptical as to whether Ged's failure was really due to the malice of the workmen. "It is more than probable, that the great difficulty, nay impossibility of casting so large a surface perfectly true, was the cause of its being unsuccessful, and any Alteration in a second Edition rendered it also useless. Within these few years another person under this Idea, in another form, endeavoured to print the Bible, and actually composed half a sheet of it with Types cemented together to remain always ready for use, like Copperplate, and this is said to be in the possession of a Stationer upon Tower Hill; but it was found impracticable, as well from the great Expense of the prodigious number of Types required, as also from the whole sheet or page becoming useless, in case a single letter was faulty or misplaced, in fact, the futility of it is plain."[31] Johnson was, perhaps, biased through his anxiety to show the merits of his own system. Half a century later the futility of stereotype was by no means plain.

For some years stereotype made no further advances in this country. In Germany its main principles were described in a volume published in Erfurt in 1740,[32] and again in the German *Encyclopædia* which appeared in Frankfurt in 1778. Meanwhile, in 1775, Benjamin Mecom of Philadelphia had cast plates for several pages of the New Testament.[33]

The patent[34] granted to Andrew Foulis and Alexander Tilloch, Glasgow printers, in 1784, marks the beginning of modern stereotype printing. In 1800 Earl Stanhope visited these two inventors in order to learn the process and afterwards, with the help of Andrew Wilson, a London printer, improved upon it; his "plaster process" was perfected in 1802. Further patents were taken out in later years by Applegath, Brunel and others, but no considerable alteration was made in the process until 1846, when papier mâché took the place of plaster for the moulds.

The process was not immediately adopted by the general printer. The reason given in the *Monthly Magazine* for April 1807 was probably sound, with the book industry still in a rather undeveloped stage: "it does not appear that more than twenty or thirty works would warrant the expense of being cast in solid pages; consequently the cost of the preliminary arrangements would greatly exceed the advantages to be attained." The writer argued that it would be cheaper to keep the type standing. He agreed, even so, that the Oxford and Cambridge University Presses had been wise to cast plates for Bibles and prayer books. A counter-statement appeared in the issue for May giving the arguments in favour of stereotype. In the first place, it saved the wear of type. It avoided the expense of recomposition, and although the expenditure on paper and press-work would be the same in the end the payment could be spread over a longer period. Stereotype plates were easier to store than a dead stock of printed paper. Every page, moreover, had a separate plate, so that all the pages were equally beautiful, whereas by the old method the type deteriorated towards the end. The taking of a permanent cast gave security against error. Finally it was claimed that the public would gain by a 25 to 40 per cent reduction in the prices of "all books of standard reputation and sale," comprising, according to this writer, three-quarters of all the book printing of England, Scotland and Ireland. This seems to suggest that stereotype moulds should be taken of *all* books in order to spread out the publication of single editions, not merely to prepare for possible future editions.

Argumentation as to the merits or otherwise of stereotype was to go on for many years. Hodgson's criticism, a quite plausible one, was that this method was no more insurance against error than any other, "for the readers of stereotype proofs are certainly no more infallible than those of other proofs." There was, he urged, an extra danger, that errors might remain uncorrected through several editions.[35] Babbage, on the other hand, thought it the ideal system of producing works demanding absolute accuracy, such as mathematical tables.[36] On the whole, the printers who had tried both methods agreed that stereotype gave the greater accuracy. It was found, in any case, that if alterations were required part of the plate could be cut away, and types inserted.[37]

By 1840 it was generally agreed that stereotype was profitable only where large numbers were concerned. One writer emphasised that it should never be resorted to except on very rare occasions; it was a fallacy to suppose that in ordinary instances it was a saving, for the plates were always liable to accident and could be repaired only by great loss of time and expense.[38] Another author was of quite a different opinion. He maintained that the principal advantage of stereotype after its accuracy was that publishers of large works need not print more than a few volumes at a time, in this way avoiding the locking-up of capital in large quantities of paper.[39]

Against the possible saving of paper, of course, there had to be set the cost of producing the stereotype moulds. That was not a costly process, but it was an extra one. The type had to be set up in the usual way and corrected. Then a cast of plaster of paris was taken from it, "prepared from that which is found in Nottinghamshire, and said to be the best, being called gypsum-in-the-rock."[40] The metal plate was taken from this cast. If, after all, no further copies of the work were wanted this was pure waste. For the invention to be used profitably everything depended upon the good judgment of the publisher. The saving where a new impression was called for was no slight one: the casting of plates was far less expensive than the founding and composition of individual types; there was, moreover, a total abolition of proof-correcting for the second impression, with all that it involved in time and money.

It is, of course, sufficient, as well as cheaper, to store the modern papier-mâché moulds and leave the actual casting of the plates until they are definitely known to be wanted. The plaster moulds were easily broken, so the casting was normally undertaken straight away. According to Edward Cowper, in 1828, Clowes had on his premises between 700 and 800 tons of stereotype plates belonging to various booksellers. Their value was estimated at £200,000.[41] In 1843 the stereotype department of the same firm contained plates "whose estimated value is not much less than *half a million sterling!* And even the plates, valued as old metal, are estimated at seventy thousand pounds!"[42] Each single plate weighed about 7 lb., and in all they were reckoned to weigh 2,500 tons. A single plate would print one page of a book, so that a ton of them would print a complete work of 320 pages. The stock which Messrs. Clowes held in 1843 would therefore be enough for 2,500 such works.

Full advantage has since been taken of the economies offered by the use of stereotype. It has become a matter of normal routine to take a mould of flong or wet papier mâché of any work of which a second impression seems likely to be wanted. At the end of the nineteenth century the cost of making such moulds amounted to between 4s. 6d. and 6s. a sheet. That is to say, in the case of an edition of 500 copies in medium 8vo the moulding cost £7 10s. of the total expenses of £135, £17 10s. representing the cost of the actual casting (which could really have been left until the second impression was called for). After this outlay, any succeeding impression of 1,000 copies could be produced for £92 10s., the original charge of £31 5s. for composition having been paid once and for all.[43]

The Decline of Type-founding

The cutting-out of the process of composition for later issues had its effects not only upon the compositors but also upon the type-founders. Individual founts of type would obviously last longer as stereotype came more into use. But the growing volume of publications in general more than compensated compositors and founders alike. A far more disturbing factor to the type-founder was the introduction in the closing years of the century of the linotype and monotype machines, which not only set up type mechanically, but also produced it. It was not long before the linotype machine had reduced the amount of ordinary type required for newspaper printing to negligible quantities. The monotype machine had almost as drastic an effect on book production. A great proportion of twentieth-century books are set up mechanically and therefore make no demands upon the specialist type-founder. Even the type for expensive hand-composed volumes is now more often than not produced on a monotype or similar machine and stored until wanted for use. It could well be said in 1926 that, owing to the increase in the use of type-setting machines, type-founding was a diminishing trade.[44] And, setting aside the type-founder's point of view, one can only be thankful that this was so. In that very same year, in spite of all these changes, the Oxford University Press still found it necessary to stock over a million pounds of metal. It included some 550 founts of type in about 150 different characters, including Sanskrit, Greek, Roman, Hebrew, Arabic, Syriac, Ethiopic, Amharic, Coptic, Armenian, Chinese, Tibetan, Burmese, Sinhalese, Tamil, Gothic and Cyrillic.[45] To store sufficient type for the whole of the output of the printing machine at the present time would clearly demand a formidable amount of space.

Anastatic Printing

One method of saving type which seemed to offer great possibilities never won the popularity which was prophesied for it. That was anastatic printing, the "fresh raising up" of copies from a printed sheet. It was a simple process. The printed paper was moistened with a weak solution of nitric acid which saturated only the unprinted part, and was then pressed with great force on to a sheet of zinc. The acid etched the metal while the printed matter "set off" on it, so that the zinc surface represented a complete reverse copy of the work. The zinc sheet was next washed with a solution of gum and acid which wet the etched surface, but was repelled by the ink. By inking the plate in this condition it was possible to pull impressions from it on the common lithographic press. The discovery was first made about 1840 by Baldermus, of Berlin. In October 1841, the editor of the *Athenaeum* was sent from Berlin a reprint of four pages of his journal from the copy published on September 25th. According to his description in number 736, "the copy was so perfect a facsimile that, had it reached us under any other circumstances, we should never have suspected that it had not been issued from our own office; and, even with our attention thus specially directed to the subject, the only difference that we could discover was that the impression was lighter, and that there was less body in the ink, from which we infer that the process is essentially lithographic, the impression of the original page being, in the first instance, transferred by some means on to the surface of the stone or zinc plate. This, however, is but a conjecture, and our correspondent is unable to throw light on the subject." The process did not remain secret for long. The inventor himself communicated the method to Joseph Woods, who took out a patent in 1844.

Lithography

Lithographic printing itself offered similar opportunities, although from the use generally made of it its description properly belongs to a study of the methods of illustration. The art was discovered as early as 1798 by Aloysius Senefelder.[46] It consists of obtaining copies from stone or other substances upon which the matter to be duplicated has been drawn with a special ink. Senefelder's activities were based on a study of the peculiar properties of the stone: a drawing made upon it with fat ink adhered to it so strongly as to require mechanical force to remove it; the parts of the surface free from the drawing absorbed water; so that on wetting the printing surface and running over it a roller covered with printing-ink the ink attached itself to the drawing and was rejected by the rest of the stone. When, therefore, a sheet of paper was placed upon the stone and then passed under a press the printing-ink was transferred to the paper, while the original drawing-ink still adhered to the stone. The art made little progress until 1815, but after that time rose to a considerable degree of importance. Babbage suggested in 1830 that the method could be used for reprinting works which had just arrived from other countries. "A few years ago," he wrote, "one of the Paris newspapers was reprinted at Brussels as soon as it arrived, by means of lithography. Whilst the ink is yet fresh this may easily be accomplished: it is only necessary to place one copy of the newspaper on a lithographic stone; and by means of great pressure applied to it in a rolling press, a sufficient quantity of the printing ink will be transferred to the stone. . . . If printing from stone could be reduced to the same price per thousand as that from moveable types, this process might be adopted with great advantage for the supply of works for the use of distant countries . . . an English work, for example, might be published in America from stone, whilst the original, printed from moveable types, made its appearance on the same day in England."[47] One would doubtless have known from the protests of outraged publishers if this had ever been made a regular practice. There is one legitimate use in which lithography has to some extent taken the place of movable types: the printing of music. The setting up of staves, bar-lines, notes and expression-marks by means of individual pieces of type is one of the most difficult forms of type-setting. A lithographic drawing, on the contrary, produces the finished sheet easily and quickly; it may either be used as a complete process, producing lithographed music which is very cheap but rather ugly, or it may form the basis of engraved music of more beautiful appearance than could be obtained from type. Nevertheless, as we have suggested, the main function of lithography is to reproduce pictures.

(*b*) *Illustrations*

At the end of the eighteenth century the book-illustrator was offered a still limited choice of processes. There were still the two main classes of engravings: relief-blocks, standing type-high and capable of being printed in the same process as the rest of the book, and intaglio plates, which required to be printed by means of a special roller-press.

To remind ourselves what these two groups so far comprised: the typical relief-blocks were the woodcuts, unchanged in principle from those of the fifteenth century. Printed most economically as part of the ordinary type-page these illustrations were normally in black and white, but for variety the chiaroscuro process was sometimes adopted, in which by dint of using several wood-blocks for the same picture, each printing a particular colour, it was possible to produce tone-prints. The woodcut was still the cheapest means of illustration, as it was the only form which did not demand the services of a skilled artist throughout; the actual cutting away of the wood from the design could be entrusted to any careful workman. In spite of that, at the time we are discussing the ordinary woodcut was completely out of fashion. For more than a century it had been kept in the background by the more elaborate and far more costly metal engraving.

Towards the close of the eighteenth century there was a partial revival in the use of wooden relief blocks. A successful attempt was made by Thomas Bewick (1753–1828) and his followers to imitate on wood the effects of copper-plate engraving. For cutting very fine lines it was hopeless to use planks of pear, beech or other soft woods such as were used for bold woodcuts. A very hard wood, such as box, had to be procured, and one of the new school of engravers, possibly Bewick himself, had the inspiration to cut on the end-grain instead of the plank surface to give a firmer line. That, incidentally, gave an opportunity for division of labour. It is difficult to obtain large surfaces on an end grain, so that the complete engraving had to be made up of a number of small sections. The preliminary drawing would be made by a single artist, but, in magazine work especially, it appears that the engraving of the small sections was sometimes left to other craftsmen, one of whom would afterwards join them together and add the finishing touches.[48] For some years wood-engraving enjoyed considerable popularity. Bewick's illustrations to *British Birds* and to Aesop's *Fables*, both published about 1800, were no less beautiful than his former engravings on copper, and his followers, Clennell, Branston, the Thompsons and the rest, approached closely to his skill. From the publisher's point of view the wood-engraving had much to commend it. The production of an engraved block was certainly far more expensive than that of a woodcut: engraving, no less on wood than on metal, had to be performed by an artist. But, apart from that, the other costs were low; there was no expenditure on metal plates, and, a still greater attraction, as the impression was to be taken from a raised line, in the same way as the woodcut, there was no special presswork involved. On balance, therefore, the wood-engraving was considerably cheaper than one on metal.

The second class of eighteenth-century engravings, the intaglio group, consisted of copper-plate prints in their various forms. These already offered a pleasing variety. Apart from the copperplate line-engraving pure and simple there were more elaborate processes—etching, mezzotint, stipple, aquatint—capable of reproducing different types of drawings. Etching is not a branch of hand-engraving, but is a process in which the design is incised upon the plate by immersion in acid, the lines which are to appear blackest being given the longest exposure. As the lines to be etched are drawn upon the prepared copper with a needle, and have not then to be carved painstakingly with the burin, the resulting picture resembles a freehand drawing to an extent which a line-engraving could never do. The resemblance can be increased by covering the plate with a soft granulated ground, giving a flecked line similar to that of a pencil. The mezzotint, in its turn, imitates the oil-painting. Its effect is obtained by roughening the whole surface of the plate with a tool known as the "rocker," to give a rich velvety-black background to the print; the medium lights of the picture are then obtained by removing the burr with a mezzotint scraper, and for the highest lights of all it is necessary to polish the surface with a burnisher so that there is no roughness at all left to hold ink. Stipple-engraving is an imitation of pencil shading obtained by covering the plate with an etching-ground, piercing this with a roulette, biting the ground with the acid, and then proceeding as for an ordinary engraving. The aquatint process reproduces water-colour drawings. Here again it is the etching-ground which gives the print its distinctive appearance. The art in aquatint is to use a porous ground so that the finished surface shows a network of white dots.

All of these copper-plate processes, with their further variations, had by the end of the eighteenth century shown themselves capable of producing beautiful results. All of them, unfortunately, were also very expensive both to produce and to print, £10 to £20 being the quite normal cost of a single plate.

The methods of illustration in use at the beginning of the nineteenth century were thus very costly. Actually the costs seem to have been specially high in Great Britain. T. N. Longman, giving evidence before the House of Commons in 1813,[49] stated that a work containing engravings would cost nearly half as much again to publish in England as in France, because the engravings were so very expensive in this country. He could not give definite figures, but he had heard that French booksellers commented on the dearness of our books of art. Was it, perhaps, that we had fewer artists who were willing to devote their energies to book illustration? We had certainly no school of book illustrators to compare with the French engravers of the late eighteenth century—C. P. Marillier, J. M. Moreau, Augustin de St. Aubin, Nicolas Delaunay and other famous names. We had the Turner engravers, it is true, but they did not specialise in bookwork, and William Blake, perhaps our most gifted illustrator of the time, was for various reasons eyed with suspicion by the publishing trade.

Nineteenth-century Developments

In the general speeding-up of the nineteenth century some change in illustrative methods was imperative. The wooden block might be used to produce very large editions, but in the case of the copperplate this was doubtful. By the time a sheet of copper had been passed through the roller-press for an edition of five hundred it was sometimes showing signs of wear. It was probably for this reason that the woodcut and the wood-engraving increased in favour for the expensive type of book. There was no question for many years of using engravings in cheap books. Charles Knight tells us of the trouble he had in 1828 to produce his *Menageries* complete with pictures. He had to arrange a special meeting at Messrs. Clowes's works of everybody concerned, and " 'everybody' not only meant the patentee of the machine, the wood-engraver, the stationer, the ink-maker, and the ingenious overseer of the printing-office, but as many of the committee [of the Society for the Diffusion of Useful Knowledge] as I could get together. . . . Such was a part of my editorial duty at a time when the great revolution in the production of books to be accomplished by the printing machine was almost as imperfectly realised as when Caxton first astonished England by the miracles of the printing press."[50] Four years later, when he began to edit the *Penny Magazine*, he thought it would be impossible to illustrate it, for the cost of wood-engravings, he reckoned, would be greater than the probable circulation of the work would justify. Good wood-engravers were now very few, he found.[51] He evidently thought better of his decision. The *Penny Magazine* certainly was illustrated, and in 1836 the editor tells us that the engravings for 305 numbers have cost £12,000. Nor was this a dead loss. Knight records that stereotype casts of the best pictures were supplied by him for similar publications in eleven different countries, including Germany, France and Holland.[52] England, in fact, was at last an exporter of illustrations!

It was an encouraging discovery that woodcuts could be stereotyped. Actually there was no more difficulty in taking a cast of a relief block than of a forme of type. What this meant in practice can be realised from the knowledge that in 1827 there were only about twenty woodcutters in London, who were all artists paid at artists' prices. Consequently, the woodcuts for each volume of *The Library of Entertaining Knowledge*, issued in that year, cost £200 or more.[53] Stereotype could not increase the number of artists, but it could give an unlimited number of reproductions of their works. Not only did this mean that copies of the same illustration could be printed on more than one machine at a time, but also there was no longer a risk of the total loss of the drawing; there had always been a danger of splitting the wooden block by too heavy pressure in the printing process, but a cast of it could now be held in readiness. The printer was quick to seize upon these advantages. By 1843 Messrs. Clowes had 80,000 woodcuts in stock, valued at about £3 each.[54]

The engraver himself had at last to adapt himself to a commercial age. Towards the middle of the century special machines were brought into use to engrave sky, water, grass and other uninteresting parts which did not seem to demand his expert attention.[55]

In the meantime metal engraving had not lost its popularity. The copperplate, it is true, was not hard enough for modern conditions, but the discovery was made that steel could be hardened to give any number of impressions. About the year 1832 it was found impossible to distinguish between two impressions of a bank-note engraved on steel; actually one was from the first thousand impressions taken while the other was taken after seventy thousand had been printed off.[56] Prints from a steel-engraving have a cold, hard appearance as compared with those from copper, but until further inventions materialised they formed a useful substitute.

The particular invention which allowed steel-engraving to fall into disuse was under consideration as early as 1839. In the *Athenaeum* for that year there is a paragraph headed "Galvanic Engraving in Relief" which states that Professor Jacobi, of St. Petersburg, has found a galvanic process by which any line engraved on copper can be converted into relief. It was not until about 1850 that experiments led to electrotyping as an established process. The system is one whereby an electric current is made to pass through a chemical bath, dissolving a plate of metal and depositing a shell of it on to a wax mould of the original type or illustration. The resulting block is an exact reproduction of the form of the original. By its use, therefore, it is possible to reproduce all the delicate variations of the copperplate processes. It has superseded stereotype, moreover, for the reproduction of woodcuts.

Illustrations in Colour

There had been no decline in the popularity of coloured illustrations. Unfortunate as were some of the early attempts at chiaroscuro, there were too many possibilities in the process for it to be abandoned without further experiment. In the meantime, before a really satisfactory mechanical method had been discovered, a large industry of hand-tinting grew up. How big this industry was at the beginning of the nineteenth century we can begin to realise on being told that a single one of Ackermann's publications, *The Microcosm of London*, involved the hand-colouring of 104,000 aquatint plates.[57] The pictures in children's books were coloured, it is said, by children in their teens, who worked very rapidly. They sat round a table, each with a little pan of water-colour, a brush, a partly coloured copy as a guide, and a pile of printed sheets consisting of impressions from wooden blocks or copperplates. No one child painted a whole picture. One was given the task of painting the red wherever it appeared in the copy. Another followed with, say, the yellow, and so on round the table until the whole was finished.[58] There was no sudden industrial change to displace all this labour. In many of the attempts to reproduce colours by means of the printing-press which were made before about 1850 certain of the more delicate parts were left to the hand-worker. During the revival of illuminated books which was so vigorous towards the middle of the century one publisher at least, Pickering, tried to obtain a truly mediaeval effect by hand-colouring alone. The quarto edition of *Dresses and Decorations of the Middle Ages* which he published for Henry Shaw in 1845 was sold at £18 18s., but considering that the artist himself had painted and gilded every initial letter, woodcut and engraving the charge was not excessive. Benjamin Fawcett was another mid-nineteenth-century illustrator who was loath to give up hand-colouring. The first of Orpen Morris's works on natural history which he illustrated, *A Bible Natural History*, seems to have been remarkably cheap: each of the 6d. monthly parts contained eight hand-coloured engravings. The *History of British Birds*, issued by Morris and Fawcett between 1850 and 1857 in 1s. monthly parts, contained 358 hand-coloured plates. The specimens for the colourers were all painted by Fawcett's wife. Traces of colour-printing appear in other works, but it was not until 1856–60, when Fawcett illustrated Lowe's *Natural History of Ferns*, that he seems to have given up hand-colouring altogether.

There is no doubt that, for those who can afford them, hand-painted volumes hold special attractions. At the same time that is no reason for limiting the reader of more modest income to a choice between black-and-white and no pictures at all. William Savage was one of the first engravers of the century to try to cater for this section of the community. By about 1820 he had successfully printed a number of coloured wood-engravings, and soon afterwards he included a number of them in a volume describing his methods.[59] Although Savage's results were quite encouraging nobody else seems to have adopted his processes, and until about 1835 the hand-colourer was allowed to proceed undisturbed.

In 1835 the Baxter process was patented. Whereas other illustrators had devoted their attention to metal engraving or to wooden blocks, or possibly both, but never both at the same time, George Baxter had the inspiration to use metal and wood in conjunction. That is to say, he began with a metal-plate engraving and applied his oil-colours by means of wooden blocks. So great was his success that for about half a century the Baxter process ranked equally in importance with the wood-block process and with chromolithography (soon to be described). It was recorded in 1852 as having recently been carried "to a considerable degree of excellence and beauty."[60]

Charles Knight, seeing the pleasing results of applying wood after metal, tried reversing the process and colouring a wood-engraving by metal blocks. At the same time he tried to cut out several processes by printing more than one colour at a time. Instead of having a separate block for each colour he used a kind of revolving press with four faces, each face bearing a colour-block. The sheet to be printed remained still while it received the colour from each block in turn, and as the first ink was still not dry when the fourth was added the shades were properly blended on the paper itself.[61] As a process it was completely successful; it was described in 1839 as being quite capable of taking the place of hand-colouring.[62] For all that, Knight himself seems not to have used it after publishing his *Old England* (1844–5). It may be that his colour-blending had not always given the results intended. It is well known that until the discovery of aniline dyes in 1856 there was no certainty as to what hue would result from applying any particular colour to metal.

Lithographic Illustrations

So far we have neglected the art of lithography as a means of illustration. It was the only new hand-process of the century, and it was specially original as being neither a relief process nor an intaglio, but a drawing on a flat surface. The essential principles have already been given: the drawing is made with fat ink or lithographic chalk upon a lithographic stone; the stone is damped, but as fat and water do not mix the drawing rejects the water; the printing-ink in its turn will not rest upon the damp part of the stone, but is attracted to the drawing, which it reproduces on the paper laid upon it and passed through the press. Senefelder, who invented the process, found that the roller-press used for copperplates gave too heavy a pressure and was liable to break the plate. He therefore devised a new kind of press, or what might better be described as a scraper.[63] This saved the stone, but did not lighten the work to any great extent. A modern writer has expressed horror at "the ruinous waste of skilled labour, which compelled a competent man to exhaust his energies, and unfit himself for the more delicate operations of his art, by the drudgery of dragging heavy stones through the press like a common labourer";[64] but until the days of machinery this was unavoidable.

One work illustrated by lithography was published in 1807,[65] but it was ten years later that the process began to be popular, sponsored by Rudolph Ackermann. The new method certainly held great attractions, especially on account of its cheapness. When the art was fully established suitable stones, the best of them imported from Germany, could be had for prices ranging from 1d. to 4d. a pound, according to size, and lithographic ink cost only about 1s. a cake.[66] Zinc plates, which could be used as alternatives to the stones, were even cheaper, besides being more portable. A far greater factor towards cheapness was the cutting out of the whole process of engraving. The many months' careful labour with a burin were no longer necessary; the drawing was made straight on to the stone. That was a point which was elaborated by Ackermann and his colleague, Hullmandel: whereas, they stressed, other types of illustration were mere facsimiles of the originals, here we had the artist's work itself.[67] Within a few years Hullmandel added a further argument; he issued a volume of illustrations showing how easily a lithographic drawing could be restored after it had shown signs of wear.[68]

Among the patents granted in 1840 was one to Hullmandel

for a "lithotint," which he described as "a new effect of light and shadow uniting a brush or stump drawing or both combined, produced on paper, being an impression from stone prepared in a particular manner for that purpose." This seems tc have been a variation of the process generally described as chromolithography, which differs from lithography only in the use of two or more stones instead of one, all except the "key-stone" printing a particular colour after the manner of the block-print.

For the printing of the profusely illustrated books of the middle of the century chromolithography offered a cheap alternative to hand-colouring. It was used in one of the finest books of the time, *The Illuminated Books of the Middle Ages*, published by Longmans in 1844. It was not a process to be adopted without first weighing the costs, for all that. Digby Wyatt's *The Industrial Arts of the Nineteenth Century at the Great Exhibition*, which was published in parts between 1851 and 1853, will serve as an example. The work contained 160 plates. The total number of pulls required to produce the 1,300 copies, so the publisher tells us, was 1,350,500, or an average of 18,000 a week. After every pull the stone had to be cleaned and the paper carefully readjusted. The number of stones used was 1,069, and altogether they weighed 25 tons.

Photographic Processes

So far there had been something laborious about all the attempts at book illustration. The invention destined to revolutionise the whole system of reproducing pictures had already been thought out, but had not yet been applied to this particular purpose. Since about 1813 Niepce, Daguerre and others had been trying to apply the new wonder of the world, photography, to the production of printing surfaces. In 1824 Niepce found a means of engraving on stone and soon afterwards on metal by photography, calling his process heliogravure. His discovery, roughly described, was that by covering the stone or metal plate with a film of albumen it was sensitised so that the film could be hardened by exposure to light, the unexposed parts remaining soluble. On washing off the soluble parts, therefore, he was left with a plate capable of being etched to produce a "photogravure." Daguerre, meantime, experimenting with silver salts, obtained photographic images of the distinctive kind to be known as "daguerreotypes." These were the beginnings. There was little so far to give any hint as to the tremendous and sudden growth which was to spring from them after many years. The early achievements, it must be confessed, were not beautiful. They were not even cheap. The cost of hand-engraving was eliminated, it is true, but the resulting plate was an intaglio, demanding the same tiresome press-work as a copperplate. It is partly for that reason that even at the present time hand-photogravure is too expensive for use in any but the very best type of work; each separate copy still takes between four and ten minutes to print. Further, it is found that for real success the finer detail must be etched in by an artist after the photographic process is over.

For many years the book illustrator preferred to ignore the new invention. Pleasanter results, and cheaper, could be had from the other new art, lithography; and if one wanted to spend more trouble on a picture what was wrong with the Baxter process? Unobtrusively, nevertheless, the art of photography was working its way in as an aid to the established processes. "The photographic principle," it was admitted in 1852, "has scarcely yet become an accessory to the printing art. There is evidence, however, that it may become so ere long; for, by a most delicate and beautiful manipulation, an electrotype cast has actually been taken from a photographic plate, and an impression printed from it—a sunbeam paints a picture, and a galvanic current engraves it. Proofs have also been given that photography may become a handmaid to the printing art; for many scenes and views have been presented in various illustrated journals, which could not have been published in time, but for the quick mode in which the sketches are produced by photography."[69]

It was, indeed, as a handmaid that photography took its first acknowledged place in the processes of illustration. Until well past the middle of the century the artist whose work was to be engraved had himself to copy his drawing in reverse on the wooden block; once there it could be altered beyond recognition by the engraver, who about this time seems to have developed an inconvenient urge for self-expression. When it was realised that a drawing could be photographed in reverse straight on to the sensitised block the original artist could take fresh heart; his own drawing, no longer destroyed, could be produced as evidence. What was more, he was saved the tedious and uninteresting task of copying his own work. Although the new method was already known by 1850, to judge from the extract we have quoted, it did not immediately come into regular use. The process was under discussion in 1865[70] but it was not for another ten or eleven years that it became popular.

What was wanted to bring photography into common use in book production was a means of obtaining a photographic relief block, one which stood type-high and could be printed in the ordinary machine. Between 1880 and 1890 two different types of block on this principle were successfully produced—the "zinco" and the half-tone. The development was sudden, and proceeded at a rate which gave the hand-engraver little warning to adjust himself to the new demands; but, his troubles apart, it gave new life to the book and newspaper world.

Neither of the new processes was invented in England. The idea of zincography was conceived by a Bavarian, Eberhard by name. It is a black-and-white process giving a similar effect to the woodcut, its lines standing in relief in the same way. The line-block, to give it its other name, reproduces exactly the lines which the artist has drawn on paper. The drawing is photographed directly on to a zinc or copper plate; an ink-roller is passed across the photograph, the ink staying on the lines but being rejected by the rest of the plate; then, by means of a bath of acid, the plate is etched so that the lines of the drawing stand in relief. A type of drawing which would formerly have taken a number of days to produce by hand could by this new method be ready in a few hours. By its nature the line-block cannot reproduce variations of tone, but as a compromise a grey appearance can be given here and there by a mechanical use of small dots printed close together.

For a tone-print there was the other new process-block, the

half-tone. The results of this process hardly need to be described: they are seen at their worst in the illustrations of the daily newspaper. It is in the newspaper, in fact, that one can best see how the tone-effect is produced. The whole picture shows as a series of dots, the dark parts being made up of large dots and the lighter sections of smaller dots, more widely spaced. Experiments on this principle had been made about 1850 by Fox Talbot, who used gauze for his attempts, but it was Meisenbach, a German, who made the process practicable by devising the modern screen. The picture to be reproduced is photographed through a screen consisting of two glass plates, each closely ruled with black lines, put together so that the lines cross one another. The light passes through the screen, and the size of the resulting dots varies according to the proportion of light passing through the individual squares. For the most perfect reproduction a very fine screen is used, with 250 or more lines to the inch. (Unfortunately a fine screen demands very smooth, shiny paper which is not only trying to the eyes but is alien to the rest of the book.) The printing-block is obtained by copying the negative on metal and etching it.

Both of these processes were far cheaper than any former means of illustration. By about 1890 a zinc line-block from a photograph or pen-and-ink drawing cost only 6d. a square inch, the minimum charge being 5s. The cost of a half-tone block varied from 1s. to 1s. 6d. a square inch, according to the nature of the copy. The usual time for executing an order was one week, but a block was frequently made on the same day as the order was received.[71] And, a further advantage, when the block did arrive it could be printed as rapidly as type.

Not all of the modern methods are as cheap. Collotype, a process which evolved from French and German experiments from 1886 onwards, remains one of the most expensive as well as one of the most beautiful. The printing-surface is here composed of gelatine. A plate of glass is coated with a layer of gelatine containing alum, which gives a delicate grain to the surface. After exposure the plate is etched. The next stage is the inking: the art here is to keep the plate sufficiently damp, as the result depends upon the principle that the lighter parts, absorbing more water than the darker ones, will take less ink and give a lighter impression. This is the clue to the expensiveness of the process; the printer has to be constantly on the watch to see that the degree of moisture is exactly right. Moreover, as the printing-surface is flat the rate of printing is rather slow.

Photogravure had by the end of the century become recognised as one of the most artistic means of illustration, but, when printed by hand, it was a slow process. The introduction of rotary photogravure was to increase the rate of printing to six thousand or more impressions an hour. It was invented by Karl Klic, of Bohemia. In 1890 he came to England and helped to form the Rembrandt Intaglio Company, which within a few years was producing copper-coated cylinders and etching them by his methods. The cost of the cylinders, unfortunately, partly offset the cheapness arising from the greater speed.

Twentieth-century Processes

The twentieth century has developed these nineteenth-century ideas and has added to them. One of the most original of the modern developments is the process known as "offset" printing. An American named Rubel invented this system of printing indirectly from rubber, and brought his idea to England in 1907. In its best-known form the process is combined with rotary printing, the ink being transferred to a rubber cylinder from one of zinc or some other metal. An extension of the process is photo-litho-offset. A photo-lithographic plate is made by photographing the original drawing, developing the negative on a film such as is used for a line-block and inking the film with lithographic ink; on washing the film the ink is removed entirely from those parts which have not been exposed to light and stays on the rest of the film in proportion to the amount of light which has fallen on each part. For the offset process an impression of the plate (which must have been reversed for the process) is transferred to a rubber sheet, from which the actual print is made. Besides being used for illustrative purposes photo-litho-offset is often used to produce cheap reprints of

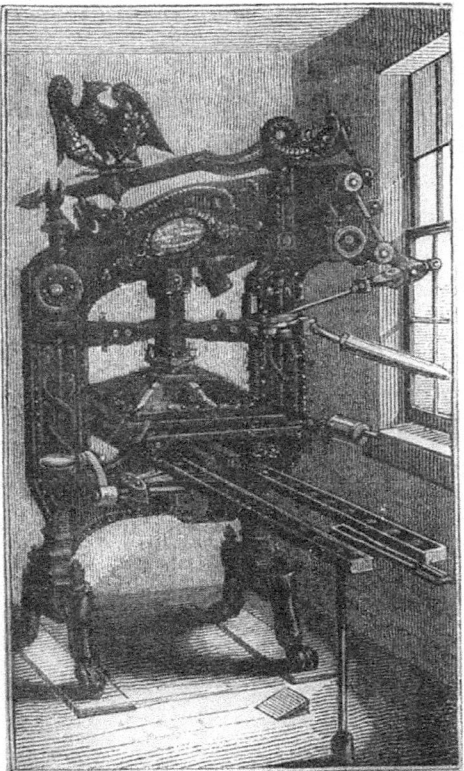

THE COLUMBIAN PRESS
From Johnson's *Typographia*, 1824

MESSRS. BACON AND DONKINS' PRINTING MACHINE
From Rees (P.), *The Cyclopaedia*, 1820

books—almost as Babbage prophesied more than a hundred years ago!

Another use of the offset printing is as an improvement on the half-tone process. The rubber, being flexible enough to reach all parts of the plate, allows a rougher plate to be used. The desire to use a pleasanter kind of paper for the half-tone process has, in fact, led to much experiment in recent years. Probably the most successful developments have been the deeply etched half-tone, in which a coarse screen is used and smoothness is given to the print by using a slightly spreading ink, and the pantone process. For the pantone a chromium-plated copperplate is used. The etching acid acts on the plate by removing the exposed parts of the chromium. The bare portions of the copper are then coated with silver and mercury, which will reject the ink, leaving it to be deposited only on the chromium, the printing-surface. Chromium will reproduce the finest of screens on quite a coarse paper.

The line-block was from the beginning capable of being printed on any kind of paper. Its modern developments have adapted it to colour-printing, the resulting prints having much in common with the earlier wood-block pictures. The process, too, is similar: the colours are put on one at a time by separate blocks, as before, but the blocks themselves are produced photographically.

The most ingenious method of colour-printing is one usually combined with the half-tone process. As its action is to split up the colours into the three primaries it is commonly known as the three-colour process. It works by a system of filtering. To photograph the red part of the picture, that is to say, the yellow and blue rays are stopped out by placing a green glass in front of the lens, so that only the red rays will reach the plate. Other plates are produced in a similar way from the yellow and blue rays. In printing they are superimposed and the colours are blended in the correct proportions; and, if exact register is obtained and the press-work is more than usually careful, the original colouring is faithfully reproduced. The Finlay process allows the light-filtering to be done on a single negative.

New processes are being introduced at an almost bewildering

rate, most of them having some affinity to the ones already described. There is, perhaps, one which is so important as a means of saving time that it calls for mention. It is akin to the mid-nineteenth century development by which the less interesting parts of an engraving were left to be put in by mechanical means. The modern variation of this is what is known as mechanical tint, or the Ben Day system. Now, instead of the artist having laboriously to draw the various kinds of suitings, curtain-weaves, and so on, he may if he wishes mark the appropriate Ben Day number on his sketch and the detail will be supplied to his order.[72]

Naturally each new method of illustration has not automatically superseded the rest. At the present day almost all the old types of illustration are still to be found issuing from the press. Lithography, perhaps, is least used in book production, having found a more suitable employment in poster-printing. Of the rest, woodcuts, wood-engravings, copperplate engravings, etchings, all are employed where they seem artistically right. Now that the woodcut is not the only possible means of illustration it offers fresh charms—and the modern woodcut can be as novel in design as any offset print. What has happened by the developments of the last century is that some appropriate means of illustration has been found for works of every description, to be sold at whatever price.

(*c*) *Ink*

Although the introduction of the printing machine was eventually to bring about a greater demand for ink, the first improvements tended rather to be ink-saving. By the old method of inking with balls much of it was wasted: the ink on the edges of the balls was not transferred to the type at all, but had to be removed later as a solid crust. The introduction of cylindrical rollers formed of a mixture of glue and treacle prevented any further waste of that kind, but it was the printing machine which was to eliminate waste altogether. In the course of their working the travelling rollers of the steam-press drew out the exact quantity of ink required and spread it uniformly over the type. An experiment was made at

Clowes's works to find what the saving actually was. "Two hundred reams of paper were printed off, the old method of inking with balls being employed; two hundred reams of the same paper, and for the same book, were then printed off in the presses which inked their own type. The consumption of ink by the machine was to that by the balls as four to nine, or rather less than one half."[73]

Until about 1820 there seems to have been no change at all from the early methods of manufacturing ink. The first improvement was a simple one: the sixth edition of the *Encyclopædia Britannica* (1823) notes an extra ingredient, soap. Its effect was to give a sharper impression in printing and to prevent the type from becoming clogged. Soap may well have been in use for some time; a recipe published in the same year includes it without special comment.[74] It had been discovered by then that the oil for the varnish could be thickened by other means than boiling.

It happened before long that the extra demand for ink, brought about especially by the wider circulation of newspapers, created a shortage of the main ingredients. Lamp-black could be bought for 1s. a barrel in 1750,[75] but its supply could not be increased sufficiently to cope with modern developments. The earlier patents for ink-manufacture were therefore concerned with the finding of a substitute. At first the alternative pigments were simple in nature: Martin and Grafton in 1821 proposed to use the soot of burnt coal-tar; Bird, in 1835, mineral earth; Gwynne and Maumene in 1853 suggested, in the first case, powdered coal, and in the other carbonised lignite. Later pigments were derived from bituminous shale and schists (1856), aniline by-product (1859), the distillation of cotton oil (1864), bone oil (1866), oxides of iron heated with carbonised peat (1868), and the tannin black from leather waste (1881).

Linseed oil was another of the traditional ingredients whose supply threatened to fail. Its price had risen gradually from 2s. 8d. a gallon in 1703 to 4s. at the end of the eighteenth century.[76] To judge by the smaller number of patents for this purpose, it was more difficult to find a substitute for oil than to suggest an alternative pigment. In 1865 Newton did manage to prepare one from glue and gelatine, but some later inventions avoided the use of oil altogether. May and Lawrence, for instance, in 1869 and 1870 respectively, produced ink from glycerine, gum and pigment. Nevertheless, linseed oil has never been superseded as the best foundation for printing-ink.

By 1859 the old methods of manufacture were too slow. That was the year of Hadfield's apparatus for the manufacture of varnish, followed shortly afterwards by Neal's grinding-mill. In 1870 Jackson patented an improved type of grinding-mill, and in 1877 Williams introduced the use of steam in boiling oil. Torrance, in 1896, obtained a patent for a grinding- and mixing-mill combined. These have all been superseded by more complicated machines, several of them of foreign design.[77]

It says much for the efficiency of modern methods of ink-manufacture that an ever-growing demand for ink since the middle of the nineteenth century has not led to higher prices. About 1860 the price quoted for ink suitable for good bookwork was 3s. a pound.[78] It is significant that by 1913 the prices quoted were for a *dozen* pounds. For bookwork and magazines they ranged from 12s. to 30s., according to quality.[79]

Variation in quality was a new and disturbing factor. To the early printer ink had been just ink; he made his own, in the best way he could, and worried no more. In the twentieth century things are very different. "The manufacture of ink has become such a complicated process that it is impossible for even the most wide-awake printer to acquaint himself with all the necessary details—even if he should feel so inclined—and he must therefore rely upon his ink maker for the information regarding the qualities and characteristics of the inks he uses. At the present time an up-to-date ink maker uses over two hundred different pigments and about one hundred and fifty different varnishes."[80] The manufacturer to-day will adapt his supply of ink for any piece of work to take account of the temperature and humidity of the pressroom, the kind and speed of the press, the kind of paper to be used and the dryness of the stock. Specialisation has here also contributed its full quota of improvement.

CHAPTER XV

Paper in the Machine Age

ONE of the most certain results of such an unprecedented growth in the textile industry as that of the late eighteenth century was surely a vastly increased supply of rags. The masses of the population, hitherto clothed in wool, could now afford frequent changes of the new, cheap cotton materials. So great was the expansion of printing, however, that at the end of the century rags were as scarce as ever they had been.

Any scarcity arising in war-time is apt to be regarded as in some way due to the upheavals of war. The shortage of rags, and hence of paper, at this time seems, accordingly, to have been generally looked upon as a necessary outcome of the Napoleonic Wars. It does not seem to have been a reduced importation of rags which was worrying the paper-manufacturers, but the growth of a new demand for rags for war purposes. Matthias Koops thought that such fears were exaggerated. "It has been imagined," he wrote in 1800, "that the present war has principally contributed to produce the scarcity of paper-stuff, which, however, does not appear to be the sole cause, because the quantity of rags used for making lint is very inconsiderable, compared to the enormous quantity at present used for the manufacture of Paper. Cartridges have usually been made on the continent of old written Paper, which heretofore has been of no other use to Paper-makers than for the fabrication of paste-boards. It appears, from various considerations, that the scarcity has originated from the extension of learning, which occasions much larger quantities of Paper for writing and printing; the large increase of newspapers and monthly publications."[1] In addition, as he pointed out, a new demand had arisen for paper for general trade purposes. Above all, "Paper-hanging, which is an invention of the middle of the seventeenth century, has, of late years, become more general; and few new-built housesare finished with walls, or wainscot, as formerly, but the surface is everywhere decorated with painted or stained Paper."

There is no doubt that the shortage of paper was acute. Lackington had prophesied a few years before this that publishers would soon have to reject works of literary value owing to its growing cost. The high price of the inferior papers used by grocers, cheesemongers and other tradesmen had already caused many thousands of volumes to be destroyed for pulp instead of being sold as remainders.[2] It was reported to a committee of the House of Commons that in July 1799, the printer to the Tax Office had three presses standing idle for want of paper; while Charles Cooke, a bookseller of Paternoster Row, gave evidence that "such is the high price of the raw material with which Paper is now made, that he could not print the detached Numbers to complete different sets of Works he had advertised to publish, without being at a greater Expense in printing the same than what he sold them for."[3]

A paper-maker told the same committee that three-quarters of the rags used in this country were still supplied from abroad. This did not necessarily mean that our new supplies were being wasted, but rather that our paper-manufacture was at last established as of world importance. England and Germany were now the largest paper-manufacturers in Europe; many of the French paper-mills, once so active, were now shut up or used for other purposes.[4] "There were, a century ago," said Koops in 1800, "in the provinces of Perigord and Angoumois 400 Paper-mills, and now there are not one hundred remaining." The French trade, according to him, although it was still considerable, had been turned into a new channel: large quantities of paper-hangings were being exported from France to America. Of the British paper the best was being made in Scotland. "Messrs. Foulis, printers, at Glasgow, are said to export annually on an average two millions of copies of books to foreign countries, and it must be presumed that they are partly indebted to the superiority of the Scotch paper, over that of Germany and the Northern countries, for the pre-eminence to which their printing-house has been raised."[5]

By 1800 about 24,000,000 lb. of rags were being annually converted into paper by our manufacturers. Koops shares our surprise that so large a proportion had to be imported to England, considering "the number of its inhabitants and their superior cleanliness in linen," but the explanation he offers is no doubt correct: English people, living on the whole fairly comfortably, could not be bothered to save rags, but burnt them.[6] If good white rags were not to be had, there was nothing for it but to use inferior ones. From 1792 onwards, therefore, a number of patents were granted for bleaching rags; and from this time, according to John Murray, our paper began to deteriorate. Much bleaching certainly tends to destroy the fibre, and the use of gypsum in the pulp and of alum in the size, which were to come next, have nothing to commend them as far as durability is concerned. Murray was soon full of gloomy prophecies: "Our modern books and manuscripts are in a state of the most rapid decay. The greater part of them will not outlive half a century; many of them not half that period."[7]

In spite of this falling back on poorer materials, the price of paper did not fall. The printing-paper which in 1793 cost 13s. 6d. a ream rose gradually in price until by 1801 it cost 27s.; paper of another quality rose in the same time from 14s. to 28s.; still another rose from 17s. to 34s.[8] How serious this was for the book trade will be realised from the publishing accounts already quoted. By 1813, according to Thomas Longman, the cost of the paper for an edition of 500 copies was roughly two-thirds of the whole expense of the publication.[9] Parliament had already given all the help possible by allowing the importation of rags free of duty, and even, from 1799, the free importation of waste paper, provided that it was torn into pieces to prevent its use for any purpose besides re-manufacture. Any other move towards a more plentiful supply of paper had to come from private initiative.

Early Experiments with Non-Rag Paper

The shortage of materials had already been foreseen in Germany. About 1756 Dr. J. C. Schäffer, of Bavaria, was experimenting with a pulp made of sawdust and shavings instead of rags. He was unsuccessful for a time, but by 1770 his theories had proved capable of practical application. His *Samtliche Papierversuche*, published in Regensburg in 1772, contains specimens of eighty-one varieties of paper made, amongst other things, from the wood of the willow, mulberry and other trees, from straw, shavings, sawdust, hop-vine, wasps' nests, nettles, thistles, potatoes, maize, peat, moss, and from walnut and tulip leaves. Most of these are in good preservation, though it must be admitted that none bear much resemblance to writing- or printing-paper as we know it. Koops made light of these achievements on the ground that a small quantity of rags had been used in each case,[10] but his own work was probably influenced by Schäffer's experiments.

The manufacture of a non-rag paper in this country dates from the year 1800, in which there was recorded a grant of a patent to Matthias Koops, of Ranelagh, gentleman, "for his new invented method of manufacturing paper from straw, hay, thistles, waste and refuse of hemp and flax, and different kinds of wood and bark, fit for printing and other useful purposes." In the same year Koops issued his famous *Historical account of the Substances which have been used to describe Events, and to convey Ideas, from the earliest Date, to the Invention of Paper; printed on the first useful Paper manufactured soley* [sic] *from Straw*. The body of the work is printed, he says, on paper made entirely from straw, and the appendix on paper made of wood, "the produce of this country, without any intermixture of rags, waste paper, bark, straw, or any other vegetable substance." At the present time both of these papers are of the same unpleasant fog-colour. Koops himself did not press the claims of his paper for printing, but he argued that if it were found suitable only for pasteboards, packing-paper and paper-hangings it could be exported cheaply and would give employment to thousands of women and children. As it happened, another half-century was to elapse before the manufacture of paper from straw became a commercial proposition, but there is no need to belittle the work of Schäffer or of Koops on that account.

The Paper-making Machine

What was wanted at the beginning of the nineteenth century was not so much a substitute for rags as a cheaper and quicker means of manufacture. By the customary method it took five or six weeks to bring paper to the marketing stage. That meant that the publisher was not sure of being able to buy a specially large quantity at short notice, and had therefore to keep part of his capital locked up in a two or three months' supply. To a growing press there could be no greater handicap than an uncertain supply of paper. It was the paper-making machine which was to provide the way out of the difficulty.

Louis Robert, a Frenchman living at Essonne, was the originator of mechanical paper-making. In 1799 he designed a machine for making a continuous sheet of paper on an endless wire cloth worked by rotary motion. There his work ended. The French had no paper-machine at all at work until 1815, and only four in 1827.[11] The scheme which was abortive in France was patented in England in 1801 by John Gamble. Three years later the patent was re-assigned to Henry and Sealy Fourdrinier, who had in the mean-time, with the help of Bryan Donkin, improved upon the original invention and set up self-acting machines at Frogmore and Two-Waters, Hertfordshire. There was no doubt about the success of the Fourdrinier. Brunel said of it, "I consider that it is one of the most splendid inventions of our age. . . . It is hardly possible to conceive the magnitude of it. When I say that it makes 1,600 miles of paper in one day, that is to say, the machines altogether, it is a monstrous thing . . . ; but it is a fact, that the 280 machines that exist can [each] make six miles a day of paper."[12] That was in 1837. Considering these eulogies, the occasion for them is the more distressing. Brunel was giving evidence before a committee of the House of Commons which had been set up to consider a petition with regard to the patent rights. The Fourdriniers, in spite of the acknowledged usefulness of their invention, had become bankrupt, and now complained that "the paper-makers employed the engineers of the patentees to construct machines, and finding that the patentees were bankrupts, they refused to pay the patent dues." From the evidence it was clear that Brunel's praises were not extravagant. It was, in fact, the committee itself which reminded Brunel of the chief service rendered by the Fourdrinier invention —the possibility of printing by means of cylinders.

Fourdrinier, in the course of his statement to the committee, remarked that about two and a quarter million pounds' worth of paper was being made annually. Whereas the full process of manufacture had formerly taken five weeks or more it now took only five days, so that manufacturers, wholesale stationers, printers, booksellers and retail stationers were all able to carry on their business with less capital. Charles Knight, the publisher, bore out this statement: "The supply," he said, "is such as to enable one with perfect ease to meet the demand, however large, without keeping any stock in hand: for example; I use about 1,500 reams of paper per month; unless this machine had been invented, I could not have gone into the market with the certainty of purchasing 1,500 reams of paper for the month's consumption; and I should have been obliged to have kept two or three months' consumption to have insured a regular periodical supply; that amounts to a large saving to a person engaged in publication."

The general opinion seems to have been that the machine-made paper was not only steadier in supply, but also of better quality than the other. John Murray, a few years before, had been rather doubtful about that, although even he agreed that some form of machinery had become necessary.[13] Those who gave evidence before the committee of 1837 had no doubts at all. George Clowes, after showing the superior merits of the new paper, made the plain statement, "in fact, we never like to make use of any hand-made paper." A stationer said that he had had about a thousand reams of hand-made paper in stock for six or seven years, and even though he had offered it at a lower price than it could be made by machine it would not sell. His explanation was, "It is manufactured by hand, and the colour is wanting, and it has not the improvements of the present day." The machine certainly saved waste. By the old method, as one witness pointed out, every sheet had to be passed to a woman whose work it was to remove knots from the surface. As that was done with the point of a knife it is easy to believe that many sheets were spoilt in the process. Then again, the outside quire of every ream still consisted, as in Moxon's day, of torn or dirty sheets. Paper made on cylinders had neither of these disadvantages.

There were now no more complaints of scarcity. Not only was the worry of securing sufficient paper to finish the work in hand now a thing of the past, but the very abundance of the supplies was offering new possibilities to the publishing world. George Clowes spoke from experience: "The paper machine, in connexion with the printing machine, without which the printing machine would have been comparatively useless, has effected a complete revolution in our business; where we used to go to press with an edition of 500 copies, we now print 5,000. . . . It has called into existence a class of cheap publications which could not otherwise have been produced. . . . We are enabled to have paper of any size that we require so that we can print a larger number of pages at one time; for instance, in printing a common demy octavo volume, instead of printing 16 pages in the sheet as we used to do, we can now obtain paper of twice the size, that is, double demy, and so print 32 pages in the same time that we used to print 16, so that we can print a book off, when it is ready for press, in half the time we used to do."[14]

The growing supplies were reflected in steadily falling prices. The price of the "fine quality" paper supplied to the Clarendon Press fell from 17d. a pound in 1814 to 12d. in 1824; that of the second quality fell from 15d. to 11d.[15] Taking the weight of the ream of the first quality as 35 lb., this represents a drop from 49s. 7d. a ream to 35s. The fall in prices was to continue. Charles Knight records that one particular kind of printing paper which cost 24s. a ream in 1831 was in 1843 sold at 15s. 6d. The paper which he used for his *Penny Cyclopædia* was 33s. a ream between 1833 and 1837 and only 24s. between 1838 and 1846.[16] But the lower prices this time were due not so much to the spread of machinery as to the reduction of taxation.

The gain to the national revenue from Fourdrinier's invention far exceeded its benefit to any of those individuals who had been so unstinting in their praise of it. By the 'thirties the excise duties on paper, at the rate of 3d. per lb., were bringing in well over half a million pounds a year.[17] The public, as Babbage showed, were actually being taxed to a still greater extent than this, "for they pay, not merely the duty which is charged, but also the profit on that duty, which the paper-maker requires for the use of additional capital; and also the profit to the publisher and bookseller on the increased price of the volume."[18] In 1837, in the general movement towards free trade, the duty was reduced from 3d. to 1½d.; hence the fall in prices from this date. Even so, the tax was still a heavy drain on the publisher's resources. Charles Knight's account of the cost of the paper for the *Penny Cyclopædia* and its supplement is illuminating in this respect: "The two works contain 15,764 pages, and the quantity of paper required to produce a single copy is 2 reams, each weighing 35 lbs. At the period of its completion, the entire quantity of paper consumed in the work was fifty thousand reams, the total weight of which amounted to one million seven hundred and fifty thousand pounds. Of this weight 20,000 Reams, or 700,000 lbs., paid the Excise Duty of *Threepence* per lb., amounting to 8,750 *l.*; and the remaining 30,000 Reams paid the reduced duty of Threehalfpence per lb. (commencing in 1837) upon 1,050,000 lbs., amounting to 6,562 *l.* The total Duty paid up to the completion of the Cyclopaedia, in 1846, was 15,312 *l.* Since that period 2,000 Reams of Paper have been used in reprinting, to correct the inequalities of the stock, making an addition of 70,000 lbs., excised at 437 *l.* But further, the Wrappers for the Monthly Parts have used 1,500 Reams of Paper, taxed at 500 *l.*, and the Milled Boards employed in binding the volumes have been also taxed about 300 *l.* The total Payment to the excise by the Penny Cyclopaedia has been sixteen thousand five hundred pounds."[19]

Whether as a direct outcome of the lowering of the rate of duty or on account of a quite independent growth in the demand for newspapers and journals, the quantity of paper being manufactured by 1850 was sufficient to bring in a higher excise revenue than ever. The duty paid in that year was £852,996 13s. 10d., amounting to about a fifth of the selling price of the paper. The actual burden of the tax was even heavier. One paper-manufacturer complained, "It costs me in labour alone, to help to charge myself with the duty on paper, about 100 *l.* a year. I make about twelve tons per week; and in consequence of these Excise Laws have to weigh every ream four times over, besides taking the number of every ream, and writing the weight on each."[20] The duty was no more popular than any of the other "taxes on knowledge," but it was not until 1861 that it was discontinued.

The Shortage of Rags in the Mid-Nineteenth Century

By 1850 the paper-manufacturer was beset by other trials. At a time when the market for his produce was greater than ever before, he was faced with an acute shortage of rags. Since 1844 the quantity of foreign rags imported had averaged about 8,000 tons a year, rising from 7,061 tons in 1844 to 10,140 in 1846 and falling again to 6,953 tons in 1849 and 8,124 in 1850;[21] the export restrictions of many continental countries prevented any adequate growth. The search for a substitute for rags now began in earnest, and led to a special correspondence between the Treasury and the Board of Trade.[22]

In the course of the correspondence Lyon Playfair gave his views on the cause of the scarcity of rags. In his opinion it was partly, though indirectly, due to the stoppages in the linen and cotton manufactures, such as the lock-outs of Wigan and Preston and the halftime working at Belfast; but, although these must have had their effects, it must be remembered that a large proportion of the supply of rags still came from abroad. His next suggestion seems more valid: the demand for paper had outrun that for manufactured linens and cottons. He realised that linen or cotton paper was necessarily a waste product; not only would the cost of cultivating flax or cotton specially for its manufacture have been prohibitive, the raw material had in any case to go through part of the process of manufacture before the fibres were sufficiently broken up for use in paper-making. That being so, it was evidently more profitable for the material to be used first for clothing or some household purpose, delaying its use for pulp. There was always a certain amount of cotton waste left over from manufacture which could quite economically be turned into paper straight away, but, as Playfair pointed out, it had been wanted of recent years for wiping the machinery on the new railways and steamboats. Above all, the Americans had become important buyers in the world rag-markets.

It was suggested that British consuls abroad should obtain information as to any other suitable materials, the one stipulation being that the cost should not exceed 2d. or 2½d. a pound. The report from India was quite encouraging: several suitable vegetable growths were mentioned, such as lily and áloe-leaved plants, which were already being used for the purpose in India, and rice straw and plantain; and it was thought that by employing cheap native labour they could be brought here at a low price. Lyon Playfair was not so optimistic. Even though the various fibres cost little enough in themselves, he reasoned, the preparation they would require would offset their cheapness; some of them in any case could not be bleached well enough for white paper.

Further Experiments with Rag Substitutes

At the time when this correspondence was being carried on new attempts to find a cheap non-rag paper were being made by private manufacturers. The successful manufacture of straw paper dates from 1853, when two Frenchmen, MM. Coupier and Mellier, worked out a process which was to be generally adopted.[23] Paper of this kind was of little direct use in the book industry, but large quantities of it have been consumed by the newspaper-press; the effect must, therefore, have been, even if not to set free more rag-made paper for the general publisher, at least to prevent further encroachment on his supplies. Meanwhile, experiments were being made with wood fibre, and in 1853 Charles Watt and H. Burgess obtained a patent for the manufacture and use of wood pulp. An exhibition of the wood paper was held at a works on the Regent's Canal; a copy of the *Weekly Times* printed on it was shown, as well as various water-colour drawings; and the Earl of Derby and various Press representatives who attended were enthusiastic as to its quality. The whole process was said to occupy only a few hours. It was claimed, indeed, that a piece of wood could be converted into paper and printed upon within twenty-four hours. Nevertheless, nobody in England was found willing to take up the manufacture, and in 1854 the inventors thought fit to take out an American patent.[24] The process was reintroduced into England by Houghton's patent of 1857.

A beginning had been made, but it had to be admitted a few years later that the cost of the chemical processes involved in preparing any of the new raw materials was still in the way of any real success. The Select Committee on Paper of 1861 described the manufacture as being in a state of "unprecedented depression."[25] That was due, it was thought, almost entirely to foreign competition. The industry still relied very largely on foreign rags: about 15,000 tons a year were being imported, representing roughly one-fifth of our annual consumption. The policy of continental countries was directed towards keeping down prices at home. To this end the export of rags was either prohibited altogether, as in Belgium and Spain, or was made subject to heavy export duties. The Zollverein was exacting a duty of £9 3s. a ton; France, £4 17s. 2d. a ton. Hamburg, on the other hand, allowed free export, and Turkey charged a duty of only 1s. a ton.[26] Most of the rags imported came from Prussia, Hamburg and Russia, although Egypt was gradually taking part of the trade of Russia. The rest came from Sweden, Denmark, Holland, Italy and other continental countries, and even from the British East Indies and Australia; but, as the committee reported, the cost of carriage from distant sources was out of all proportion to the value of the material.

It is significant that there was now no talk of scarcity of paper, with its dire effects on the book industry. The complaint now was of a too great abundance, an abundance arising from abroad and not from our own mills. The reduction of the import duty in August 1860, had been followed by a sudden influx of foreign paper against which the British manufacturer could not compete.

The imports increased from 1,468,992 lb. in the year ending March 1860, to 4,735,136 in the following year. The effect was to lower the price of English paper by 10 per cent, making some mills work at a loss and driving others to half time. The depression was deepened by an equally heavy decline in the foreign demand for British paper; exports, which had increased steadily from 11,000,000 lb. in 1855 to 20,000,000 in 1859, had fallen in 1860 to 15,000,000. The only remedy, according to the committee, was to promote real free trade conditions. "The removal of the Excise Duty on Paper will not place the English manufacturer in a position of equality with his continental rivals, so long as the export duties on rags remain in force abroad. The Committee, therefore, recommend that the British Government should continue strenuous exertions to effect the removal of all restrictions abroad upon the export of all paper making materials."

While the committee was thus regretting the inability to control the taxation of other countries an entirely new paper-making material was finding its way to England. A North African grass known either as esparto or alfalfa was introduced by Thomas Routledge into his mills at Eynsham, near Oxford, in 1857,[27] and was soon widely chosen in preference to rags for its cheapness. Esparto presented none of those difficulties of manufacture which appeared so formidable in the case of wood. There were no involved chemical processes demanding expensive equipment. The grass had simply to be picked to remove roots, weeds and other unwanted substances (a task carried on by women and girls, or, later on, by a special machine, the "willow"), to be boiled, in quantities of about three tons at a time, to be washed, and then bleached; after which there was no difference from the methods adopted for making rag paper.[28] Its success was almost phenomenal. In 1884, for example, while the rags imported amounted to 36,233 tons, valued at £487,866, the quantity of esparto and other fibres was 184,005 tons, worth £1,125,553. Spain and North Africa are the chief centres of supply of esparto. For some reason its use up to the present has been almost exclusive to the British paper-maker; foreign countries have had little success with it.[29]

Experiments in another direction were to result in a further substitute for rags. In 1860–65 and 1873 Voelter obtained patents in England for the manufacture of mechanical wood. It will be remembered that nearly a century before Dr. Schäffer had tried to make paper from sawdust, but had been handicapped for lack of suitable machinery. Voelter's method was to press blocks of wood against a revolving grindstone to reduce them to dust, then to pulp the material with water. A more durable paper, it was found, was to be made from wood cellulose: wood shavings were boiled in caustic soda ley and then washed to remove the alkali; the wood was next treated with chlorine gas and washed again to free it from hydrochloric acid; caustic acid was then added to convert it into pulp, which, after washing and bleaching, was ready for the beating engine and the machine.

By 1882 the shortage of raw materials was at an end and the United Kingdom was leading the rest of Europe in both production and consumption. Our production in that year was approximately 470,000,000 lb. and our consumption 430,000,000. Germany followed closely in both. The United States of America was already ahead, with a production of 530,000,000 lb. and a consumption of 540,000,000. These quantities included a vast number of types of paper, and it was estimated that only 6 per cent of the total would be used for books.[30]

The use of rags was not abandoned on the discovery that other materials could be turned into serviceable paper. It is generally agreed that the most durable paper is still made from linen or cotton rags, preferably soft, well-used cotton for printing purposes as linen tends to be rather harsh.[31] But modern fashions in dress and furnishing offer little reward to the rag-collector; artificial silk, of which most of the scraps would probably consist, is useless to the paper-manufacturer. What has happened is that the newer paper-materials have taken the place of rags for those publications which do not justify the use of the best paper.

In the earlier years of non-rag paper some anxiety was felt as to the permanence of the new materials. The visions of decay which had so worried John Murray earlier in the century had now, it seemed, a real foundation. In 1898, accordingly, the Society of Arts appointed a committee to investigate the problem. They found that the fibres fell into four classes: the most durable paper, the committee agreed, was still to be obtained from cotton, flax and hemp; of the rag substitutes the various wood celluloses had the longest life; next came esparto and straw celluloses; last of all, and for book purposes quite unreliable, was mechanical wood-pulp, a sawdust product.[32] A committee of the Library Association more than thirty years later came to the same general conclusions.[33] In practice these four main groups can be broken up and resorted; quite a good paper can be made, for instance, by combining esparto and wood in the same pulp.

Actually the introduction of so many alternatives has given rise to an almost endless range of papers, from the finest hand-made all-rag to the cheapest of mechanical wood. The range of prices by 1930 was very wide. Newsprint, the poorest paper of all, cost only about a penny a pound. The finest esparto printing papers were about 3d., and good machine-made "tub-sized printings" cost about 7d.[34] (The average weight of paper in a book has been estimated at 14 oz.).[35] Pre-1914 prices were, of course, lower: a good quality antique wove which in 1925 cost 4d. was then only 2½d.[36]

It cannot be said as yet that the paper on which a book is printed has often been chosen with regard to the value of the text. A paper very frequently chosen for novels is the so-called "antique" variety, a thick substance (usually of esparto) which provides in the easiest possible way the bulky volume expected by the fiction-buying public. Its lightness and bulk together condemn it, showing that it is loose in texture and full of air. But, as one authority has aptly said, its appeal to the publisher is that air is cheaper than fibre.[37] Other admittedly non-durable papers in general use are more easily justified. They have arisen to meet a special demand from the printer in connection with photo-mechanical processes of illustration. The half-tone process in particular calls for a very smooth, brilliant paper, and the china-clay surface of this art paper usually covers a base foundation.

For general book printing probably the best paper is made from a mixture of chemical wood and esparto.

Comparative Costs of Paper

All of this goes to show that in comparing publishing costs for various periods since the early nineteenth century, as far as paper is concerned one may really not be comparing examples of the same thing. It is actually more relevant economically that one should not. The ordinary book of the year 1800 was printed on hand-made rag paper; a present-day work on such paper would be one of an *édition de luxe* not truly comparable with it even though it were cheaper than the earlier volume. An abundance of other materials naturally helped to lower the price of rags. Whereas in 1891, for instance, the price of a hundredweight of rags ranged from 11s. to 22s., by 1897 they cost only between 8s. and 17s. 6d. The paper manufactured from them was sold at about 1s. 3d. a pound[38]—a more expensive variety than would be chosen for general printing purposes, although its price was only that of the "second quality" paper supplied to the Clarendon Press in 1814.

At the beginning of the nineteenth century, as we have seen, the cost of paper might amount to two-thirds of the whole expense of publication. It was certainly a formidable item in Reed and Harris's edition of Shakespeare: the whole cost of producing the work, including the editor's fees of £400, was £5,683 4s. 6d., of which the paper accounted for £3,345 3s.[39] By the time that Babbage published his volume *On the Economy of Machinery and Manufactures* (1832) the Fourdrinier had come into use, which may be the reason that the paper for the whole edition cost, so he tells us,[40] only £99 4s. 6d. (including excise duty of £22 1s.) out of the whole expense of £266 1s. Ten years later paper appears to have been just as plentiful: the first edition of Dickens's *Christmas Carol* (1843) cost £805 8s. 5d. to produce; the paper cost only £89 2s. of this, but its proportion to the total was affected by three unusually heavy items—colouring plates, binding and advertising—which together amounted to over £468.[41] Round about 1850, according to specimen accounts, the paper for an edition of 1,000 copies cost rather more than a quarter of the whole expense of production.[42] That was before the abolition of the tax and before the use of esparto and wood-pulp. The effects of these show clearly in later accounts. An edition of 500 copies of an octavo work of 272 pages was estimated in 1891 to cost £64 17s. 8d.; the paper was put down at £7 13s. One thousand copies of a rather larger volume were estimated at £112 3s. 4d., of which the paper cost £19 10s.[43] Forty years later the paper ordinarily cost a still smaller proportion of the whole. An estimate in the thirties of the cost of 1,500 copies of an octavo volume of 288 pages gives a total of £262 17s.; only £18 18s. of this applies to paper.[44]

In the course of a century, therefore, the share of paper in the total cost of producing a work may be said to have fallen (at a very broad estimate) from two-thirds of the whole to less than one-tenth. Other factors have not remained entirely unchanged, it is true; a higher expenditure is normally made on advertising now than in former times; printers' wages, again, have raised type-setting costs. On balance, nevertheless, it is clear that the cheapening of books in modern times owes not a little to the experimenter with wood and grass.

CHAPTER XVI

Modern Bookbinding

UNTIL beyond the middle of the eighteenth century it was still the fairly general practice for the customer who wanted his book bound to make special arrangements for the work to be carried out. Yet while the sale of volumes in loose quires, or merely stitched, allowed the future owner scope for expressing his own ideas in the matter of binding, it had its drawbacks. Most people, after all, buy a book with the intention of reading it, and not as a museum piece; they are apt to wax impatient at being offered a choice between a collection of loose sheets, tiresome to read and liable to tear before they are at last given up to the binder, and a wait of three weeks or more while the volume goes through all the processes involved in giving it a stiff cover. In the days when bookbinders were still few the delivery of a work in loose quires was specially tantalising. The Reverend William Clarke once had occasion to remonstrate with William Bowyer, the printer, on the subject. Writing in 1742 from Buxted, in Sussex, he pointed out: "We are as distant almost from the mechanical as the liberal arts, and it is as easy to find an orator as a bookbinder among us. In such a situation, you may be sure, the appearance of Lysias *in sheets* gave us some disorder: a country tailor could never have taken measure of him, who are commonly our ablest artists. In short, there was nothing to be done, without returning him back again to London, and desiring that he may make his next visit in a more elegant and ceremonious manner, *bound and lettered.*"[1]

The alternative form of issue, in which the sections were stitched together and the book given a thin paper cover, was no more popular. We have already mentioned one of the unaccountable differences between the continental and the English book market until recently, that while French and German purchasers were content to buy paper-covered books English people would seldom take a volume that was not in a stiff cover. John Murray in 1876 gave this before the Royal Commission on Copyright as a fact of his own experience.[2] While, therefore, binders' lists of the early nineteenth century were still quoting prices of 2½d. a volume upwards for stitched paper covers, by this time the paper cover had been superseded almost entirely by plain paper boards, still designed as a purely temporary covering, but very often the only cover which the volume was destined to receive. A medium-sized octavo volume could be bound in "common boards" for as little as 4d.[3] For the customer who had no intention of giving himself any further trouble a rather more elaborate style quickly followed the use of plain boards: "extra boards" signified a cover on the same plan, but made more attractive by the use of patterned papers.

Certain types of literature had now for many years been obtainable ready bound in leather as an alternative to the sheet form. At the beginning of the nineteenth century the leathers most generally used were calf and sheepskin. Parchment, once so popular, had at last been relegated to the binding of account-books. The main use of roan, or sheepskin, was for school-books; it was cheaper than calf and demanded less artistic workmanship; and it was probably on that account that before long sheepskin work came to be given to workmen other than those who were intrusted with the finer materials.[4] Those who were content with this cheaper leather could reap the benefits of mass production. The "quarterly book," the extra copy which it was customary for the bookseller to supply free of charge on an order for 24, was not charged for by the binder if sheepskin or some cheaper binding were chosen, provided that all the work was of the same kind and sent at the same time. This concession did not apply to calf bindings, except in the case of Bibles plainly bound.[5] Nevertheless, it was calf which was most in use for regular binding, and morocco for the finest books; sheep was used only for the cheapest work.[6]

Cloth as a Binding Material

There was still room for another kind of covering-material. From leather to paper was a long step; what was wanted was some attractive substitute for leather which would come mid-way in price between the two. What was more natural than for the binder to turn to the new, cheap cotton fabrics? Various attempts were made to use them, but the untreated dress materials were found unsuitable. They were too soft to be easily workable, and, what was worse, the glue came through. The same objections applied to silks and satins, but there was a revival of their use round about 1820 for the kind of volume supplied for drawing-room perusal. By 1822 Pickering had found a satisfactory red cloth which he used regularly for his publications,[7] but it was not until 1825 that a book cloth specifically so called was put on the market. It was produced by Archibald Leighton from white calico, which he bought in Manchester and glazed and dyed on his London premises. There were two methods of binding in cloth in these early years: it could be used for quarter-binding a volume with paper sides or the whole volume could be covered with it.[8] There was as yet no attempt at ornamental lettering on cheap bindings, and the effect of a paper label on a rather dreary-looking cover did not at first make for popularity. Book production in general has tended to cling closely to tradition, and the new shiny cloth was too unlike anything that had been used for it to be readily accepted. Something was done to bring it into favour by making it not merely a substitute for leather, but an imitation of it. The grained "morocco cloth" of the eighteen-thirties was a far more successful competitor against boards. This embossing too was at first performed solely on Leighton's premises, although by the time Robert Leighton entered the business in 1836 other houses had set up embossing machinery of their own, obtaining their dyed cloth from Leightons. Embossing as carried on in those days was a laborious process employing four men. The pattern was engraved on a gunmetal cylinder and transferred in reverse upon one made of compressed paper, strung upon an iron spindle. Red-hot irons were placed inside the gunmetal cylinder, being changed for others as soon as they were cold, and by a great effort of manual labour the cloth was passed between the two cylinders and received the impress of the metal one.[9]

The discovery in 1832 of a quick means of stamping gold-lettering and ornaments on binding-cloth was the greatest triumph for the new material.[10] This again was mainly the work of Archibald Leighton. It saved the cost of adding leather backs for taking gold-tooling, and in the opinion of H. G. Bohn the idea would have brought in a considerable income if it could have been patented.[11] Cloth bindings had come to stay, although it was not until 1838 that Leightons were able to give up dyeing and calendering and to buy finished material from the first manufacturer of bookbinders' cloth, Thomas Hughes of Bunhill Row.[12] There were many variants of it before the modern buckrams, canvases, rexines and the rest came on the market. One new material produced in 1846 was advertised in strange company: its patent[13] was granted for improvement in the manufacture of "caps, bonnets, book-covers, curtains and hangings, show cards or boards, labels, theatrical decorations, and coffins" by the use of flocked fabrics; that is, cotton or linen cloth flocked on one side to represent wool. An early attempt at producing artificial leather for bookbinding was made by Eugene Carless, who in 1855 was using cotton cloth and a rubber solution for the purpose.[14] This actually was a bad time for the cotton trade, owing to the shortage created by the Crimean War. Another bad setback came a few years later with the cotton famine of 1860–63. With cotton at 2s. 5½d. a pound in December 1863, as compared with 6d. to 7d. in 1860, the cloth binding lost for the time its main attraction to the publisher. There was nothing for it but to return to binding in boards until conditions improved.

The Introduction of Machinery

The actual covering of a book is, after all, only one of a large number of operations, all of which are reflected in the final cost of the binding. If the labour-cost of folding the sheets, sewing them, hammering them and so on were to remain unchanged the amount of the saving merely from using cloth instead of leather might be disappointing. After about 1830, too, when the printing machine made it possible to turn out more and more copies of a work in a given time, by some means the binder had to keep up with the new rate of output. His was not an industry for which mechanism at first offered obvious advantages. Unlike the work of the pressman, which could be relegated to a single machine, bookbinding involved many separate processes, all completely independent of one another. By 1820 the first operation, folding, was usually being carried on by women. It was easy work, the sheets being folded into 2, 4, 8 or more by means of a slip of ivory or box-wood. When folded the sheets had to be gathered together in correct order and beaten on a stone with a heavy hammer to make a solid block, and then they were pressed. Next came the sewing of the sections together, after which the back of the book was glued and then rounded with a hammer. At this stage the volume was ready for the boards to be stuck on: the cords round which the sewing had been carried were threaded through holes in the boards and the ends of the cords hammered smooth. After being pressed the book was ready for the cutting-press. If the leaves were not to be gilded, marbled or sprinkled the next procedure was to add the head-band, an ornament of thread or silk twisted round a roll of paper. All was now finished except the actual covering. The leather for this had to be moistened in water and cut to the size of the book, the edges being pared off on a marble stone. Then it was smeared with paste and stretched over the boards; and it was on the pressing which followed that the neatness of the book depended. There were still a few processes: the end-papers had to be pasted in, the cover had to be glazed with white of egg and polished with a polishing-iron; pieces of morocco might then be added to receive the lettering, or gold letters and ornaments might be worked straight on to the cover. Most of these operations seem to have been carried on by the same man, for although bookbinders were now usually fully occupied throughout the year it was not long since the trade had been a part-time occupation for the general stationer.[15]

It was impossible to devise a machine to carry out all these operations. Individual processes might lend themselves to mechanical treatment, but the cost of setting up as many machines as there were processes was in the early days of mass-production far beyond the resources of the ordinary binder. It paid him better to employ more and more labour to cope with his growing work, giving as much of it as possible to women, whose time was cheaper. In 1830 there were not quite 600 journeymen bookbinders employed in London. In 1862 there were 1,545, including 24 children under the age of 13.[16] According to the 1861 census the industry as a whole was now occupying 3,691 males and 4,063 females. But by that time it had been found profitable to introduce machinery.

One small improvement had, in fact, been made at the beginning of the century. To the Society of Arts it seemed so far from trivial that the inventor, J. I. Hawkins, was awarded a silver medal. The idea was for a machine for cutting paper and the edges of books, cutting the three edges of a book at one fixing in the press.[17] Charles Stimpson of Boston in 1831 secured an American patent for an equally simple matter—the addition of a board to the cutting-press to act as a gauge, to save marking the edges of the paper.[18] The close cropping so noticeable in many books of the period may have had something to do with the use of these new machines by ill-practised hands. Or a modern writer is perhaps correct in suggesting that this frequent "bleeding" of books, as cutting into the letterpress is technically called, was an intentional means of raising the profits on bookbinding.[19] Not only did the cropped volume require less binding-material, but the sale of shavings was no small item. A century before the bookbinders had petitioned Parliament on the subject of millboards: formerly these had been made by the binders themselves from the shavings cut off the edges of books in the process of binding, "which generally is about the sixth part of the whole quantity of paper in every book," but now that millboards were being made from old ropes used in shipping the petitioners pointed out that the shavings of books were being wholly employed in making white paper.[20] That being so, might there be an inducement to raise the proportion rather above one-sixth? These odd scraps mounted up. By the middle of the nineteenth century the weight of the paper shavings sold by the London binders amounted to about 350 tons a year.[21]

The almost certain result of introducing a machine of any kind in the early part of the century was a storm of protest from the employees. In the bookbinding trade, apart from this early cutting-machine, no machinery at all was brought into use until about 1828, but the usual objections were then soon being raised all over again. The machine in question was designed to do away with one of the heaviest of the hand-processes. It was a rolling machine, a kind of iron mangle which did the work formerly carried on with heavy beating hammers. For all that, the men wanted to return to the harder work. Nearly five hundred of them pointed out in a petition sent to the employers in December 1830[22] that the number of journeymen bookbinders out of work was rapidly growing, and they claimed that the rolling machine was directly responsible for the distress. Some employers, according to this paper, had in commiseration gone back to the old methods. That may be, but one feels loath to believe that the rolling-press itself displaced much labour. There was really very little mechanism about it, for its two rollers were worked by hand. The journeyman placed a small number of folded sheets between two tin plates and passed them between the rollers; a boy on the other side received the sheets, laid them in heaps and returned the tin plates to the man,[23]—a quicker process, certainly, than hand-beating, but something more leisurely than the movement of, for example, the printing machine.

Seeing that the first machine was moderately successful the bookbinders gradually introduced others, necessarily on the plan of a machine to each individual process. In 1843 the works of Messrs. Westleys and Clark contained paper and board-cutting machines as well as rolling machines. The "cloth-cylinder" room contained 2 machines for giving to the cloth a granulated or speckled appearance; and in the embossing shops there were 3 powerful machines for pressing designs on to the flat covers.[24] None of the machines so far were very involved in design, nor were any of them yet run by steam-power; but such mechanism as there was had already led to reorganisation of the more progressive firms. Whereas in earlier times all the individual operations were generally carried on in one room, and many of them by one man, the up-to-date bindery had now a separate department for each of the main styles of binding. Messrs. Westley and Clark's factory in Shoemaker Row, for instance, a building 6 storeys high, comprised a board warehouse, a cloth warehouse, an embossing warehouse, a cloth-cylinder room, embossing shops, a counting-house, a boarding-shop, a roan- or sheep-shop, a "Pinnock" room (appropriated to the sewing and covering of the 9d. books called *Pinnock's Catechisms*), blocking-shops, a leather warehouse and still more. It was found convenient to classify the departments according to the type of binding to be carried on rather than the kind of labour required; to have, that is to say, all the workpeople required for binding in boards on one floor, those dealing with leather-bindings on another and those binding in cloth on yet another, each department having its own group of women and girls for the preliminary work of folding and sewing. Altogether the firm employed from 250 to 300 hands. It was described by a Government commissioner as admirably conducted.[25] There was still room, as there remains to-day, for the small bindery, but already it could be said that to set up in a "respectable way" required capital; the new tools and presses were expensive, and the booksellers were apt to demand credit.[26]

Other machines were invented in time for the Great Exhibition of 1851. It was reported then that book production so greatly exceeded that of any former period, and had caused the application of so much machinery to bookbinding, that it could fairly be said to have become a manufacturing business.[27]

The binder's great handicap was that although the individual machines might be fairly cheap he needed many different kinds of them before his works could be considered fully equipped. Round about 1860 a rolling machine could be bought at prices ranging from £18 to £60; a backing machine cost £55; millboard-cutting machines were from £10 to £15 each; and arming presses might be had for various prices between £12 and £63.[28] All these taken together would go only a short way towards binding a book, but their cost was already as high as the printer need pay for a complete and efficient printing machine, workable by two boys. Bookbinding machinery was still in most cases worked by manual labour. Nevertheless, Charles Knight was able to claim at about this time that the new contrivances had not only cheapened books, but had enabled the publisher to give them a permanent cover, ornamental as well as useful.[29]

Steam-power was late in being introduced into this particular industry. Even the heavy blocking-press, which stamped patterns on the covers, was at first laboriously worked by means of a lever, but by 1862 steam engines had been introduced for the purpose in many establishments. Some of the new folding machines, too, were being worked by steam.[30]

The folding machine was not an immediate success. It consisted of a series of tables or shelves, each fitted with a folding knife. A child could mind it, and it worked four times as fast as hand-folding; but in 1862 it was described as not yet sufficiently well adjusted for book work.[31] That did not matter greatly to the employer when women and children could be engaged to do the work by hand for very low wages. In 1845 women folders were in some cases being paid as little as 5s. 6d. for a 55-hour week, and learners 2s.[32] Piece-rates combined with long hours brought them a better return, but when the Factory Acts set a limit to their working hours some other means had to be found of getting the folding done by a given time. The women naturally resented the change. Until the Act of 1867 one provincial printer used to employ casual labour for the work: the women used to come in and fold for a day and a night once a month and in this way earn from 10s. 6d. to 14s. When this was no longer allowed a very expensive folding machine was bought, capable of doing the work of ten women.[33] "It is a very hard thing of the gentlemen in London," was the immediate outcry, "that they cannot let poor women like us earn a little extra money sometimes."[34] One way out of the difficulty was to let the women take the work home. The 1901 census figures, the first to give the numbers of those working at home, show that 274 women bookbinders were so employed. On inquiry by a group of social workers it was found that much of this work was folding, especially of thin paper Bibles and prayer books. But it was not a very popular arrangement with the employers; the women were too prone to send back the work covered with teacup stains.[35]

As the century advanced and the annual volume of publications steadily increased other types of machinery were tried, until by about 1890 there were machines for over half of the main processes. There were machines for folding, sewing, gathering, nipping, cutting, rounding and backing, as well as for several of the finishing operations. So far none of them were capable of great speed. The newer folding machines, it is true, could deal with between 1,000 and 2,000 sheets an hour, a great advance on hand-folding. The gathering machine, on the other hand, seems merely to have allowed the hand process to continue, removing the cause of fatigue: by the old method the gatherer walked up and down picking up a sheet at a time from the piles on a long table; now a number of gatherers sat at a round table which was covered with piles of sheets; the table was made to revolve, and the gatherers took a sheet from each pile as it passed them. The main advantage to the employer seems to have been the saving of space and the prevention of shirking on the part of the workers.[36] Higher speeds were to come in the last decade of the century with an influx of American machinery. While the foreign linotype and monotype machines and the new rapid printing machines were giving rise to some apprehension among employees in the printing trades there were equally disturbing developments in bookbinding. Foremost among the new American machines were the Sheridan case-maker (1897), the Dexter folding machine (1898), and the Crawley rounder and backer, invented about 1900, which successfully combined the two processes in one operation. The various folding machines will fold about 12,000 16-page sections an hour, and gathering machines work at an approximate rate of 7,800 books an hour. There are various types of sewing machines which will sew 60 sections a minute, whereas it takes a woman a day to sew 2,000 or 3,000 of them. Book-back gluing machines save both time and glue; their output is equal to that of from 3 to 5 hand-workers. The machine-minder has simply to take a number of books and place them on the feed-table. From there they are automatically carried over a roller, which glues the backs, and then over a brush, which distributes the glue between the sections. As for the combined rounding and backing machines, they work as fast as the books can be fed in. But even now some firms prefer to do these two processes with an ordinary hammer, believing that it gives better results.

By the end of the nineteenth century cheap labour was no longer the main consideration; speed was a matter of far greater concern. According to one employer, "When we see a good machine we try it, and we do not think of the cheapness or dearness of the labour it may displace."[37] As it happened, labour was reapportioned rather than displaced. Although women were not required to mind the new self-feeding folding machines, openings were provided for them on other processes newly mechanised. The gloom which was cast over the men by the introduction of the rounding and backing machine was soon dispelled; it was found that even though there was less to do in these branches there was more "lining-up" and other work than before, so that nobody was turned off on that account.[38]

Publishers' Casings

Almost before the idea of bookbinding machinery had been entertained it had occurred to somebody that it would be much easier to make a large number of separate covers and merely stick them on. The idea was mentioned in a bookbinding manual issued in 1835,[39] and it was already being practised. Joseph Shaylor, in one of his papers written about that time, describes the rush of getting new novels ready for the distributing agents. Formal notice was given to the trade that a novel would be ready at noon upon a certain day, and "punctually at that hour the sheets which had been previously ordered were handed to the novel dealers who were waiting for them. Then commenced the race for the libraries, as it was a recognised arrangement that whoever arrived first with the books ready bound should supply the librarian with the copies he required. Some of these distributing agents prepared the covers for binding beforehand, thus forestalling most of the other competitors." It was quite easy to have the cases ready; the printer had only to send a dummy copy of the book made from the actual paper being used, and this he could do as soon as he knew how many pages the book would make. By 1850 houses such as the Remnants, the Leightons and the Westleys were casing volumes in cloth at the rate of 1,000 in 6 hours, provided that the cases were previously made, and the making of the cases themselves took less than 2 days.[40]

A bookbinder trained on the traditional methods must no doubt have been shocked at the suggestion that the whole of the strength of the binding should be sacrificed to speed; the binding as he knew it was firmly worked on to the book by lacing the cords or tapes through the boards; how much strength could one expect from a pasted strip of mull? The answer was that the public did not ask for strength in bookbinding. For all ordinary books they were content with attractively coloured covers which would stand a moderate amount of use; and these the publishers were more than content to supply. Casing, as distinct from binding proper, has been the normal form of covering provided by the publisher for more than a century. That is not to say that true binding has died out; far from it, but as in earlier times it is now a matter for special arrangement.

The advantages of the publisher's casing are speed and cheapness. In regular binding little can be done to forward the work of covering until all the processes of folding, gathering, sewing, rounding and backing have been carried out. In casing, on the other hand, a great mass of covers can be produced in readiness while all this other work is in progress, and can be finished off even to the lettering. All that is needed then is for the covers to be attached by means of a piece of mull and for the end-papers to be pasted down, a simple enough process, nevertheless one which lends itself to division of labour. By the year 1900 one firm was apportioning the work among 6 people: the first girl glued; the second laid on the boards; a man cut the corners; another girl turned in the ends; a fourth turned in the fore-edges; and finally a fifth girl put the volumes through the rolling machine.[41] The larger the

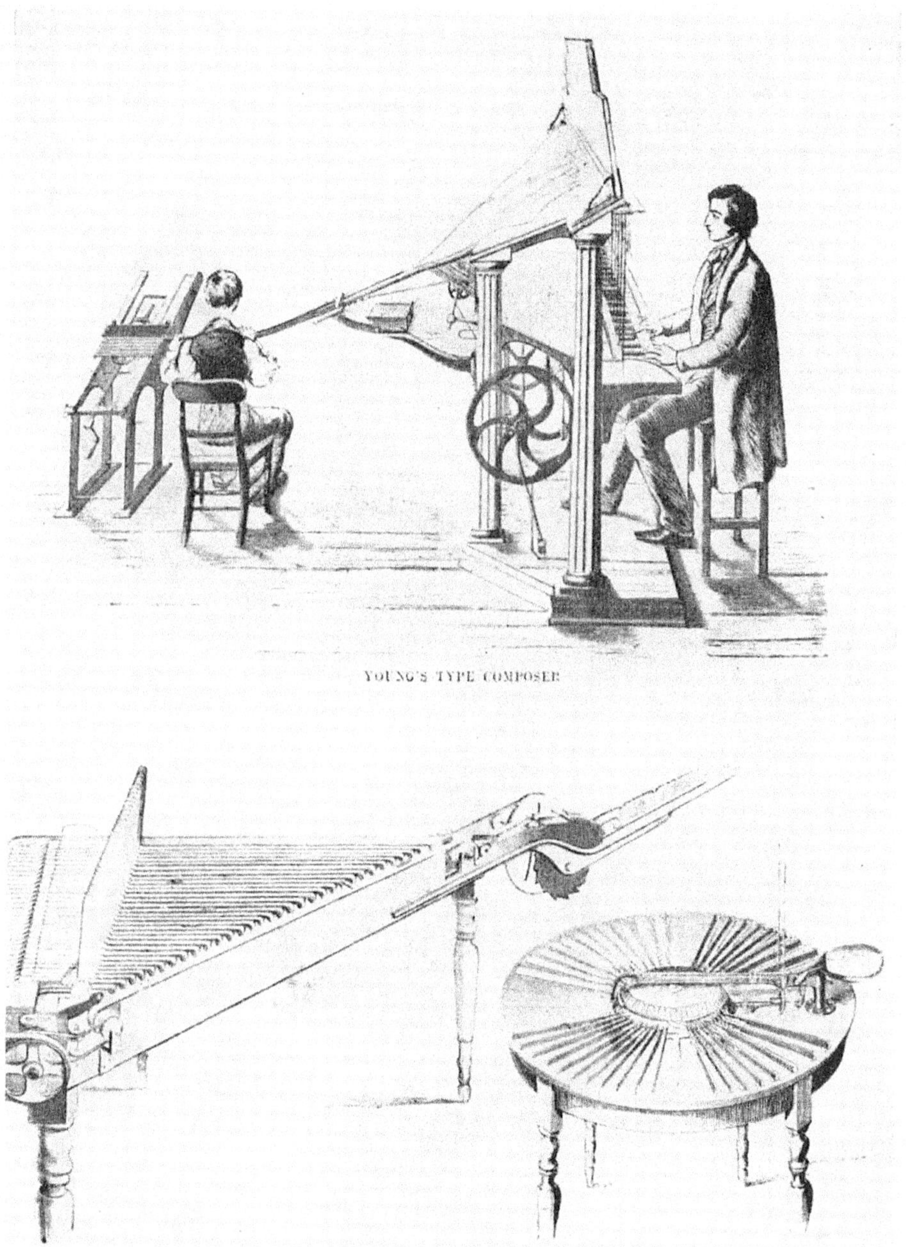

YOUNG'S TYPE COMPOSER

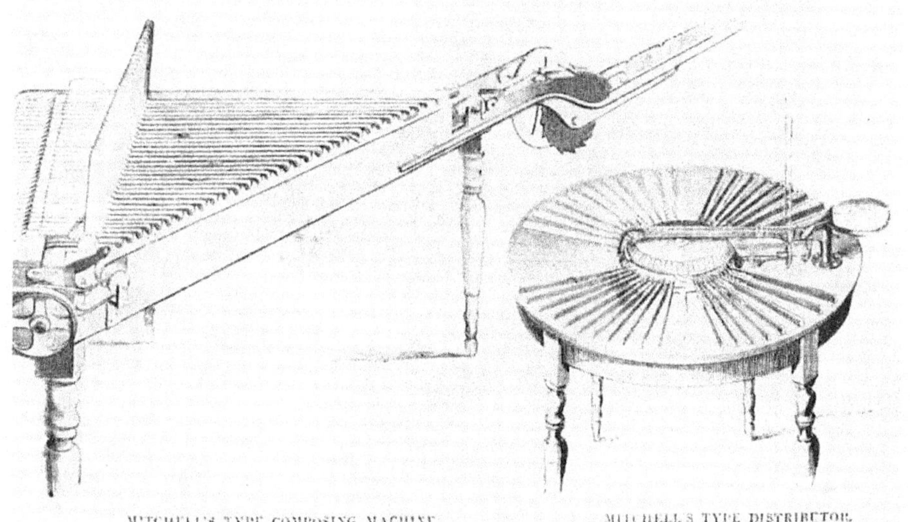

MITCHELL'S TYPE COMPOSING MACHINE.

MITCHELL'S TYPE DISTRIBUTOR.

TYPE COMPOSING AND DISTRIBUTING MACHINES

From *The National Encylopaedia*

order, the higher the saving that could be effected. It was calculated about 1890 that if an edition of 350 copies of a novel were ordered the binding could be done for 30s. for 100 volumes. For 1,000 copies the rate would be only 27s. for 100, or a little over 3d. a volume.[42] Some of the modern case-making machines will make 2,000 cases an hour, and there are casing-in machines which will stick on 15 or 20 covers a minute.

It is interesting to see how the cost of publishers' casing compares with earlier binding expenses. The cost of extra boarding a fairly small volume in 1832 was 6d.[43]—nearly twice as much as a publisher's casing would cost in 1890. The boarding of the 6,000 copies of Dickens's *Christmas Carol* issued in 1843 cost £180, or rather more than 7d. a copy.[44] An estimate made in 1852 of the cost of producing a work to be sold at 4s. 2d. a copy allowed a little more than 5d. a volume for binding; for another work, to be sold at 25s. 6d., more elaborate covers were thought to be called for, and roughly 2s. a volume were allowed for them.[45]

The low costs which prevailed until 1914 were not long maintained after the war. The good quality book cloth which until 1914 was only about 5d. a yard was in 1925 about 1s.; straw-boards, too, had risen from about £5 to £8 or more a ton. These together with labour costs are the principal expenses to be reckoned, and wages had more than doubled in the present century. On the basis of 1,000 or more copies binding costs were approximately double the pre-war figure; improved machinery had probably kept them from soaring even higher.[46] But the economies to be derived from machinery are limited. Despite the numerous new developments by which even such small processes as gluing and end-papering are performed mechanically, the nature of the industry necessarily demands a separate machine for each of the many operations, and the volumes have to be passed from one process to the next by hand.

Modern Leather Bindings

Publishers' cloth casings obviously do not meet the whole demand. The Great Exhibition of 1851 would not have been truly representative of Victorian taste if it had not included sumptuous leather bindings costing anything up to £75 each. The amount of gold leaf used every week by the London binders was about 3,600,000 square inches.[47] Most of the high cost of the hand-tooled bindings can be attributed to the workmanship, but the leather itself almost doubled in price during the century. On that account the method of half-binding, in which only the backs and corners are of leather, became more popular. It is very economical, as the corners can be cut from the flanks of the skin which would be wasted in cutting full covers. But the desire for cheap effect has been partly gratified by the use of inferior leathers. Is it a mere coincidence that the deterioration of leather bindings becomes more marked in volumes bound since 1830, shortly after the introduction of bookbinding-cloth, or was there an attempt to compete with the new material by using skins really unfit for the purpose? The Society of Arts reported in 1901[48] that hardly any sound calf had been used since 1830; the calf bindings of the latter part of the century were excessively thin and of poor quality. Although the sheepskin of the early part of the century was still in good condition, since 1860 sheepskin as sheepskin was hardly to be found, and through being grained in imitation of more expensive leathers it was in very bad condition. Even morocco bindings had been less reliable since 1860. The recently introduced Niger morocco, a Nigerian red goatskin, was an excellent material used in high-class binding, but was expensive. The demand for low-priced morocco bindings was being met by the use of so-called Persian morocco, which was being imported from India by thousands of skins at a time; and these had been used for more than half of the modern books which were in a bad state of decay. Part of the trouble, it was agreed, was due to the dyes. Earlier leathers and the modern Niger morocco were tanned with sumach, which did not damage the skin, whereas most of the modern skins were dyed with sulphuric acid. But as a present-day writer has said, neither the leather manufacturers nor the binders are wholly to blame for this; the demand for delicate and evenly coloured skins has compelled the manufacturers to produce an artificial material from a natural product.[49] If a book sells more readily for a pretty cover the bookseller can hardly be expected to issue a warning that in a few years' time that cover will be no more.

The Dust Cover

In the matter of covers there is an additional expense to the publisher which did not fall upon him until the closing years of the nineteenth century—the cost of the dust-jacket. The plain sheet of paper which once gave adequate protection to the cover has given way, generally speaking, to an ornate affair apparently designed as a clue to the contents of the book. In the case of novels especially as much artistry may be devoted to the loose wrapper as to the illustrations themselves. But it is a questionable point as to how much of the artist's fees and how much of the extra cost of printing should be accounted a binding expense. In so far as a brightly coloured wrapper tends to create appetite for the book its cost would perhaps more appropriately be included among the charges for advertising.

CHAPTER XVII

Modern Labour Conditions

On April 1, 1828, Jacob Unwin wrote in his diary, "Very busy; five men at work."[1] It was then about two years since he had founded the Gresham Press, starting with one hand-press, so that in a small way he had already achieved a measure of success. Nevertheless, if the size of his firm were to be regarded as typical of the times there could have been little advancement at all on sixteenth-century conditions. This was not quite the case.

For the first few years of the nineteenth century the printing industry had been in a depressed condition, owing, it was alleged, to the paper duty imposed in April 1801. In spite of that, there were a number of firms larger than would have been allowed in the time of the Stationers' Company's stringent rules. One printer gave evidence before the House of Commons that he had 3 presses working, with 17 employees. Another had 23 men working on 4 presses. In normal times they each employed over 40 compositors and pressmen, and one of the firms had 9 presses.[2] The university presses, too, were gradually extending; by 1818 the Cambridge Press had 13 presses in use, and employed about 30 pressmen.[3] But so far the growth had been anything but spectacular. Round about 1830 Jacob Unwin was not the only printer who was busy in a small way. One printer has left a description of the small printing-office off Ludgate Hill in which he worked. He shared a room with 4 others: 3 apprentices and a journeyman almost past work. "There were twelve apprentices in all, nine of whom wrought in a room by themselves upon the best work the house afforded.... Much of the press-work was monopolised by a machine in the cellar, driven by an Irish engine of flesh and blood—and potatoes—who turned the handle for half-a-crown a day, finding his own steam; and the whole of the reading was ground off for a pound-a-week by a young parson waiting for a 'call'."[4]

Until the coming of machinery the large firm really had few advantages in the matter of economical production over the smaller establishment. It obviously made for efficiency to split up the work of the compositor, reader, pressman and warehouseman among different men, but the printing-office did not need to be very large to allow for this. Even so, it was a size which was seldom to be reached in the provinces for many years to come. The provincial printing-house had quite commonly only two men, or perhaps one, to undertake every single process—a state of affairs which existed in some London workshops.[5]

Once the various processes of book production had been mechanised it was of first importance that there should be sufficient employees and work to keep the machines constantly running. That would not necessarily mean increasing the size of the firm at all: the printing works which set up one of Applegath's machines could dispense with the services of pressmen altogether; young boys could do all the minding that was needed. But the installation of machines, if it is justified, leads to quicker and cheaper output, and therefore to a larger volume of trade; and this was certainly true of the industries engaged in producing books. The growth came later than in the newspaper and periodical branch (so far as the division was already clear), but when it did come it affected every part of the trade, from type-founding to bookbinding.

The Rise of Factories

The first firm to print books by machinery was that of Messrs. Clowes. By 1840 it had 19 Applegath and Cowper's machines at work, as well as 23 hand-presses and 5 hydraulic presses.[6] They were not all in constant use on bookwork: the *Penny Magazine* and other periodical literature accounted for part of their output; but there seems to have been no appropriation of machines to particular work. To house all these machines a large factory had grown up, consisting of several lofty buildings surrounding a lower one which contained the engine-room and the larger printing machines. The rooms in the outlying blocks were given up to a variety of uses: there were composing-rooms, readers' rooms, type-making shops, stereotyping shops, paper warehouses, hand-printing shops, machine-printing shops, wood-block store-rooms and stereotype-plate store-rooms. The type-foundry itself was a double room holding 30 men and boys. It contained 18 furnaces, each 3 feet in height. The stock of type to be found in the fount-case at any one time weighed about 80,000 lb., and the paper warehoused in piles 20 feet high averaged about 7,000 reams—roughly a month's supply. Composing-rooms accommodating an aggregate of 200 men were situated in different parts of the premises.[7]

The bindery of Messrs. Westleys and Clark, we have already noticed, was just as detailed in organisation by this time, but as far as printing works were concerned it was some years before another English firm approached the size of Messrs. Clowes'. For works on a large scale it was necessary to turn to the Continent. Although the printing machine had largely owed its origin to English activity, French and American printers had not been idly watching. The most important French printing-house, l'Imprimerie Royale, in 1840 had 6 steam presses at work besides 120 hand-presses. It had its own type and stereotype foundries and employed up to 450 workmen. The Propaganda at Rome was still larger.[8] By 1850 the Imperial Printing Office at Vienna had spread over 5 blocks of buildings and possessed about 50 printing machines, 50 printing-presses, 25 copper-plate presses, 40 lithographic presses and 80 type-founding machines; it had about 150 tons of type and turned out 300,000 printed sheets a day. For all this nearly 1,000 employees were being maintained.[9]

As late as 1866 there was not a single English firm with as many employees as the Viennese establishment. Of the firms which provided information for the Children's Employment Commission Messrs. Clowes's printing-works was still the largest, with 568 employees, all males. The Spottiswoode family were close rivals: the New Street Square firm of Spottiswoode and Co. had 450 men and the Government printing-office of Eyre and Spottiswoode had 388. There were two other London firms employing round about 400 people, but some of these were females.

At the other extreme were a number of printing-offices with from 20 to 40 workpeople. There was already one Manchester firm with over 300 employees, but most provincial offices were still quite small.[10] Steam-power was only just beginning to penetrate into some of them. Even the firm of Jarrold and Sons of Norwich, one of the best known, was still turning out much of its work by means of 7 or 8 hand-presses and printing off only the larger editions in the machine-room.[11]

To judge from recent statistics the optimum size of the various types of firms engaged in book production is quite small. Of the printing, bookbinding, stereotyping, engraving and connected firms which sent in returns for the eighth census of production (1968) only 12 employed 750 or more people (with an average of 1,212). Only 30 firms had between 400 and 749 employees and 28 had between 300 and 399. Of the total of 4,332 establishments which supplied the information over 3,000 had fewer than 25 workpeople. The total number employed on average during the year was 154,462. The 1930 census had shown less than 1,000 firms with fewer than 25 workpeople, but on that occasion firms with 10 employees or less did not have to make a return.

Working Conditions in the Factories

Nevertheless, although the full growth up to the present time may seem somewhat insignificant compared with that of the great engineering concerns or the textile mills, the change to a factory system had been sudden enough to cause the stress so often associated with an industrial revolution. The rapid increase in the demand for books and periodicals was met in its earlier years only partly by installing machinery. For the rest the growing output depended on long working hours (compensated, it is true, by high wages) and on the employment of more children.

The worst conditions were to be found in connection with the newspaper and periodical press, whose issues had to be ready for publication at a given time, but by 1840 Blue Books were being produced in a similar rush and bustle. Things had been much more leisurely earlier in the century. "One of the most vivid of my recollections at this period [*c.* 1800], and indeed of some years after," soliloquises Charles Knight, "is that of the extremely easy mode in which the majority of the trading classes struggled with the cares of obtaining a livelihood. It is not within my remembrance that anybody worked hard."[12] This statement probably requires considerable modification, but it was probably true enough of the printing trade. Even the printing of parliamentary papers, as urgent a job as any, seems to have been carried on in comfort. Hansard himself, the Government printer, was said to arrive at the office an hour before his men in times of stress to see that the rooms were clean and the fires burning brightly for them.[13]

By about 1840 the working conditions of those engaged on Blue Books had completely altered. Work now did not begin until noon, and it was about 8 in the evening before all the processes of composing, proof-reading, correcting and press-work were going on together and the din of the printing-office was at its height. "The banging of mallets, the sawing of 'furniture,' the creaking of the old press, the shuffling feet of messengers, the bawling of twenty voices, and the endless gabble of reading-boys" continued until half-past nine or ten. There was a short break then for supper, a substantial one of pork and mutton pies, "slap-bang" or boiled beef, plum pudding, together with bread, cheese and beer. Towards midnight the last beer arrived, the boy who brought it declaring his intention to "go in for the horizontal in less than no time." For the printer there was no such hope. Work now began with increased intensity, and there was no sign of flagging until about three in the morning. Even then the work did not stop, although it had become half-hearted and was no longer accompanied by lively conversation. By morning the atmosphere was smoky and stiflingly hot. It needed all the powers of hot coffee to rouse the men sufficiently to carry on until the arrival of the 11 o'clock beer, brought in by the same boy with the "same unwashed face as yesterday." Try as they might, the men could not keep up the same rate of progress on the second day. The 5 o'clock tea had lost its refreshing qualities. Even the candles burned red in the smoky air, and gave only half the light they should have done.

From now on reading-boys and apprentices tended to be missing when they were called for, to be discovered at last snoring in some dark corner; some of the men, too, were stretched under their frames asleep. But by the end of the second night the whole volume was standing in type, and only the corrections remained to be done. Lots were drawn to decide who should be allowed to go home to bed, and the rest had to stay to finish the work. "A young fellow fresh from the country, when left in this predicament, presents but a sorry spectacle to the view," said one of those who had shared this experience. "A vigil of it may be more than fifty hours, passed in an atmosphere that would poison a vulture, has added twenty years to his aspect, and, indeed, he will never thoroughly regain his former look. He begins to wander in his speech—answers incoherently to questions, and staggers about in a semi-somnolent state—and does the last necessary office to his last sheet more like a prize-fighter collecting his exhausted forces for the last 'round' than anything else I can compare him to." However, by noon of the third day a small number of damp copies of the Blue Book were ready to lie on the table of the House of Commons, and all was well.[14]

Somewhat similar conditions seem to have prevailed in the printing of periodicals, but in regular bookwork there was not usually such a state of rush. It was during the last three months of the year that pressure was at its heaviest in this trade, in preparation for the Christmas demand. The Children's Employment Commission of 1862 found that at such times night work was frequent, even for boys, with no lessening of the next day's hours; several boys mentioned working all night at least once a week.[15] The difficulty was that the machine boys were needed all the time the machine was working, so that night work for men necessarily involved bad hours for the children. Some of them, it is true, did manage to snatch a sleep occasionally in the pit under a machine which was not working while the man in charge was substituting one forme for another. But none of the boy witnesses seemed at all discontented with their lot. The boys at Clowes's works in Southwark regularly began work at 7 o'clock in the morning.

They were due to finish at 8 in the evening, but it was often 10 or 11 before their work was done, as they had to deliver proofs. "They have to go to different parts of London," the foreman explained; "as far as St. John's Wood, for example; they walk both ways."[16] And yet it was not unusual for boys who had regular work in the day at one office to obtain night work at another.[17] It was not only printing-offices which were involved in the pressure: during the 6 weeks before Christmas the employees in many of the London bookbinding works, children included, worked from 7 in the morning until 10 at night.[18]

For the older workers long hours as distinct from continuous night work were no new thing. Thomas Gent recalls in his autobiography that round about 1710 he quite often worked from 5 in the morning until 12 at night, frequently without food from breakfast time until 5 or 6 in the evening.[19] The urgency in this case was the need to be ready for the hawkers; more often it was some impatient author or editor who demanded instant attention. George Steevens, for instance, when he was producing his edition of Shakespeare's *Plays* (1766), not only worked himself with the utmost perseverance but exacted just as much activity from his printers. He gave his whole attention to the work for 18 months; and "during that time, he left his house every morning at 1 o'clock with the Hampstead patrole, and, proceeding without any consideration of the weather or the season, called up the compositor and woke all his devils." Arriving at the chambers of Mr. Reed "he was allowed to admit himself, with a sheet of the Shakespeare letter-press ready for correction, and found a room prepared to receive him: there was every book which he might wish to consult; and on Mr. Reed's pillow he could apply, on any doubt or sudden suggestion, to a knowledge of English literature perhaps equal to his own."[20] William Wilberforce, too, was apt to be somewhat exacting. In 1797, when Messrs. Cadell and Davies were publishing his *A Practical View of the Prevailing Religious System of Professed Christians*, he suddenly pressed for publication by the end of the week. Luke Hansard, the printer in charge of the work, did his utmost, and was able on the Thursday to tell the publishers'

"I wrote you, last night, a hasty statement of this Business. At between 9 & 10 I sent Mr. Wilberforce 24 pages of proof—at between 10 & 11—40 more. At between 1 & 2 this morning, all the aforesaid were received back. At every other hour since 8 this morning I have continued sending more. And now (1 o'clock) *all* the Text is sent."[21] The printer and his men presumably became accustomed to such demands, and it was well past the middle of the nineteenth century before the working hours in their establishments became the subject of Government inquiry. One of the reasons given then for late work was this unreasonableness of authors, who seemed to think nothing impossible where printers were concerned.[22]

By the time of the Government inquiry a certain amount of night work was unavoidable; modern Fleet Street problems had arrived. The trade unions, which, as we shall see, had since the beginning of the century become possessed of considerable bargaining power, were unable to eliminate it; all they could do was to try to regulate the payment for it. Actually a large number of men were said to prefer working at night, quite apart from the extra pay to which it entitled them: they were brought less into contact with their employers and they had time in the day for their own devices. In any case, they could usually afford to pay somebody else to work instead of them for one night in the week, leaving them with only five nights to work. Day work exclusively throughout the year was now unknown in any printing-office. It was either supplemented at various seasons by extra hours, which carried it to 10 or 12 at night, or it was carried on throughout the night and perhaps through the following day as well, involving 2 days and 1 night of continuous labour. For day work the usual hours were now from 8 or 9 in the morning until 8 in the evening. On Saturdays work normally stopped at 2 o'clock, but in some offices this half holiday had been partly compensated for by beginning work each day half an hour earlier than was the case before the free afternoon was granted.[23]

The long working hours were usually spent in unhealthy surroundings. Sanitation was not a matter which greatly interested either the master printer or his men. The building in which Blue Books were manufactured, although extensive enough, was by 1836 already almost a ruin. Two hundred men were employed there, as well as a large number of boys, and the oldest employee, who had never been away from the office for a whole week at a time for nearly half a century, could not remember that a single sixpence had ever been spent on cleaning.[24] Thirty years later the state of printing-offices was said to be almost uniformly bad. Composing-rooms generally were overcrowded and ill-ventilated in comparison with present-day standards. Even the rooms which housed the most up-to-date machines were dirty, close and unhealthy. There was one London machine-room whose roof was so low that a hole was cut in the ceiling for the head of the boy who was "laying-on" to go through.[25] The reader, on a higher stage of the social hierarchy, might have been expected to occupy a fairly pleasant office. He, too, it appears, was as a rule to be found in a small den, black and unwhitewashed, ill-lighted and ill-ventilated. Any opening in the window or door he took care to paste over lest it should admit any air; and here he was to be found almost without a break throughout the whole period of his employment.[26] Bookbinding works were just as unhealthy, but the worst evils had been overcome by using gas-pans to heat the tools instead of charcoal braziers.[27]

Insanitary working conditions were bound to leave their mark on the employees. On the whole the printers' readers suffered least. Although they might spend the daytime in a dark, stifling room most of them lived in the suburbs, so that they at least breathed pure air on the way home even if they shut it out as soon as they arrived. For all that, they had an unhealthy appearance; they were "commonly pale and thin, of a depressed and anxious aspect, very sensitive to the influence of temperature, of a nervous or irritable temperament, with a dainty yet not a very bad appetite." They had a tendency to contract consumption.[28] So, too, had the compositors. The mortality rate from consumption among printers was double that of the community as a whole, and at ages 45 to 55 the general rate of mortality was twice that of agricultural labourers. But apart from this one tendency compositors were a moderately healthy group, although marked by pallor. They kept the old tradition alive by drinking heavily, but their besetting sin was generally admitted to be snuff-taking. Their habit of "chewing type" when correcting had its own ill effects on the system, as the type dust which they swallowed contained a harmful amount of antimony, arsenic and lead.[29]

Factory Legislation for the Book Industry

In accordance with the Government's general industrial policy an attempt was made to protect the women and child workers while leaving the men to their own devices. The Children's Employment Commission, reporting in 1866 on the long hours which prevailed throughout the printing and kindred trades, the Sunday work, the irregular meal times and the generally insanitary conditions, recommended that the Factory Commissioners should be given power to deal with the abuses. In 1867, therefore, the printing, bookbinding and paper-making trades were brought under control by the Factory Acts Extension Act. The statutory hours for women and young persons were thus fixed at from 6 o'clock in the morning until 6 in the evening, or from 7 until 7, with an hour and a half for meals; on Saturday work was to stop at 2 o'clock. In printing works male young persons over the age of 13 were to be allowed to work at night for 6 nights in any fortnight, a night's work constituting 10 hours.[30] A special exception was made for bookbinders: young persons of 14 and upwards, and women, could still be employed for up to 14 hours on any one day so long as this did not happen on more than 96 days in the year, and provided that the total hours worked in any one week did not exceed 60. This concession left some uneasiness in the minds of the Commissioners, and when the working of the Acts was reviewed 9 years later there was a suggestion that the bookbinding trade should be brought under the same regulations as the rest; but one of the Commissioners, after investigation, was not in favour of the change. "I think that the modification is absolutely necessary," he said, "because the work of bookbinders depends upon printers;

printers depend upon authors, and bookbinders come last of all, and the work never goes to the bookbinders till the very last moment."[31] As to the complaint that binders were working too much overtime, the present late hours were not overwork; what frequently happened was that the work could not be begun until 9 or 10 in the morning, so that it was thrown to the end of the day.[32]

The conditions of women and young people were thus from 1867 onwards strictly regulated by law. In so far as the factories which employed them were from henceforth liable to inspection the men's working conditions, too, may have been somewhat improved. The men's own struggles to shorten their hours and improve their wages can hardly be discussed apart from their trade-union activities, but the improvement in the health of compositors by the end of the century was said to be a direct result of the introduction of composing machines. "The pallid, wearied 'comp,' " it was claimed in 1897, "with 'his nose in the space-box' for 8 or 9 hours a day; with his frequent over-indulgence in stimulants, distinctly attributable to the fatiguing nature of his calling; his weak chest and chronic cough . . . all these are things of the past."[33]

For whatever reason, adult compositors in recent times have a better health record than any other group of men employed in printing. The sickness experience of printers was the subject of a special investigation made by the Industrial Fatigue Research Board in 1929, and this was one of the facts to be most definitely established. Stereotypers, electrotypers and lithographic machine printers are rather less healthy, but the highest sickness rate is among machine printers and warehousemen. The one disease which attacks every group is tuberculosis. Although printers as a whole compare favourably in their general death-rate with all occupied males their death-rate from tuberculosis exceeds the average for all males at every age, often by a very considerable amount. No explanation of this has yet been found. It has been suggested that printers suffer from exposure to lead dust and from inadequate ventilation; but, seeing that compositors begin their working life unfavourably as regards morbidity experience and become more healthy in later years, a third suggestion seems more likely to be true, that the printing trades attract, among others, persons of low physique.[34]

Social Changes during the Nineteenth Century

In the course of the nineteenth century, then, there had been a complete change in the general character of the book industry. Instead of being carried on, as it was formerly, by small groups of people in almost a domestic atmosphere the trade had become more an object of mass organisation, wholly impersonal. It was a development bringing about other social changes besides the ones we have noticed.

During the eighteenth century there had been a tendency for boys of good education to be attracted as apprentices to the printing and publishing trades. Parents were frequently able and willing to pay a premium for their sons' introduction to the trade, and this practice continued into the nineteenth century. In 1829, for instance, Jacob Unwin noted in his diary that John Derham, his apprentice, had brought £46 premium with him.[35] The general bookseller and printer in a country town would be content with a very small premium, and would engage to board and lodge his apprentice during the whole of the seven years for which he was bound; and in such a business the boy would gradually learn every essential part of the printing trade besides finding ample time in the evenings for his own reading.[36] An apprentice on such terms had really a better chance of a good all-round training than some of the London entrants to the trade could hope for. In London there was a growing tendency to specialise, spending perhaps the whole of the seven years on one process. Round about the year 1840 the boy who wanted to enter the book industry had to make up his mind whether he wanted to be a compositor, a type-founder, an engraver, a binder, a publisher or a retail bookseller. His parents' circumstances might determine the choice for him. He was ill-advised to choose the publishing branch unless he had a good financial backing: the premium required in a first-rate house varied from £200 to £500, and even when he had finished his training he had little hope of success unless he had considerable private means.[37] The premium for an apprentice to an engraver varied according to the talent of the master; a man who was very high in the profession would expect about £500, but a smaller sum would be accepted in the minor branches.[38] The aspiring compositor and the bookbinder's apprentice were usually expected to bring £50 with them, and the retail bookseller from £50 to £100.[39] Type-founding, on the contrary, which had formerly been one of the most exclusive trades, had come down in the social scale: the premium had dropped from £100 to £30 or £50 or none at all; a boy who showed a genius for type-cutting would be admitted without further ado.[40] The demand for a premium was in fact being waived in a number of cases. There were already numerous examples, for instance, of publishers and booksellers who had made large fortunes without having been apprenticed at all. But this was still felt to be rather irregular. "There are few persons in decent circumstances," it was generally agreed, "who would wish to expose their children to the trials, temptations, and sufferings which those fortunate individuals have had to wade through."[41]

Where the master printer, publisher or bookseller could afford to do without the premium he may sometimes have preferred not to accept it. To judge from the case of Jacob Unwin the premium pupils were apt to take up an attitude far from subservient. Jacob was apprenticed in 1816 to a printer-bookbinder-stationer of Houndsditch. He appears to have worried his employer by receiving friends during work time and talking to them for 20 minutes or more. On one occasion, according to an entry in Unwin's diary, the master hinted that this must stop, as it was hindering business. Whereupon, noted his apprentice, "I remonstrated on the subject, and having paid a handsome premium to be treated as one of the family, expected to be called if anyone wanted me. And said it was in general on business, which was as much for his own advantage as mine. He appeared very sore about it. However, the next day two friends called and I was sent for as usual." No wonder that the premium system fell into abeyance!

A succession of strikes on the part of printers' journeymen at the beginning of the century had already caused some of the London master printers to change the terms of apprenticeship. By the regular form of agreement the master had gained considerably from taking apprentices. There was the trouble of teaching them, it is true, but after about three months a boy could usually make himself useful, and for some years out of the seven he was as competent as a journeyman. The one drawback was that the master was expected to look after the general welfare of his apprentices, bringing them up with his own family and making himself responsible for their health and morals. When his journeymen began to fail him he looked for a way of securing more of this cheap labour without its obligations. He found the solution in a system of outdoor apprenticeship.

From the early years of the century, therefore, outdoor apprentices came to be employed in increasing numbers. They lived at home with their parents, were charged no premium, and from the beginning were given a few shillings a week as wages. There was really very little difference between this arrangement and ordinary child labour, except that at the end of the 7 years the outdoor apprentice ranked equally with the premium pupil as a fully fledged journeyman.

As the factory system developed in the book industry outdoor apprenticeship became the normal form. When the number of boys attached to any one firm ran into dozens it was perhaps too much to expect of the head of the establishment that he should regard them all as members of his own family and take them to live with him. And where night work was to prove so profitable it was fortunate for the master printer that he was not solely responsible for the health of his young employees. Actually, for the period the conditions were quite good. There was none of the infant labour which one associates with the early textile factories: it was reported in 1843 that few, if any, children under 10 or 11 years of age were employed in the printing trades, and the majority were apprenticed at 14 or 15 for 7 years.[42] In bookbinding, too, the boys were apprenticed at the age of 14. Although in some of the more important firms they received no wages at all in the first year, they paid no premium; and in their second year they were paid 5s. a week. From then until the end of the 7 years the amount rose by 2s. a week after each 12 months.[43]

By the 'sixties indoor and outdoor apprentices in printing works were fairly equally divided. In principle the master was in both cases bound to provide board and lodging for the boys and to watch over their conduct, but where his outdoor apprentices were concerned he delegated the duty to the parents or guardians, who entered into an agreement for the purpose. According to a special report by Dr. Edwin Smith the conditions of both types were usually satisfactory: the food supplied to the resident boys was good and abundant and there seemed to be no deficiency among the others. In his first year an outdoor apprentice might receive only 4s. a week, quite insufficient to keep him; but by the end of his period he would be paid £1 or more, which was a large sum for his age. Indoor boys received pocket-money of £5 or £6 a year. Overtime was rewarded by extra pay. On occasion the apprentices in book offices might be required to work throughout the night after a full day's work, but as far as possible this seems to have been confined to the older boys; and after all, as Dr. Smith pointed out, by the time the apprentice was drawing near to the end of his training he was generally equal to a journeyman not only in capability for work, but also in powers of endurance. The general cheerfulness of the report is moderated by a final description of the boys, especially the ones from the country: "usually they are pale and thin, with sunken features and large pupils." Nevertheless, from the records available it appeared that only 1 boy out of 162 had died during his term of apprenticeship.[44]

Until the invention of the printing machine the apprentice was the lowest worker in the scale. Now there was a new, even lower stratum. The apprentice was regarded as superior to the machine-boy, the boy who laid the paper on the machine and took it off again. He was not apprenticed at all. Very little skill was needed for the work, and the boys were in consequence drawn from a lower class than the rest; they were noted for being very ignorant and disorderly.[45] It was really no wonder if they were ill-behaved. They seem to have had quite the worst of the new system. They began work at 12 or 13 years of age at about 5s. a week. Quite frequently they had to work for a period extending over two days and a night with only brief intervals for rest, and as they were generally children of poor parents and therefore dependent upon their own earnings their main food during the whole time, according to Dr. Smith, often consisted of bread and butter. If a boy attracted attention by his alertness there was a chance of his being offered a regular apprenticeship; or he might find more remunerative work elsewhere. For the rest, so it was casually expressed, the only future was to be "thrown out of employment and left to fall into crime."[46]

The introduction in this way of a wholly illiterate class had a parallel development among the compositors. From the middle of the century there were complaints from the masters of the old school of the bad effects on the art of printing which had arisen from the multiplication of newspapers and periodicals. A host of compositors had been called into existence whose only idea of typography, it was alleged, was to pick up as many thousand types in an hour as could be managed. Their training, though adequate for newspaper printing, was not such as to fit them for the more exacting work on books.[47]

It is understandable that as an apprentice was drawn more and more into the hub of business he tended to become a routine worker skilled in only one small process. Under the old conditions, when he was in everyday contact with the master printer or one of the journeymen and had time to stand and stare, he could pick up many hints. Now in some of the bigger offices, it was alleged, nobody had time to bother with him. Unless one of the journeymen happened to be particularly well disposed towards him the new apprentice was simply told to take a composing-stick in his hand and set up "that pi"; for the rest he was left to his own resources.[48] All that was expected of the entrant to the trade by the 'seventies was a sufficient knowledge of reading to allow him to understand the copy,[49] and the education which the master was too busy to provide had now to be left to outside bodies.

Technical Education

About the year 1880 the City and Guilds London Institute began a series of technical classes for members of the printing and allied trades and instituted a graded system of examinations. The results were promising, although the number of students was very small as compared with those in continental schools. Vienna had a school of printing in which 400 or more students were enrolled and to which over 100 firms sent their apprentices; it was maintained jointly by the master printers and the Government. The Municipal Council of Paris was in process of erecting special buildings for a school of book production, and there were a large number of foreign cities which had set up complete printing-offices for the use of technical classes. Manchester was the only English town which could boast of such a training-office.[50]

By the early thirties a quite elaborate system of technical education had grown up. The City and Guilds London Institute had extended its work, and together with the Stationers' Company and the Printing Industry Technical Board held examinations annually in composing, machine printing, lithography, bookbinding, costing, warehousing and other specific branches. The Associated Booksellers' Association examined in book production and book distribution; and the Master Printers' Federation and other trade societies had examinations of their own. An apprenticeship scheme drawn up by the Joint Industrial Council of the Printing and Allied Trades of the United Kingdom in 1924 provided that apprentices indentured under the scheme should attend a suitable day or technical school or school of art for a whole day and two shorter periods a week until the age of sixteen, and for two years after that they were to attend evening classes at least twice a week.[51] Many local education authorities by this time were providing suitable schools and classes, and a few firms had arranged for technical classes on their own premises. Where a full-time course is desirable some trade unions and employers' associations have agreed that the time spent at a technical school shall count as up to two years' apprenticeship. In one case, that of the electrotyping and stereotyping industry, it was provided in 1921 that apprentices should attend classes for a number of years depending upon the age at which they were indentured; those entering at the age of 14 were to attend for 4 years. In the matter of technical education the printing industry was by 1935 ahead of most other trades,[52] while by 1972 the Booksellers' Association, mindful of its responsibilities under the Industrial Training Act of 1964, was so up-to-date in its approach as to provide training courses in management, middle management, supervision, and "training the trainer."

Modern Terms of Apprenticeship

Apprenticeship, it will have been noticed, remained the normal means of entry to the printing trades. Seven years was still the usual period, beginning at the age of 14, so that recruits were mostly drawn from the elementary schools. By 1915 premiums were unusual, but £10 to £25 would sometimes be paid on behalf of an apprentice who wanted all-round knowledge.[53] It was found in 1926 that only 279 apprentices out of 10,209 covered by the returns had been asked to pay a premium; they were nearly all compositors, letterpress machine minders or lithographic printers.[54] The usual rate of wages for an apprentice by this time was from 10s. to 15s. in the first year rising to 25s. to 45s. in the final year. Apprentices, in fact, were not so cheap as they once had been, taking into consideration the amount of time which had to be given to them for educational purposes; that may be why nearly one-third of the employers who sent in returns in 1926 were completely without them.

It was found in 1915[55] that comparatively few bookbinders wanted to serve the full term of apprenticeship; they wanted better wages early, even though they could not hope to do so well in the end; but in the agreement signed in 1935 between the British Federation of Master Printers and the National Union of Printing, Bookbinding and Paper Workers provision was still made for a seven years' apprenticeship for bookbinders. For the retail book trade the system is now almost unknown.

These various changes in the position of the new entrant to the book industry were partly determined, as we have seen, by general industrial developments. Technical changes had led to enforced specialisation. No longer, as in early days, could a boy be sent to a "stationer" to learn all that there was to know of printing, binding, publishing and retail bookselling. He must choose in future some specific branch: composing, lithography, electrotyping, or binding perhaps. But there was another change from early nineteenth-century conditions which was really a return to a far earlier state of affairs. In the sixteenth and seventeenth centuries, we remember, the Stationers' Company had enforced a strict limitation of apprenticeship. During the nineteenth century there came to be imposed restrictions no less exacting, but they were the rulings not of the Stationers' Company but of collective agreements between organisations of employers and employed. The apprenticeship system imposed by the unions became so irksome in some quarters that in 1966 suggestions were made before the Royal Commission on Trade Unions and Employers' Associations that it should be abolished. And it was the trade unions which were to insist upon the regulation of those other important aspects of working life which we have so far neglected to discuss.

CHAPTER XVIII

The Rise of the Trade Unions

IN its earlier years the Stationers' Company, though vested with all the power and dignity of a city company, retained, as we have seen, much of the character of the traditional craft gild. Although to the casual observer the activities of the corporation might seem to be spent in attendance on the Lord Mayor, in pageantry, or in banqueting, the individual member of the Company could have shared no such delusions. All, from apprentices to master printers, found the whole of their working lives fully regulated by its decisions; output, materials, trading conditions were all ordained by its officers, with occasional interference from the national Government. This regime was accepted almost without question. Each young apprentice had an equal chance with every other of rising through the journeyman stage to the dignity of master printer. The regulation which appeared to favour the master might one day benefit him, so why bear malice? In practice, as he knew, the by-laws of the Company which were the most irksome to individuals were those which put bounds to the ambitions of the masters themselves; those which limited the number of presses they might keep, which kept down, in the interests of the journeymen, the number of copies in any one impression, and so on. It was not until hopes of achieving the mastership had receded from the ordinary journeyman that a need was felt for some form of association able to put forward the claims of a permanent body of workers. Hence, although the Stationers' Company continued to be accepted by the men as a suitable central organisation for the enrolling of apprentices and for other ceremonial duties, more intimate matters began to be reserved for discussion at meetings of journeymen only.

We have already noticed the feeling of dissatisfaction among the journeymen printers of the seventeenth century at the growing exclusiveness of the Stationers' Company. In or about 1640 they petitioned the House of Commons on the matter, claiming that the master printers had converted the Company's charter to their own use, whereby the petitioners were made "perpetuall bondmen to serve some few of the rich all their lives upon such condicions and for such hire, and at such times, as the Masters think fit."[1] In 1666 they were petitioning again, this time against the multiplication of apprentices.[2] Here they had hit upon a vexing problem which two hundred years later was still to be unsettled. But it was of little use for the journeymen to try to enforce their rights in the Company at a time when their masters themselves were fighting for recognition. This was the period when the master printers were combining to challenge the supremacy of the booksellers in the Stationers' Company. In the presence of this greater conflict the claims of an association of yeomanry, if it had existed, could scarcely have received attention.

During the eighteenth century, as we saw, the journeymen appealed successfully at various times for the establishment of a regular scale of wages. From about 1770 onwards the rise of the modern newspaper revived the discussions on wages and created a series of new industrial problems. It was an experimental period with, as yet, none of the organisation which smoothes the way of the modern newspaper press. When it was still uncertain how long any new venture would last it was useless to engage a number of extra compositors, so that the prompt issue of papers necessarily involved night work. The question of payment for overtime immediately arose. There were technical innovations, too, demanding recognition in wage schedules and not capable of being settled by reference to tradition. Between 1785 and 1793, for instance, the method of layout for newspapers changed completely; in the same few years minion type was introduced, small capitals came to be used for particular paragraphs, and most of the double letters and the long *s* were discarded.[3] Moreover, as newspapers were still produced in the ordinary printing-houses by men occupied at times on bookwork, with its own system of number publication, it was impossible to segregate the problems of the newsmen from the rest. Even in the binderies new conditions were arising. Binding was no longer only a matter of carrying out the special orders of individual customers; it was now more often a question of putting a whole edition into boards for a publisher impatient of delay. There was no lack of material for discussion at meetings of workers.

During the eighteenth century it was still inexpedient to form a trade union with the avowed purpose of improving working conditions. The Government still seems to have reasoned that any movement towards compulsory wage-revision should be made by its own officers; any attempt on the part of the workers was regarded as sedition. It was on that account that the tailors, for instance, were by an Act of 1721 forbidden to combine at all (quite ineffectually, as it happened), and that the numerous associations which did spring up during the century took the less aggressive form of friendly societies. That was perhaps the more natural development. A whole branch of the activity of the mediaeval gild and of the company which had succeeded it had been devoted to friendly-society activities. The printing trade, again, had had its additional little social groups from earliest times: the "chapel" met regularly, for drinking purposes if for none other, before arbitration regarding hours and wages had ever been attempted. A combination of two or three such chapels and the choice of a public-house as the official headquarters for the Saturday-night meetings were all that was required for the establishment of a regular friendly society.

Early Trade Societies

Three of the new trade societies formed in connection with the book industry were soon in trouble with the law. They were associations of bookbinders—the "Friends," established in 1780, the "Brothers," 1783, and the "City Brothers," 1785, united after a short time as the London Consolidated Society of Journeymen Bookbinders. Their first public activity was an agitation for the reduction of hours. On April 25, 1786, twenty-four bookbinders were indicted at Clerkenwell Sessions House for unlawful conspiracy on the charge that they "did unlawfully conspire, combine and agree together to take from, lessen, and diminish one hour in each day's work; . . . and afterwards did, on the same day, unlawfully assemble and meet together, and form themselves into an unlawful society to support each other in such unlawful purpose." Early in the following year the trial was transferred to the Court of King's Bench. The outcome was that nineteen men were discharged and the other five were sentenced to two years' imprisonment in Newgate. Before the two years had expired one of the men died. Sir Matthew Bloxham, one of the sheriffs of London, thereupon interceded for the other four, and they were released; and as a further result the men were given the one-hour's reduction for which they had fought.[4] This was the second reduction in the course of the century, but the hours were still long if judged by modern standards. In the middle of the century the recognised hours of the bookbinding trade, in common with many handicraft trades, were from six in the morning until nine at night. Since then they had already been cut down by one hour, and now, in 1787, the working day was timed to end at seven. Seven years later another hour was taken off, but this time by peaceful agreement with the masters.[5]

In the meantime an association of compositors had been formed. From the rules of "The Phoenix," which met at "The Hole in the Wall" Tavern, Fleet Street, it appears that the body was established on March 12, 1792. The pressmen had their own friendly society with a history as unfortunate as that of the bookbinders. They held a meeting, it seems, to discuss the old vexed question of apprenticeship, their aim being to limit the number of apprentices to three for seven presses. As a result five members were indicted at the Old Bailey for conspiracy. The prosecuting counsel said of the society, "It was called a friendly society, but by means of some wicked men among them this society degenerated into a most abominable meeting for the purpose of a conspiracy; those of the trade who did not join their society were summoned, and even the apprentices, and were told unless they conformed to the practices of these journeymen, when they came out of their times they should not be employed." Conspiracy was the terror of the age. The judge, with such a lurid picture painted for him, could do no other than sentence each of the defendants to two years' imprisonment.[6] However, in the following year the newsmen were free from interference in their attempt to obtain an advance of wages, a move which had the full support of the book printers but was nevertheless regarded in later times as the beginning of the division of the compositors into two branches of one trade.[7] Early in 1793 the book hands were successful on their own account in claiming payment for the head and direction lines of pages.

The Combination Acts

By 1799 the fear of conspiracy, fostered by events on the Continent, had reached its height. The Combination Acts of 1799 and 1800 were an attempt to uproot it by making any trade society illegal. It was not, therefore, until their repeal in 1824–5 that a trade union could lawfully be established. For all that, it was in 1801 that there was formed the first printers' union on modern lines: the object of this First Trade Society of Compositors was "to correct irregularities, and to bring the modes of charge from custom and precedent into one point of view, in order to their being better understood by all concerned."[8] It comprised about one-third of the compositors then employed in London, whether on newspapers or books. In the same year the book hands obtained an advance of one-sixth on all work, the establishment wages since 1786 having varied between £1 1s. and £1 7s. It says much for the tactics of the society in such a time of suspicion that by 1805 its members had managed to obtain the co-operation of the employers in forming an Arbitration Committee, consisting of eight representatives from each side, for the regulation of compositors' wages. The elaborate scale drawn up by the committee was altered slightly in 1810, and then formed the basis of charges until 1847.[9]

The newspaper compositors had by now found a special grievance. On May 19, 1809, they addressed a circular "To the Proprietors of Newspapers," signed by 198 men, asking for an advance of one-fifth; they had had no share in the concession of 1801, they argued, although their work had become considerably heavier through the introduction of so much small type. A second circular was issued in June. The master printers, in reply, protested against a suggestion which offered no reciprocal benefit. In answer to the request for £2 8s. a week for morning paper hands and £2 3s. for workers on evening papers they said, "Their claims to high wages do not rest on the difficulties in obtaining the necessaries of life, but on the disagreeable hours of labour. They make more money than falls to the lot of 39/40ths of the men in Britain, and they can procure not only all the necessaries of life, but even more of its comforts than ninety-nine out of every hundred men in Europe. It is lamentable to see men so insensible to the blessings of their situation." In the next year the question arose again, and this time the men gave force to their plea by tendering a fortnight's notice. On the last day of the fortnight eleven of the twelve newspaper proprietors agreed to their demands. Unfortunately, the twelfth was the most influential of them all, the proprietor of *The Times*, and he prosecuted eleven of his compositors on a charge of conspiracy. On sentencing the men to terms of imprisonment varying from nine months to two years Sir John Silvester dilated on their evil deed: "Prisoners," he said, "you have been convicted of a most wicked conspiracy to injure the most vital interests of those very employers who gave you bread, with intent to impede and injure them in their business; and, indeed, as far as in you lay, to effect their ruin."[10] One of the men died in prison, but another of them, unreformed by his sentence, lived to help in the formation of the London Union of Compositors in 1834. The experiences of 1810 cast a gloom upon the members, but apart from this one incident the association, illegal or not, had a peaceful existence. By 1820 it had gathered in 193 members—about one-third of the London compositors at that time.

In reality the Combination Acts had not had the full effect that was intended. The Act of 1800, it was said not long before its repeal, was "in general a dead letter upon those artisans upon whom it was intended to have an effect—namely, the shoemakers, printers, papermakers, shipbuilders, tailors, etc., who have had their regular societies and houses of call, as though no such Act was in existence;

and in fact it would be almost impossible for many of those trades to be carried on without such societies, who are in general sick and travelling relief societies; and the roads and parishes would be much pestered with these travelling trades, who travel from want of employment, were it not for their societies who relieve what they call tramps."[11] According to evidence given in 1824 master printers in general would have scorned to take advantage of the Combination Acts. They preferred an amicable settlement of wages by masters and men in consultation. The compositors who had been imprisoned for combining were in their opinion the victims of misunderstanding; their masters considered them to be some of the most respectable in the trade.[12]

Although there is little record of prosecution under the Combination Acts an Act far more dangerous to the worker was still in force. The maximum sentence under the Combination Acts was three months' imprisonment; the long sentences given in *The Times* case were not for the offence of combining but for conspiracy at common law. The sanction for this was derived from the Elizabethan Statute of Artificers, then still in force, whose thirteenth clause provided that persons who undertook to do any piece of work and left without finishing it, unless for non-payment of wages, were liable to imprisonment. Hundreds of strikers were prosecuted under this law, so that the repeal of the Combination Acts alone would have been little reassurance. The really important clause of the Act of 1824 was the one providing that persons combining for an increase of wages or for the improvement of working conditions should no longer be liable to an indictment for conspiracy.[13]

The spread of socialism in the meantime had been encouraged rather than checked by this repressive policy. To get away from the more insistent problems of modern industrial life self-supporting communities were being planned, on the lines of the one formed at New Lanark by Robert Owen. In 1821 a meeting of journeymen printers was held to consider the proposals of George Mudie for a similar colony. The distress in which labour found itself was due, they decided, to the inventions of the preceding thirty years, and it was feared that continued progress would be accompanied by still more unemployment. By co-operating on the system of the New Lanark community it was hoped to bring about stability. But what was to be the place of a large number of trained printers in such a community was not expressly stated.[14]

The London Society of Compositors

From 1826 onwards there was no restriction on the formation of trade unions, and on May 1st of that year the London General Trade Society of Compositors was established. This was the opening of the so-called "revolutionary period" of trade-union history, a time of frequent commercial depressions, unemployment and strikes, but the development of printers' unions has been singularly free from revolutionary actions of any kind. The committee system which they had been so early in adopting was partly responsible for that. The business of the London General Trade Society of Compositors, for instance, was conducted by a committee of eight, which met every Monday night. From 1832 onwards members who were dissatisfied with the decisions of their own committee could refer the matter in dispute to the Union Committee of the London Trade Societies of Compositors, consisting of six members of each of the two existing societies of compositors, to which all important trade questions were to be referred.[15] The Union Committee met once a fortnight. It was a committee of final appeal and consultation only, without any legislative authority. Through its influence the problems of apprenticeship and unemployment led, not to strikes, but to the appointment of special committees to work out a peaceful solution. It was not that there was no provision for extreme action: any member of two years' standing was entitled to strike pay of 2s. a week, raised to 5s. after five years' membership; but so successful was the committee system that these sums were allowed to accumulate. One of the early committees, indeed, took upon itself with great dignity to criticise the ungentlemanly procedure of some unions: "Unfortunately almost all Trades Unions hitherto formed have relied for success upon extorted oaths and physical force. . . .

The fault and the destruction of all Trades Unions has hitherto been that they have copied the vices which they professed to condemn. While disunited and powerless they have stigmatised their employers as grasping taskmasters; but as soon as they were united and powerful, then they became tyrants in their turn, and unreasonably endeavoured to exact more than the nature of their employment demanded, or more than their employers could afford to give. . . . Let the Compositors of London show the Artisans of England a brighter and better example; and casting away the aid to be derived from cunning and brute strength, let us, when we contend with our opponents, employ only the irresistible weapons of truth and reason."[16]

The irresistible weapons of truth and reason had certainly served them well so far. Quite early in their corporate existence, as we have seen, the compositors had negotiated successfully for an increase in wages, obtaining an advance of one-sixth on all book printing (thus raising time rates to 33s. a week). In 1810, at a general meeting held at Stationers' Hall, it was agreed that book hands should receive another increase of one-seventh. A most complicated scale of piece rates was agreed upon. For example, works in the English language were to be composed at different rates according as they were printed with or without space lines; within these two main groups the charges per 1,000 letters were to vary according to the size of type used; works in Hebrew, Arabic, Syriac and other languages were to be paid for at double rates; and special charges were fixed in full detail for footnotes, marginal notes and tables.[17]

On the terms of the new scale the skilful compositor could afford to take every Monday as a holiday, and the idle day, "St. Monday," became a recognised feature of the trade. The master printer who had a piece of work urgently to be carried through on that day was in a sorry plight. If he had no journeyman at all who was paid weekly wages, and therefore could not keep St. Monday, there was nothing for it but to do the job himself with the help of an apprentice.[18]

By the Scale of Prices payment for overtime work was to count from ten o'clock at night, the normal working week for time workers being 60 hours. In practice the compositors' unions did not countenance the working of overtime at all except in special circumstances. That was perhaps why the more ambitious workmen sometimes preferred not to join a union. One printer, at least, chose to work in a small printing-house in which the scale of charges was ignored. A 60-hour week was not long enough for him. In 1833, therefore, he was working from 6 in the morning until 10 at night, or even until midnight, and was consequently earning more than he would have done in a larger establishment.[19] When he did move, a year later, to a printing-house run on union lines, he found the restrictions most irksome. "I wrought for the first week," he complains, "with all the energy of which I was capable, and at the end of it had eighty-two hours to charge, and which, of course, I expected to be paid for. The general bill paid eightpence an hour, owing to an unusual number of blank and short pages, for which compositors charge the same as for those full of matter; and I looked as a matter of course for 2*l.* 14s. 8d." The sum actually given him was £2, with a note saying "on the shelf, 22 hours," meaning that he could work 22 hours less in the next week and still receive full pay. By the end of 6 weeks, with 70 hours unpaid for, he was disgusted with the whole system: "The reader will see," he argued, "that the operation of this execrable system of management is to reduce the character and efficiency of the best workman to that of the worst, or at least to the average standard, and to clap an extinguisher on industry and emulation: it is, in fact, the compositors' scheme of protection, and has the inherent vice of all schemes of protection, inasmuch as it is fit for nothing but to secure to the idle and inefficient workman a greater share than he has a right to of the rewards of the more industrious and effective, at the expence of the latter."[20] Nevertheless, although the compositors' unions might curb the too ambitious, they did aim at making overtime rates payable at an earlier hour. One of the questions discussed by the Union Committee in 1833 was whether compositors receiving stated weekly wages were "bound to light up candles before the usual time, without receiving extra pay."[21]

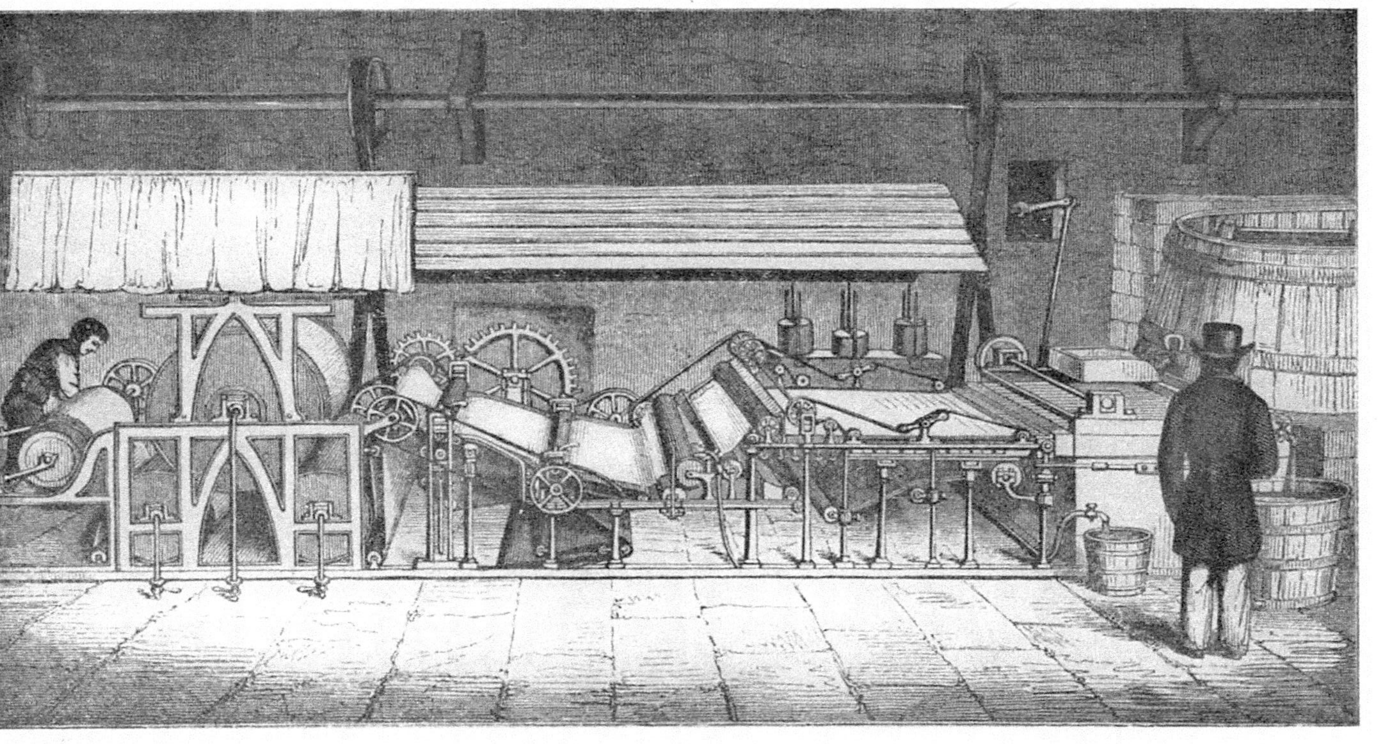

PAPER-MAKING MACHINE

From Tomlinson (C.), *The Useful Arts and Manufactures of Gt. Britain*, c. 1845

But it was not until 1866 that overtime charges were advanced to 9 o'clock instead of 10.

On May 1, 1833, the committee of the London General Trade Society of Compositors issued an address claiming that never since the establishment of the society had a member left on account of its mismanagement or illiberality. Since 1826 the numbers had steadily increased, and although payments had been promptly made to those injured in protecting the rights of the trade the society's funds were in a healthy condition. The reason offered was that the union was not weakened by conflicting aims; its sole purpose was to protect the wages of labour.

One of the duties of the Union Committee of the London Trade Societies of Compositors in 1834 was to draw up a commentary on the compositors' scale of wages. The commentary, when written, was agreed to be clear and informative, but in 1847 the journeymen members of the Conference of Master Printers and Compositors pointed to its serious defect: "it was the compositors', not the masters' and compositors' book. Master printers would not acknowledge it because journeymen made it; and thus, while it has been a valuable guide to the compositor, it has been of no service to him as an accepted authority by his employer."

The Extension of the Trade Union Movement

A number of other societies had already been formed in various parts of the country, but they were little more than relief organisations for the unemployed. The Northern Union, formed in 1830, had more resemblance to the London Society. Its objects were the maintenance of a fair standard rate of wages, the limitation of the number of apprentices and the relief of members in search of work. According to a complaint made at the time many employers expected their men to work for long periods of overtime without extra pay; and as to the other problem of the day, the only limit to the number of apprentices was the employers' own convenience. The union was unable to improve the position, but for fourteen years it managed to prevent matters from becoming worse.[22]

There might be individual critics of union policy, but there was no fear that the various associations would fail for lack of members. In 1834 it was found expedient to form a new society of compositors. The newspaper compositors had appealed to the Union Committee for a separate jurisdiction, but the committee decided against them: the wages of newsmen, the committee argued, did not depend upon a union among themselves, but upon the co-operation of the bookmen; without the aid of the bookmen, who had resolved not to accept employment on newspaper work during a dispute, the newsmen could not hope to bargain successfully. The solution was found in forming a general union of compositors, the London Union, governed by a trade council of 24 members. At the first quarterly meeting a membership of 1,580 was reported. About that time, too, other societies connected with the book industry were formed, notably the Association of Pressmen (1834), the Bookbinders' and Machine Rulers' Consolidated Union (1835) and the London Printing Machine Managers' Trade Society (1839). At their annual meeting of 1837 the London compositors referred to similar unions in Ireland and Scotland, and in Brighton, Bristol, Oxford, Cambridge and other English towns. During the year the Association of Master Printers had been re-established, the Council of the compositors "knowing not whether they should call upon the trade to lament or to rejoice at this circumstance."

At the first annual meeting of the London Union of Compositors (February 1835) it was reported that £245 8s. 1d. had been paid to members engaged in disputes and that £65 10s. had been paid to the Operative Builders towards the carrying on of their own struggle. During the next few years several loans were made to other unions. The fourth annual report, for instance, mentions sums of £50 each lent to the Curriers and to the Associated Typefounders' Society and £200 to the Glasgow Compositors. It was owing to the fear of strikes that employers tended to be hostile to the whole movement. One Dublin printer objected so strongly to coercion that he gave up most of his printing and turned to publishing. He objected, too, to the minimum wage demanded by the unions, arguing that if he paid high wages to men who were inefficient he could not pay the rest what they deserved; the compositors were by no means equal in capabilities, and an inferior one caused so much trouble in proof-correcting that the total expense might be five times as great as it need have been. But he admitted that although other unions had resorted to violence there had been no intimidation on the part of the printers. "It is merely that they can compel you to do the thing," he complained. "They say, 'If you do not do it, we will leave you in a fortnight, and leave your business at a stand.' " In his opinion matters had become far worse since the repeal of the Combination Acts: "It was explained to the men . . . that they were not breaking the law by giving warning and leaving any employer, and therefore, they have gone on from that time in a partial way ever since, taking advantage of that opinion; it has gone on from one thing to another. It is much worse now than at any former time."[23]

The problem which seems most to have vexed the unions at that time was the one of unemployment. It was said in 1828 that of the 3,500 compositors and pressmen in London there were throughout the year more than 800 out of work.[24] The growth of outdoor apprenticeship and the breaking of the old limits as to the number of apprentices to be maintained were held to be chiefly responsible for the low demand for journeymen's labour. As one unemployed compositor explained it, "Fathers and mothers, all of 'em, think that printing is a light and genteel business; and the consequence is, they are for everlastin' a-bringing their sons to be bound apprentice. There's three times the number of boys brought up to this trade that there's any occasion for."[25] A return prepared in 1840 by the Union Committee of the London Trade Societies of Compositors showed that in London there were 534 apprentices employed to 1,343 journeymen; it was suggested that an immediate effort should be made to limit the number to one in four. That was a generous allowance in comparison with the former rulings of the Stationers' Company and the Government on the same question, but it was useless to hope for Government enforcement of any maximum in a period of *laisser-faire*. But in any case, judging from the general state of the trade at the time, one would say that apprenticeship was not the real trouble. The whole of the country's trade had been stagnant since 1815, and unemployment had become a national problem.

National Associations

It was partly as an attempt to overcome the problem of unemployment that from about 1843 onwards the innumerable small local societies began to amalgamate into great national unions, such as the Miners' Association of Great Britain and Ireland. From that time the general industrial policy of the unions was modified: the proneness to strike gave way to more constructive friendly society activities. The printers' unions, it is true, had held by their resolve to avoid hasty action. As one authority has aptly said, "The student of the reports of the larger compositors' societies, from the very beginning of the century, will be struck, not only by the moderation, but also by the elaborate Parliamentary formality—one might almost say the stateliness of their proceedings."[26] Concerning moderation, then, they had little to learn. Even the relief of distress, one of the main functions of the unions then taking shape, was not new to them. On the formation of the London Union of Compositors in 1834 it had been agreed that 25s. a week should be allowed as unemployment relief. Nevertheless, the amount of social work which could be done by local societies on subscriptions of about 4d. a month was obviously limited. Amalgamation was to provide new opportunities.

Before there was any suggestion of amalgamating the existing societies of compositors an attempt was made in 1837 to turn the London Union into a national federation. Branch associations of compositors were to be established outside London, each with a corresponding secretary. Strictly local minor disputes could be settled by the branch itself, but any question of wages or hours was to be referred to the Trade Council of the London Union. The intention was to prevent provincial workers from offering to do the work of men on strike elsewhere.[27] By 1844 the unemployment problem was beyond the control of local societies. The difficulty of keeping the provincial unemployed away from London broke down any objections which the London compositors might have to merging their society in a national organisation. The National Typographical Association was therefore formed, with sixty branches grouped into five districts: the South-eastern (including London), the South-western, the Midland, the Western (comprising all Ireland), and the Northern (comprising all Scotland). By the following April 1,751 men had joined the London section, while the national membership was 4,320.

The total income of the National Typographical Association in its first half-year (1844–5) had been £1,637 17s. 8½d., of which it was reported at the end of the period that £713 had already been spent.[28] Most of that amount went in strike payments. In the fourth half-year it was reported that over ninety disputes had been referred to the executive; that and the growing number of unemployed had led to the doubling of subscriptions. The unemployment problem was no nearer solution. Just as the sixteenth-century poor had flocked to London for relief, so in the nineteenth a rumour that London compositors were earning vast sums led to as great a migration: "journeymen poured in from almost every part of the empire," bringing their families with them. In London, therefore, "the enormous sum of £1,200" had to be spent on unemployment relief—a considerable proportion of the society's total income.[29] The general discontent at the shortage of work led to a lack of interest in the union. It was reported to the twelfth quarterly delegate meeting, 1848, that Dublin was no longer a branch, Liverpool had only one-half of its former membership, Edinburgh had now only 50 members, many of the smaller societies had broken away altogether, and in London there were 700 men who had paid no subscriptions for many months. In the face of financial ruin the association had no choice but to dissolve. The London branch in 1848 accordingly reconstituted itself as the London Society of Compositors, a local society quite independent of any other.

During its short existence the National Typographical Association seems to have had some restraining influence on the policy of the master printers. It was reported in 1849 at a meeting in Sheffield for the formation of a new union that while the association existed there were in one town 10 journeymen and 5 apprentices; there were now 44 apprentices but still only 11 journeymen.[30] Charles Knight was himself about that time struck with the numbers of children employed: "There are manufactories in London," he wrote, "whence hundreds of reams of vile paper and printing issue weekly; where large bodies of children are employed to arrange types, at the wages of shirt-makers."[31] The growth of juvenile employment was an incentive towards re-amalgamation of the local unions. The Provincial Typographical Association, afterwards the Typographical Association, was the outcome, formed for "the limitation of the number of apprentices, restriction of the hours of labour, regulation of the standard of wages, and a general supervision of all matters affecting the interests of the printing profession."[32] The London Society of Compositors maintained its independence of the new body, and so for some time did the societies of Manchester and Birmingham; otherwise the association was nationally representative. All the same, its membership was small: in 1850 it had only 603 members as compared with 1,800 in the London Society of Compositors and 420 in the Bookbinders' and Machine Rulers' Consolidated Union. Ten years later its membership had risen to 1,473, but the London Society had meanwhile grown to 2,650.

Although the Typographical Association had as its main object a drastic reduction in the number of apprentices, it must not be thought that the society was opposed to apprenticeship as such. On the contrary, it was a strict rule that membership should be confined to those who had served a seven years' apprenticeship to the trade, or at least to the connected trades of bookbinding and stationery. Quite soon even the bookbinder and stationer were required to work only at printing if they wished to retain membership; but whether they worked as compositors or pressmen was of no concern. From these entrance requirements it is obvious that there was no intention of abolishing apprenticeship altogether; the object was to do away with boy labour beyond the amount needed to keep up a regular supply of journeymen. The rule which the Association tried to enforce was that not more than two apprentices should be kept unless four journeymen were employed, when the number might be increased to three, but on no account to four or more.[33] Not much effect could be expected from such a regulation unless it could be enforced in printing-houses other than the ones directly influenced by the Association. In 1855, therefore, we find the union trying to persuade the London Society of Compositors of the urgency of the question; it advocated the sending of missionaries throughout the provinces "for the purpose of rousing the profession to the necessity of making more efficient provision for protecting our labour, and for limiting the number of apprentices in localities where no restriction now exists."[34] The London Society itself already had its ruling on the subject. According to the London Scale of Prices of 1810 and its various amendments to 1889 the maximum number of apprentices was fixed, "in accordance with the custom of the Trade," at one to every three journeymen employed.[35]

Unemployment

If all this precaution had any effect at all on the volume of unemployment it does not appear in the statistics of benefit paid. Between 1848 and 1866 the London Society of Compositors was paying unemployment benefit of 8s. a week; although during that period the membership remained fairly constant at a little over two thousand the average sums paid annually in relief rose from £196 10s. 7d. in 1848–52 to £491 16s. 9d. in 1858–62. In 1897 the number of members had risen to 10,780—but the amount given as unemployment benefit (at 12s. a week) had grown to over £12,215.

Work on behalf of the unemployed did not end with the payment of a weekly allowance. Some of the men, with little prospect of making a living at home, were anxious to try their fortunes in the colonies, and the unions encouraged them in the idea. Both of the main printers' unions formed societies for the purpose: the Compositors' Emigration Aid Society, in connection with the London Union, in 1852, and the National Typographical Emigration Society, for the provinces, in 1854. The National Society failed before the end of the year because "the passage money was given, instead of being lent"; the offer of a fair-sized sum of money for the asking was too good to miss, and once it was spent emigration was out of the question. The Emigration Aid Society met with the same problem. Their loans of £15 or £30 were sometimes spent on other purposes than the one intended, and the committee soon had to resort to fining members who did not emigrate within a specified time.[36] There seemed no end to the difficulties. Perhaps the one which gave the Society the most apprehension was the new threat mentioned in a half-yearly report for 1853: "The Committee having ascertained, upon undoubted authority, that the Society would be responsible for the support of the wives or families of any members emigrating without them, beg to announce that under no circumstances whatever will advances be granted to married men about to emigrate without either their wives or families." One wonders how many irate wives had already confronted the members of the committee.

Questions for Arbitration

Apart from questions of this nature the printers' unions had resumed a fairly peaceful course. The disputes with which the London men at least were connected were seldom of their making. In 1849, for instance, the sympathies of the London Society were aroused by the plight of the secretary of the Sheffield Trades' Committee and three of its members, who had been prosecuted for inciting two members of the Sheffield Razor Grinders' Union to destroy machinery. The Society contributed £20 towards the defence. In the same year a committee of the bookbinders appealed for help for a number of girl bookfolders and sewers who were striking against an elaborate system of fines, and the London Society granted £30 towards their support. For its own part it would probably have settled such a difference by arbitration, according to its traditional policy. At that very time the Society was working for the establishment of a regular arbitration committee. In 1848 the Masters' Association had proposed that such a committee should be appointed, but wanted it composed entirely of master printers, six to be chosen by the masters and six by the compositors; the compositors in reply had asked for a mixed committee of masters and journeymen, but the masters refused to entertain the idea. The journeymen won their point seven years later: the masters agreed to the appointment of an annual arbitration committee consisting of three employers and three journeymen, presided over by a barrister as chairman.

Outside London disputes were more frequent. The second and third half-yearly reports of the Provincial Typographical Association (1849–50) mention strikes in several districts. In South Shields and Halifax there had been successful strikes against an excessive number of apprentices; one in Cardiff had put an end to the employment of jobbing men on news work without extra pay; while another in Wakefield broke out on the threat of a wage reduction, but failed owing to the availability of non-union men.

For some years apprenticeship continued to be one of the main subjects of disagreement, but by about 1860 the half-yearly reports of the Association show an increasing number of the disputes to have been settled without strikes. If a district were notoriously overburdened with boy labour its printers were liable to be refused admission to the Provincial Typographical Association until improvements had been made. In 1864 the Plymouth men were rejected on those grounds, but the Association granted £26 towards the work of reformation and the London Society of Compositors contributed £30. The introduction of the first composing machine intensified the problem. In 1868 the Hattersley was introduced into a Bradford office, and although the firm already had its full quota of apprentices four more were appointed to work the machine. No attention was paid to the demands of the union and the office was accordingly "closed." But the apprenticeship rule was really impossible to enforce. A few months after this incident the Stafford Branch altered its own rules on the subject to agree with those of the Provincial Typographical Association. The revised code was sent to a local printer to be set up in type, but when he read the proof he refused to produce such an objectionable rule, and ordered the type to be distributed and the men to leave either his firm or the society. Three men decided to give up their positions.

From about 1865 the printers' unions were increasingly occupied with the matter of working hours. In that year the Manchester Branch of the Provincial Typographical Association obtained a reduction from 59 hours a week to 55. Ashton, Bury and Bolton straightway demanded the same, but the employers refused, saying that with shorter hours they could not compete against Manchester's more up-to-date machinery. Once begun, the movement for improved hours spread rapidly, and in the thirty-fifth half-yearly report of the Provincial Typographical Association the Executive Committee found it necessary to caution the branches against entering upon such movements without consent from headquarters. The London Society of Compositors, too, had entered into negotiations, and in 1866 managed to reduce the hours to 60 a week. But one wonders how far the individual members were interested in the changes. In 1860 the committee of the London Society had cause to recommend that "members holding regular situations, and being in full work, should not take work in other offices after eight o'clock at night, or on Sundays."

Besides obtaining a reduction of hours the London Society in 1866 succeeded in raising the establishment wages to 36s. A man employed on piece work might earn more. Thirty years before this a good worker could easily obtain up to 2 guineas a week,[37] and now, although the usual payment to piece workers was from 30s. to 36s., there was one office in which the men averaged £9 a week, working almost day and night on parliamentary reports.[38] But the best and most regular workmen were usually on the "establishment"; the employer had to pay them whether they were busy or not, so they were provided with work first, and generally with the work that would cost more at piece rates.[39]

In January 1872, while negotiating for another wage increase, the executive committee of the London compositors urged the need for a 54-hour week so plausibly that it was granted. Whether the individual members were really anxious for the reduction is doubtful. The first ballot on the 8-hour question (1888) had surprising results. Four questions were asked: "Are you in favour of an eight hours limit of the day's work—total forty-eight hours per week? Are you in favour of a total cessation from work on Saturdays? Are you in favour of Parliament enforcing an eight hours day by law, or enforcing a Saturday holiday by law? Are you in favour of obtaining either of these privileges by the free and united efforts of the organised trades of the kingdom?" By an overwhelming majority the men opposed each of the suggestions. Can it be that they had misread the questions? At all events, when a second ballot was held later in the year the majority were in favour both of an 8-hour day and of obtaining it by Act of Parliament. The Lithographical Association, too, wanted an 8-hour day, but not by parliamentary interference; the members preferred to rely on their own efforts.[40]

Meanwhile the question of composing machines was coming to the fore. At the delegate meeting of the Typographical Association (as it was now called) held in 1877 the Liverpool Branch objected to the employment of boys on the Hattersley machine as distributors. It was explained that this had been sanctioned only on the understanding that the boys should not be taught composition or any other branch of the trade. The Southport men, at least, made no complaints; their representative said that the boys might as well be employed on sewing machines for any harm they did to the trade. But in 1888 the proprietor of a Bolton works introduced a machine of his own invention and straightway dismissed two journeymen and took on extra apprentices. As he insisted that he would go on employing as many boys as he pleased his office was declared closed.

If composing machines were to be operated by union men, as was the aim, a scale of wages had to be drawn up to meet the special conditions. The Typographical Association in 1893 agreed upon maximum and minimum rates for each of the three composing machines in use. The London Society of Compositors was occupied with the same problem, but reached no final settlement until 1898.

There was evidently still no lack of differences of opinion, although strikes were infrequent. A witness before the Royal

Commission on Labour of 1892–4 said that in the printing trades there had been no general strike "in the ordinary acceptance of the term" for some years. "We have had strikes in this way," he added, "that if an employer departs from the scale which has been mutually agreed upon, then there has been a difficulty." "You refused to go to work?" "We have done with it."[41]

Unions of Specialised Bookworkers

By the end of the century the book industry was employing a more varied body of workers than ever. Besides the compositors, pressmen and bookbinders there were machine minders, stereotypers, lithographic printers, engravers, type-founders, as well as printers' warehousemen, lithographic stone preparers and others still more remotely concerned with the actual production of books. Then, as a further complication, several of the groups included a few women workers. No one union could give adequate representation to all interests. Gradually, therefore, as the numbers in each branch of the trade grew sufficiently, more specialised associations were formed. Some did not survive for long, but among those in existence in 1892 several had been founded twenty or more years before. The Society of Day-Working Bookbinders of London and Westminster, for instance, dated from 1850; the Caxton Printers' Warehousemen's Association had been formed in 1860, the London Society of Lithographic Printers in 1869.[42] Those engaged in the work of illustration were not numerous enough to form a union until the 'eighties: the Society of Lithographic Artists, Designers, Engravers and Process Workers was formed in 1885 with only 252 members among its ten branches. A rival organisation arose in the following year, the National Society of Lithographic Artists, Designers and Writers, Copperplate and Wood Engravers (London), but it was soon found advisable for the two bodies to come to a working agreement, which was brought to an end by the collapse of the London society in 1898.[43]

Considering the widespread concern at the employment of children it is rather amusing to find a well-organised union among the offending boys themselves. A witness before the Children's

Employment Commission of 1862, speaking of the general troublesomeness of machine boys, said, "They have a society of their own, with stricter rules even than that of the men, and they are more strictly looked up; they insist upon all their members taking the regular holidays, and send boys round in pairs to apply for work during those times at any place where they think their rules are being infringed, in order to find out about it."[44]

The success of the women's organisations varied from one branch of the industry to another. There was one trade, bookbinding, which women had entered in full force by the middle of the century, and in which certain tasks regularly fell to their lot without opposition from the men. That being so, the Society of Women Employed in Bookbinding (1874) had nothing to hinder its success. It must be agreed, nevertheless, that women on the whole lacked interest in union activities, and this probably accounts for the early end of the Bookfolders' Union (1892). In the actual printing processes their failure was due to an insincere welcome held out to them by the main typographical unions. A conference was held in 1886 at which the men resolved "that while strongly of opinion that women are not physically capable of performing the duties of a compositor, this conference recommends their admission to membership of the various Typographical Unions, upon the same conditions as journeymen, provided always the females are paid strictly in accordance with scale."[45] The rule was adopted both by the Typographical Association and the London Society of Compositors. It was a masterly stroke, for the only reason for employing women was the lower wage which they would accept. By 1900 only one woman had been able to join a compositors' union, and she had not long remained a member.[46]

At the end of the century the London Society of Compositors, the Typographical Association and the Scottish Typographical Association were still the most considerable printers' unions. These three together with the Bookbinders' and Machine Rulers' Consolidated Union accounted for 27,000 of the 46,000 members of printers' and allied workers' unions in the British Isles. The other 19,000 were divided among 45 small unions, the whole being gathered for general trade purposes into the Printing and Kindred Trades' Federation of the United Kingdom, formed in 1898. The total membership was small compared with other trades. Engineering unions at that time had 287,000 members; 200,000 textile-workers had joined unions, together with 148,000 in the building trades and 347,000 miners. A writer at the time, admitting the success of the Typographical Union in the large towns, said that in the smaller places unionists in printing firms were rare. It was quite common, he thought, for apprentices to serve their time without knowing of the existence of trade unions. In his opinion the infrequency of strikes was due not so much to satisfactory working conditions as to a knowledge of the weakness of the societies;[47] but to judge by results the unions had not failed. The Royal Commission on Labour found that all the recent wage increases in the printing and allied trades were due to trade-union efforts. The wages of lithographic stone and zinc preparers in particular had been very low, but many employers had now accepted the scale drawn up by their society, ranging from 25s. to 30s. a week. By the formation of the Printers' Labourers' Union, again, wages had been raised to 20s. for a 54-hour week, with 6s. 6d. a night extra; formerly the men had earned only 12s. or 14s. a week, with 4s. for night work.[48]

The Eight-hour Day

English printers had secured a 54-hour week many years before their Parisian brethren, who in 1889 were still working for 60 hours.[49] On the other hand, the London compositors were in 1892 financing the bookbinders in a struggle for a concession which they themselves had not yet obtained—an 8-hour day. Several bookbinding firms had agreed to the introduction of a 48-hour week as soon as the suggestion was put to them in 1890, but those employers who were connected with the Bookbinders' Section of the London Chamber of Commerce had made a reservation that extra payment for overtime should not begin until 54 hours had been worked.[50] When the new terms had been unconditionally accepted, in 1892, the bookbinders' representatives claimed that the employers had no cause to regret their action. There was little fear that profits would fall, for various reasons, "principal among them," they said, "being what economists are pleased to call 'greater efficiency of management,' but more painfully known to ourselves as 'increased supervision,' which, unfortunately, is so intense at times as almost to make life unlivable. This condition, supplemented by a natural saving of gas, fuel, wear and tear of plant, an increase in their previous prices, &c., tend to place employers in a position at least as good as that which existed previous to the reduction in the hours of working."[51]

Later Developments

By the beginning of the present century the experimental period was well over. Unions existed even in the minor branches of the industry, and had worked out a regular routine. But before long there was a happening which aroused unpleasant publicity, arising from the lists of "fair" houses issued by the London Society of Compositors. In 1912 the firm of Vacher and Sons, having been omitted from the Society's list, brought an action against it for libel, and for conspiracy to induce persons not to deal with them. The defendants pleaded that under the Trade Disputes Act, 1906, the action was not tenable. Lord Justice Vaughan Williams gave judgment that the act was done in contemplation or furtherance of a trade dispute by the trade union as such, and that it was therefore within the rights of the union—a decision which was affirmed in the House of Lords in the following year.[52]

Such incidents have been rare, and the unions have been free, after settling minor difficulties, to form international friendships. The London Society of Compositors had paved the way with its financial assistance to foreign unions. In 1891, for instance, the union had granted £510 towards the German printers' strike and £110 to the Typographical Association of Vienna, following those grants within a few years by gifts of £10 each to the Carmaux Glass Workers, the Dock Labourers of Hamburg and the Typographical Association of Cape Town. In more permanent co-operation the lead seems to have been taken at the end of the century by the Society of Lithographic Artists, Designers, Engravers and Process Workers, who attached themselves to the International Federation of Lithographers and Kindred Trades.[53] Several relationships of this kind have been formed. Their object, in the words of an agreement between the Printing Machine Managers' Trade Society of London and the International Printing Pressmen and Assistants' Union of North America, was to provide "a means for the interchange of trade advice, the exchange of transfer cards, and to encourage and develop the true brotherhood which should exist between members of Trade Unions so closely allied."[54]

In point of numbers the two main societies of compositors long continued to hold the foremost position. In 1910 the members of the Typographical Association numbered 21,436 as compared with 12,230 in the London Society of Compositors and 5,027 in the Bookbinders' and Machine Rulers' Consolidated Union. The Amalgamated Society of Lithographic Printers of Great Britain and Ireland and the Amalgamated Society of Lithographic Artists, Designers, Engravers and Process Workers had about 4,500 and 1,600 respectively, but there were a number of unions with fewer than 200 members, such as the London United Society of Plate Printers, the Book Edge Gilders' Trade Society, the Amalgamated Type-Founders' Trade Society and the Lithographic Stone and Plate Preparers' Amalgamated Society.[55]

The variety of unions within the trade led to irritation and inter-union disputes on demarcation questions. These were aggravated by technical changes such as the introduction of composing machines and the consequent rise of unions of less-skilled workers. The situation began to be eased in 1911 when four unions of bookbinders amalgamated as the National Union of Bookbinders and Machine Rulers. Further amalgamations followed, but agreement between the letterpress craft unions proved more difficult to achieve. The National Society of Operative Printers and Assistants and the National Union of Printing and Paper Workers, for instance, could only compromise in 1914 with a "defensive alliance". On the whole, federation had greater success than amalgamation, and by 1914 the constitution of the Printing and Kindred Trades

Federation freely recognised the growing local federations.

In industry as a whole, not excluding the printing and allied trades, the years 1911–13 were disturbed by strikes and general unrest, but by 1914 all the major unions in the printing industry were parties to written agreements designed to foster peaceful co-existence. The advantage of this was clear during the labour shortages of the 1914–18 War, when the usual rules relating to overtime and demarcation of work were relaxed without undue difficulty. The war caused no serious decline in union membership; by 1920, indeed, the membership of the unions affiliated to the Printing and Kindred Trades Federation had steadily increased from the pre-war figure of 75,000, the main growth being in unions of semi-skilled and women workers.

Although the printing industry expanded during the inter-war period, fears of unemployment led to increased union pressure for strict regulation of entry into the skilled grades, and the trade continued to occupy a modest position in union statistics. In 1936 the whole of the union members of the printing and allied trades amounted to 126,518 as compared with 1,291,909 in the transport group, 582,865 in metals and 569,409 in mining. The printing trades ranked as eighth out of the total of nineteen main classes, although the statistics included members of the newspaper and periodical press.[56] In spite of that, "Mr. Peter Pendulum," the conscientious worker who keeps strictly to the clock, probably remained as much the typical printer as he had been in 1880: "Our friend is a strong believer in the Trade Society, and a firm supporter of all its rules. He not only attends every meeting when he does not work late, but he has got bound up at home, as part of his family library, all the annual reports from the days of Mr. R. Thompson to those of Mr. Self. He can tell you when every advance or change in the scale took place, and the names of all the chairmen at the annual meetings for the past thirty years."[57]

Since 1919 discussion between employers and employed had been simplified by the existence of the Joint Industrial Council of the Printing and Allied Trades of Great Britain and Ireland, as an association of members of the British Federation of Master

Printers and of trade unions affiliated to the Printing and Kindred Trades' Federation of the United Kingdom. Its objects were to secure complete organisation of employers and employed and to promote good relationship between them; to establish uniform working hours and conditions; to assist in the maintenance of such selling prices as would give reasonable remuneration to employers and employed; to settle apprenticeship problems; to deal with general matters of health; and to encourage social intercourse and the establishment of welfare departments. The Council was actively concerned in 1937 with the reduction of printers' hours from forty-eight to forty-five. Nevertheless, "the function of the Joint Industrial Council, in our view," runs a statement in the report for 1936–7, "is not to settle differences, but to assist the parties to settle their own differences. The negotiating of hours, wages, etc., is not, and never has been, the function of this Council. The greater success which it has had in comparison with other Joint Industrial Councils is in a great measure due to the fact that it has refrained from acting as a negotiating body."

Post-War Developments

The Second World War inevitably caused a temporary decline in union membership, but by the end of 1946 the membership of the Printing and Kindred Trades Federation, at 219,000, was higher than in 1939.

A problem which became more acute after the war, with government calls for increased productivity, was that of restrictive practices, often a result of demarcation. It was alleged in 1965 by the National Board for Prices and Incomes[58] that demarcation between craft and non-craft unions was largely to blame for a situation in which paper being transferred from one department to another might have to change hands at a certain line on the floor, and machine minders might decline to carry out certain tasks on the machines in their care. Another practice not conducive to speed was that of "pegging" output, fixing, for instance, the time to be taken for oiling and cleaning machines, regardless of circumstances. The Board was hopeful that such difficulties would be overcome if union leaders would continue their efforts towards amalgamation, already showing signs of success. "We have heard it said," it announced, "that the appearance of a single craft union and a single non-craft union is a practical possibility. We hope . . . no more than a penultimate step to a final objective of creating one union for the whole industry."[59] This might have seemed unlikely: no fewer than nine unions were parties to a wage settlement of May 1965; they ranged from the National Union of Printing, Bookbinding and Paper Workers, with 172,165 members, to the Association of Correctors of the Press, with 1,449.[60]

The Royal Commission on Trade Unions and Employers' Associations, 1965–8, was less optimistic than the Board, complaining that some of the unions concerned still maintained an unreasonably negative attitude to the need for change. Having invited the Printing and Kindred Trades Federation, the Society of Graphical and Allied Trades, the National Graphical Association, and the Society of Lithographic Artists, Designers and Engravers to submit their views on various comments made by employers the Commission regarded it "both as significant and as a matter for regret" that none of them accepted the invitation.[61]

The main difficulty, as seen by another government investigation, was that in British printing plants the loyalty of the workers went first to the union and only secondly to the firm. In various other countries, in contrast, management within each firm maintained and exercised the right to manage, with varying degrees of consultation with shop floor representatives.[62] One reason seemed to be that the British production workers were nearly 100 per cent organised (as in Holland, where union membership was legally enforced), whereas in Italy, Western Germany and the United States membership was less general.

As a result of successful recruiting by the Association of Scientific, Technical and Managerial Staffs a special branch of that union was formed in 1970 for clerical and administrative workers in book publishing. They had previously been limited to membership of the National Society of Operative Printers, Graphical and Media Personnel (NATSOPA) or, earlier, of the National Union of Journalists.

More recently, in 1973, *The Times* has announced a major new development in union organisation: "The Printing and Kindred Trades Federation is to be abolished and replaced by a Printing Trades Coordinating Bureau. The new body will leave individual unions free to negotiate their own wage agreements with employers, rather than jointly with the Newspaper Publishers Association and the Newspaper Society, as in the past. . . . The bureau will have a less powerful conciliation service for inter-union disputes. Conciliation committee decisions will not be binding on the parties."[63]

CHAPTER XIX

The Cost of Books in the Age of Mechanical Power

Technical Costs

We have already formed some idea of the general tendencies in book-production costs since the days of hand-printing and of hand-made paper. The use of esparto and wood, no less than the machinery introduced to deal with it, reduced the charge for paper in the course of a century from being about two-thirds of the cost of an edition of moderate size to barely one-tenth. Savings in the cost of composition were effected on the one hand by the introduction of composing-machines and on the other by the taking of stereotype moulds in readiness for a new impression. The resort to casing in place of the hand-worked binding not only reduced the cost of covering a book to a few pence but also made it possible for the binder to keep pace with the accelerated output of the printing-press. Illustrations, again, too dear at one time to be included in any but expensive volumes, became available for all types of publication. The course of prices has not, of course, been downward in every particular. From 1914 to 1935 production costs more than doubled; increases in the prices of materials were only partially offset by new and improved machinery and were accompanied by wage increases to printers and bookbinders. The cost of labour is the one item which in modern times has steadily increased.

In a search for still greater economies of production there has been a partial return to the early form of industrial organisation, in which various processes were under one control. Benjamin Disraeli, on a visit to Edinburgh in 1825, was particularly impressed by Oliver and Boyd's establishment, which he described to John Murray II as "one of the completest I have ever seen. They are booksellers, bookbinders and printers, all under the same roof; everything but making paper. . . . I never thought of binding," he added; "suppose you were to sew, &c., your own publications?"[1] Had he but known, there were already firms in France working on a still larger scale. The works of Alfred Mame & Co. in Tours, for instance, was combining printing, publishing, copper and steel engraving and binding, and was by 1850 producing 15,000 volumes a day.[2] Now that it is customary for large editions to be issued ready covered in mass-produced casings it is convenient for publishers to run their own binderies. The firm of Longmans is one of those which some eighty or ninety years ago established a bindery, working for the book trade generally as well as binding its own publications.[3] Other binderies are attached to printing works, and it was in order to compete with such joint establishments that in 1924 the printing-house of Unwin Brothers entered into a working agreement with the bookbinding firm of Messrs. Key and Whiting.[4] But for a combination rare even in the sixteenth century one must turn to the Oxford University Press, which in 1870, already maintaining its own binderies, took over the Wolvercote Paper Mill.[5]

The antagonism which existed from the beginning between the type-founder and the stereotype founder prevented for some time what would seem to be a natural amalgamation. In 1842 there was still nobody who undertook both processes. The explanation offered was that the two branches of the trade were opposed to one another, "inasmuch as the more books were cast in plates the less necessity would exist for the moveable types, and vice versa";[6] but to the lay mind that would offer a still greater argument for the combination of the two to make sure of constant employment in one process or the other. The introduction of composing machines partly solved the problem by reducing the need for separate foundries. Large printing establishments now have their own stereotyping and electrotyping departments, but there are still firms which specialise in the work and undertake it on contract for the trade.

One aspect of the book trade which in 1813 was described as its great disadvantage could not be altered by any of this reorganisation. A publisher pointed out then that before it was known whether 50 copies of a work would sell it was necessary to provide 200 or 300; he could think of no other branch of manufacture liable to so heavy a risk.[7] He had in mind the trade custom of paying the printer in multiples of 250, but in any case the cost of composition for a smaller edition would have raised the price of the individual volume to a prohibitive degree. But publishers already seemed fairly capable of judging what would sell; T. N. Longman, giving evidence before the same committee, said that the edition usually comprised 750 copies, and that about one work in ten sold off completely.[8]

One of the economies of modern printing could not have been brought about but for the conveniences of present-day transport. It is no longer possible to acquire suitable premises in the neighbourhood of St. Paul's Cathedral for a rent of £3 a year—or even the equivalent of that sixteenth-century charge in modern currency. Nor is it feasible for the user of up-to-date machinery to imitate John Jarrold and his partner, who in 1810 established a printing-press on a farm at Dallinghoo, using for the purpose the granary and one or two rooms of the old farmhouse.[9] Printing at its cheapest is now to be had in provincial towns, where most bookwork is carried on: lower rents allied with lower labour costs more than compensate for the cost of carriage.[10]

All of these together make up the technical costs of book production. But there are other expenses to be taken into consideration before one is in a position to fix the selling price of an individual book. Generally speaking the published price nowadays must be fixed at not less than three times the actual manufacturing cost. The remainder is accounted for fairly equally by the cost of distribution (booksellers' discounts and travellers' commissions) and by a balance which covers advertising expenses, the author's remuneration, the publisher's working expenses and the publisher's profit.[11]

The book trade was not to be left behind in the trend towards computerisation. In 1969 A. & C. Black, publishers of *Who's Who*, faced as usual with hundreds of hours of expensive hand composition in making the annual alterations, took the bold step of having the latest edition converted to coded punched tape. The data were then transferred to magnetic tape to produce a print out for the editorial staff, for the new material to be added.[12] Meanwhile the Oxford University Press had installed an efficient computer system at Neasden for handling booksellers' orders, and for accounting and stock control.[13] The innovations were not all immediately satisfactory; there were the usual complaints of computer errors (or rather, human errors) leading to delays in delivery, to incorrect invoices, and so on. "Teething troubles is a mild description of the chaos we suffered," said the Chairman of the Hamlyn Group of the International Publishing Corporation in 1970; "but this was in 1967. Our computer services are no longer troublesome, but remain unacceptably expensive."[14] Mr. Julian Blackwell summed up the situation by saying that in general the paper makers, printers and binders had introduced new methods, including the use of computers, in trying to increase productivity and absorb increasing costs; but that, nevertheless, paper was much the same as before, the efficient traditional printer was still competitive, and the new technologies in binding were making little change. To him one of the most welcome contributions of the computer was its help in finding the most economic routes for the Book Centre's Publishers and Booksellers Parcel Delivery Service, established in 1969.[15] And he quoted appreciatively the quip of Mr. Dana Pratt, associate director of Yale University Press, that if the computer had preceded the book, the book would have been hailed as a technological invention, "portable, durable, requiring no electricity, and, moreover, it's cuddly"—far-fetched, but not altogether silly.

The Cost of Distribution

The normal rate of discount to booksellers throughout the nineteenth century was 33⅓ per cent of the nominal retail price. In addition it was usual to charge for 25 copies as 24, or in cases of low-priced books 13 as 12, or 7 as 6½[16] There was a further concession to chosen booksellers in the form of invitations to the sale dinners, the periodical bargain sales for the trade. They were not new institutions. There is still in existence a catalogue of the stock of Mrs. Elizabeth Harris, to be sold in 1704 at "The Bear in Avey-Mary-Lane . . .: Where the Company shall be entertained with a Breakfast; and at Noon with a good Dinner, and a Glass of Wine: and then proceed with the Sale in order to finish that Evening."[17] By the middle of the nineteenth century not only were remainders sold at great reductions at the dinners but new publications were offered at 10 or 15 per cent below trade prices, often with an allowance of long credit.[18] One of the best known sales was Murray's annual dinner, held regularly for fifty years at the Albion Tavern in Aldgate Street. The proceeds usually amounted to more than £20,000.[19] On one of these occasions (1816) John Murray sold 7,000 copies of the third canto of *Childe Harold* and 7,000 of *The Prisoner of Chillon.*[20] This was a tribute both to Byron's appeal as a writer and to the attractions of large discounts. The publisher himself naturally had no intention of losing by the system; prices were fixed high enough in the first place to allow for these concessions. The same thing was happening in America. According to the *Publishers' Weekly*, 1877, there was a tendency to issue new books at lower prices, "but the passion for large discounts," it was stated, "is by no means eradicated, and books are still often published at much higher price than the normal rate, simply to permit a large discount. This holds especially true in Juveniles."

The existence of wholesale terms showed that at last the division between publishing and bookselling was an established fact. Until the mid-eighteenth century, we remember, there was little practical distinction between the terms "bookseller" and "publisher." By 1757 the two functions were recognised as independent, but the business of booksellers was still held to be "to purchase original copies from Authors, to employ Printers to print them, and publish and sell them in their Shops; or to purchase Books from such as print them on their own Account, or at Auctions, and sell them at an advanced Price: But their chief Riches and Profit is in the Property of valuable Copies."[21] In 1852 Luke Hansard still referred to "the Charge on the Publisher (the Bookseller)" as though the terms were equivalent,[22] although Charles Knight, in his reminiscences of the period, mentioned that the greater number of city booksellers did not carry on the business of publisher pure and simple. They were factors of books for the London collectors and agents for the country booksellers. But most of them still seem to have been publishers to the extent of being shareholders in the Chapter Books, so called because the business concerning them was carried on at the Chapter Coffee House.[23] It was not only the older firms which combined the two activities; Messrs. Chapman and Hall, who began business in 1830, opened first a retail bookshop but began publishing periodicals the same year. And, at risk of labouring the point, one may perhaps mention that in a manual published in 1839 the bookseller was described as "a person of considerable importance in the republic of letters, more especially if he combines those particular branches of the trade denominated *Proprietor* and *Publisher*."[24]

The division, even when it was complete, did not at once begin a period of impersonal relationships between publisher and retailer. The London publishers, it seems, had open accounts with almost every retail bookseller in the kingdom. Accounts were settled at regular intervals, but if at any time a retail shopkeeper had taken an inconvenient amount of ready money he was at liberty to deposit it with a publisher, who undertook to pay bills as they fell due and in general to act as banker.[25] The whole system was different from the German method of distribution. Since 1600, when the annual *Easter Catalogue* began to be issued, it had been arranged for all new German books to appear at the Easter Fair at Leipzig. Every bookseller of any importance had an agent there, and it was to the agent he applied, and not to the publisher, for any book he wanted to buy; wherever the books were printed, it was through the Leipzig commissioners that they had to be bought.[26] There was no one such market in England, but the need for a central clearing station had already been felt; late in the eighteenth century, therefore, the firm of Simpkins had been founded as wholesale distributing agents,[27] to be followed by similar firms. In addition the general publishers who received a heterogeneous assortment of orders from their country clients came to employ a special collector, whose sole duty was to go from one publishing-house to another collecting books to make up the country orders.[28] It is the practice now for publishers to send travellers to canvas for orders for new books before publication.[29]

The costs of distribution, therefore, which in the days of simple barter were almost non-existent, have grown with increasing specialisation until they now cover a remuneration to the retail bookseller, to the wholesale agent and to the publisher's own travellers.

Advertising Costs

The first two items which make up the balance of expenditure after technical costs and distribution costs have been accounted for, namely advertising costs and the payment to the author, had a development very similar. In the sixteenth century the cost of advertising had been the mere outlay of energy involved in writing a placard and fixing it to a post. During the next hundred years advertisements were accepted by the literary journals at 6d. or 1s. a time. As for the author's remuneration, we have seen that in the early days that was an item apt to be overlooked altogether. But after 1710, at least, authors took to withholding their copies until sufficient inducement was offered to part with them; and where advertising was concerned conditions began to favour the publisher who could make a good display.

When the nineteenth century opened advertising on the part of publishers was still undeveloped. The main publicity came from the summaries of new publications which were given in the weekly, monthly and quarterly reviews. The duty of 3s. 6d. which in 1815[30] was imposed on advertisements (irrespective of size) came at a time when newspapers were just beginning to be recognised as a valuable advertising medium for the book trade. It was estimated by a writer in the *Edinburgh Review* that quite one-third of the £173,821 realised from the tax in 1830 came from publishers' announcements. The duty of 3s. 6d. nearly doubled the charge for each entry.[31] In spite of that, Constable could write in 1825, "Advertisements in the ordinary way in newspapers, you may depend upon it, *always pay.*"[32] None the less, there were rejoicings when the tax was in 1834[33] reduced to 1s. 6d. and finally, in 1853,[34] repealed altogether.

It was soon realised that a single insertion in a newspaper was of little use. By the time a work had been fully advertised quite a formidable amount had been spent. One bookseller, Owen Rees, gave evidence in 1818 that in the preceding twelve months his firm had paid £4,638 7s. 8d. on advertising in newspapers alone.[35] The cost of advertising a new work was estimated at about £30; for later editions, when the book was already in demand, a smaller sum was sufficient.[36] About 1850 it could be said that £20 was the minimum and £150 the maximum usually spent in advertising a new book, but that the outlay quite often reached £200 or £300. One publishing-house varied the amounts between £70 and £150; another generally limited itself between £25 and £100; and a third rarely exceeded £60. From 1830 to 1832 the firm of Messrs. Colburn and Bentley spent £27,000 on advertising. Another firm was paying £3,000 or more a year.[37] It was an expense partly saved to German publishers by the Leipzig Börse: the agents were in the habit of sending copies of new publications throughout Germany for display in the bookshops, taking them back after six months if not sold. A few French and American publishers, too, had adopted the system, but those English publishers who had tried sending books into the country on sale or return were dissatisfied with the results; the unsold books were too often shop-soiled or damaged in transit.[38]

By the inter-war years the expenditure on advertising had become directed into several main channels. Press announcements still took the first place, although for their insertion the publisher might have to pay at the rate of about £8 an inch. Next there came prospectuses of forthcoming works, describing the volumes in greater detail; they were sent to booksellers and also to individual purchasers likely to be interested. There were, again, the house-organs issued regularly by publishers, sometimes costly to produce and, like the prospectuses, running away with large sums in postage. Display material for bookshops, consisting of showcards, streamers for window display, and so on, the hire of poster-spaces in lifts and on station platforms, and the provision of the posters were all items not to be ignored. The picture jackets which served to protect the bindings of novels might be as effective a means of advertising as any, and might cost up to £25 for the edition. Copies of books sent out for review must presumably be included in advertising costs, although the resulting paragraphs may be little to the publisher's taste. These were all parts of a routine system towards which £50 for an individual book was a modest outlay.[39] We have taken no account of the extraordinary methods sometimes adopted, as when Arthur Bullen tried to popularise W. W. Jacobs's *Many Cargoes*. This he did by employing sandwichmen dressed for the purpose as riverside sailors, complete with pipes.[40] But it may be that the least expensive item of all, the publisher's imprint, carries more weight than some of the most spectacular devices. It is fairly true now, as it was in 1840, that "the reading public can tell the *character* of any book from the name of the Publisher by whom it is issued."[41]

Round about 1840 the author who could undertake his own advertising was being advised to publish by commission. He had only to send the books, ready printed, to a publisher and call every six months for the proceeds less a commission of 7½ per cent.[42] As a method of publication it has fallen rather out of favour, although, as one publisher reminds us, many learned works of research would never have been issued at all if they had to wait for a publisher to finance them on their purely commercial merits.[43] Dickens's unfortunate experiences over *The Christmas Carol* (1843) may have helped to render the system unpopular. It is common knowledge that his final cleavage with Messrs. Chapman and Hall followed his demand to issue the work on a commission basis, to his eventual disappointment.

The Author's Remuneration

Where commission publication is not adopted the author's remuneration may take the form of a single payment for the copyright, a share in the profits, a combination of the two, or a royalty on the number of copies sold. In the early nineteenth century it was quite common for an author to sell his copy outright, one author at least being offered a sum which he found embarrassingly high. That was in 1813, when Lord Byron wrote in his diary, "Mr. Murray has offered me one thousand guineas for 'The Giaour' and 'The Bride of Abydos.' I won't. It is too much: though I am strongly tempted, merely for the say of it."[44] Thomas Moore raised no such objections when Longmans offered him £3,000 for a poem to be of the same length as *Rokeby*; within three years, in 1817, his *Lalla Rookh* was ready for publication on the agreed terms.[45] The system which John Murray II usually recommended was the division of profits, which Hallam, Milman and others had found advantageous. He was specially proud of the results in the case of J. W. Croker's *Stories from the History of England* (1816), selling at 2s. 6d. a copy: Croker himself would have accepted 20 guineas for the work, but having agreed to take a half of the profits instead he was soon in possession of £700.[46] John Murray III, too, was in favour of half-profit terms, with the result that Layard's *Nineveh and its Remains* (1848) brought its author about £1,500 a year for some years instead of the lump sum of £200 which he had been willing to take.[47] The writer of renown sometimes preferred to lease his copyrights for limited periods on payment of an agreed sum. Lord Lytton, for instance, in 1853 assigned to the firm of Routledge a ten years' right of publication of nineteen of his novels, receiving in return the sum of £20,000. The arrangement succeeded so well that the bargain was renewed for a further period at £1,000 a year.[48] A record payment for a novel was the sum of £10,000 paid to Disraeli in 1880 by Longmans for the copyright of *Endymion*.[49] One can think of several twentieth-century writers of wider appeal, but it is more usual now for the author's remuneration to take the form of a royalty calculated on the price of the book.

This varies according to circumstances, but in general is 10 per cent, whether on a hardback or paperback (Penguins started with 4 per cent, but now have a higher rate). It appeared in 1957 from a questionnaire circulated by the Society of Authors to its members (of whom only 600, or one in five, replied) that fewer than 8 per cent of them earned more than £1,500 a year from writing; 40 per cent earned £260 or less. This did not distinguish between full-time authors and those who wrote in their spare time, for prestige or simply for pleasure.

The outstanding writer, even if his publications do not include a best-seller, may be fortunate enough to win a literary award. Literary prizes in the United Kingdom began in 1806 with the institution of the annual Newdigate prize for a poem by an Oxford University undergraduate. They have grown in number and importance until there are now more than sixty, some of them of considerable monetary value. Some of the awards are administered by the National Book League, the Society of Authors, the British Academy or other institutions or societies, but they tend to be offered more and more by individual publishers anxious to find promising writers. Some of the most lucrative are the Young Writers Award (£2,500) given by the New English Library Ltd., the Robert Pitman Literary Prize (£1,000) awarded annually for a first book by a British author, the Booker Prize for fiction (£5,000) sponsored by the Publishers' Association and Booker McConnell Ltd., and the biennial Religious Book Award (£1,000), which was inaugurated by Wm. Collins Sons in 1969 to celebrate the hundred and fiftieth anniversary of the company's foundation. Three major annual awards announced in 1971 were sponsored, not by a publisher, but by Whitbread's Brewery, and are administered by the Booksellers' Association; they consist of £1,000 each for a novel, a biography and a volume of poetry (altered in 1972 to a children's book). But the most encouraging awards for the young writer are probably those which provide an incentive for further work, such as the prize offered in 1972 by *The Times Saturday Review*, in conjunction with Jonathan Cape, for an original detective story (£500 plus a £500 contract commissioning a further novel) and Butterworth's Scientific Fellowships for authors, awarded annually to encourage the writing of a scholarly work on mathematics or science; these provide for allowances against royalties to compensate for loss of income while writing the book, together with £750 on acceptance of the work.

This is only a brief note of the many awards offered each year. In one case, at least, a prize competition organised by T. Fisher Unwin had results beyond the expectation of either the author or the publisher. One of the entrants was a new writer, Ethel M. Dell, whose contribution, *The Way of an Eagle*, had already been declined by eight publishers. This time it was successful, and was published in 1912; by 1915 it had had twenty-seven printings, sold under the slogan "the novel with the ugly hero," and in due course it became responsible for half the turnover of the firm.[50]

Success from literary awards has not come to the ordinary writer. The fifty or so annual grants from the Arts Council, ranging from £400 to £1,000, go some way towards helping the rank and file, but long before these were available authors had begun to cast resentful eyes on the public library system, whereby a single copy of a work might be used by a hundred or more readers.

Public Lending Right

The so-called "public lending right" agitation began openly in 1951, with John Brophy's article in *The Author* entitled "A proposal to increase authors' incomes through the libraries". His suggestion was that borrowers from public and circulating libraries should pay a fee of one penny for each volume they borrowed. The Society of Authors was in favour of the scheme, but it was left to A. P. (afterwards Sir Alan) Herbert to take the lead with his memorandum *Public Lending Right: Authors, Publishers and Libraries*. In 1959, through his efforts, the Society launched a full-scale campaign. Publishers were sympathetic, and in the following year the Authors and Publishers Lending Right Association was formed. Librarians held back through apprehension as to the administrative work likely to be involved and through anxiety as to the source of the money. Herbert's proposal was simple but controversial: he wanted a Libraries (Public Lending Right) Bill to be drawn up, "to provide for the just remuneration of authors and publishers for books supplied to the public lending libraries" by amending the Copyright Act of 1956. Under it an authors' and

ROAN-BINDING SHOP—MESSRS. WESTLEYS AND CLARK'S FACTORY
From Dodd (G.), *Days at the Factories*, 1843

publishers' association would be set up, with a council drawn from the Ministry of Education, the Society of Authors and the Publishers' Association; the council would administer the funds received from the libraries, which would contribute either $6\frac{1}{3}$ per cent of their annual book-expenditure or some other sum to be agreed. The publishers would receive part of the proceeds and the rest would be distributed among authors who were members of the association. The Library Association's reaction was that authors would be worse off than before, because libraries would have less money to spend on books. In 1962 Herbert revised his suggestions, proposing in a pamphlet *Libraries: free for all* that registered public library readers should pay 7s. 6d. a year; half of the proceeds would be the public lending right fee and the rest would be retained by the libraries towards improvements in service and staffing. This, too, was opposed by the Library Association.

From 1964 the Government was brought into the discussion. Miss Jennie Lee, Minister with special responsibilities for the arts, was sympathetic but unable to act; but in 1966 Lord Goodman, Chairman of the Arts Council, reminded its Literature Panel of its responsibilities with regard to authors as well as to literature, and a working party was set up to discuss the whole question. The working party took quick action, first examining the arrangements for public lending right which were already functioning in Denmark and Sweden and then, in 1967, submitting proposals based on the Danish system to the Department of Education and Science. These proposals, published in 1968 as *The Arts Council and Public Lending Right*, were for an annual government grant to be made available, based on the total expenditure of public libraries on books, and for payments to be made to authors and publishers in accordance with the library books in stock each year. The Library Association still objected. In 1969, following questions and discussions in Parliament, Miss Lee stated that the Government did not intend to implement the Council's plan; but, at her instigation, the Department of Education and Science offered a new suggestion, that libraries should pay an extra sum when buying books, based on a scale of the average library life of the various categories. Yet another scheme had meanwhile been produced by the Arts Council: the Government would provide funds for a 15 per cent royalty on each copyright book bought by a library, to be divided three to one between author and publisher. This was rejected by Miss Lee's successor, Lord Eccles, in 1970, but he set up a working party "to consider how any amendment of the Copyright Act, 1956 to add lending to the public acts restricted by copyright might be implemented." Its suggestion, in 1972, was that all libraries except the British Museum should be subject to public lending right payments on purchases, the money being collected by a Lending Rights Society which would issue licences in return for an annual fee based on the library's book expenditure.[51] This time it was a group of authors, the Writers Action Group, which was to dissent, claiming that no scheme would work unless it was financed by central funds and related to loans.

Meanwhile the Society of Authors continued to press for an appropriate amendment of the Copyright Act and the Library Association continued to oppose any scheme which would reduce library book funds, whether directly or indirectly.[52] There seemed to be a deadlock, but in November 1973 a private member's Bill was introduced into the House of Commons, with backing from all three parties in the House, for the establishment of Public Lending Right by amending the Copyright Act of 1956. If the General Election of 1974 had not intervened it would have restricted public lending by copyright and would have required that the right should be enforced only by licensing bodies representing the copyright owners and by negotiating with the libraries on their behalf. Further legislation has since been introduced without success. (The right was conceded in New Zealand in 1973 and in Australia in 1974.)[53]

Establishment Charges

Publishers' working expenses, the last costs to be considered, are high, amounting for most firms to 25 per cent or more of the turnover.[54] In the case of Murray *v.* Walter and another, heard in the King's Bench Division in 1908, John Murray provided the information that 16⅔ per cent of his turnover went to establishment charges.[55] For the book which was the occasion of his libel action, *The Letters of Queen Victoria*, the amount was calculated at £2,000.

Total Costs

There were yet other heavy charges in the publication of the *Letters* to justify the price of £3 3s. for the three volumes. The corrections alone had come to four times the cost of composition, and they had been included in the general costs instead of being laid to the charge of the editors, as lawfully they might have been. Many letters at Windsor Castle had had to be specially copied, involving a payment of over £900 to amanuenses. Moreover, as the proofs were to be read by very distinguished persons they had to be printed on special paper. The total costs, including advertisements but excluding establishment charges and payment to the editors, came to a little over £7,060. The editors received £5,392.

The technical costs, the expenses of advertising and the payments to the editors for this particular work thus amounted to about £12,452. It is interesting to compare its cost with that of another expensive work issued rather more than a century before, Johnson and Steevens's edition of Shakespeare (1803).[56] That was in twenty-one volumes, whereas *The Letters of Queen Victoria* were in three; but the edition of Shakespeare's works was only one-eighth of the size of the other. The quantity of paper required was approximately the same, but as the earlier edition was smaller its cost of composition was relatively high. The total cost of the Shakespeare volumes was £5,683 4s. 6d. The technical and advertising costs amounted to £5,283, including £3,345 3s. for paper, £1,719 14s. for printing and £62 0s. 1d. for advertising. The difference in the editorial fees can be explained by the very different work involved. For the earlier publication they were only £400 as compared with £5,392 for the other.

Comparisons of book-production costs at different times cannot be made with complete accuracy unless firstly the volumes compared contain the same number of pages and are of the same format.

That is not all. The large edition costs relatively less than the smaller one, but is it right to compare an edition of 1,000 copies published in 1800 with another of 1,000 published 100 years later? In 1800 an edition of that size was considered fairly large; in 1900 a work of the same importance might have run into ten or more times the number of copies. Small type, again, is more expensive to set than large, so that 16 octavo pages of brevier cost more than 16 octavo pages of pica; and footnotes, diagrams, mathematical symbols or anything else out of the ordinary all add to the price. Two volumes of the same size which cost the same total amount to produce might still, therefore, show discrepancies making up that total. More especially is that true of works published at different periods. For instance, Babbage's *On the Economy of Machinery and Manufactures*, published in 1832, cost 2s. 3d. a volume,[57] which was the estimated cost of producing a travel-book of the same size in 1890.[58] The details of the first show that the paper for each volume cost about 8d., the extra boarding 6d. and the composition and presswork 8½d. The paper for the later one cost only 4½d. and the casing 4d., but the cost of printing had risen to 9d.

In 1906 *The Times* published the costs of various works which had been issued with its co-operation.[59] They show clearly the economies of printing large editions. The estimate given in 1890 for a travel-book of 320 pages was for an edition of 1,000 copies. One of these other works, Busch's *Memoirs of Bismarck*, was in three volumes averaging 497 pages, but by publishing 5,000 copies the printing cost was reduced to 5·7d. a volume compared with the 9d. of the former work. A larger work still, *The War in the Far East*, in 672 pages, cost only 5·86d. for printing each of the 5,230 copies; but the maps for each volume cost an extra 18·65d. and the illustrations an extra 5·12d., which accounted for the high cost of technical production of 3s. 9d. a volume. Advertising cost £246. The price was fixed at £1 1s., and the profits on sales amounted to £1,100, of which £800 went to the authors and £300 to the publisher. A more recent estimate, for a book of 100,000 words and 212 pages, was made in 1970 by the Secretary of the

Edinburgh University Press: printing, £2 a page; paper, at £8 a ream, £112; binding, £225; jacket, about £60; correction costs, up to £30. This gave a basic manufacturing cost of £1,015, or a unit cost of 10s. 2d. The price, at 50s., allowed for an average discount over the whole sale of 40 per cent, with author's royalty 10 per cent, administrative, editorial and production overhead 7s., plus promotion, invoicing, postage and packing costs. Nearly 1,750 of the edition of 2,000 had to be sold before the basic costs and overheads were recovered.[60]

Publisher's Profit

The publisher's profit depends very largely, of course, on the whim of the public. All that the publisher can do is to fix the price he thinks low enough to guarantee a sale for the whole edition, allowing himself a margin but vesting his hopes of large profits in the reprints which may follow. He naturally has no guarantee of any profit at all. At the close of the eighteenth century the profit yielded by an edition of 1,000 copies of an octavo volume was generally about £100, according to the experience of Messrs. Cadell and Davies.[61] But John Murray II, having paid Washington Irving 3,000 guineas for *The Voyages of Columbus* and 2,000 guineas for *The Conquest of Granada*, had in 1831 to report a gross loss on the two of £2,250.[62] His successor, John Murray III, had also to admit to disappointing sales. In 1846–7 he published Herman Melville's *Typee* and *Omoo* in his 2s. 6d. series. "Of *Typee*," he reported, "I printed 5,000 copies and have sold 4,104. Of *Omoo*, 4,000 and have sold 2,512. Thus I have gained by the former £51 2s. and by the latter I am a loser of £57 16s. 10d."[63] The 21-volume edition of Shakespeare which was published in 1803 took nine years to sell at its price of £11 11s. and produced a total profit of £375.[64] Even *The Letters of Queen Victoria*, whose sales had by May 1908 brought in £18,971, gave a profit of only £600 or £700 to the publisher.[65]

It is clear that the publisher's profit depends very largely on his skill in fixing prices. The prices of books depend in the long run, as the prices of all else, on the cost of production. Competition tends to lower them, but in its absence there may be an inducement to limit output in order to raise prices and aggregate profit. That has been illustrated by the history of the book trade.

Book Prices

From about 1780 until the end of the first quarter of the nineteenth century the prices of new books were rising steadily. This was the period of scarce paper and of growing labour costs unrelieved as yet by any economy in the methods of production. A hundred years earlier the published price of an ordinary octavo volume had been 5s. or 6s. Now it was anything from 10s. to 14s.; the duodecimo had risen to 6s. or thereabouts and the quarto was frequently £2 2s. It was not entirely a matter of technical costs of production. In 1813, for instance, there were five editions of Cowper's poems on sale, each in two volumes: one in octavo with plates at £1 6s., one in octavo without plates at £1 1s., two foolscap octavo editions, one at 14s. and the other, of inferior print and paper, at 7s., and a duodecimo stereotype edition at 9s.[66] They could scarcely have been sold at a profit for less because of the large amount which had been paid for the final two years' copyright. This was an unusually hard bargain. In other cases the raising of prices seems to have been due to the deliberate policy of the publishers, who chose to limit the size of their editions in order to secure higher returns from the well-to-do. Almost as much was admitted by T. N. Longman in his evidence before the House of Commons in 1813;[67] and this, at all events, was the opinion of one of the first publishers to adopt different tactics.[68]

When, in 1826, Charles Knight and his associates founded the Society for the Diffusion of Useful Knowledge the policy of cheap publication of new works was shown to be practicable. So far such cheap books as there were had been the production of the new men in the trade, men who could not, perhaps, pay large sums for copyright, and who in any case thought it worth while to cater for the humbler sort of readers. These lesser publishers—Bell, Cooke, Lane and the rest—rendered good service to the growing middle classes with their cheap reprints of works whose copyright had lapsed. In the 1790's, for instance, one could buy for 6d. a complete work in Cooke's series of British poets. But the reader who wanted anything new had to buy it in an expensive form which did not necessarily appeal to him. The new society remedied that in the case of works of a scientific nature; and its policy of cheap publication led to the issue, in 1833, of the *Penny Cyclopædia*, in weekly parts at 1d. a time. At that price 75,000 copies were sold. In 1834 it was decided to double the rate of issue, but at the new charge of 2d. a week the sale fell to 55,000. After three years the work was issued four times a week, but soon, whether through an unwillingness to spend 4d. a week on literature or to loss of interest, there was a regular fall in demand until, in 1843, only 20,000 issues were sold.[69]

In the meantime, in 1827, Constable had begun to publish his *Miscellany*, a series of original works which he offered at a price then associated only with reprints. "His three-and-sixpenny volumes," says Knight, "and his grand talk of 'a million of buyers,' made the publishing world of London believe that the mighty autocrat of Edinburgh literature had gone 'daft.' And so the Row sneered, and persevered in its old system of fourteen-shilling octavos and two-guinea quartos."[70]

By 1850 the famous yellow-backs and other pocket-editions were on sale at the railway bookstalls at 1s. or 2s. a copy. That was nothing to the cheapness which was to come. In 1909 the Secretary to the Federation of Master Printers, giving evidence before the Law of Copyright Committee, spoke of the large number of books being sold at 6d. and 7d. each, consisting mostly of reprints of works whose copyright had expired. Any one of Dickens's works, it was alleged, could be bought complete for 1d. One of the publishers present questioned that statement, but was assured that such books were being issued by more than one publisher as "street copies."[71]

Successful as were most of the early bookstall editions, they did not all pay their way. John Murray III told Gladstone in 1852 that his own experiment in cheap literature, the Home and Colonial Library, at 2s. 6d. a volume, had met with so little encouragement that he had been obliged to abandon it.[72] Actually, most of the established publishers still seem to have been reluctant to lower their prices to any great extent even for a second edition, when the first demand had been satisfied. "In the same manner," Charles Knight recalled, "it is within the memory of living persons that there was an invariable high price for fish in London, because the wholesale dealers at Billingsgate always destroyed a portion of what came to market, if the supply were above the average. The dealers in fish had not recognised the existence of a class who would buy for their suppers what the rich had not taken for their dinners; and knew not that the stalls of Tottenham Court Road had as many customers ready for a low price as the shops of Charing Cross for a high price. The fishmongers had not discovered that the price charged to the evening customers had no effect of lowering that of the morning. Nor had the booksellers discovered that there were essentially two, if not more, classes of customers for books—those who would have the dearest and the newest, and those who were content to wait till the gloss of novelty had passed off, and good works became accessible to them, either in cheaper reprints, or 'remainders' reduced in price."[73]

The difficulty was that under the existing copyright system it paid the publisher best to limit the size of his editions and so to keep up prices. That was mentioned time and time again in the evidence given before the Copyright Commission of 1876–8, and not always as a fault to be remedied. John Murray went so far as to deny that books were dear at all. He agreed that for the best of them the general public had to wait, but he argued that this was only to be expected; the newest fashions were not reduced in price until a year or so after they were first produced, and the same was true of books. The opposite view, as expressed by Sir Charles Trevelyan and others, was that it was not merely a case of waiting; by the time the expensive edition had been exhausted and had been followed by a "student's edition" or some other issue of more moderate price the work was becoming too stale for the long-postponed "people's edition" to be of much value. Trevelyan agreed with other writers that if cheaper editions were published at the outset authors would find themselves equally well compensated by the royalties on the larger number which would be sold.[74] As things were it seemed that the only way for book-buyers to be served cheaply was for the bookseller to share with them part of the discount which he was allowed by the publisher. This in many cases he was willing to do, and during part of the nineteenth century was allowed to do; but at what cost of strife and argumentation we shall see later on.

It is interesting to find that in France, too, prices were for a time kept artificially high. According to Georges Maillard, addressing the Law of Copyright Committee of 1909,[75] the normal price of a book in France had for some years been 3 francs. At that price, as he put it, "there was such over-production that the number of readers was no longer sufficient"; in order to secure a demand, therefore, prices were reduced to 1 franc, in so far as the publisher thought he could sell a sufficiently large number to make that price remunerative. In England, in spite of an ever-increasing output of pocket editions at from 6d. upwards, there has been no drastic reduction such as this in the prices of ordinary new publications. Nevertheless, there was a tendency between the wars for books to become cheaper in spite of heavier costs of labour and materials. The reason given by one publisher was that editions were rather larger than before and that publishers were working on a smaller margin.[76] As opposed to this, where fiction was concerned there was a powerful force at work against price-reduction. The great majority of novel-readers did not buy their books but borrowed them from the circulating libraries. Experience showed that having paid subscriptions for the privilege they would not think of including a 3s. 6d. novel in their order lists; nothing under 7s. 6d. will satisfy them.[77] The publisher, therefore, who thought to widen his market by lowering prices might find that he had instead cut off part of the demand which already existed. From 1908 prices of non-net books, mainly novels, *were* reduced, but by the circulating libraries themselves, after representations made to the Publishers' Association by Mudie's, W. H. Smith & Sons and Boots. Investigation among publishers showed that 90 per cent of the first year's sale of these books took place in the first month after publication; the Council of the Association accordingly agreed to their sale at second-hand prices after three months.[78]

The demand from circulating libraries is not one which can be lightly disregarded, but publishers no longer consider these institutions to be an unmixed blessing. It is felt that subscribers, unless on a "guaranteed book" basis, are liable to be put off with inferior substitutes for the works which they really want in order to make use of the library's surplus stocks of cheaper volumes.[79] Opinions have changed since T. N. Longman had been asked by the Copyright Committee of 1813 whether the circulating library system was not injurious to the bookselling trade. "I think the contrary," he had said. "It tends to diffuse a taste for reading; having read a book, you have a desire to possess it, in many cases: besides that, the numerous societies which exist, each taking a copy, creates a considerable demand."[80]

Prices of books, as of all else, have increased during recent years. Sir John Benn recalled, in 1973, that in 1925 the Nations of the Modern World Series sold for one guinea a volume. They had risen to three guineas. Other works, too, were three times the original price.[81] But this must be compared with an increase of seven to ten times in the price of other commodities. The business of fixing book prices is very subtle. Sir Stanley Unwin gave an instance of an art book in two volumes which he considered good value at three guineas the set, but which the booksellers would not buy at two guineas; he changed the price on the jackets to three guineas per volume, or six guineas the set, and told the booksellers that they could sell it at half price and pay two guineas for it themselves. "The stock just melted away."[82]

The Sizes of Books

Closely linked up with the question of prices of books is the matter of their size. It would be difficult to say whether the modern pocket editions owe their popularity more to their cheapness or to their convenience to handle. The two attractions grew up together, fostered by such enterprising publishers as John Bell, whose duodecimo edition of Shakespeare's works (1774) aroused so much criticism from his fellow publishers and won so great a welcome from the public. Big volumes were necessarily expensive. Cowper found, in issuing his Homer, that the quarto edition appealed only to the rich; the bulk of readers were clamouring for an octavo edition which they could afford to buy.[83] John Murray II was well aware of the new tendency. Writing in 1818 to James Hogg, the Ettrick Shepherd, he said, "With regard to the projected quarto edition of 'The Queen's Wake,' I am not sorry that it is at an end; for you will gain more, I think, by one in royal octavo. But I really think that you ought to print a thousand in demy octavo to sell for 9s., and throw off no more in the larger size than you are confident of obtaining subscribers for—otherwise you will absolutely stop the sale of your book by printing it in a form that is neither customary nor useful, and retard at the same time the advancement of your own fame."[84]

Number Publication

However confident Hogg may have been of obtaining subscribers, subscription publication had had its day. Too many writers had found, in common with J. H. Prince, that to go about soliciting for subscriptions was "a most *painful undertaking* to a *susceptible* mind."[85] What was now more acceptable to all concerned was the system of number publication. It had the same general appeal as the cheap reprints of standard works put on the market by John Bell and others. The new 6d. editions of the poets were followed very closely, in 1779, by Harrison's *Novelists' Magazine*, issued in weekly numbers at 6d. a time and selling at the then remarkable rate of 12,000 copies a week. It seems to have been a means of publication very profitable to the distributing agents. When, round about 1830, Baines of Leeds issued in 6d. parts the *History of the Wars of the French Revolution* which had been such a dismal failure in its two-volume quarto edition its circulation, so Constable was told, was over 20,000 copies, and the wholesale price to the hawkers was only 2½d. a number.[86]

Far from being limited to reprints of earlier novels, publication in weekly numbers became the accredited system for new works. Dickens's novels are the example which comes first to the mind, but other works of a much more formidable nature were issued on the same plan. By 1842 it could be said that thousands of volumes of a learned description had been bought in weekly parts by readers who would otherwise have had no means of access to them at all.[87] In fact, one had to be a person of very firm will to escape buying them. The hawkers were most persistent. "As in Birmingham and other great towns," it was said, "there is a beggars' register, which describes the susceptibilities of the families at whose gates beggars call, even to the particular theological opinions of the occupants, so the canvasser has a pretty accurate account of the households within his beat. He knows where there is the customer in the kitchen, and the customer in the parlour. He sometimes has a timid colloquy with the cook in the passage; sometimes takes a glass of ale in the servants' hall; and, when he can rely upon the charms of his address, sends his card boldly into the drawing-room. No refusal can prevent him in the end leaving his number for inspection."[88] But generally speaking it seems the system was not so common in the south of England as it was in the midlands and the industrial north.[89] And even in those districts the reader who was willing to wait a whole week for the next instalment of a novel was before long able to buy it, complete with household hints, children's pages and other attractions, in a weekly illustrated magazine. It seems all the more strange that there has been a revival of number publication since the Second World War. Cookery manuals, children's encyclopaedias and other reference works are being published in weekly or monthly parts, but at prices unlikely to attract the same kind of reader as before.

Paperbacks

A new source of cheap reading matter has been developed during the present century. The economy arising from printing long runs of works in uniform sizes has led to what some have regarded as a revolution in publishing, the rise of the so-called "paperback." The large-scale production of cheap books had progressed rather slowly from the pocket-editions of the mid-nineteenth century to the "street copies" (George Newnes' Penny Library of Famous Books and the rest) of the turn of the century. Next came the 6d. or 9d. paper-covered novels which were available from newsagents and railway bookstalls until after the 1914–18 war. They existed at the same time as "colonial editions," works of fiction obtained from their original publishers in sheet form, at 1s. or less each, in batches of 500 or 1,000 copies; the new publisher had them bound in paper or sometimes cloth for sale in the colonies at 1s. 6d. or 2s.[90] The original publishers profited from the larger printing-runs made possible in this way without the need to undertake export business themselves. Some of them complained that the cheap cloth-bound reprints threatened the profitability of the 6s. novel, but Heinemann admitted that the 6d. paper-covered novel had not had the same ill effect, but actually yielded considerable profit to authors and publishers.

There is some difference of opinion as to the origin of the paper-back in its modern form. Sir John Benn, at the fiftieth anniversary celebrations of Ernest Benn, Ltd., which was founded in 1923, stated that his father was first in the field, with his publication of Benn's Sixpenny Library, the Ninepenny Novels and the Augustan Poets. The more general view is that they began in 1935, when Allen Lane, director of the Bodley Head, optimistically began to publish paper covered reprints at 6d. a volume. The first ten, all of which appeared in July 1935, were calculated to appeal to a wide public; they included Ernest Hemingway's *A Farewell to Arms*, Eric Linklater's *Poet's Pub*, Compton Mackenzie's *Carnival* and Mary Webb's *Gone to Earth*. Twenty thousand copies of each of the ten were printed, and the publisher estimated the break-even point at 17,500. In spite of his personal visits to booksellers up and down the country to introduce the series, sales were disappointingly small until he approached Woolworths, who decided to take the risk of a large order.[91] By January 1936, following the publication of the first twenty reprints, Penguin Books Ltd. was formed, to take full responsibility for this already successful venture.

The need for rapid printing during the Second World War was met by new techniques of high-speed production by rotary machines fed with continuous web paper. This development was to make possible the phenomenal increase in paperback production which has since taken place, and which to a large extent has divorced it from traditional publishing. The production of long runs of many titles of identical format reduces to a minimum the cost of making ready the printing machines and the attached folding machines. It is estimated that, for works of 256 pages, a web-fed rotary press with a folding attachment will produce editions of 25,000 copies of about 115 titles a year, and a smaller rotary machine about fifty titles.[92] For books designed to be read and thrown away there is no reason to slow down production for the sake of niceties of appearance.

The works chosen for the Penguin series, both general and special, have from the beginning been of a high standard which Sir Allen Lane was determined to maintain. It is told of him that at one time he became worried about the permissiveness of some of his editors. "One book particularly affronted him and he could not persuade his editors that they were wrong, and the printed copies lay in its [*sic*] thousands in his warehouse at Harmondsworth awaiting distribution. After a certain midnight with a friend and a lorry he broke into his own warehouse, collected the copies and burned them in the darkness on his farm near Reading. No one mentioned that title again."[93]

By 1950 there were getting on for 1,000 paperbacks in print, in 1960 nearer 6,000 and by 1962 between 9,000 and 10,000.[94] Penguin Books were still in the lead, but the 1962 figure was accounted for by 133 publishing-houses, of which some 40 per cent were under American control. Pan Books (issued by Macmillan and Collins) were then second in importance in the British market, followed by Corgi and the New English Library; both of the latter were under American control.[95] Penguin Books were almost alone at that time in including original works, as distinct from reprints, in their lists.

The days of the 6d. Penguin have long passed, and, whereas hardbacks are at roughly four times their pre-war prices, thus reflecting the decline in the value of money, the ordinary Penguin at 25 new pence has increased ten times. An important factor in raising the price of paperbacks has been an increase of "quality" ones, including specially commissioned original works, which are published in smaller editions and therefore at higher costs. It was estimated in 1961, for instance, that the total printing and paper costs of 5,000 copies of a standard-sized paperback worked out at £86 per thousand; for 20,000, 50,000, 100,000 and 200,000 it was £51, £35, £29 and £26, respectively.[96] (In the United States, by then, the first printing of a paperback designed for mass circulation was seldom less than 100,000, and was often much higher.[97])

In March 1971 the *Financial Times* published a survey of current annual sales of paperbacks. Penguin, Fontana, Pan and Corgi headed the list, with approximately 35, 20, 18·5 and 15 million volumes, respectively; the total sales of the eleven leading imprints were 132·25 million, valued at about £23 million. The conclusion drawn was that although, in monetary terms, the turnover was still less than one-third of that of the hardbacks, the "upstarts" were by then profitable and powerful, and "increasingly able to call the tune."

The tendency in recent years has been for publishers of students' text-books to issue a paperback edition at the same time as the hardback, and the saving to the purchaser is derived simply from the reduced cost of binding. Sometimes the hardback edition is quite small, intended mainly to ensure that the work is reviewed. But, in any case, the "quality" paperback has attained the dignity of a real book. It is significant of the latest trend that in 1971 the Oxford University Press decided to reverse its previous practice with regard to orders; it announced that in future, if the bookseller did not specify which edition he wanted, he would be supplied with the paperback one, on the assumption that this was what the customer required.[98]

CHAPTER XX

Copyright and Competition

WHETHER or not the Copyright Act of Queen Anne was an effective bar to piracy, it did at least establish its illegal nature. For fourteen years after the publication of a work, and for still another fourteen if the author were still alive, it was risky for any unauthorised person to issue a rival edition of it in this country. In 1814[1] the period was extended: copyright was to be observed for twenty-eight years absolutely and to continue further for the life of the author. A further modification in 1842[2] fixed the term at the life of the author and seven years, or forty-two years, whichever was the longer. But the clause of this Act which was most appreciated by publishers was the one which forbade the importation of foreign reprints of British books into England or her colonies.

Foreign Competition in English Works

The earlier Acts had, in fact, conferred only a partial monopoly upon the original publisher. Foreign publishers were quite within their rights in reprinting English copyright works straight away and sending their copies to compete with ours. And this, it seems, was found most profitable.

Complaints of foreign competition were made repeatedly. A bookseller reported to the House of Commons in 1802 that the high price of books printed in England had induced publishers abroad to print copies of their own instead of continuing to import ours. He himself had been approached by an agent from Paris who wanted to be supplied with a copy of each forthcoming edition of Thomson's *Seasons* with a view to reprinting them abroad; as a bribe it was suggested that copies would be delivered to the original publisher cheaper than he himself could produce them. Another bookseller showed an actual copy of Addison's *Cato*, printed in

Berlin, which could be sold at 4d., although the same work printed in England could not have been sold at less than 1s. At that very time there were said to be about two hundred English works in process of being reprinted in Paris, to be sold at half the price of the originals. That was possible because, as Luke Hansard pointed out, the wages of journeymen printers on the Continent were considerably lower than here. America, in spite of transportation difficulties, was staking a claim in the works of English authors. One Boston printer had already arranged to print new English books in France for the American trade. He thought that by getting copies of a work as soon as it came out and setting three or more presses to work on it in a printing-house at Havre, a convenient port for transmission to America, he might easily be first in the United States market.[3]

America was at the beginning of the century the principal foreign market for English books. Our booksellers were finding this a useful means of disposal of the remainders which they refused to reduce in price at home.[4] But even before the war of 1812 completely suspended the trade it had greatly diminished. All the standard English works were being printed in America, and printed well, at a much lower cost than they could be imported.[5] English publishers, naturally aiming at the highest profit to themselves, and assured of their monopoly at home, were not necessarily intent on selling as cheaply as possible. Their American colleagues, on the other hand, having only their low prices to assure them of a market, developed a keen competition among themselves. The great aim was to be the first in the field. It was to that end, it seems, that Kirk, the American publisher, negotiated with John Murray II in 1817 for the establishment of what is now known as the advance sheets system. Admitting that the American non-recognition of foreign copyrights was exasperating to English publishers he suggested as a remedy an arrangement "founded on principles of reciprocity and confidence": the division, in short, of the profits arising from the first republication of new works in America with the publisher in England who first sent out the copy. His proposal was that Murray should supply the sheets of any works of general interest as soon as they were printed, and that the service should be repaid by one-third of the net profits.[6]

Four years later Murray received an application from a French publisher, M. Galignani, for the exclusive rights of printing Byron's works in France. Murray's rather brusque answer was that for the copyright of these works which were being printed abroad so freely he himself had given the author more than £10,000. All the same, he was willing to give the coveted rights for a payment of £250. He mentioned further that he had just received a new tragedy by Lord Byron, for which he had paid £1,050, and also three new cantos of *Don Juan*, which had cost him £2,100. If the French publisher cared to make an offer for the exclusive French rights of these it would be considered. Galignani offered £100 for the assignment of these new works, but pointed out that a pirated edition of Byron's works had already been issued by another publisher, and was being sold for 10 francs. He ignored the matter of payment for the earlier publication.[7]

For these French editions of English works our compositors were in great demand. In 1826, when employment was at a low ebb in London printing-houses, an unemployed compositor was advised, "Take yourself over to Paris while you have got the mopuses to get there. I know, for a certainty, that plenty of work is to be had there. I saw a letter from a chap yesterday, who is doing well, and says there's room for more hands. The work is English—mainly pirated editions of Scott, Byron, and others; and as English hands can get them out faster than the Frenchmen, of course they have the preference."[8] The printer did as he was recommended, and within a few days found himself in Paris setting up Scott's *Woodstock*, which had not yet been published in England, from what were obviously corrected proofs. The novel was published in France at half a crown a volume within a few days of its publication in London at half a guinea a volume. The next work to be undertaken was Cooper's *Last of the Mohicans*, to be followed by a pocket edition of Byron's works and other popular books, reprinted as soon as they appeared in England. "The want of an international law of copyright was the occasion of our prosperity," the compositor explained; "and the question of printer's piracy, though it was not very profoundly discussed amongst us, was, whenever alluded to, invariably settled on the principle that 'whatever is, is right.' The whole of my companions agreed on this point, though they were perpetually disputing upon every other."[9]

English publishers were not the only ones to be treated in this way. In Germany each state had its own law of copyright, and a work was secured against piracy only in the state in which it was printed. But the German language was common to the whole Confederation, and an author popular in one state was likely to be popular in all. The best books were reprinted straight away in neighbouring states, and as the pirate paid nothing for copyright he could easily undersell the original publisher. The copyrights of unsaleable books were, of course, scrupulously observed.[10]

Where French so-called piracy was concerned English authors had no need to feel resentful, for they had the means of preventing it. The French copyright law of July 19, 1793, unlike our own, was extended to writers of any nationality who chose to publish a book in France, so the author, if he wished, could arrange for simultaneous publication in both countries. Apart from a convention with Prussia in 1836 it was not until 1838 that the British Government recognised the rights of foreign authors; the International Copyright Act then allowed for Orders in Council giving the authors, in the case of works to be specifically mentioned, the sole liberty of printing them within the British Dominions for a term not to exceed that to which British writers were entitled. But it was still true that books could be printed in a foreign land and sold in England at a cheaper rate than they could be printed here.[11]

Copyright Conventions

International copyright began with a series of conventions with individual countries. A treaty of 1851 between the United Kingdom and France extended the copyright protection already obtained for a publication in one country to the other. It was confirmed by an Act of 1852,[12] which allowed for similar agreements with other powers. Conventions followed in quick succession, to be superseded by the Berne Conventions of 1886 and 1908, the Brussels Convention of 1948 and, in 1952, the Universal Copyright Convention, which was ratified by the United States.

Not the least appreciated clause of the early conventions was the one reducing the tax on volumes imported from the participating countries. For imports from all other countries the tax was 52s. 6d. a hundredweight, adding in many cases 1s. or more to the price of the individual book. The Society of Arts made a fervent appeal for the duty to be remitted altogether. It was important, the memorial ran, that we should be able to receive accounts of industrial and scientific investigations abroad. The language difficulty alone was great enough; there was no need to make matters worse by taxing books on import.[13] Although there was no immediate response to this the successive conventions were at least a stage nearer the abolition of the tax.

The one important country before the twentieth century which steadily remained aloof from copyright agreements was the United States. In the middle of the nineteenth century not only were we imposing the maximum tax on American books but America was retaliating with a 10 per cent duty on our publications, or 20 per cent if the works in question were printed in America at the time.[14] The practice, moreover, of reprinting English works immediately after their publication in England continued unabated. The Boston Society for the Diffusion of Knowledge began in 1831 its cheap series issued as the American Library of Useful Knowledge, but the first great wave of cheap books in America came in the 1840's in the form of "extras" to the literary newspapers.[15] Taking into consideration the saving both on payments to the author and on transportation, the prices of the United States reprints throughout the North American continent were far lower than those of the imports from the United Kingdom. Canadian booksellers could not be expected to order books from England if much cheaper copies were available close at hand. On that account the Foreign Reprints Act of 1847[16] did little more than legalise a trade which was already being carried on. Its purpose was to enable the colonies to take advantage of English copyright books made in foreign states, but to exact a customs duty on them for the benefit of the authors concerned—a benefit which, incidentally, was very slight.[17]

There was a fairly general opinion that if England and America could be united in one system of copyright the extension of the market would allow books to be published at a lower price. McCulloch was doubtful whether that would happen. Although he agreed that larger editions allowed for economy in production he argued that publishers would still fix the prices which seemed to offer the greatest profit. That might lead to a reduction of the number of copies printed so that their rarity might make them saleable at higher prices.[18] In a system of free competition that would not happen, as events of the next few years were to prove. For a time the prices of English books were low enough to secure a large part of the American trade. A period of very cheap literature in England during the 1860's coincided with one of increased production costs in the United States, a result of the cotton famine and the Civil War. In 1867 a comment was passed in the *Round Table* that "A cheapness of book-making which seems to us almost incredible is now established in England"; an example was given of an English edition of the *Waverley Novels* which was on sale in New York at 25 cents a volume, which America could not at that time have produced and sold for less than 75. That was only a passing phase. Soon after 1870 there began a second flood of cheap American reprints, which again overflowed on to the Canadian market.

Forceful objections were made in Canada to this latest influx: if an American publisher could issue English works without restriction why could not a Canadian enjoy the same privilege? The Foreign Reprints Act of 1847 no longer met the case. It was an Act authorising Canadian reprints which was wanted. It came in 1875: the Canadian Copyright Act allowed British authors to secure copyright in Canada, and advantage was taken of it straight away. From a return made in November 1876 it appeared that thirty-one works of British authors had already been published under the Act, and they were selling at lower prices than either the English editions or the American reprints.[19]

In Herbert Spencer's opinion the Canadian Act was mischievous in principle. One of its rulings was that in order to obtain copyright in Canada the work must be set up afresh in that country. (The old Star Chamber decree, it seems, had revived in a new form!) Spencer was one of those who argued in favour of extending the area of copyright in such a way that a work could be set up once and for all in one country and allowed to circulate in two.[20] As between England and America that would have been an impossible arrangement, according to G. H. Putnam, the American publisher. At every hint of a copyright convention American printers had protested, afraid of losing part of the work of type-setting. It had been suggested that stereotype plates could be sent to America to overcome the need of resetting the volume there, but that implied using English type and composition in place of American. Those printers who were constantly pressing for the protection of the American printing industry would not consider the idea.[21]

A number of American authors and publishers, it appears, would have welcomed an international copyright convention. As things were there was a tendency to publish English works in preference to American, for which the authors would have wanted payment. This was felt to be a check on the growth of American literature. Nor was the publication of English works quite as profitable as once it had been. Competition was now felt to be so disastrous that publishers had made an agreement among themselves to recognise the priority of right to the republication of a British work as existing in the American publisher who first procured the copy. The result was almost equal to that of an international convention. As American publishers were by this voluntary agreement secure from competition at home it was worth their while to rival each other abroad in their offers for early sheets of important works. The English author of some renown at last found himself able to bargain for the disposal of his American rights. All the same, his returns were not necessarily equivalent to what could have been expected under a convention, and there was still no protection at all for a successful book by a new author.[22]

The criticism that copyright tended to increase the price of books by more than the amount of royalty payable to the author certainly seems to have been justified. It was reported to the United States Senate in 1875 that, of seventy-five English books reprinted in America, the average price in dollars of the English copies was \$5.60, whereas the American reprints were only \$2.40. Incidentally, when it came to price-cutting of reprints of foreign works the English were just as successful. Of fifty-seven American books which had been reprinted in England the total price of the American originals was \$121.05, but that of the English reprints was only \$36.06.[23] The price of a copyright work tended to be greater when, as in England, the importation of other copyright copies from abroad was prohibited. As T. H. Farrer remarked in his evidence, under such a system of monopoly there was no motive whatever for selling at such a price as would unite cheapness to the public with profit to the author; it was not true that it was the interest of the seller to follow the market, for, however great the demand, it might not be to the interest of the publisher to sell a large number of copies. To illustrate his argument Farrer quoted the prices of various editions of *Daniel Deronda*: "The price in England of the first edition was 42s., of a subsequent edition 21s.; the price in the United States, published by Appleton in two volumes, was 11s. 6d., one volume in paper 5s. 9d.; the price in Canada of the English edition, as given to me, is 52s. 6d.; the price of the edition published in Canada, and published, be it remembered, as a copyright edition with the consent of the author, under the recent Act, is 6s. 3d.; the price of the same book, published by Baron Tauchnitz in four volumes in paper, and published with extremely nice print and paper, which also must be copyright, since we have a copyright treaty with Germany, is 6s. 8d. for the four volumes."[24] "I know no reason," he argued, "why the English who are rich enough to travel abroad should be able to buy the Tauchnitz editions while those who are obliged to stay at home cannot do so."[25]

Quite apart from these copyright works, which were not allowed to compete in the English market, German competition was becoming a disturbing factor to the English publisher. It was first felt in the production of children's picture-books. According to a

London publisher, as soon as the German printers saw Kate Greenaway's *Under the Window*, printed from engraved blocks, they set to work on the same lines, and actually employed English artists to make designs for similar works. These they offered to English and American booksellers so cheaply that not even the American tariff could keep them out. The quality of workmanship was quite equal to our own. Competition in letterpress printing was so far on a much smaller scale, but, as this publisher remarked, "a publisher is not a philanthropist"; offered cheap workmanship in Germany and Holland, and faced with trade disputes at home, he would obviously take advantage of foreign efficiency. Another London publisher thought that the disadvantage of having the work done so far away would outweigh this, but yet another who was asked for his opinion thought that if trade unions continued to raise costs the foreign printing would increase.[26]

The printers' unions were well aware of this possibility. Their representative before the Law of Copyright Committee of 1910 accordingly asked for an "employment" clause to be inserted in the Copyright Act similar to the one in the American Act, which refused copyright to any work not printed from type set up in the United States. It was generally felt by the Committee that it was a contingency not likely to arise to any great extent except in times of strikes, and a question asked by Mr. Macmillan implied that publishers had no desire to cut off what might then be a great convenience to them.[27] Publishers were indeed to find it a great convenience, and not only during strikes. The rapid expansion of colour printing, in particular, was to encourage international co-operation in the more ambitious types of publishing. For an art book, especially, considerable economy was to result from printing all the coloured plates in one country, leaving the text to be added separately in the co-operating countries in their own language.[28]

The general provisions of the Copyright Act of 1911,[29] later modified by legislation of 1956, are fairly common knowledge. From July 1, 1912, the duration of copyright (with certain exceptions) was to be for the life of the author and fifty years after, provided that when twenty-five years had elapsed after the author's death it should be legal for any person to reproduce the work on giving written notice of his intention and on paying to the owner of the copyright royalties for every copy sold at the rate of 10 per cent on the publication price. So ended for a time the arguments of two centuries between those who, like Alexander Macmillan, asked for perpetual copyright on the plea that "what is everybody's business is nobody's business,"[30] and those who argued that as much competition as possible should be encouraged for the sake of lower prices. But in the meantime the question of prices had caused long and bitter warfare on grounds still to be discussed.

Photographic Reproduction

The use of photographic processes in producing new editions of books has already been mentioned. Publishers are less happy about the enormous increase in photocopying, without recompense to themselves, by industrialists, students and others. Provisions for "fair use" seem to be loosely interpreted when, for instance, the United States Court of Claims can cite nearly a million pages of articles from medical journals which were photocopied in one year by the National Institute of Health.[31] In the United Kingdom, too, the spate of photocopies of periodical articles is a threat to the continued publication of certain specialist journals; book-publishing is also affected to an irritating degree. Mr. Ronald Barker, secretary of the Publishers' Association, told the International Publishers' Conference in 1970 that in one year some 55,000 photocopies of extracts from books had been made by about 400 libraries in the United Kingdom. Although he disclosed that a paper-coating had been invented which could defeat the practice, the Conference resolved that its members would seek greater control of the situation both in their own countries and internationally.

It was announced in August 1973 that a departmental committee of the Department of Trade and Industry was to be set up to enquire into the working of the copyright law, partly in relation to the changes needed to enable the United Kingdom to ratify the

1971 Paris text of the Berne Copyright Convention, and partly to consider various urgent problems. Although it is expected that these will include the photocopying question, it will be difficult to find a remedy for the type of blatant misuse of photographic reproduction reported in 1969 by British publishers visiting Korea and Taiwan.[32] They found bookshops crammed from floor to ceiling with pirated copies of works typical of the stock of an academic bookshop, priced at about 40 per cent of their price in the United Kingdom. Likely customers were frequently offered further reductions, particularly of titles copied also by other offenders.

The Home Market

In the home market, too, the effect of expanding trade had been to introduce competition as an almost new factor in the publishing business. The older tendency had been to form partnerships for the issue of any work likely to be expensive. John Dunton, we remember, had found a new partner for almost every venture. The Stationers' Register throughout the eighteenth century had something of the appearance of a stock register, with its notes of quarter-shares owned by one publisher, eighths owned by another and hundredths by yet another. A convenience of the system was that any publisher could relinquish his part of the control without upsetting in any way the agreement with the author. With regard to Scott's works, for instance, Archibald Constable told William Davies in 1813, "It would be a matter of some convenience to me at present to sell three 16ths of these Works—but I will not part with them unless I get my price & your House be the purchasers—our friends Messrs. Longman and Co. have ¾ths of the Minstrelsey. ¼ of the Lady of the Lake ¼ of Marmion & one half of The Lay—the only Works in which Ballantyne & Co. have an Interest are The Lady of the Lake ½ & The Lay ¼ or ⅛."[33] The names of the shareholders were given on the title-page with strict attention to precedence. "With regard to the Order of the Names in the Imprint," reasoned Messrs. Cadell and Davies on sharing the publication of Dr. Beattie's works in 1806, "as Mr. Longman happened to commence business a Year or two before us, the Attention here paid to Etiquette, places not only his Name, but Mr. Hurst's, Mr. Rees's, and Mr. Orme's also before ours—1st Longman &c., 2d Cadell & Davies, 3d Murray, 4th Mawman."[34] Incidentally, the names of firms in themselves illustrated the search for safety in numbers; the firm of Longman was in 1807 officially described as Longman, Hurst, Rees, Orme, Brown and Green. Even so eminent a publisher as John Murray II had no desire to secure absolute independence: "I should be very glad," he wrote to Sir Walter Scott in 1818, "if, when you and your friends are making arrangements with Constable, you thought of me; for I fancy that neither of us have any objection to publish good books in conjunction. Perhaps a word from you might yet induce Ballantyne to ask for my junction in the 'New Tales of my Landlord.' "[35] The time was coming when publishers would not be so anxious to pass on part of their risks. From the 'sixties onwards the risks borne by publishing and other companies were greatly reduced by the provisions for limited liability. Although Latham's edition of Johnson's *Dictionary* was published in 1866 by a partnership it was the very rarity of such a form of publication by that time which called attention to it.

After the Second World War, in particular, the book trade was to be involved in the general search for economy through large scale production and distribution, achieved by partial or complete amalgamation with other firms. One of the most recent mergers took place in 1970 between the Longman group and Penguins, followed by an announcement that Longman General, Longman Young Books and Allen Lane the Penguin Press would remain distinct imprints, but administratively they would form a division of the Penguin Publishing Company. This organisation, together with Collins, Hutchinsons, Routledge and one or two other publishing groups, by then accounted between them for some 30 per cent of Britain's total sales.

Other publishing-houses have preferred to remain independent but, in some cases, to enlarge their business by opening branches abroad. The Oxford University Press began as early as 1896 with the establishment of an autonomous American branch in New

York, followed within the next twenty years by branches in Canada, Australia, India and South Africa and, after the Second World War, in Pakistan, Africa and the Far East. Some of these are mainly distributing centres for the books published in Oxford and London, but acting as publishers of educational books to meet local requirements.[36]

Sales Promotion

With the growth of competition came more intensive advertising. By 1830, according to Charles Babbage, several of the great publishers found it convenient to be the proprietors of reviews, magazines or even newspapers; and, as he pointed out, it was scarcely to be expected that their editors should criticise very harshly the works in which their own employers were financially interested. A sufficient number of publications were reviewed with care to win the confidence of the public, and under shelter of this, Babbage alleged, a host of ephemeral productions were brought into undue popularity.[37] It was not always that the author himself was in favour of advertisement. Professor Millar on one occasion had objected even to including a preface in one of his works, on the ground that it would seem like "puffing." "To make a preface to a book," he expostulated to John Murray, "appears in the same light as to make a number of bows and scrapes as you enter a room. It always puts me in mind of what Hamlet says to the player who acts the part of the murderer—'Leave off thy damnable faces, and *begin.*' "[38] If a serious preface was to cause him embarrassment what would he have said to the extravagances of press advertising? Coleridge, at least, was well aware of the possibilities of the Press; he professed that quite two-thirds of his reputation as a writer was due to anonymous critics in reviews and magazines.[39]

From about the year 1800 there was a steady rise in the output of new periodicals all over the country. One publishing-house was in 1800 already advertising in *The Times*, *The Herald*, *The Morning Chronicle*, *The True Briton*, *The Porcupine*, *The Sun*, *The Star* and the *St. James's*.[40] Those of them which were issued by the book-publishers were obvious channels for advertising forthcoming works from the same firms, and the attractions of a healthy advertisement revenue were great enough to find space for rival announcements. That is not to say that other publishers watched the issue of such periodicals with no qualms whatever. As Thomas Cadell wrote to William Blackwood in 1820, "I am fully sensible that you endeavour as much as possible to prevent the insertion of objectionable matter in the Magazine [Blackwood's] so as to steer clear of offending your own connections, but as you are unacquainted with many with whom I have literary transactions I must own, my dear Sir, I am in constant dread of reading some mention of them of a nature they may consider such as might prove highly detrimental to my interests, and truly unpleasant to my feelings."[41] The daily newspaper, with its wider circulation, was to provide far greater opportunities for publicity. While publishing was still something of a co-operative concern these Press notices were probably adequate. Even a general invitation to "Buy more books" would have reacted favourably on all. Monthly lists and other individual house organs were to be an outcome of the new competition.

Now that the publishing-houses were no longer their own sole distributors there was a risk, it seems, that the most skilful advertising might be brought to nought to suit the ends of the wholesale dealers. The book calculated to bring in the biggest profit was liable to be pushed in preference to any other. If, it was alleged, a country bookseller sent in an order for a dozen copies of a particular work the answer given him, in many cases, would be, "This is a very inferior book; we have, therefore, sent a similar work by a more popular author, which we have charged at 3d. per copy *less* than you must have paid for the other." The country bookseller was said to be duly impressed by this expert advice, and to act accordingly.[42] But it was a system which could not long be expected to work. The new reading public had definite demands. As a witness before the House of Commons went out of his way to explain, "There are classes which you cannot reach, unless you go to them with something which is the nearest thing to what they want."[43]

That being so, the publisher's business was to persuade those classes as to what they did want. One means of doing this was to link up a number of books in such a way that the reader who was impressed with one volume would straightway want the rest. We have noticed already how John Newbery tempted the appetite of his child readers by referring to one book incidentally in the text of another. The modern link was an external one: the issue of a collection of distinct works under a general series title. By 1850 the new railway bookstalls were covered with the shilling volumes of the Railway Library, the Parlour Library, the Popular Library and the Shilling Series. At that time, indeed, the only chance of making cheap books pay was said to be to issue them in series form: to some extent they advertised one another, and the publisher profited from the purchaser's dislike of having an incomplete set of books.[44]

The sale of books in sets opens the way to yet another form of advertising, the free gift system. It is not often that one comes across such a tempting offer as the one made by Harrison, who promised to give a square pianoforte to every purchaser of his entire *Musical Magazine*;[45] but it is not unknown, although still somewhat rare, for a set of the classics or of an encyclopædia to be offered complete with a case to put them in.

Advertising at its most vigorous preceded the publication in 1950 of Thor Heyerdahl's *The Kon-Tiki Expedition.* Sir Stanley Unwin described the arrangements in his autobiography; they included a special article in *The Times*, serial rights sold to various newspapers, personal letters to leading critics, full briefing of booksellers with facts about the expedition (together with models of the Kon-Tiki raft for window display), and a television programme featuring the author in person and a model of the raft.[46] In contrast to all this effort, on finding that there was no demand for his three-volume edition of *Praeterita* he simply had new title-pages printed calling the work *The Autobiography of Ruskin*; it sold out immediately.[47]

Twentieth century sales promotion has largely taken the form of book exhibitions, of which the most popular between the wars were those sponsored by the *Sunday Times.* They have been followed by others, general and specialised. One of the most ambitious during recent years was the open-air "Book Bang" held in Bedford Square, London, in June 1971, sponsored by the National Book League. In spite of inclement weather over 40,000 people attended, attracted partly by the personal appearance of many famous authors. Sales at the time brought in some £12,000, but it is difficult to estimate the number of works noted down at an exhibition and bought later on at individual bookshops. One is equally unaware of the long-term effects of the Children's Book Show held annually since the fifties by the Children's Book Group of the Publishers' Association. A special Book Train now brings in hundreds of excited children to the show from other towns, and leading children's authors and illustrators give their time. It is good fun, but it is impossible to say whether it inspires a lasting enthusiasm for books in children who do not already possess it.

National book sales, as distinct from exhibitions, have a more general appeal. They began after a sub-committee of the 1948 Book Trade Committee of the Booksellers' Association and the Publishers' Association suggested that controlled sale of both publishers' and booksellers' overstocks by means of a National Sales Week might contribute substantially to solving the problem of overstocking. The sales have since become popular annual events. They are held by licence of the Publishers' Association, which allows any individual publisher to exclude any of his titles from the sale; otherwise the bookseller may sell off any of his stock (during the official sale period only) at less than the published price. In order to preserve good public relations booksellers may not offer remainders as sales items, and no book in the sale may be remaindered within six months.

Book *tokens* have from 1932 onwards provided a more constant means of sales promotion. The system was devised by the Associated Booksellers as an alternative to the thousands of postal orders given as Christmas presents. While they simplify present-giving, they provide the trade with a means of reaching the more reluctant book-buyer. The procedure is now organised by Book Tokens, Ltd., and tokens can be sold and exchanged only by booksellers recognised by them for the purpose. According to an interim report (1970) of a professional market research survey carried out for Book Tokens Ltd. in London and two other cities, booksellers are not so aware as they should be of the advantage of the system to themselves. They regard the scale of tokens as a service to customers rather than a source of profit; hence the promotion of tokens by retailers is thought to be minimal. (This may be because, unlike the gift-vouchers of individual stores, a book-token is seldom spent in the shop which issued it.) Nevertheless, in spite of competition from record tokens and from vouchers offering a wider choice, the sale of book-tokens shows no decline. Over 2 million book token cards were sold to booksellers by Book Tokens, Ltd. in the year ended April 30, 1973, an increase of 23 per cent over the previous year, and over £2 million worth of the stamps were sold, an increase of 11 per cent.[48]

By one means or another sales promotion has thus become a major activity in the book trade. The Oxford University Press is one of the firms best able to work out its own arrangments for this on a large scale. The Promotion Department of its London business had by 1970 a staff of sixty-five, responsible between them for sales in the United Kingdom, Eire, the West Indies, Latin America, Europe, the Middle East, and countries in Africa where there was no branch. There were agencies in Germany, the West Indies and Latin America; three travellers covered the rest of Europe and the Middle East, and three English language specialists called on institutions teaching English as a special language. Other travellers visited booksellers throughout the United Kingdom.[49] Not many publishers could operate on this scale, but, as we have seen, there was still plenty of scope for those with ingenuity.

Competitive Prices versus *Re-Sale Price Maintenance*

A more obvious way to tempt the public is to lower prices. This has been tried since the end of the eighteenth century only to a limited extent. Cheaper production arising from mechanical methods has been partly offset so far as initial publication is concerned by the monopolistic tendencies of the Copyright Acts. Although the cost of a very large edition works out at much lower for the

TYPE FOUNDRY

From Dodd (G.), *Days at the Factories*, 1843

individual volume than that of a smaller edition the gain to the publisher tends, as we have mentioned, to be greater if the edition is limited and the price kept proportionately high. In the case of works whose copyright has expired this does not apply; the thought of a rival edition induces the publisher to make his own as attractive as possible, and, other things being equal, a great attraction is a low price. Reprints of the classics, for instance, vie with one another for cheapness. In spite of that, price-cutting on the part of the individual bookseller has always been eyed with concern. However willing the publisher may be to allow his own efficiency of production to be reflected in his prices he has been strangely loath to allow the retailer any latitude at all in price-fixing. It is not a new problem. As early as 1772 a bookseller in New England, Henry Knox, received a letter from Thomas Longman saying that complaints had been made that Knox was underselling his neighbours. "A trade carried on upon such terms," Longman protested, "must be destructive to us both, but I hope that you will satisfy me in your next that this is not the case."[50]

Longman may have managed to subdue the trading instincts of Henry Knox, but neither he nor anybody else could alter the determination of James Lackington to sell at the lowest prices he could afford. Established in London as a second-hand bookseller, he not only sold second-hand books cheaply but he also offered remainders at half price in defiance of trade usage. What *was* a remainder he seems to have decided for himself in a quite arbitrary way. His policy, he tells us, was to sell everything cheaply, both to attract new customers and to retain the ones he had already found. He was not successful straight away. Many of those who came to his shop assumed that the volumes he offered were imperfect; customers writing from the country, too, inquired anxiously whether such-and-such items from his catalogue were *really* the best editions, were *really* in calf, and were *really* elegantly bound. "Oh, my friend!" he sighs, "I *really* was afraid for some years that I should be *really* mad with vexation."[51] However, once his policy was known he could hardly keep pace with the demand. By 1803 he could claim to selling more than a hundred thousand volumes a year. His difficulty was to obtain the stock to sell. The principal publishers tried to boycott him. Those private people, again, who had libraries to dispose of argued that if Lackington sold so cheaply he himself would not pay much. They chose to offer them to booksellers who sold at high prices, and presumably could afford to give more for them.[52] In fact, Lackington found that quite the opposite was true. By selling cheaply he himself could pay more. If he were to sell at high prices, he argued, he would be ten times longer in selling his books; his extra expenses on warehousing and on fire-insurance, together with the loss of interest on money lying in dead stock, would leave him less to pay out for new purchases.[53]

It was difficult for the publishers and the more conservative booksellers to know what to do to combat such practices. Lackington, it seems, was not the only offender. A resolution had been passed by over six hundred members of the trade that no new work should be retailed at more than 10 per cent under the publisher's price, but a number of booksellers, for the sake of quick returns, were accepting less than half of the 25 per cent profit to which they were entitled. Their plea, following Lackington's precedent, was that the copies were remainders, and in face of that argument the publishers were powerless. It had never been decided what in fact was a remainder. If the ban on price-cutting was to have any effect at all this point had to be cleared up. In 1829, accordingly, the leading booksellers and publishers met at the Chapter Coffee House to agree upon a definition. They decided that the term "new work" was to comprehend books published or reprinted within the preceding two years or protected by copyright.[54]

Now that the one element of uncertainty had been removed publishers and booksellers were quick to combine and to draw up regulations inflicting penalties upon such booksellers as did not subscribe to their policy. If one may credit the complaint of William Pickering, himself a noted bookseller, private jealousies were allowed too much sway; several retailers lost their trading privileges without having infringed the regulations in any respect. Pickering himself disapproved of the regulations as being against the public interest, but having, he says, followed a bad example and become a party to them he felt bound to conform to the dictates of the trade. It had never been said of him that he sold books below the regular price or that he had even sold to others who did so; "but on the bare *suspicion* that FOURTH parties have procured books which originally came from his shop, at a cheaper rate than was deemed proper, he is denied those privileges of the Trade to which he has by servitude a just and legal right."[55] Worse than that, the trade committee circulated a placard bearing his name and that of a few others, calculated to ruin their reputations. On applying to various publishers for copies of their works Pickering was met with curt refusals. John Murray reported, "Cannot supply Mr. Pickering, if he pays twice the value of the books I would not; I will not give a reason—I would not sell any body a book that sold Mr. Pickering one." Longmans, Rivingtons, J. M. Richardson and one or two others replied quite courteously that the orders of the committee would not allow them to supply him, but one firm ended a lengthy refusal with the remark, "We must make a distinction between those who act *nobly* and those who do not."[56]

The few isolated booksellers who agreed with Pickering were helpless against such a powerful combination. Babbage put forward a scheme for breaking it up which seems to have attracted little attention. He suggested a counter-association of authors who should employ a printer to act as retail agent for their books. Each author would retain the liberty of putting any price he thought fit on his productions, so that the public would still have the advantage of price-reduction produced by competition between authors on the same subject.[57] Possibly the thought of the strain of fixing a price for their works and bearing the risk of their publication in addition to that of writing them was enough to deter the authors from putting the scheme into practice. Publishers have their uses after all!

For a time there was a lull. Then, in 1848, a new Booksellers' Association was formed and the struggles began all over again. Trouble arose this time over a bookseller named Bickers, accused of passing on part of his discount to his customers. Gladstone made a strong protest at the boycott which followed, but John Murray III tried to justify the action by pointing out the peculiar nature of the book trade. The big discount allowed to the booksellers, he said, was in consideration of the long credit given to the public. It was difficult to do away with that credit, for as books were a luxury they were the first expense to be curtailed in times of depression; it was a less noticeable form of economy than dispensing with servants or a carriage.[58] He did not explain why booksellers should be thought incapable of running their own businesses without help, and why publishers should "follow the retail dealer into his own shop," as *The Times* had it, "and insist on dictating the disposal of the profits."[59] Gladstone at least was not convinced by Murray's argument, and in the course of the debate in the House of Commons on the paper duty he spoke of this "most important struggle in progress in the book trade," in which attempts "of a most imprudent and most unwarrantable character" were being made to keep up the price of books.[60] The whole system of bookselling in this country, except in so far as the new cheap editions mitigated the evils, he declared to be a disgrace to our civilisation. "The truth is," he said, "that monopoly and combination have gone near, if not to the extinction of the trade itself, to reduce the sale of books to a minimum."

It was by no means strange that Gladstone took the matter so seriously. He had already shown himself an ardent enthusiast for free trade, and was bent on continuing the policy which under Peel had led to successive tariff reductions and to the repeal of the Corn Laws in 1846. By 1850 the principle of free trade was well established; there remained only a few duties on foodstuffs and manufactures, and these Gladstone was to sweep away in 1853 and 1860. Little wonder, then, that in 1852 he had scant sympathy for so monopolistic an association as this of the booksellers. J. R. McCulloch shared his feelings. Admitting that retailers had difficulties of their own, "I cannot, however, imagine," he wrote to John Chapman, "that, after the assize of bread has been put down, and a system of free competition introduced into the sale of almost all articles, a wretched monopoly should be permitted to narrow and debase the trade in books."[61]

Chapman, a bookseller and publisher, was himself at war with the Association, whose members had closed their accounts with him as an answer to his deliberate underselling. On May 4, 1852, he held a meeting of authors to discuss the position, with Charles Dickens in the chair. Naturally enough, a large part of the discussion turned on the question of free trade. A few of those present doubted whether competition and free trade really applied to books at all. A book, they argued, could not compete with itself. Nor could books on the same subject be said to compete with each other, for the sale was determined not by the price but by the intrinsic worth. This argument was soon refuted. It was pointed out that if the retailer were free to fix his own prices the element of competition between different copies of the same work would straightway be present. The resolution carried by the meeting was that free trade principles applied to books as to all else; that the principles of the Booksellers' Association were opposed to free trade and were tyrannical and vexatious in their operations.[62]

Another attempt to ascertain the views of authors was made by John W. Parker and Son. The firm sent the following inquiry to each of a hundred writers: "If a retail bookseller, of ascertained credit and respectability, applies to your publisher for copies of any book in which you are directly or indirectly interested, which he is ready to purchase on the terms at which the publisher has offered them to the trade at large, but with the avowed intention of retailing his purchases at a smaller profit than that provided for between the wholesale rate and the retail price fixed for single copies, do you consider the intention to sell at a low rate of profit a good and sufficient reason why the publisher should refuse to supply him with books which he is ready to purchase and to keep in stock at his own risk?" The authors who were asked for their opinion included Dickens, J. S. Mill, Darwin, Herbert Spencer, Tennyson, Carlyle, Charles Kingsley and F. W. Newman. Almost without exception they were against any interference with retail policy. Mill, indeed, replied, "I think that there is no case in which a combination to keep up prices is more injurious than in the sale of books." Professor de Morgan held that the system of artificial prices had received its death-blow in the repeal of the Corn Laws; the only question for publishers now was whether they would accept the new system for their own benefit or see the growth of a new race of publishers and retailers who were prepared to serve the general public.[63]

The publishing fraternity seemed to resent the charge of being protectionists but could produce no evidence to the contrary. John Murray, writing to *The Times* on April 1st, did admit that an analogy could be established between free trade and the bookselling question, but asked why competition should be confined to the retail booksellers: the author and the publisher fixed their own price, and were protectionists in the fullest sense of the word. He did not, as one might expect, go on to suggest the extension of competition into the realms of publishing, but broke away into an attack on the undersellers, who were willing to sell at 15 or even 10 per cent profit. "They are solitary upstarts," he complained, "who by this means endeavour to filch away the customers from old-established houses, and thus to carve out for themselves a short road to opulence."

The concluding article in *The Times* cleverly summed up the situation: "It is exceedingly amusing, and should be not a little instructive, to see how piously the name and theory of actual 'Protection' are eschewed by the advocates of the Association. As if conscious that such doctrines, purely avowed, would be the ruin of their cause, they earnestly proclaim themselves Freetraders, but argue that theirs constitutes an exceptional case to the overruling principles of free trade. They declare one and all, with great statistical display, that upon less than the present profits the booksellers 'can't live.' If this is indeed the case, there can be no necessity for an Association to prevent them from doing so. If a bookseller *must* charge 25 per cent profit, he will do so under the operation of necessity much more surely, and far more naturally, than under the dictation of the Executive Council. It is certainly possible, as Mr. W. Longman predicts, that books under such freedom of trade might be sold 'at one price in one street and at another in another,' according as one dealer found it practicable to 'live' upon less than another; but this, we take it, is a very general aspect of wholesale trade. To put the whole case in a very few words, the natural course is for publishers to supply all comers with all they ask for at the trade or wholesale price, and leave the price to the public to be regulated, as in all other trades, by the arrangements of the retailers. Whether this might create any material changes of business we cannot take upon ourselves to say; but it is, at any rate, not likely to cause so much embarrassment as an artificial protective system."

Argumentation seemed likely to go on for ever. Publishers, booksellers, authors and the general public all joined in the fray, sending their comments, invited and uninvited, to the daily press. Apart from *The Times*, the *Economist* and one or two other papers, the general attitude of the editorials was in favour of re-sale price maintenance. Authors, on the other hand, and the public generally, wanted cheapness. Meanwhile the various booksellers who wanted to cut prices found their own way of doing so. If a customer showed signs of going away without making a purchase, on the plea that the book he wanted was too dear, the shopkeeper would simply cut open a few of its leaves or allow a drop of ink to fall on it; the volume could then be sold as second-hand.[64]

The dispute was eventually submitted to arbitration. In April 1852 the Booksellers' Association convened a special conference and asked Lord Campbell to preside over it. After hearing the case for both sides he judged, with the support of Dean Milman and George Grote, that the association was an illegal conspiracy. A publisher had no right, he ruled, to refuse to sell to any man in the trade or to dictate the prices at which his publications should be retailed. The publishers and booksellers accordingly dissolved their association.

For thirty years or more after this decision booksellers were free to sell at the prices they thought most profitable to themselves. Publishers were still not too pleased at the idea. William Longman, for instance, giving evidence before the Copyright Commission in 1876, was in favour of continuing the $33\frac{1}{3}$ per cent discount to the trade on the ground that a lower profit would not allow the retail trade to make a living. He agreed, all the same, that in London and most of the large towns books could be bought at from 5 to 20 per cent below the prices given on the covers.[65] In John Blackwood's opinion retailers could not possibly be prevented from taking off the discount.[66]

Government Enterprise

One problem had thus been settled, to the dissatisfaction of the publishers, on free trade principles. While its discussion was in progress certain publishers were at war in another direction, this time against the Government and with free trade as their watchword. Their indignation had been aroused by the action of the Irish Education Commissioners. That body, in a way "inconsistent and contradictory in a Government which proclaims its devotion to the principles of free trade," had in 1848 taken to printing books in Ireland and selling them in England at very low prices. It was not to be tolerated. The firms of Longman and Murray wrote immediately to Lord John Russell to protest. "It would be a novel feature in the internal economy of this country," they argued, "more especially since free trade has been in the ascendant, were Her Majesty's Government to take possession of the Isle of Wight, or of some other district, to grow corn upon it, to construct bakehouses, and to supply the people with bread, at less than its cost price, making up the deficit by taxes levied on those very agriculturists whom the Government had thus done its best to destroy. . . . Yet, in what respect is the production and sale of books by Government, at less than they cost, more reasonable and proper?" In 1850 they wrote again, complaining that the books supplied by the Commissioners to schools in England amounted to about a fourth of the whole. A year later a third letter of protest was sent, this time because a mathematical work produced by the Government had been introduced into the schools under the Board of Ordnance. What chance had private individuals, it was asked, against such palpable favouritism? The reply to this one-sided correspondence was long overdue. When it came it ran as follows: "Sir, I am desired by Lord John Russell to acknowledge the receipt of your letter of the 20th inst. and of the accompanying memorial. I am, Sir, Your obedient servant, Arthur Russell."[67]

The Net Book System

The book trade had been one of the last to throw over the restrictions which had grown up around it. It was to be one of the first to return to them. In September 1887 there was issued a prospectus of a proposed Authors' and Booksellers' Association, whose primary object was to be the production of new and standard books for sale to the public at net prices. It was not to be exactly a revival of the old system. The idea was to narrow the margin between the cost of production and the price asked of the public so that the price fixed *could* only be net. With lower profits all round, it was claimed, there would be less unfair competition. But the suggested means of cutting down profits ran counter to modern practice in the book trade: some of the middlemen were to drop out; "either the publisher must print his own books or the printer must turn publisher, and thus one large profit, and perhaps the least deserved profit, must be given up." If this had been practicable would not publishers of their own accord have gone back to the organisation of Caxton's time and undertaken to print their own books?

Net books were to come, but not in that way. It was Frederick Macmillan who was to take the lead. He wrote to *The Bookseller* in 1890 suggesting the publication of net books, inviting comments from those interested in the scheme. Those interested were in fact numerous enough to supply many newspapers with sufficient material for many days. Very little encouragement was given to the suggestion. Booksellers nearly all condemned it. Publishers wished that something might come of it, but thought it a vain hope. All the same, in spite of the doubtful reception of his plan Macmillan resolved to experiment, and in a most ingenious way. Two of the most trenchant critics of the fixed discount system in the earlier controversy had been the economists McCulloch and John Stuart Mill. How appropriate, then, to secure the leading economist of the day as an actual participator in a net book scheme! It was a stroke of genius on the part of Frederick Macmillan to write to Alfred Marshall for permission to publish *The Principles of Economics* on a net basis. Marshall was quite agreeable. The book was published in July 1890 at 12s. 6d. net instead of the 16s. originally decided upon; the trade price was fixed at 10s. 5d. with a further discount at settlement averaging 5 per cent, and the "odd copy" (the twenty-fifth book given free on an order for twenty-four) was abolished. Much as the "discount-booksellers" disliked the arrangement they were bound to conform to it. Those who tried to cut prices found their accounts closed straight away. It was no use to try to boycott the work, for a public was eager to have it; and to show displeasure by ordering only one copy at a time instead of ten would be to nobody's loss besides the booksellers', who would be sacrificing 5 per cent of their profits.[68]

The choice of a work less assured of a demand might have led to a different result. As it was the success of the first attempt encouraged the same publishers to issue fifteen more net books in 1890, sixty in the next year and increasing numbers in following years. Other firms were quick to follow the example. In 1891 net books were being published by Messrs. Philip and Son, Fisher Unwin, Longmans, John Murray, Methuen, and yet others.

As before, the attempt to enforce net prices led to the formation of a booksellers' association. In 1890 the London Booksellers' Society was formed, to be merged five years later in a new body, the Associated Booksellers of Great Britain and Ireland. One of the first acts of this association was to express approval of net prices and to call upon publishers to enforce the system by more stringent regulations. The Publishers' Association of Great Britain and Ireland was formed in the same year.

Various schemes were shortly to be put forward by the Associated Booksellers and the Publishers' Association for the more effectual prevention of underselling. The one adopted was drawn up in 1899 by the Publishers' Association, which advocated that books should more generally be published at net prices; that those booksellers who agreed to sell at the fixed prices were to be allowed trade terms, but all others should be charged the full published price.

In 1905 *The Times* Book Club was founded, and it was not long before it had adopted a policy reminiscent of James Lackington's of a century before. Clean copies which had been in circulation for about a month were offered for sale at 10 per cent discount; and there was an understanding that borrowers might keep any book on payment of a reduced price. It was the old disputable point of what was a new book and what was not. An agreement was reached in 1906 that a net book should not be sold as second-hand within six months of its publication, and that new net books should not be reduced in price for a year. Once again the Press had a controversial topic for discussion. *The Times*, as the interested body, led the way in a revived attack on publishers' monopolies. The public showed a lively interest in the subject, and long lists of signatures were obtained to a memorial against the net book agreement. The agreement might have broken down (for popular feeling was obviously against it) had not *The Times* in 1907 published an exaggerated statement. It was in connection with *The Letters of Queen Victoria*, published by Murray at £3 3s. "Artifex," in a letter in *The Times*,[69] accused Murray of excessively overcharging for the book, which he reckoned to have cost the publishers about 9s. a copy: £1 in his opinion would have been a quite high enough price. In the libel action which followed it was brought to light that "Artifex" had overlooked some of the heaviest expenses of publication, including the whole of the advertising costs. Murray was vindicated and awarded £7,500 damages.

In passing, it is interesting to note that a similar war had been in process in America since 1902. A combination of the American Publishers Association and the American Booksellers Association had been fighting the department stores on this very question of price-cutting. On June 1, 1908, a decision was given in the Supreme Court that no publishers had the right to dictate the price at which books should be sold. Combination for such a purpose was judged to be in restraint of trade, and offenders were rendered liable to heavy damages.[70]

Apart from one or two minor modifications the working of the net book system was long accepted. Although the reading public, no doubt, might still have protested against its restrictions if asked to think about them, publishers and booksellers on the whole seemed well content with the arrangement. One of our booksellers voiced a general opinion when he said that "The Net Book Agreement is not only the safeguard of the bookseller, but also an assurance to the publisher that his accounts can be paid, because the margin of profit has been made a reasonable one.[71] And Messrs. Constable & Co. were amongst those supporting the agreement because, "were it abolished, the retail bookseller would slip back into the condition of apathetic incompetence . . . from which it raised him. . . . We believe that it is in our interest, no less than in that of the public, to have educated and intelligent booksellers; and it is certain that the precarious livelihood of the bookseller in the days before the Net Book Agreement was in force prevented either education or intelligence, so base was the trade and so miserable were its rewards."[72]

On the whole net books seemed an established fact. But by 1938 a number of book clubs had been successfully formed, with the avowed aim of guiding their members' choice of reading. One or two of these societies had already introduced a practice by which books published in the ordinary way at as high a price as 10s. 6d. were sold at 2s. 6d. to members. "The booksellers have intimated that some new arrangement must prevail. A meeting of the interested parties has been arranged. . . ."[73]

The controversy was ready to break out anew when war intervened. It was to revive in full vigour in due course as part of the general problem of resale price maintenance. In 1962 the regulation of book prices under a revised net book agreement of 1957 was considered as a central issue under the Restrictive Trade Practices Act of 1956. The verdict was that the agreement was not contrary to the public interest.

With the position thus legally established, in 1973 the Council of the Publishers' Association, on behalf of all the signatories of the Net Book Agreement of 1957, authorised the registration of the agreement with the Commission of the European Communities in accordance with the Treaty of Rome.

Internationalism in the Book Trade

The lead taken by the Oxford University Press from 1896 onwards in establishing branches abroad was soon to be followed by other publishers, foreign as well as British. By the sixties publishing-houses in America, France, Spain and other countries had opened branches in the United Kingdom and elsewhere to act as sales agents and, to some extent, as publishers. That was the beginning of an important international development in which, by 1970, over thirty American companies had branches or subsidiaries in the United Kingdom, mainly publishing academic or technical works, and fourteen British publishing-houses had been entirely taken over by American companies. It was calculated that by then about £40 million of British book sales a year were by companies owned or partly owned by American interests.[74]

We have already noticed a parallel development, the growth of international co-operation in book production, particularly in the printing of art books and other expensive publications. This was only the first step towards a complete merger of various publishers throughout the world (including a number of publishers of encyclopaedias and other reference works) into great combines such as Time-Life and the McGraw Hill International Book Company, based in America, and Hachette, based in France. In face of this intensified competition, the Publishers' Association may or may not have been reassured to learn from the managing director of the McGraw Hill Publishing Company that American companies regard British publishing not as British, but as world publishing with Britain as the centre.[75]

CHAPTER XXI

The Volume of Production since the Beginning of the Nineteenth Century

THE book industry at the beginning of the nineteenth century was still on a small scale. Pamphlets and reprints apart, the yearly average of under a hundred new books which had remained fairly constant from 1666 to 1756 had risen for the period 1792–1802 to 372, and for the next twenty-five years to about 580,[1] but it is doubtful whether the total number of volumes had risen in the same proportion. T. N. Longman, the publisher, thought that it had not. Giving evidence before the Copyright Committee of 1813 he said that the variety of publications had greatly increased in the last ten years but he doubted whether sales had been larger than before.[2] Nor did the immediate prospects seem very bright. These were the early days of a depression fated to last for several years. A large number of printers were thrown out of employment, partly, it was said, owing to the general state of the times, partly to the expense of publishing in a period of rising prices, and partly to the heavy burden of the copyright law of deposit.[3]

There was still little in the way of an educated reading public. The new moneyed classes, the merchants, were not great readers; yet they were the people upon whom, now that books were becoming so dear as to be "articles of fashionable furniture more than anything else," the well-being of the book trade depended. In spite of Southey's contemptuous remark, they seem to have been customers worth having. "I have seen," he goes on to tell his friend (1806), "a Wiltshire clothier who gives his bookseller no other instructions than the dimensions of his shelves; and have just heard of a Liverpool merchant who is fitting up a library, and has told his bibliopole to send him Shakespeare and Milton and Pope, and if any of these fellows should publish anything new to let him have it immediately."

The growing dependence of the booksellers on the commercial classes had its drawbacks: a general trade depression was liable to bring the book trade to a standstill. Even the nobility, the former standby of the booksellers, were forced to withdraw their custom because their rênts were not forthcoming. That at least was the conclusion arrived at by Thomas Cadell and William Blackwood.[4] During the crisis of 1826 Constable and other publishers were in serious difficulties,[5] and nearly every London printing-house had a notice on the door saying, "Compositors and pressmen need not apply."[6] Again in 1842 business declined, and John Murray wrote, "I am very sorry to say that the publishing of books at this time involves nothing but loss, and that I have found it absolutely necessary to withdraw from the printers every work that I had in the press, and to return to the authors any MS. for which they required immediate publication."[7]

It was to be some time before the reading habit could spread to the general population. Something had been done towards it by the National Society for Promoting the Education of the Poor and by the British and Foreign School Society, established in 1811 and 1814 respectively, but the Government inquiry of 1816 showed how little it was. There were still 3,500 parishes in England and Wales without a school of any description. Less than three-quarters of a million children were being educated in all the schools together, endowed and unendowed.[8] The year 1833 saw the first Government grant for education, and six years later there was set up the Committee of the Privy Council on Education, but there was still no compulsory scheme for the whole population. On finding then, that the average output of new books had risen by the middle years of the century to over 2,600 we must turn elsewhere for an explanation. Three offer themselves immediately: between 1801 and 1851 the population of Great Britain had almost doubled;[9] since 1780 wages generally had increased by 50 to 100 per cent;[10] and in the second quarter of the century the average price of new works had fallen from 16s. to 8s. 4½d.[11] Encouraged by this new cheapness, the demand for food for the mind was so catching up with the demand for material food that the 1861 census showed as many people to be engaged in producing books and newspapers as there were employed as bakers (54,000), and only 14,000 fewer than the butchers!

The Elementary Education Act of 1870 was to create in due course an entire population able, even if unwilling, to read books. Several years were to pass before those who in 1870 were of school age could be expected to have much direct influence on the book market, but the provision of school textbooks was an immediate call upon the trade. That may account for the exceptionally good state of the London printing trade between 1870 and 1875.[12] Even in the worst years of the general trade depression of 1879 onwards the printing industry of London suffered only slightly, owing, it was thought, to the incentive given by the Education Acts.[13] The printers of Salisbury, Bristol, Derby and one or two other places were also unaffected by the depression. Although several branches of the Typographical Association, especially Cardiff, Liverpool and York, sent in very gloomy accounts of the years 1879 to 1885 the general feeling was that the trade was in a fairly healthy condition compared with other industries.[14]

The decline of illiteracy and rise in family incomes in a population still growing explains well enough the rise in the number of new publications until in 1901 they totalled 6,044. Since that date there has been a steady increase (due partly to the rise of the woman author) to the 12,379 of 1913 and then, after the setback of the war periods and a few years following, to the record figure of 26,154 for the year 1964.[15] Taking into account reprints and new editions, there was a fairly steady upward trend from 13,046 titles published in 1947 to 33,489 in 1970, with only a slight fall in 1971 to 32,538. In monetary value the growth was greater still: for 1907 the works published totalled 9,914 (as compared with 30,073 German publications, 10,785 French ones and 9,620 American ones);[16] they were valued at £1,360,000,[17] whereas the 15,393 works published in 1930 were worth £4,841,000.[18] Although, that is, the publications of the year 1930 had risen by nearly half as much again compared with those of 1907 their monetary value was more than three times as great. This can be only partially explained by post-war inflation; any attempt at comparison with present-day values would be liable to error.

Times have changed since John Murray II wrote to Byron, with regard to *The Corsair* (1814), "I sold on the day of publication—a thing perfectly unprecedented—10,000 copies."[19] The present-day tendency towards standardisation is very evident in the book trade. Just as, in spite of the wide range of colours procurable by the modern dyer, it is found profitable to choose only a few of them as the "correct wear" for a season, there are a small number of books at a time which are "correct reading." To issue a best-seller is a natural aim—the larger the edition the cheaper the production cost of the individual volume; but, as one publisher has pointed out, the general effect is that "year by year, while the success of the successful grows more fantastic, the failure of the failures grows more marked."[20] To him the growing figures of modern book-production are no cause for congratulation, but are "ominous evidence of collective insanity,"[21] to be remedied only by a rationing of output.

With the increasing specialisation of learning more and more publications are likely to appeal only to a select few. Each new discovery in science, each improvement in technology, calls for its own monograph which may interest only an infinitesimal part of the population. To supply the wants of a constant number of readers in an ever-branching system of knowledge it is necessary for the number of new publications to increase in something like geometrical progression. The purely "general reader" may still exist among people of leisure, but for men of particular studies or special hobbies it is the best-seller which provides one of the few common grounds for conversation.

Publishers have not always fully estimated the demand for a work which was to become a best-seller. For instance, A. S. M. Hutchinson's *If Winter Comes* (1921) had a first printing of 5,000 copies, a large edition but not large enough; within a year 100,000 copies were required. This record was to be greatly exceeded after the Second World War. *The Kon-Tiki Expedition* reached over half a million copies by 1949. Monsarrat's *The Cruel Sea* (1951) had a demand reaching nearly half a million copies in its first five months. Another work in great demand, *The Diary of Anne Frank*, had by 1971 reached a million copies in the Pan paperback edition (so far, fewer than thirty British paperbacks had reached that distinction). Sales of the *New English Bible* (1970) rose to more than 2 million in the first six months, while the sales of J. R. R. Tolkien's trilogy, *The Lord of the Rings*, had exceeded 4 million by the time of his death in 1973. These are still exceptionally high figures, and the more restrained output of the Edinburgh University Press is more typical of the general publishing house, "with average runs of 2,500, an occasional 5,000, and a rare 10,000 as a highly speculative venture."[22] In contrast, students' textbooks have a more assured demand, and the firm which is fortunate enough to obtain a contract for publishing Open University basic textbooks (Macmillan in the first instance) can safely print 50,000 of each, to meet the demand from the general public as well as from the students concerned.

Providing books (largely "quality" paperbacks) for 200,000 or more university students has been one of the more rewarding ventures of recent years. And the new demand is not only from registered students. Mr. John Prime, a general bookseller in King's Lynn, speaking at the annual Booksellers' Conference in 1970, gave an account of his experiences in this small town in a mainly agricultural area, without a university or training college within forty miles. He had sold about 100,000 books of all kinds in two years, and was convinced that, quite apart from the university trade, his biggest potential market was from young people under twenty-five, the most literate generation the country had ever known. To make his point he gave a vivid description of "Hell's Angels" roaring up on motor-cycles to buy paperbacks and motoring manuals, and barefoot maidens buying Leonard Cohen's poems for their long-haired boy friends.[23]

In spite of the other attractions offered to a twentieth-century population—motor cars, cinemas, wireless and the rest—the output of recreational works has only recently shown a decline. The works of fiction, for instance, published between 1926 and 1930 amounted to 17,507 as compared with an output of 11,914 for 1921–5. Novel reading is a convenient pastime for the tired city worker travelling home from his office, and the extent to which it can compete with the solving of crossword puzzles or with gazing out of the window depends very largely on the amount of effort involved. Even the thriller would be unattractive for the purpose if it took the form of a heavy quarto volume printed in small type. To some extent this was realised in the early days of railway travel. The "railway libraries" of the mid-nineteenth century were among the first of the modern pocket-editions. The type used for them, unfortunately, was ill-suited for reading in a dimly lighted compartment. There had already been one move towards clearer type: the advertisement of Bell's edition of Shakespeare (1787) called attention to the abolition of the long "s," and a general change to the new form of the letter can be seen in the periodicals issued between 1802 and 1808;[24] but the problem of the legibility of print in relation to fatigue did not receive full consideration until the present century, with the investigations of the Committee on Type Faces (1922) and of the Medical Research Council (1926).

The growth in output is reflected in the number of employees connected with the paper, printing and stationery trades. In 1935, according to the fifth census of production, there were 249,023 male employees (235,452 in 1930) and 151,713 females (144,551 in 1930). Only a small proportion of the total employees, of course, was occupied on book production. It is doubtful whether there were any printing-houses engaged wholly upon the printing of books. The total number of printing firms in the late thirties was about 8,000, of whom about 4,000 were members of the British Federation of Master Printers, but only about 50 of them were engaged principally on book-printing. Of the rest there were perhaps 300 who, though primarily general printers, fairly frequently printed books.[25] Similarly, although there were at that time some 1,400 publishing-houses,[26] the majority of the 17,000 new publications of the year 1937 came from about

200 firms. The census of production of 1958 shows that there were still only 61 firms of 25 or more employees which were mainly engaged on printing books, while the census of 1968 shows a drop to 58.

Between 1919 and 1939 the annual issues of books by the public libraries alone rose from under 60,000,000[27] to some 188,000,000,[28] followed by a remarkable increase by the seventies to over 600,000,000. This would not have been possible without the removal of rate-restrictions by the Public Libraries Act of 1919, but it is a development not altogether welcome to the publishers. As one of them once said, "Most people have not yet learned to regard books as a necessity. They will beg them, they will borrow them, they will do everything, in fact, but buy them. People who would be ashamed to cadge for anything else they wanted, who will unhesitatingly pay 8s. 6d. apiece for a dozen gramophone records, or 12s 6d. each for stalls at a theatre, will think twice, if not three times, before spending 5s. upon a book which will last a lifetime."[29] That would seem to be an important factor. Books *do* last a lifetime, and modern houses are small. Added to that, most modern books take only an hour or two to read. The voracious reader who had to keep all he read would, if he could afford to buy all he wanted, before long find himself without room to turn. He would not be impressed by the early nineteenth century idea of books as "articles of fashionable furniture," or by the "positive effort to promote books as decorative background to a home" made in 1970 in a supplement to *Homes and Gardens*. But it is a sad fact that many bookshops have gone out of existence during the last twenty years, including about 800 closed between 1956 and 1958 and not replaced.[30] In Leeds the general bookshops dwindled during the sixties from seven to three. Several reasons have been offered: shortage of capital, the unprofitability of single sales, the rise of library suppliers as competitors with local bookshops, and a new development beyond the control of the book trade—a big increase in high street rents, and the consequent removal of bookshops to premises off the main flow of business. The formation of a Charter Group of the Booksellers' Association has done much to raise the standards of individual members of the group, providing them with economic information and consultancy services. More recently, the Oxford University Press together with Messrs. B. H. Blackwell Ltd. have formed a jointly owned subsidiary called University Bookshops (Oxford) Ltd., which provides co-operative help to some of the smaller bookshops and has a controlling interest in several others.[31] But, for all their efforts, the fact remains that the general reader borrows far more books than he buys.

Even the volumes which one borrows have been bought by somebody. In 1971–2, for instance, the public libraries of Great Britain spent nearly £16 million on books,[32] an amount which their borrowers very possibly would not have exceeded on their own account. And if an occasional publication does fail, its promoter may console himself with Thomas Fuller's reflection that "Learning hath gained most by those books by which the printers have lost." If he can.

References

CHAPTER I

INTRODUCTION

1. *Quoted in* Brassington (W. S.), History of the Art of Bookbinding, p. 64.
2. West (A. F.), Alcuin and the Rise of the Christian Schools, p. 73.
3. Madan (F.), The Early Oxford Press.
4. *Quoted in* Putnam (G. H.), Books and their Makers, I, 366.
5. Copinger (W. A.), *in* Bibliographical Society Transactions, I, 39.
6. Acts of the Privy Council, July 18, 1550.
7. Duff (E. G.), Century of the English Book Trade, p. xv.
8. Arber (E.), Transcript of the Stationers' Register, II, 746.
9. *ib.*, III, 41–42.
10. Ames (J.), Typographical Antiquities; ed. Herbert, III, 1454.
11. Letters and Papers of the Reign of Henry VIII, vol. 17, March 1542.
12. Putnam, *op. cit.*, II, 169.

CHAPTER II

THE DEMAND FOR BOOKS

1. Philobiblon (1344); translated by J. B. Inglis, 1832.
2. *See* Adamson (J. W.), A Short History of Education.
3. Rogers (J. E. T.), Six Centuries of Work and Wages, I, 165.
4. Leach (A. F.), Educational Charters, p. 148.
5. Lupton (J. H.), A Life of John Colet, D.D., p. 285.
6. Leach (A. F.), The Schools of Medieval England, p. 331.
7. Leach (A. F.), English Schools at the Reformation, p. 7.
8. *ib.*, pt. 2, p. 82.
9. Lupton, *op. cit.*, p. 279.
10. Stow (J.), Survey of London; ed. by Henry Morley, 1893, p. 101.
11. Leach (A. F.), English Schools at the Reformation, pt. 2, p. 34.
12. *ib.*, pt. 2, p. 92.
13. Arber (E.), Transcript of the Stationers' Register, II, 791.
14. Leach (A. F.), English Schools at the Reformation, pt. 2, p. 39.
15. Harrison (W.), Elizabethan England; ed. by Lothrop Withington, p. 255.
16. Rogers, *op. cit.*, IV, 602.
17. Historical Manuscripts Commission, Report II (1871), App. p. 132.
18. *ib.*
19. Leach (A. F.), English Schools at the Reformation, p. 92.
20. *ib.*, pt. 2, p. 300.
21. Camden Society, Letters of Eminent Literary Men, p. 66.
22. Harrison, *op. cit.*, p. 74.
23. *ib.*, p. 219.

24. Plomer (H. R.), *in* Bibliographical Society Transactions, III, 219.
25. Nash, Works; ed. Grosart, III, 105.
26. Lansdowne MS. 43, fol. 187.
27. Sandys (*Sir* J. E.), Scholarship, *in* Shakespeare's England, I, 247.
28. Strype, Memorials of Archbishop Cranmer, 1848, App. XX.
29. Letters and Papers of Henry VIII, vol. 16, May 1, 1541.
30. State Papers Domestic, Elizabeth, vol. 48, art. 6.
31. Pepys (S.), Diary, July 23, 1666.
32. The Bibliographer: a Journal of Book-Lore, vol. 2, 1882, p. 64.
33. Dunton (J.), The Life and Errors, vol. 1, pp. 154–7.
34. *ib.*, p. 177.
35. *ib.*, p. xxix.
36. *See, for instance*, Brinsley (J.), Ludus Literarius, 1612; *and* Hoole (C.), New Discovery of the Old Art of Teaching Schoole, 1660.
37. Account of Charity Schools (annual).
38. Knight (C.), Passages of a Working Life, vol. 1, p. 26.
39. Adamson (J. W.), A Short History of Education, p. 219.
40. Rogers (J. E. T.), History of Agriculture and Prices.
41. Tucker (J.), Instructions for Travellers, 1757, p. 19.
42. Nichols (J.), Literary Anecdotes, vol. 5, p. 471.
43. *ib.*, vol. 2, p. 61.
44. Dibdin (T. F.), The Bibliomania, 1809, pp. 34–9.
45. Pope (A.), Moral Essays, Epistle 4.
46. Dibdin, *op. cit.*, p. 46.
47. Nichols, *op. cit.*, vol. 1, p. 288.
48. Lackington (J.), Memoirs, 10th ed., p. 242.
49. Foote's Author, act 1, scene 2.
50. Lackington, *op. cit.*, p. 242.

CHAPTER III

THE DIVISION OF LABOUR IN THE BOOK INDUSTRY

1. Unwin (S.), The Truth about Publishing, p. 119.
2. State Papers Domestic, 1637–8, vol. 376, nos. 13 and 14.
3. Moxon (J.), Mechanick Exercises, 1683, vol. 2, p. 353.
4. Almon (J.), Memoirs, 1790, p. 13.
5. *Based on* Plomer's Dictionary of the Printers and Booksellers who were at Work in England, Scotland, and Ireland from 1668 to 1725; ed. by A. Esdaile.
6. *Based on* Plomer's Dictionary . . . 1726–75.
7. Smith (G.) and Benger (F.), The Oldest London Bookshop, pp. 5–9.
8. Harleian MS., 5910, fol. 137.
9. Wither (G.), Schollers Purgatory, 1625, p. 10.
10. Nichols (J.), Literary Anecdotes, vol. 2, p. 461.
11. Dunton (J.), The Life and Errors, vol. 1, p. 62.

12. Almon (J.), Memoirs, p. 62.
13. *ib.*, pp. 182, 184.
14. *ib.*, p. 232.
15. Arber (E.), Transcript of the Stationers' Register, July 14, 1617.
16. Walwyn (W.), The Fountain of Slaunder Discovered, 1649, p. 26.
17. Palmer (S.), A General History of Printing, 1733, p. 141.
18. Nichols (J.), Literary Anecdotes, vol. 5, p. 198.
19. Palmer, *op. cit.*, p. 287.
20. *ib.*, p. 292.
21. Moxon (J.), Mechanick Exercises, 1683, vol. 2, p. 264.
22. *In* The Postman, September 27, 1711.
23. Nichols, *op. cit.*, vol. 2, pp. 228–9.
24. *ib.*, vol. 2, p. 385.
25. Walpole (H.), Journal, May 15, 1773.
26. Wither (G.), Schollers Purgatory, 1625.
27. Curwen (H.), A History of Booksellers, p. 23.
28. Dunton (J.), Life and Errors, vol. 1, p. 168.
29. *ib.*, p. 179.
30. *ib.*, p. 200.
31. Curwen, *op. cit.*, p. 27.
32. *ib.*, p. 28.
33. Collins (A. S.), Authorship in the Days of Johnson, p. 181.
34. Nichols (J.), Literary Anecdotes, vol. 8, p. 296.
35. *ib.*, p. 301.
36. Boswell (J.), Life of Johnson, I, 105.
37. Nichols, *op. cit.*, vol. 2, p. 730.
38. Almon (J.), Memoirs, pp. 41–2.
39. Lackington (J.), Memoirs, p. 221.
40. *ib.*, p. 229.
41. Nichols, *op. cit.*, vol. 1, p. 656.
42. *ib.*, vol. 3, p. 4.
43. Smiles (S.), Memoir and Correspondence of the late John Murray, vol. 1, p. 26.

CHAPTER IV

THE STRUCTURE OF THE INDUSTRY

1. Ames (J.), Typographical Antiquities; ed. Herbert, 1790, vol. 3.
2. Report on Patents (Lansdowne MS. 48).
3. State Papers Domestic, Elizabeth, vol. 190, art. 48.
4. State Papers Domestic, Charles I, vol. 364, art. 111.
5. L'Estrange (*Sir* R.), Considerations and Proposals in Order to the Regulation of the Press, 1663.
6. Journey to England, 1663, p. 16.
7. Plomer (H. R.), Dictionary . . . 1668–1725, p. 175.
8. *ib.*, pp. 135, 301.
9. Welford, Early Newcastle Typography, p. 24.

10. Nichols (J.), Literary Anecdotes, vol. 1, pp. 288–312.
11. *Based on* Plomer's Dictionary . . . 1726–75.
12. State Papers Domestic, James I, vol. 80, art. 52, fol. 98.
13. Arber (E.), Transcript of the Stationers' Register, IV, 533.
14. State Papers Domestic, Charles II, vol. 243, p. 181.
15. Madan (F.), Oxford Books, vol. 2, pp. 526–30.
16. Walford, Antiquarian, vol. 8, p. 133.
17. The Life and Bibliography of Andrew Brice, pp. 42–3.
18. Nichols, *op. cit.*, vol. 4, pp. 589, 591.
19. Knight (C.), The Old Printer and the Modern Press, 1854, p. 253.
20. Wheeler (G. W.), *in* Oxford Bibliographical Society Proceedings and Papers, vol. 2, pp. 25–8.
21. Nichols, *op. cit.*, vol. 5, p. 169.
22. Dunton (J.), The Life and Errors, vol. 2, p. 512.
23. Welsh (C.), A Bookseller of the Last Century, pp. 337–47.
24. Straus (R.), Robert Dodsley, *bibliog.*
25. Straus (R.), The Unspeakable Curll, *bibliog.*
26. Return of the Number of Literary Works . . . entered at Stationers' Hall, B.P.P. 1826–7, XX.
27. Meidinger (H.), *in* Journal of the Royal Statistical Society, July 1840.
28. Arber, *op. cit.*, II, 43.
29. State Papers Domestic, Charles I, no. 301, art. 105.
30. Dunton (J.), The Life and Errors, vol. 1, p. 175.
31. Welsh, *op. cit.*, p. 254.
32. Plomer, Dictionary . . . 1668–1725, p. 215.
33. *ib.*, p. 79.
34. *ib.*, p. 41.
35. *Quoted in* Dredge (J. I.), Devon Booksellers.
36. Notes and Queries, II, Series XI, 45.
37. Welsh, *op. cit.*, p. 22.
38. Nichols, *op. cit.*, vol. 2, p. 358.

CHAPTER V

COPYRIGHT

1. Putnam (G. H.), Books and their Makers, II, 412.
2. *ib.*, II, 363, 370.
3. Dibdin (T. F.), Typographical Antiquities, vol. 2, p. 477.
4. Lowndes on Copyright, p. 5 *n*.
5. Rapin's Acta Regia, p. 308.
6. *ib.*, p. 309.
7. Rymer's Foedera, 1704–32, vol. 15, p. 150.
8. Dugdale's Origines Juridiciales, 1680, p. 59.
9. Rymer's Foedera, vol. 15, p. 255.
10. Camden Society, Egerton Papers.
11. Dugdale, *op. cit.*, p. 59.
12. *ib.*, p. 60.

13. Arber (E.), Transcript of the Stationers' Register, II, 15.
14. Lansdowne MS. 48, art. 76, fol. 176.
15. *ib.*, fol. 180–1.
16. *ib.*, fol. 184.
17. State Papers Domestic, Elizabeth, vol. 15, art. 38–40.
18. Lansdowne MS. 48, fol. 189–94.
19. *ib.*, fol. 173–4.
20. Arber, *op. cit.*, I, 248.
21. Rymer's Foedera, vol. 16.
22. Arber, *op. cit.*, III, 42.
23. Rymer's Foedera, vol. 19, p. 577.
24. Arber, *op. cit.*, IV, 13–14.
25. *Printed in* Cooper's Annals of Cambridge, III, 142–5.
26. State Papers Domestic, James I, vol. 153, fol. 71.
27. *Reprinted in* Arber, *op. cit.*, IV, 35–8.
28. Arber, I.
29. Putnam (G. H.), Books and their Makers, II, 361.
30. Arber, II, 43.
31. *ib.*, I, 259.
32. *ib.*, I, 306.
33. *ib.*, IV, 148.
34. Greg (W. W.) and Boswell (E.) eds. Records of the Court of the Stationers' Company, 1576 to 1602; from Register B, p. 59.
35. *ib.*, p. 34.
36. Arber, I, 101, 184.
37. *ib.*, I, 126.
38. *ib.*, I, 182.
39. 13 and 14 Car. II, c. 33.
40. Stationers' Company, Orders, 1692, p. 34.
41. Dunton (J.), The Life and Errors, vol. 1, p. 52.
42. 8 Anne ch. 19.
43. Hume (D.), Letters; ed. J. Y. T. Greig. Letter to Francis Hutcheson, March 16, 1740.
44. B.M. 357, c. 2 (80), 1735.
45. *ib.*, c. 2 (74).
46. Burrow (*Sir* J.), Reports of Cases Adjudged in the Court of King's Bench, vol. 4, 2303–2408.
47. Cobbett's Parliamentary History, vol. 17.
48. Nichols (J.), Literary Anecdotes, vol. 2, pp. 475–6.
49. *ib.*, vol. 4, p. 588.
50. Campbell (R.), The London Tradesman, 1757, p. 133.
51. *ib.*, p. 136.
52. Boswell (J.), Life of Johnson (Routledge), vol. 1, p. 197.
53. Lloyd's Evening Post, Oct. 2, 1765.

References

CHAPTER VI

EARLY TRADE AND LABOUR ORGANISATION

N.B.—Much of the material on which this chapter is based is derived from Arber's Transcript of the Stationers' Register. Specific references have been omitted, as the dates given in the text form a sufficient guide to each particular entry.

1. Sheavyn (P.), The Literary Profession in the Age of Elizabeth, p. 102.
2. Putnam (G. H.), Books and their Makers, II, 106.
3. *ib.*, II, 364.
4. *ib.*, I, 450.
5. Duff (E. G.), *in* Bibliographical Society Transactions, vol. 5, p. 88.
6. Duff (E. G.), Century of the English Book Trade, p. xxii.
7. Arber (E.), Transcript of the Stationers' Register, I, 114.
8. Mumby (F. A.), The Romance of Book Selling, p. 31.
9. Brassington (W. S.), History of the Art of Bookbinding, p. 125.
10. Plomer (H. R.), Abstracts from the Wills of English Printers and Stationers.
11. Letters and Papers of the Reign of Henry VIII, vol. 17.
12. *Printed in* Arber, I, 30.
13. State Papers Domestic, Elizabeth, vol. 15, art. 38–40.
14. Arber, I.
15. *ib.*, I, 488.
16. Nichols (J.), Literary Anecdotes, II, 575.
17. *ib.*, II, 577.
18. *ib.*, II, 578.
19. *ib.*, II, 580.
20. Knight (C.), Passages of a Working Life, vol. 2, p. 58.
21. Wither (G.), Schollers Purgatory.
22. Arber, II, 13.
23. *ib.*, I, 590.
24. The Charter and Grants of the Company of Stationers, *etc.*, 1741, p. 24.
25. Stationers' Company, The Orders, *etc.*, 1678, p. 6.
26. Mellottée (P.), Histoire Économique de l'Imprimerie, p. 208.
27. Dunning (T. J.), Some Account of the London Consolidated Society of Bookbinders, p. 98.
28. Nichols, *op. cit.*, vol. 5, p. 4.
29. *ib.*, vol. 1, p. 307.
30. Mellottée, *op. cit.*, p. 234.
31. Ames (J.), Typographical Antiquities; ed. Herbert, vol. 3, p. 1672.
32. Arber, IV, 22.
33. *ib.*, IV, 533.
34. Stationers' Company, Orders, 1678, p. 21.
35. The Charter and Grants of the Company of Stationers, *etc.*, 1741, facing p. 40.
36. Knight (C.), The Guide to Trade: the Printer, 1838, p. 9.
37. Select Committee on Artizans and Machinery, Second Report, p. 56.

38. Rogers (J. E. T.), History of Agriculture and Prices.
39. Jacob (G.), City-Liberties, 1732, p. 152.
40. Gent (T.), Life, 1832, p. 67.
41. Stationers' Company, Orders, 1678, pp. 12–13.
42. Dunton (J.), The Life and Errors, vol. 1, p. 202.
43. The Charters and Grants, *etc.*, p. 27.
44. Stationers' Company, Orders, 1678, p. 17.
45. *ib.*, pp. 8–10.
46. *ib.*, pp. 13, 15.
47. Stationers' Company, Orders, 1692, pp. 32–4.
48. Nichols, *op. cit.*, vol. 2, p. 577.
49. Curwen (H.), History of Booksellers, p. 100.
50. The Charter and Grants, *etc.*, 1741, pp. 28–30.
51. *ib.*, facing p. 40.
52. *ib.*, p. 40.
53. Arber, II, 882.
54. Mellottée, *op. cit.*, pp. 196–9.
55. Moxon (J.), Mechanick Exercises, vol. 2.

CHAPTER VII

LABOUR SUPPLY AND CONDITIONS OF EMPLOYMENT

1. Moxon (J.), Mechanick Exercises, 1683, vol. 2, p. 213.
2. *ib.*, vol. 2, p. 373.
3. Knight (C.), The Guide to Trade: the Printer, 1838, p. 38.
4. Moxon, *op. cit.*, vol. 2, pp. 260–1.
5. Whittock (N.), and others, The Complete Book of Trades, p. 35.
6. Putnam (G. H.), Books and their Makers, vol. 1, p. 206.
7. *ib.*, vol. 2, p. 396.
8. Plomer (H. R.), Abstracts from the Wills of English Printers and Stationers, p. iii.
9. Arber, I.
10. State Papers Domestic, Charles I, vol. 364, art. 111.
11. Nichols (J.), Literary Anecdotes, vol. 2, p. 286.
12. Whittock and others, *op. cit.*
13. Dunton (J.), The Life and Errors, vol. 1, p. 49.
14. Nichols, *op. cit.*, vol. 2, pp. 286–8.
15. Arber, II, 881–2.
16. *ib.*, II, 43–4.
17. *ib.*, IV, 534.
18. Gent (T.), Life, 1832, p. 17.
19. Select Committee on Artizans and Machinery, 1824, Report.
20. To the Booksellers of London and Westminster (printed sheet in Add. MS. 27799, fo. 97).
21. Mellottée (P.), Histoire Économique de l'Imprimerie, p. 242.

22. Greg (W. W.) and Boswell (E.) eds. Records of the Court of the Stationers' Company, 1576 to 1602, p. 1.
23. *ib.*, p. 3.
24. *ib.*, p. 12.
25. Arber, IV, 22–23.
26. George (M. D.), London Life in the Eighteenth Century, pp. 164–5.
27. Gent (T.), Life, pp. 18, 90.
28. Plomer (H. R.), Dictionary . . . 1726–75, p. 239.
29. Walpole (H.), Journal of the Printing Office at Strawberry Hill, pp. 79–80.
30. London Society of Compositors. A Brief Record of Events, *etc.*, p. 8.
31. Knight (C.), The Guide to Trade: the Printer, pp. 36–7.
32. Dunning (T. J.), Some Account of the London Consolidated Society of Bookbinders, p. 94.
33. Moxon (J.), Mechanick Exercises, vol. 2, 356–66.
34. Mellottée, *op. cit.*, p. 167.
35. Reed (T. B.), Old English Letter Foundries, pp. 36–8.
36. Gentleman's Magazine, vol. 10, 1740, pp. 239–41.
37. Gent (T.), Life, p. 16.
38. Gray (G. J.) and Palmer (W. M.), Abstracts from the Wills . . . of Printers . . . of Cambridge, *etc.*, p. 120.
39. Add. MS. 6880.
40. Franklin (B.), Autobiography, pp. 54–5.
41. Cox (H.) and Chandler (J. E.), The House of Longman, p. 81.
42. Mellottée, *op. cit.*, p. 167.
43. Hone (W.), Every-day Book, August 5, 1825.

CHAPTER VIII

PREMISES AND EQUIPMENT

1. A convenient account of these technical processes is given in Esdaile (A.), A Student's Manual of Bibliography.
2. Arber, I, 454.
3. Plomer (H. R.), Abstracts from the Wills of English Printers and Stationers from 1492 to 1630, p. 22.
4. Duff (E. G.), The Printers, Stationers and Bookbinders of Westminster and London from 1476 to 1535, p. 33.
5. Plomer, *op. cit.*, p. 35.
6. Arber, I, 103.
7. *ib.*, I, 531.
8. *ib.*, I, 129.
9. Greg and Boswell, *op. cit.*, p. 48.
10. *ib.*, p. 87.
11. *ib.*, p. 58.
12. Moxon (J.), Mechanick Exercises, vol. 2, pp. 10–11.
13. Dunton (J.), Life and Errors, vol. 1, p. 61.
14. Nichols (J.), Literary Anecdotes, vol. 9, p. 99.

15. Dunton, *op. cit.*, p. 500.
16. Gent (T.), Life, p. 15.
17. Moxon, *op. cit.*, vol. 2, pp. 19–31.
18. *ib.*, vol. 2, p. 32.
19. *ib.*, vol. 2, p. 74.
20. Cunningham (W.), Growth of English Industry and Commerce, vol. 2, p. 65.
21. Haynes (M. W.), The Student's History of Printing, p. 23.
22. *ib.*, p. 39.
23. Plomer, *op. cit.*, p. 27.
24. Haynes, *op. cit.*, p. 46.
25. Moxon, *op. cit.*, vol. 2, p. 37.
26. *ib.*, vol. 2, p. 270.
27. Gray (G. J.) and Palmer (W. M.), Abstracts from the Wills . . . of Printers . . . of Cambridge, p. 71.
28. *ib.*, p. 83.
29. Nichols, *op. cit.*, vol. 8, p. 364.
30. *ib.*, vol. 2, p. 454.
31. Blades (W.), The Pentateuch of Printing.
32. Reed (T. B.), History of the Old English Letter Foundries, pp. 19–20.
33. Moxon, *op. cit.*, vol. 2, p. 168.
34. *ib.*, vol. 2, p. 171.
35. The Young Tradesman, 1839, p. 413.
36. State Papers Domestic, 1637–8, vol. 376, nos. 13 and 14.
37. Pollard (A. W.), Early Illustrated Books, p. 224.
38. Isaac (F.), English Printers' Types of the Sixteenth Century, p. 1.
39. *ib.*, p. 10.
40. *ib.*, p. 6.
41. Reed, *op. cit.*, pp. 92–3.
42. Blades (W.), Life of Caxton, I, 39.
43. Plomer (H. R.), A Dictionary of the Booksellers and Printers . . . 1641 to 1667, p. 36.
44. Moxon, *op. cit.*, vol. 2, p. 227.
45. Nichols, *op. cit.*, vol. 4, p. 146.
46. *ib.*, vol. 8, p. 414.
47. *ib.*, vol. 2, p. 418.
48. Isaac, *op. cit.*, p. 2.
49. *ib.*, p. 1.
50. *ib.*, p. 35.
51. Moxon, *op. cit.*, vol. 2, p. 81.
52. Nichols, *op. cit.*, vol. 2, p. 359.
53. Curwen (H.), A History of Booksellers, p. 48.
54. Hart (H.), Notes on a Century of Typography at the University Press, Oxford.
55. Strype, Life of Parker, p. 382.
56. Rogers (J. E. T.), History of Agriculture and Prices, IV.
57. Arber, I, 470.

58. Moxon, *op. cit.*, vol. 2, p. 17.
59. Nichols, *op. cit.*, vol. 8, p. 364.
60. Gray (G. J.) and Palmer (W. M.), Abstracts from the Wills, *etc.*, p. 70.
61. *ib.*, p. 83.
62. Walpole (H.), Journal, p. 96.
63. *ib.*, p. 88.
64. Plomer (H. R.), Short History of Printing, p. 191.
65. Luckombe (P.), The History and Art of Printing, 1771, p. 232.
66. *ib.*, p. 246.
67. British Museum, A Guide to the Processes and Schools of Engraving, p. 22.
68. Duff (E. G.) *in* Pollard (A. W.), Early Illustrated Books, pp. 223–5.
69. *ib.*, p. 227.
70. *ib.*, p. 233.
71. *ib.*, p. 238.
72. Duff (E. G.), The Printers, Stationers and Bookbinders of Westminster and London from 1476 to 1535, p. 33.
73. *ib.*, p. 57.
74. Pollard (A. W.), *in* Bibliographical Society's Transactions, vol. 6, p. 32.
75. Nichols (J.), Literary Anecdotes, vol. 8, p. 626.
76. Pollard, *op. cit.*, p. 30.
77. Smith (G.) and Benger (F.), The Oldest London Bookshop, p. 17.
78. Welsh (C.), A Bookseller of the Last Century, Appendix.
79. Nichols, *op. cit.*, vol. 2, p. 488.
80. *ib.*, vol. 2, p. 247.
81. *ib.*, vol. 2, p. 250.
82. Whitehall Evening Post, July 6, 1727.
83. Nichols, *op. cit.*, vol. 8, p. 653.
84. The Young Tradesman, p. 120.
85. Mitchell (C. A.) and Hepworth (T. C.), Inks, p. 136.
86. Bridge (*Sir* F.), The Old Cryes of London, p. 78.
87. Moxon, *op. cit.*, vol. 2, p. 75.
88. Rogers (J. E. T.), History of Agriculture and Prices.
89. Plomer (H. R.), Short History of English Printing, p. 138.
90. Reed (T. B.), Old English Letter Foundries, p. 149.
91. Arber, I, 575.
92. Unwin Brothers, Unwins: a Century of Progress, p. 19.

CHAPTER IX

THE SUPPLY OF PAPER

1. McKerrow (R. B.), Introduction to Bibliography, p. 98.
2. Jenkins (R.), *in* Library Association Record, September 1900, p. 480.
3. Haynes (M. W.), The Student's History of Printing, p. 26.
4. Mentioned in the prologue to Bartholomaeus de Glanville, De Proprietatibus Rerum, printed by De Worde in 1495.

5. Fuller's "Worthies," under Cambridgeshire.
6. Aubrey, Brief Lives; ed. by Andrew Clark, vol. 2, p. 323.
7. Norden, Speculum Britanniae, 1593, p. 37.
8. State Papers Domestic, Elizabeth, vol. 185, no. 69.
9. Arber, II, 815.
10. Nichols (J.), The Progresses of Queen Elizabeth, vol. 2, p. 582.
11. Nichols, History of the County of Leicester, 1795.
12. Smiles (S.), The Huguenots, p. 338.
13. *ib.*, p. 127.
14. Discourse of the Common Weal of this Realm of England; ed. by E. Lamond, pp. 63–6.
15. State Papers Domestic, Elizabeth, vol. 185, no. 69.
16. State Papers Domestic, Charles I, vol. 331.
17. Middlesex County Records, vol. 3, p. 167.
18. Hall (H.), History of the Custom-Revenue in England, vol. 2, pp. 239, 241.
19. *ib.*, vol. 2, p. 244.
20. Davenant (C.), Report on Public Accounts (Works, vol. 5), p. 355.
21. Smiles, *op. cit.*, p. 158.
22. Bohun (E.), The Diary and Autobiography: entry for 1689.
23. Historical Manuscripts Commission, 13th Report, House of Lords Papers, App., pt. 5, p. 435.
24. *See* Patent Office. Abridgments of the Specifications relating to Paper, *etc.*
25. Patent Roll, 2 Jac. II, pt. 10, no. 17.
26. The British Merchant.
27. The Case of the Paper-Traders, Humbly offer'd to the Honourable House of Commons, 1697.
28. The Case of the poor Paper-Makers and Printers, farther stated, 1712.
29. Reasons for Amending the Clause for a Drawback to be allow'd to the Universities, &c., 1712.
30. Reasons for Altering the New Duty of Thirty Per Cent ad Valorem upon Books Imported, *etc.*, 1713.
31. Journals of the House of Commons, vol. 17.
32. Nichols (J.), Literary Anecdotes, vol. 2, p. 699.
33. Treasury Board Papers, CCC, no. 7.
34. The Library, vol. 9, p. 132.
35. Nichols, *op. cit.*, vol. 8, p. 717.
36. Introduction to Bibliography, p. 106.
37. Rogers (J. E. T.), History of Agriculture and Prices, vol. 4, pp. 606–7.
38. Arber, II, 767.
39. Greg and Boswell, *op. cit.*, p. 51.
40. Gray (G. J.) and Palmer (W. M.), Abstracts from the Wills . . . of Printers . . . of Cambridge, *etc.*, p. 70.
41. Rogers, *op. cit.*, vol. 4, p. 593.
42. *ib.*, vol. 7, pt. 1.
43. Welsh (C.), A Bookseller of the Last Century, p. 243.
44. *ib.*, p. 358.

FAST SINGLE-CYLINDER JOBBING MACHINE.

STEAM LITHOGRAPHIC MACHINE.

HOE'S FAST 10-FEEDER AMERICAN PRINTING MACHINE.

PRINTING MACHINES
From *The National Encyclopaedia*

45. Putnam (G. H.), Books and their Makers, II, 361.
46. Moxon (J.), Mechanick Exercises, vol. 2, p. 337.
47. *ib.*, pp. 353–5.
48. Reed (T. B.), Old English Letter Foundries, p. 172.
49. State Papers Domestic, Elizabeth, vol. 48, art. 6.
50. Histrio-Mastix, 1633, fol. 1.

CHAPTER X

BINDING MATERIALS

1. Arber, I, 158, 274.
2. *ib.*, I, 70, 100.
3. Lansdowne MS., 74, 75.
4. Arber, II, 185.
5. 24 Henry VIII, c. 1.
6. Hall (H.), History of the Custom-Revenue, vol. 2, p. 243.
7. Rogers (J. E. T.), History of Agriculture and Prices, vol. 5, p. 607.
8. Walpole (H.), Journal, p. 88.
9. 21 Henry VIII, c. 8.
10. 22 Henry VIII, c. 6.
11. Rogers, *op. cit.*
12. Esdaile (A.), A Student's Manual of Bibliography, p. 192.
13. Epstein (M.), The English Levant Company, p. 238.
14. Gray (G. J.) and Palmer (W. M.), Abstracts from the Wills . . . of Printers, Binders and Stationers of Cambridge, from 1504 to 1699, p. 27.
15. *ib.*
16. Gibson (S.), Abstracts from the Wills . . . of Binders . . . of Oxford, *etc.*, p. 17.
17. *ib.*, p. 22.
18. Gray and Palmer, *op. cit.*, pp. 56–8.
19. The Case of the Book-Binders of Great Britain, 1712.
20. The Case of the Paper-Makers of Great Britain, 1712.
21. The Case of the Book-Binders of Great Britain . . . relating to the Excessive Duty resolved to be laid on Mill-Boards, 1712.
22. 9 Anne, c. 11.
23. 10 Anne, c. 26.
24. Rogers, *op. cit.*, vol. 7.
25. The Case of the Tanners, which use Leaden-Hall Market, *etc.*, 1711.
26. Reasons for Taking off the Draw-Back on Tann'd Calves-Skins, 1711.
27. *Quoted in* Horne (H. P.), The Binding of Books, p. 201.
28. Welsh (C.), A Bookseller of the Last Century, pp. 173, 204.
29. *ib.*, p. 117.
30. Sadleir (M.), The Evolution of Publishers' Binding Styles, p. 11.
31. Welsh, *op. cit.*, pp. 329, 332.

CHAPTER XI

FINANCIAL ORGANISATION AND TERMS OF PUBLICATION

1. Gray (G. J.) and Palmer (W. M.), Abstracts from the Wills and Testamentary Documents of Printers . . . of Cambridge, p. 58.
2. *ib.*, p. 62.
3. Plomer (H. R.), Abstracts from the Wills of English Printers and Stationers, p. 38.
4. Plomer (H. R.), Short History of English Printing, pp. 100–1.
5. Lansdowne MS., no. 48.
6. Putnam (G. H.), Books and their Makers, II, 433.
7. *ib.*, II, 276.
8. Arber, II, 761.
9. Dunton (J.), The Life and Errors, *etc.*, vol. 2, p. 465.
10. Arber, III, 567.
11. *ib.*, IV, 82.
12. *ib.*, IV, 245.
13. Aldis (H. G.), *in* Cambridge History of English Literature, vol. 4, ch. 18.
14. Arber, III, 664.
15. Select Committee on the Copyright Acts, 1818, Evidence of Owen Rees.
16. Memorials of Archbishop Cranmer, 1848, Appendix XX.
17. Camden Society, Trevelyan Papers, 1857, I, 171.
18. Arber, V, liii.
19. *ib.*, III, 350.
20. *ib.*, IV, 174.
21. Stationers' Register, 1640–1708, vol. 1, p. 15.
22. Bowes, Cambridge Books, Note to no. 105.
23. Select Committee on the Copyright Acts, 1818.
24. Moxon (J.), Mechanick Exercises, vol. 2, 381.
25. Putnam, *op. cit.*, I, 448–9.
26. Bouchot, The Book, p. 174.
27. Curwen (H.), A History of Booksellers, p. 69.
28. Nichols (J.), Literary Anecdotes, vol. 2, pp. 95–7.
29. Ralph (J.), The Case of Authors by Profession or Trade (1758).
30. State Papers Domestic, Charles I, vol. 275, art. 28.
31. Plomer (H. R.) in Bibliographical Society Transactions, vol. 3, p. 214.
32. Dunton, *op. cit.*, p. 60.
33. Arber, III, 211.
34. *ib.*, III, 435.
35. Nichols, *op. cit.*, vol. 8, p. 293.
36. Curwen, *op. cit.*, p. 81.
37. Arber, IV, 88.
38. Sheavyn (P.), The Literary Profession, *etc.*, p. 85.
39. Mumby (F. A.), The Romance of Book Selling, p. 131.
40. State Papers Domestic, James I, vol. 109, pp. 106–7.

41. Straus (R.), Robert Dodsley, p. 64.
42. General Evening Post, August 4, 1750.
43. Nichols, *op. cit.*, vol. 5, p. 688.
44. *ib.*, vol. 2, p. 186.
45. *ib.*, vol. 8, p. 348.
46. Collins (A. S.), The Profession of Letters, p. 97.
47. Straus, *op. cit.*, p. 23.
48. Nichols, *op. cit.*, vol. 1, p. 470.
49. *ib.*, vol. 1, p. 466.
50. Collins, *op. cit.*, p. 106.
51. Nichols, *op. cit. passim.*
52. *ib.*, vol. 2, p. 529.
53. *ib.*, vol. 2, p. 530.
54. *ib.*, vol. 2, p. 113.
55. Stackhouse (T.), The Bookbinder, Book-Printer and Bookseller Confuted, 1732.
56. Gentleman's Magazine, vol. 4, 1734, p. 489.
57. Plomer (H. R.), A Dictionary of Printers . . . 1668 to 1725, p. 20.
58. Cox (H.) and Chandler (J. E.), The House of Longman, p. 5.
59. Nichols, *op. cit.*, vol. 2, p. 459.
60. *ib.*, vol. 2, p. 277.
61. Lackington (J.), Memoirs, p. 129.
62. *ib.*, p. 207.
63. Notes and Queries, vol. 11, pp. 377, 418.
64. Welsh (C.), A Bookseller of the Last Century, p. 358.
65. Mumby (F. A.), Publishing and Bookselling, p. 239.
66. Welsh, *op. cit.*, p. 243.
67. *ib.*, p. 357.
68. *ib.*, p. 358.
69. Nichols, *op. cit.*, vol. 2, p. 262.
70. Memoirs of John Almon, 1790, p. 42.
71. Smiles (S.), Memoir and Correspondence of the late John Murray, vol. 1, pp. 81–2.
72. Lackington, (J.), *op. cit.*, p. 217.
73. Longman (W.), Tokens of the Eighteenth Century connected with Booksellers and Bookmakers, *etc.*

CHAPTER XII

THE SALE OF BOOKS

1. Arber, III, 501–10.
2. 25 Henry VIII, c. 15.
3. Ames (J.), Typographical Antiquities; ed. Herbert, vol. 1, p. 445.
4. Oxford Historical Society, The Day-Book of John Dorne.
5. Ames, *op. cit.*, vol. 1, p. 376.
6. Parish Accounts of St. Margaret's, Westminster.
7. B.M. Add. MS., 28, 196.

8. Churchwardens' Accounts, St. Michael's, Cornhill, pp. 123, 129.
9. *ib.*, pp. 156, 185.
10. Greg and Boswell, p. 51.
11. McKerrow (R. B.), Introduction to Bibliography, p. 133.
12. Churchwardens' Accounts of Marston, Spelsbury, Pyrton, p. 18.
13. Churchwardens' Accounts, St. Michael's, Cornhill, p. 176.
14. *Printed in* Arber, IV, 35–8.
15. B.M. Add. MS., 28, 196.
16. Churchwardens' Accounts, p. 67.
17. Arber, I, 222.
18. *ib.*, I, 449, 572.
19. Rogers (J. E. T.), History of Agriculture and Prices.
20. Arber, I.
21. Knight (C.), The Old Printer and the Modern Press, p. 221.
22. Rogers (J. E. T.), *op. cit.*, vol. 7, pt. 1.
23. 8 Anne, c. 19.
24. Memoirs of a Printer's Devil, 1793, p. 104.
25. Lackington (J.), Memoirs, p. 132.
26. Newbery (J.), Private Memorandum Book, *quoted in* Welsh (C.), A Bookseller of the Last Century.
27. Journal of Humphry Wanley; *in* Nichols (J.), Literary Anecdotes, vol. 1, p. 90.
28. Osborne (T.), Catalogue to the Harleian Collection, 1743–4, Preface to vol. 3.
29. Impartial Protestant Mercury, January 10, 1681–2.
30. Heath (R.), Epigrams, 1650, "To my Bookseller."
31. Dunton (J.), Life and Errors, vol. 2, pp. 496–8.
32. Nichols, *op. cit.*, vol. 8, p. 464.
33. Hill (J.), The Book Makers of Old Birmingham, pp. 39–40.
34. Welsh (C.), A Bookseller of the Last Century, p. 107.
35. Nichols, *op. cit.*, vol. 2, p. 109.
36. Collins (A. S.), Authorship in the Days of Johnson, p. 250.
37. Lackington (J.), *op. cit.*, p. 89.
38. Boyle (J. R.), Early History of the Town and Port of Hedon, p. cix.
39. Arber, II, 70.
40. *ib.*, 138.
41. Plomer (H. R.), A Dictionary of the Printers . . . 1668 to 1725, p. 173.
42. Arber, III, 19.
43. Campbell (R.), The London Tradesman, 3rd ed., p. 134.
44. Nichols, *op. cit.*, vol. 2, p. 64.
45. *ib.*, p. 122.
46. Lackington, *op. cit.*, p. 132.
47. Swift (J.), Journal to Stella, April 27, 1711.
48. Arber, I, 94.
49. *ib.*, I, 184.
50. *ib.*, I, 348, 390.
51. *ib.*, III, 88.

52. Ashton, Chap-Books of the 18th Century.
53. Arber, I, 94.
54. Greg and Boswell, p. 2.
55. Putnam (G. H.), Books and their Makers, II, 279.
56. Greg and Boswell, p. 45.
57. *ib.*, p. 22.
58. Arber, II, 748–9.
59. Universal Spectator, February 26, 1736–7.
60. Penny London Morning Advertiser, March 21, 1744.
61. Lackington (J.), *op. cit.*, pp. 210–11.
62. Arber, I, 454.
63. British Museum, Catalogue of the Pamphlets . . . collected by George Thomason, vol. 1, p. vi.
64. *ib.*
65. Putnam, *op. cit.*, II, 304.
66. Fox's Acts and Monuments, 1576, p. 1108.
67. Ames (J.), Typographical Antiquities; ed. Herbert, vol. 3, p. 1585.
68. Hall (H.), History of the Customs-Revenue, vol. 2, p. 240.
69. State Papers Domestic, Elizabeth, vol. 33, art. 66.
70. Rymer's Foedera, vol. 18, p. 8 (note).
71. Nichols (J.), Literary Anecdotes, vol. 2, p. 699.
72. Six Centuries of Work and Wages, p. 149.
73. Dunton (J.), The Life and Errors, vol. 1, p. 222.
74. Gray (G. J.) and Palmer (W. M.), Abstracts from the Wills . . . of Printers . . . of Cambridge, *etc.*, p. 98.
75. Lansdowne MS. 68, art. 32.
76. State Papers Domestic, Elizabeth, vol. 15, art. 38–40.
77. Oxford Historical Society, Publications, vol. 5.
78. Lackington (J.), *op. cit.*, p. 89.
79. Reprint of the Barnstaple Records, vol. 2, p. 100.
80. Arber, II, 50.
81. Historical Manuscripts Commission, II, App., p. 102.
82. Bibliographical Society Transactions, 1898, pp. 182–3.
83. Ballad Society, Captain Cox, his Ballads and Books, p. 29.
84. Annual Register, 1761, p. 207.
85. Nichols (J.), Illustrations of the Literary History of the 18th Century, 1817, vol. 1, p. 424.
86. Campbell (T.), Diary of a Visit to England in 1775; edited by S. Raymond, 1854.
87. Lackington (J.), *op. cit.*, p. 247.

CHAPTER XIII

THE APPLICATION OF MECHANICAL POWER TO PRINTING

1. 39 George II, cap. 79.
2. Patent No. 1748, April 1790.

3. Cowper (E.), On the Recent Improvements in Printing, 1828, p. 3.
4. Vol. 5, p. 26.
5. Patent Office, Abridgments of the Specifications relating to Printing, *etc.*, p. 22.
6. *ib.*
7. *ib.*
8. The Sister Arts, p. 87.
9. Hoe (R.), A Short History of the Printing Press.
10. [Smith (C. M.)], The Working-Man's Way in the World, pp. 73–4.
11. Hoe, *op. cit.*
12. Select Committee on the Copyright Acts, 1818, Minutes of Evidence.
13. Cowper, *op. cit.*, p. 1.
14. Besterman (T.), *ed.* The Publishing Firm of Cadell and Davies: Select Correspondence and Accounts, 1793–1836, pp. 107–11.
15. Evidence of Owen Rees.
16. Cowper, *op. cit.*, p. 3.
17. S.P.C.K., The History of Printing, 1855.
18. No. 3757.
19. Cowper, *op. cit.*, p. 4.
20. *ib.*, p. 5.
21. No. 3868.
22. Cowper, *op. cit.*, p. 4.
23. The Times, July 29, 1847.
24. Cowper, *op. cit.*, p. 4.
25. No. 3974.
26. *op. cit.*, p. 5.
27. No. 4194.
28. *op. cit.*, p. 6.
29. Wilson (F. J. F.) and Grey (D.), A Practical Treatise upon Modern Printing Machinery, *etc.*, 1888, p. 48.
30. Dodd (G.), Days at the Factories, 1843, pp. 354–5.
31. In the Technical Library, St. Bride's Institute.
32. Harrild and Sons, List of Prices of Printing Machines, *etc.*
33. Knight (C.), Passages of a Working Life, vol. 1, p. 163.
34. The Printer's Tragedy.
35. Unwin Brothers, Unwins: a Century of Progress.
36. Children's Employment Commission (1862), Fifth Report, p. 3.
37. Hoe (R.), A Short History of the Printing Press.
38. Wilson and Grey, *op. cit.*, p. 204.
39. No. 4664.
40. No. 8428.
41. No. 9300.
42. Dodd (G.), Curiosities of Industry: Printing, p. 8.
43. No. 9731.
44. Nos. 1287 and 155.
45. No. 1639.
46. Dodd, *op. cit.*, p. 8.

47. The Times, Printing in the 20th Century, p. 17.
48. Typographical Circular, June 1893.
49. *ib.*, May 1893.
50. *ib.*, December 1878.
51. *ib.*, 1893.
52. *ib.*, November 1878.
53. *ib.*, May 1893.
54. Cloister Press, Print, 1936.
55. Typographical Circular, October 1893.
56. December 28, 1901.
57. Wilson (F. J. F.), Typographic Printing Machines, *etc.*, 3rd ed., p. 47.
58. *ib.*, p. 87.
59. Wilson and Grey, *op. cit.*, p. 204.
60. Harrild and Sons, A General Catalogue of Machinery, *etc.*, 1913.
61. [Dorrington (C.)], Composing Room Lectures, p. 7.
62. Unwin Brothers, Unwins: a Century of Progress, p. 30.
63. Wilson and Grey, *op. cit.*, p. 450.
64. Wilson, *op. cit.*, p. 181.
65. *ib.*, p. 187.
66. Unwin Brothers, *op. cit.*, p. 38.
67. Census of Production, 1907.
68. The Times, Printing in the 20th Century, p. 149.
69. Third Census of Production, 1924.
70. Fourth Census of Production, 1930.

CHAPTER XIV

THE ACCESSORIES OF MODERN PRINTING

1. The Young Tradesman, 1839, p. 414.
2. Babbage (C.), On the Economy of Machinery and Manufactures, 1832, p. 169.
3. Besterman (T.), *ed.* The Publishing Firm of Cadell and Davies: Select Correspondence and Accounts, 1793–1836, p. 22.
4. No. 1748.
5. No. 2931.
6. No. 2979.
7. No. 3194.
8. No. 4664.
9. No. 4826.
10. No. 4850.
11. No. 5685.
12. No. 6076.
13. No. 7585.
14. No. 9731.
15. No. 9802.

16. Dodd (G.), Days at the Factories, pp. 330–3.
17. *ib.*, p. 328.
18. Southward (J.), Progress in Printing and the Graphic Arts during the Victorian Era, p. 60.
19. Dodd (G.), Curiosities of Industry: Printing, p. 4.
20. The Times Printing Number, 1912.
21. Proposals for Establishing a Graduated Scale of Sizes for the Bodies of Printing Types, and Fixing their Height to Paper, *etc.*, 1841.
22. Select Committee on Printing (Houses of Parliament, *etc.*), 1855, Minutes of Evidence.
23. No. 1266.
24. Johnson (H.), An Introduction to Logography, 1783, p. 9.
25. *ib.*, pp. 5–6.
26. *ib.*, p. 64.
27. The Times, Printing in the 20th Century, p. 14.
28. The Sister Arts, p. 88.
29. Lottin, Catalogue des Imprimeurs de Paris, p. 87.
30. Ged (W.), Biographical Memoirs, 1781.
31. Johnson, *op. cit.*, p. 10.
32. Kurze doch nutzliche Anleitung von Form- und Stahl-Schneiden.
33. Hodgson (T.), An Essay on the Origin and Progress of Stereotype Printing, 1820, p. 44.
34. No. 1431.
35. Hodgson, *op. cit.*, p. 167.
36. Babbage (C.), On the Economy of Machinery and Manufactures, 1832, p. 56.
37. Dodd (G.), Days at the Factories, 1843, p. 345.
38. [H: T.], The Perils of Authorship [*c.* 1841], p. 19.
39. The Young Tradesman, 1839, p. 324.
40. *ib.*
41. Cowper (E.), On the Recent Improvements in Printing, 1828, p. 2.
42. Dodd (G.), Days at the Factories, p. 358.
43. Society of Authors, The Cost of Production, 1891, p. 47.
44. Ministry of Labour, Report of an Enquiry into Apprenticeship . . . 1925–6, I, 51.
45. Some Account of the Oxford University Press, 1468–1926, p. 28.
46. Patent No. 2518.
47. Babbage, *op. cit.*, p. 58.
48. Poortenaar (J.), The Technique of Prints, p. 28.
49. Committee on Acts respecting Copy Rights of Printed Books, 1813.
50. Knight (C.), Passages of a Working Life, vol. 2, pp. 115–16.
51. *ib.*, vol. 1, p. 244.
52. *ib.*, vol. 2, p. 223.
53. Knight (C.), The Old Printer and the Modern Press, p. 244.
54. Dodd (G.), Days at the Factories, p. 359.
55. Poortenaar, *op. cit.*, p. 55.
56. Babbage, *op. cit.*, p. 52.

57. Lewis (C. T. C.), The Story of Picture Printing, *etc.*, p. 14.
58. Tuer (A. W.), Pages and Pictures from Forgotten Children's Books, p. 6.
59. Savage (W.), Practical Hints on Decorative Printing, with Illustrations Engraved on Wood and Printed in Colours at the Type-Press.
60. Dodd (G.), Curiosities of Industry: Printing, p. 20.
61. Quarterly Review, December 1839: the Printer's Devil.
62. Jackson (J.), A Treatise on Wood Engraving, 1839.
63. Senefelder (A.), A Complete Course of Lithography, *etc.*, 1819.
64. Lewis, *op. cit.*, p. 120.
65. Smith (J. T.), Antiquities of Westminster, 1807.
66. Richmond (W. D.), The Grammar of Lithography, 1880.
67. Hullmandel (C. J.) and Ackermann (R.), The Art of Drawing on Stone, *etc.*, 1824.
68. Hullmandel (C. J.), On Some Important Improvements in Lithographic Printing, 1827.
69. Dodd (G.), Curiosities of Industry: Printing, p. 24.
70. The Art Student, 1865.
71. Southam (A. D.), From Manuscript to Bookstall, p. 49.
72. Preston (J. F.) and Arch (E.), Advertising, Printing and Art in Commerce, pp. 223–8.
73. Babbage, *op. cit.*, p. 46.
74. Savage, The Preparation of Printing Ink, 1823.
75. Rogers, History of Agriculture and Prices, vol. 7, pt. 1.
76. *ib.*
77. Mitchell and Hepworth, Inks, pp. 145–64.
78. Harrild and Sons, List of Prices of Printing Machines, *etc.* [*c.* 1860].
79. Harrild and Sons, A General Catalogue, 1913.
80. Hochstetter (R.), The Relation of the Printer to the Ink Maker, 1914.

CHAPTER XV

PAPER IN THE MACHINE AGE

1. Koops (M.), Historical Account of the Substances which have been used to describe Events, *etc.*, 1800, p. 13.
2. Lackington (J.), Memoirs, 1795, p. 246.
3. Parliament, Report on Mr. Koops' Petition, 1801.
4. Koops, *op. cit.*, p. 60.
5. *ib.*, p. 73.
6. *ib.*, p. 74.
7. Murray (J.), Practical Remarks on Modern Paper, 1829, p. 77.
8. Committee on the Booksellers' and Printers' Petition, 1801, Report.
9. Committee on Acts respecting Copy Rights of Printed Books, 1813, Evidence.
10. Koops, *op. cit.*, p. 77.
11. Dodd (G.), Curiosities of Industry: Paper, p. 3.
12. Select Committee on Fourdrinier's Patent, 1837, Report.

13. Murray, *op. cit.*, p. 65.
14. Select Committee on Fourdrinier's Patent, 1837, Report.
15. *ib.*
16. Knight (C.), Passages of a Working Life, vol. 2, p. 332.
17. Parliament, Return of the Number of Pounds Weight of Paper Made, *etc.*, 1834.
18. Babbage (C.), On the Economy of Machinery and Manufactures, p. 170.
19. Knight (C.), The Struggles of a Book against Excessive Taxation, 1850.
20. Chapman (J.), Cheap Books, and how to get them, 1852, p. 3.
21. Parliament, Table showing the Total Quantity of Foreign Rags imported, *etc.*, 1861.
22. British Parliamentary Papers, 1854, LXV.
23. Watt (A.), The Art of Paper-making, p. 80.
24. *ib.*, p. 17.
25. British Parliamentary Papers, 1861, XI.
26. Return of the Names of those Countries in Europe which permit of the . . . Export of Rags, *etc.*, B.P.P., 1861, LVIII.
27. Clapperton (R. H.), Paper and its Relationship to Books, p. 19.
28. Watt, *op. cit.*
29. Clapperton, *op. cit.*, p. 35.
30. Mulhall (M. G.), Dictionary of Statistics, 1892.
31. Clapperton, *op. cit.*, p. 27.
32. Royal Society of Arts, Report of the Committee on the Deterioration of Paper, 1898.
33. Library Association, The Durability of Paper [1930].
34. Clapperton, *op. cit.*, p. 22.
35. Mulhall, *op. cit.*
36. Unwin (S.), The Price of Books, p. 3.
37. Esdaile (A.), A Student's Manual of Bibliography, p. 41.
38. Conference between Representatives of the Employers of Carded Labour and a Deputation from the Original Society of Paper-makers, 1897.
39. An Address to the Parliament of Great Britain, on the Claims of Authors to their own Copy-Right, 1813, p. 182.
40. *ib.*, p. 166.
41. Waugh (A.), A Hundred Years of Publishing, p. 66.
42. Chapman (J.), Cheap Books, and how to get them, 1852, p. 11.
43. Society of Authors, The Cost of Production, 1891.
44. Thring (G. H.), The Marketing of Literary Property, 1933, p. 225.

CHAPTER XVI

MODERN BOOKBINDING

1. Nichols (J.), Literary Anecdotes, vol. 4, p. 442.
2. Copyright Commission, 1876–8. Minutes of Evidence, p. 61.
3. Associated Master Bookbinders, Price List, 1813.
4. Dodd (G.), Days at the Factories, 1843, p. 365.

5. Associated Master Bookbinders, Price List, 1813.
6. Whittock (N.) and others. The Complete Book of Trades, 1842, p. 36.
7. Robert Leighton *in* The Bookseller, July 4, 1881.
8. The Bookbinders' Manual, 1829.
9. The Bookbinder, vol. 1, 1888, p. 50.
10. *ib.*
11. *ib.*
12. *ib.*, p. 101.
13. December 31, 1846.
14. Repertory of Patent Inventions, Enlarged Series, vol. 28, p. 52.
15. The Book of English Trades, 1821, pp. 25–7.
16. Children's Employment Commission (1862), Fifth Report, p. 8.
17. Repertory of Arts, Manufactures and Agriculture, 2nd Series, vol. 9 (1806), p. 195.
18. Repertory of Patent Inventions, *etc.*, vol. 15, p. 154.
19. Harrison (T.), The Bookbinding Craft and Industry, p. 72.
20. The Case of the Bookbinders, 1711.
21. Bookbinders' Trade Circular, December 1850, p. 16.
22. The Reply of the Journeymen Bookbinders to Remarks on a Memorial addressed to their Employers on the Effects of a Machine introduced to Supersede Manual Labour, 1831, pp. 6–8.
23. Dodd (G.), Days at the Factories, p. 369.
24. Penny Magazine, September 1842.
25. Children's Employment Commission (1843), Second Report, p. 134.
26. Whittock and others, *op. cit.*, p. 38.
27. Exhibition of the Works of Industry of all Nations, 1851, Reports of the Juries, p. 423.
28. Harrild and Sons, List of Prices of Printing Machines, *etc.*
29. Knight (C.), Passages of a Working Life, vol. 2, p. 162.
30. Children's Employment Commission (1862), Fifth Report, p. 8.
31. *ib.*
32. Journeymen Bookbinders of London and Westminster. Appeal . . . to the . . . British and Foreign Bible Society . . . on the Subject of Cheap Bibles, 1849, p. 2.
33. Factory and Workshops Act Commission, 1876, Minutes of Evidence, No. 13480.
34. *ib.*, No. 13475.
35. MacDonald (J. R.) *ed.*, Women in the Printing Trades, 1904, p. 100.
36. Zaehnsdorf (J. W.), The Art of Bookbinding, 1880, p. 4.
37. MacDonald, *op. cit.*, p. 97.
38. *ib.*, p. 48.
39. Arnett (J. A.), Bibliopegia, or the Art of Bookbinding, 1835.
40. Exhibition of the Works of Industry of all Nations, 1851, Reports by the Juries, p. 423.
41. MacDonald, *op. cit.*, p. 52*n*.
42. Society of Authors, The Cost of Production, 1891, p. 10.
43. Babbage (C.), On the Economy of Machinery and Manufactures, p. 166.

44. Waugh (A.), A Hundred Years of Publishing, p. 66.
45. Chapman (J.), Cheap Books and how to get them, 1852, p. 11.
46. Unwin (S.), The Price of Books, 1925, p. 3.
47. Bookbinders' Trade Circular, December 1850, p. 16.
48. Society of Arts, Report of the Committee on Leather for Bookbinding, 1901.
49. Harrison (T.), The Bookbinding Craft and Industry, p. 79.

CHAPTER XVII

MODERN LABOUR CONDITIONS

1. Unwin Brothers, Unwins: a Century of Progress, p. 20.
2. Committee on the Booksellers' and Printers' Petition, Report, 1801–2.
3. Select Committee on Copyright Acts, 1818, Minutes of Evidence.
4. [Smith (C. M.)], The Working-Man's Way in the World, p. 166.
5. Knight (C.), The Guide to Trade: the Printer, 1838, p. 17.
6. Quarterly Review, 1840.
7. Dodd (G.), Days at the Factories, 1843.
8. Meidinger (H.), *in* Journal of the Royal Statistical Society, January 1841.
9. Dodd (G.), Curiosities of Industry: Printing, 1852, p. 17.
10. Children's Employment Commission (1862), Fifth Report.
11. Jarrolds, The House of Jarrolds, 1823–1923, p. 47.
12. Knight (C.), Passages of a Working Life, 1864, p. 48.
13. Knight (C.), The Guide to Trade: the Printer, p. 4.
14. [Smith], *op. cit.*, pp. 276–9.
15. Children's Employment Commission (1862), Fifth Report, p. 3.
16. *ib.*, p. 15.
17. *ib.*, p. 5.
18. *ib.*, p. 8.
19. Gent (T.), The Life of Mr. Thomas Gent, Printer, of York, p. 12.
20. Nichols (J.), Literary Anecdotes, vol. 2, p. 651.
21. Besterman (T.) *ed.*, The Publishing Firm of Cadell and Davies: Select Correspondence and Accounts, 1793–1836, p. 114.
22. Children's Employment Commission (1862), Fifth Report, p. 18.
23. Privy Council, Sixth Report of the Medical Officer, 1863, Appendix by Dr. E. Smith, p. 395.
24. [Smith], *op. cit.*, p. 242.
25. Children's Employment Commission (1862), Fifth Report, p. 2.
26. Privy Council, *op. cit.*, p. 388.
27. Children's Employment Commission (1862), Fifth Report, p. 8.
28. Privy Council, *op. cit.*, p. 388.
29. *ib.*, pp. 399–403.
30. Factory Acts Extension Act, 1867, schedule XVII.
31. Factory and Workshops Acts Commission, 1876, Evidence, No. 400.
32. *ib.*, No. 403.
33. Southward (J.), Progress in Printing and the Graphic Arts during the Victorian Era, p. 56.

34. Industrial Fatigue Research Board, Report No. 54.
35. Unwin Brothers, Unwins: a Century of Progress, p. 21.
36. Knight (C.), The Guide to Trade: the Printer, 1838, pp. 3, 9.
37. Whittock (N.) and others, The Complete Book of Trades, 1842, p. 42.
38. *ib.*, p. 219.
39. *ib.*, pp. 38, 43, 390.
40. *ib.*, p. 458.
41. *ib.*, p. 43.
42. Children's Employment Commission (1843), Second Report, p. 133.
43. *ib.*, p. 134.
44. Privy Council, *op. cit.*, p. 384.
45. Children's Employment Commission (1862), Fifth Report, p. 7.
46. Privy Council, *op. cit.*, p. 408.
47. Knight (C.), Passages of a Working Life, 1865, vol. 3, p. 137.
48. The British Typographia, 1887.
49. [Dorrington (C.)], Composing Room Lectures, 1878, p. 2.
50. The British Typographia.
51. Ministry of Labour, Report of an Enquiry into Apprenticeship . . . 1925–6, I.
52. Board of Education, Educational Pamphlet No. 103, 1935.
53. Board of Trade, Report of an Enquiry . . . into the Conditions of Apprenticeship, *etc.*, 1915.
54. Ministry of Labour, *op. cit.*
55. Board of Trade, *op. cit.*

CHAPTER XVIII

THE RISE OF THE TRADE UNIONS

1. Abstract of the Grievances of the Poor Freemen and Journeymen Printers to the House of Commons [*c.* 1640].
2. The Case and Proposals of the Free Journeymen Printers in and about London, 1666.
3. Committee of the News Society of Compositors, 1820, Report.
4. Bookfinishers' Friendly Circular, 1845–51, p. 5.
5. Dunning (J. T.) *in* Social Science Association. Report on Trade Societies, p. 23*n*.
6. An Account of the Rise and Progress of the Dispute between the Masters and Journeymen Printers exemplified in the Trial at Large, *etc.*, 1799.
7. Report of the Committee of the News Society of Compositors, 1820.
8. London Society of Compositors, A Brief Record of Events, *etc.*, p. 153.
9. *ib.*, pp. 20–1.
10. The Times, December 13, 1810.
11. A Few Remarks on the State of the Laws at Present in Existence for regulating Masters and Workpeople, p. 84.
12. Select Committee on Artizans and Machinery, 1824, Second Report, Evidence of Richard Taylor, printer, p. 52.

13. George (M. D.), The Combination Laws reconsidered, *in* Economic History, No. 2, May 1927.
14. Report of the Committee appointed at a Meeting of Journeymen, chiefly Printers, to take intó Consideration certain Propositions, submitted to them by Mr. George Mudie, having for their Object a System of Social Arrangement, *etc.*, 1821.
15. London Society of Compositors, *op. cit.*, p. 25.
16. London Society of Compositors, Annual Report, February 2, 1835.
17. London Society of Compositors, The London Scale of Prices for Compositors' Work . . . 1810, *etc.*
18. Knight (C.), The Guide to Trade: the Printer, 1838, p. 6.
19. [Smith (C. M.)], The Working Man's Way in the World, p. 169.
20. *ib.*, pp. 185–7.
21. London Society of Compositors, A Brief Record, *etc.*, p. 31.
22. Typographical Association, A Fifty Years' Record, p. xiii.
23. Select Committee on Combinations of Workmen, 1838, Second Report, Evidence of P. D. Hardy, pp. 21–47.
24. Morning Herald, June 13, 1828, Letter from "Verax."
25. [Smith], *op. cit.*, p. 19.
26. Webb (S. and B.), History of Trade Unionism, 1926, p. 196.
27. London Society of Compositors, A Brief Record, *etc.*, p. 44.
28. National Typographical Association, First Half-Yearly Report, 1845.
29. Fourth Half-Yearly Report, 1847.
30. Typographical Association, A Fifty Years' Record, p. 2.
31. Knight (C.), The Old Printer and the Modern Press, p. 280.
32. Typographical Association, *op. cit.*, p. ix.
33. *ib.*, p. 4.
34. London Society of Compositors, A Brief Record, *etc.*, p. 74.
35. London Society of Compositors, The London Scale of Prices, *etc.*, 1889, p. 30.
36. The London Society of Compositors, A Brief Record, *etc.*, p. 74.
37. The Young Tradesman, 1839, p. 324.
38. Privy Council, 6th Annual Report of the Medical Officer, 1863, Appendix by Dr. E. Smith, p. 397.
39. *ib.*
40. Royal Commission on Labour, 1892–4, Evidence (22590).
41. Evidence before group "C" (22940–1).
42. Royal Commission on Labour, Rules of Associations of Employers and of Employed, 1892.
43. Society of Lithographic Artists, *etc.*, A Record of Fifty Years, 1885–1935.
44. Children's Employment Commission (1862), Fifth Report.
45. Conference of the Typographical Societies of the United Kingdom and Continent, London, 1886.
46. MacDonald (J. R.) *ed.*, Women in the Printing Trades, p. 26.
47. Gaskell (F.), The Experience and Practice of a Master Printer, 1890, p. 40.
48. Royal Commission on Labour, Fifth Report, 1894, p. 287.

49. London Printing Machine Managers' Trade Society, Report, 1889, p. 13.
50. Amalgamated Committee of the Bookbinding Trade of the Metropolis on the Eight Hours Movement, Preliminary Report, 1891.
51. *ib.*, Final Report, 1892.
52. Times Law Reports, vol. 28, p. 366; vol. 29, p. 73.
53. Society of Lithographic Artists, *etc.*, *op. cit.*
54. Printing Machine Managers' Trade Society, Report for 1916, p. 28.
55. U.K. Tables showing the Rules and Expenditure of Trade Unions, *etc.*, 1911.
56. Chief Registrar of Friendly Societies, Report for 1936.
57. [Dorrington (C.)], Printing-Office Characters, 1881, p. 6.
58. National Board for Prices and Incomes, Report No. 2, 1965, p. 15.
59. *ib.*, p. 20.
60. *ib.*, pp. 23–4.
61. Royal Commission on Trade Unions and Employers' Associations, 1965–8, Report, par. 300.
62. National Economic Development Office, Printing in a Competitive World, 1970, pp. 19–21.
63. *The Times*, May 24, 1973.

CHAPTER XIX

THE COST OF BOOKS IN THE AGE OF MECHANICAL POWER

1. Smiles (S.), Memoir and Correspondence of the late John Murray, vol. 2, p. 187.
2. Dodd (G.), Curiosities of Industry: Printing, 1852, p. 16.
3. Cox (H.) and Chandler (J. E.), The House of Longman, p. 40.
4. Unwin Brothers, Unwins: a Century of Progress, p. 54.
5. Some Account of the Oxford University Press, 1468–1926.
6. Whittock (N.) and others, The Complete Book of Trades, p. 457.
7. Committee on Acts respecting Copy Rights of Printed Books, 1813, Evidence, p. 26.
8. *ib.*, p. 14.
9. Jarrolds, The House of Jarrolds, 1823–1923, p. 8.
10. British Institute of Industrial Art, Notes on Printing Considered as an Industrial Art, 1926, p. 4.
11. Unwin (S.), The Price of Books, p. 2.
12. *Bookseller*, May 2, 1970.
13. Oxford University, Report of the Committee on the University Press, 1970, p. 86.
14. *Bookseller*, July 11, 1970.
15. *Aslib Proceedings*, III, 1970.
16. Chapman (J.), Cheap Books, and how to get them, 1852, p. 20.
17. *Quoted by* Peet (W. H.) *in* Notes and Queries, 7 S. IX., 301.
18. Chapman, *op. cit.*, p. 21.
19. Paston (G.), At John Murray's, p. 70.
20. Smiles, *op. cit.*, vol. 1, p. 369.

21. Campbell (R.), The London Tradesman, 3rd ed., 1757, p. 128.
22. Committee on the Booksellers' and Printers' Petition, 1801–2, Report.
23. Knight (C.), Passages of a Working Life, 1864, vol. 1, p. 275.
24. The Young Tradesman, new ed., 1839, p. 36.
25. Whittock and others, *op. cit.*, p. 40.
26. Annual Register, 1824, p. 217.*
27. Simpkins: being some Account of . . . the House of Simpkin, Marshall, *etc.*, 1924.
28. Whittock and others, *op. cit.*, p. 40.
29. Unwin (S.), The Truth about Publishing, p. 177.
30. 55 George III, cap. 185.
31. Babbage (C.), On the Economy of Machinery and Manufactures, 1832, p. 170.
32. Constable, Archibald Constable, III, p. 341.
33. 3 and 4 William IV, cap. 23.
34. 16 and 17 Victoria, cap. 63.
35. Select Committee on Copyright Acts, 1818, Minutes of Evidence.
36. An Address to the Parliament of Great Britain on the Claims of Authors to their own Copy-Right, 1813, p. 181.
37. Chapman, *op. cit.*, p. 7.
38. *ib.*, p. 6.
39. Constable & Co., Publishers' Advertising, 1930, pp. 22–3.
40. Waugh (A.), A Hundred Years of Publishing, 1930, p. 264.
41. [H: T.] The Perils of Authorship [*c.* 1840], p. 20.
42. *ib.*
43. Unwin (S.), The Price of Books, 1925, p. 10.
44. Smiles, *op. cit.*, vol. 1, p. 222.
45. Cox and Chandler, *op. cit.*, p. 22.
46. Smiles, *op. cit.*, vol. 1, p. 340.
47. Paston (G.), At John Murray's, p. 78.
48. Mumby (F. A.), The House of Routledge, pp. 57, 59.
49. Cox and Chandler, *op. cit.*, p. 32.
50. Unwin (S.), The Truth about a Publisher, 1960, p. 93.
51. Public Lending Right: Report of the Working Party appointed by the Paymaster General, 1972.
52. A fuller account is given in Alan Day's article "Public Lending Right" in *New Library World*, August 1973.
53. *Bookseller*, July 21, 1973.
54. Unwin (S.), The Price of Books, p. 7.
55. The Times, May 6, 1908.
56. An Address to the Parliament . . . (*op. cit.*), p. 182.
57. Babbage, *op. cit.*, p. 166.
58. Society of Authors, The Cost of Production, p. 31.
59. The Times, October 26, 1906.
60. *Bookseller*, April 25, 1970.
61. Besterman (T.) *ed.*, The Publishing Firm of Cadell and Davies: Select Correspondence and Accounts, 1793–1836, p. 115.

62. Smiles, *op. cit.*, vol. 2, p. 260.
63. Paston, *op. cit.*, p. 52.
64. Committee on Acts respecting Copy Rights of Printed Books, 1813, Evidence, p. 2.
65. The Times, May 6, 1908.
66. An Address to the Parliament . . . (*op. cit.*), p. 181.
67. Committee on Acts respecting Copy Rights of Printed Books, 1813, p. 4.
68. Knight (C.), The Old Printer and the Modern Press, 1854, pp. 238–40.
69. Knight (C.), Passages of a Working Life, vol. 2, p. 203.
70. *ib.*, vol. 1, p. 278.
71. Law of Copyright Committee, 1909, Evidence of H. V. Stow, p. 168.
72. Paston (G.), At John Murray's, p. 114.
73. Knight (C.), The Old Printer and the Modern Press, pp. 225–6.
74. Copyright Commission, 1876–8, Evidence.
75. Evidence, p. 126.
76. Unwin (S.), The Truth about Publishing, p. 52.
77. The Times, Printing in the 20th Century, p. 79.
78. Kingsford (R. J. L.), The Publishers' Association, 1896–1946, p. 45.
79. Unwin, *op. cit.*, p. 191.
80. Evidence, p. 11.
81. *Bookseller*, February 3, 1973.
82. Unwin (S.), The Truth about a Publisher, p. 158.
83. Southey, Life, VI, p. 213.
84. Smiles, *op. cit.*, II, p. 4.
85. The Life of J. H. Prince, written by Himself, 2nd ed., 1807, p. 240.
86. Constable, Archibald Constable, III, p. 364.
87. Whittock (N.) and others. The Complete Book of Trades, 1842, p. 40.
88. Knight (C.), The Old Printer and the Modern Press, p. 217.
89. *ib.*
90. Unwin (S.), The Truth about a Publisher, p. 90.
91. *Bookseller*, July 11, 1970.
92. Pratten (C.) and Dean (R. M.), The Economies of Large-Scale Production, 1965, p. 35.
93. Sir Robert Lusty in a B.B.C. interview, quoted in the *Bookseller*, July 11, 1970.
94. Paperbacks in Print, May 1960 and June 1962.
95. Findlater (R.), What are Writers Worth?, 1963, p. 14.
96. Pratten and Dean, *op. cit.*, p. 36.
97. Escarpit (R.), The Book Revolution, 1966, p. 131.
98. *Bookseller*, February, 6, 1971.

CHAPTER XX

COPYRIGHT AND COMPETITION

1. 54 George III, c. 156.
2. 5 and 6 Victoria, c. 45.
3. Committee on the Booksellers' and Printers' Petition, 1801–2, Report.
4. *ib.*

5. Committee on Acts respecting Copy Rights of Printed Books, 1813, Evidence, p. 9.
6. Smiles (S.), Memoir and Correspondence of the late John Murray, vol. 2, p. 27.
7. *ib.*, p. 116.
8. [Smith (C. M.)] The Working Man's Way in the World, 1857, p. 21.
9. *ib.*, pp. 59–60.
10. Annual Register, 1824, p. 218.*
11. Report to the Union Committee of the London Trade Societies of Compositors, 1838.
12. 15 and 16 Victoria, c. 12.
13. Memorial addressed by the Society of Arts to the Government respecting Remission of Duty on Foreign Books, *etc.*, B.P.P. 1852, LI.
14. Chapman (J.), Cheap Books, and how to get them, 1852, p. 15.
15. Shove (R. H.), Cheap Book Production in the United States, 1937, pp. v–vii.
16. 10 and 11 Victoria, c. 95.
17. Copyright Commission, 1876–8, Report, p. xxxii.
18. McCulloch (J. R.), Commercial Dictionary, 1862, Article "Books."
19. Copyright Commission, 1876–8, Report, p. xxxii.
20. *ib.*, Evidence, pp. 284–8.
21. *ib.*, p. 89.
22. *ib.*, Report, pp. xxxvi–xxxvii.
23. Correspondence between the Foreign Office and H.M. Representatives Abroad . . . on the Subject of Copyright, 1872–5, pp. 34–6.
24. Copyright Commission, 1876–8, p. 204.
25. *ib.*, p. 209.
26. Daily Chronicle, December 20–2, 1893.
27. Law of Copyright Committee, 1910, pp. 164–5.
28. Economic Development Committee for Newspapers, Printing and Publishing, Imports and Exports of Print, 1967.
29. 1 and 2 George V, c. 46.
30. Copyright Commission, 1876–8, Evidence.
31. *Bookseller*, March 18, 1972.
32. Book Development Council, Report of the Publishers' Missions to Korea and Taiwan, 1969.
33. Besterman (T.) *ed.*, The Publishing Firm of Cadell and Davies, Select Correspondence and Accounts, 1793–1836, p. 36.
34. *ib.*, p. 35.
35. Smiles, *op. cit.*, vol. 2, p. 8.
36. Oxford University, Report of the Committee on the University Press, 1970, p. 20.
37. Babbage (C.), On the Economy of Machinery and Manufactures, 1832, p. 268.
38. Smiles, *op. cit.*, vol. 1, p. 11.
39. Coleridge (S. T.), Biographia Literaria, p. 26.
40. Besterman, *op. cit.*, p. 123.

41. *ib.*, p. 61.
42. [H: T.] The Authors' Advocate, 1837, pp. 11–12.
43. Select Committee on Newspaper Stamps, 1851.
44. Chapman, *op. cit.*, p. 9.
45. Collins (A. S.), The Profession of Letters, 1928, p. 59*n*.
46. Unwin (S.), The Truth about a Publisher, 1960, pp. 286–8.
47. *ib.*, p. 158.
48. *Bookseller*, April 14, 1973.
49. Oxford University, *op. cit.*, p. 70.
50. Cox (H.) and Chandler (J. E.), The House of Longman, p. 12.
51. Lackington (J.), Memoirs, 10th ed., 1795, p. 212.
52. *ib.*, p. 214.
53. *ib.*, p. 215.
54. Annual Register, 1829, p. 190.
55. Pickering (W.), Booksellers' Monopoly, 1832.
56. *ib.*
57. *op. cit.*, p. 268.
58. Paston (G.), At John Murray's, p. 112.
59. March 30, 1852.
60. Hansard, May 12, 1852.
61. A Report of the Proceedings of a Meeting (Consisting chiefly of authors) held May 4th, at the House of Mr. John Chapman . . . 1852, p. 12.
62. *ib.*
63. John W. Parker & Son, The Opinions of Certain Authors on the Bookselling Question, 1852.
64. Chapman, *op. cit.*, p. 32.
65. Copyright Commission, 1876–8, Evidence, p. 31.
66. *ib.*, p. 44.
67. Longman & Co. and John Murray, On the Publication of School Books by Government at the Public Expense, 1851.
68. Macmillan (*Sir* F.), The Net Book Agreement, *etc.*, 1924, pp. 14–16.
69. The Times, October 19, 1907.
70. *ib.*, June 3, 1908.
71. Wilson (J. G.), The Business of Bookselling, 1930, p. 73.
72. Constable & Co., Publishers' Advertising, 1930, pp. 4–5.
73. The Observer, February 20, 1938.
74. *Bookseller*, September 26, 1970.
75. *ib.*

CHAPTER XXI

THE VOLUME OF PRODUCTION SINCE 1900

1. All the Books Printed in England since the Dreadful Fire, 1666, to . . . (1685).
   Complete Catalogue of Modern Books, Published from the Beginning of the Century to 1756.

Modern Catalogue of Books (for 1792–1802).
London Catalogue, 1800, *etc.*

2. Committee on Acts respecting Copy Rights of Printed Books, 1813, Evidence of T. N. Longman.
3. Select Committee on Copyright Acts, 1818, Evidence of R. Taylor.
4. Besterman (T.) *ed.*, The Publishing Firm of Cadell and Davies: Select Correspondence and Accounts, 1793–1836, p. 64.
5. Knight (C.), Passages of a Working Life, vol. 2, p. 43.
6. [Smith (C. M.)] The Working Man's Way in the World, p. 18.
7. Smiles (S.), Memoir and Correspondence of the late John Murray, vol. 2, p. 494.
8. Select Committee to Inquire into the Education of the Lower Orders, 1816.
9. 1801 census, 10,942,646; 1851 census, 20,814,042.
10. Bowley (A. L.), Wages in the Nineteenth Century.
11. Statistics compiled by Charles Knight from the London Catalogue of Books and the Annual Catalogue of New Books; *in* Passages of a Working Life, vol. 3, p. 194.
12. Royal Commission on Depression of Trade and Industry, 1886, Second Report, Appendix, pt. 2; Answers from the London Society of Compositors.
13. *ib.*
14. Typographical Circular, February 1885.
15. English Catalogue of Books and Bookseller, January 2, 1965.
16. Law of Copyright Committee, 1910, Evidence, 3901.
17. First Census of Production of the United Kingdom, 1907.
18. Fourth Census of Production, 1930.
19. Smiles, *op. cit.*, vol. 1, p. 223.
20. Faber (G.), A Publisher Speaking, 1934, p. 94.
21. *ib.*, p. 95.
22. *Bookseller*, April 25, 1970.
23. *Bookseller*, June 6, 1970.
24. Committee on Type Faces, 1922; A Note on the Legibility of Printed Matter, by L. A. Legros.
25. An unofficial estimate by Mr. L. J. Cumner, Assistant Secretary of the British Federation of Master Printers.
26. English Catalogue of Books, 1937, List of Publishers.
27. Library Association Record, 1919, p. 162.
28. *ib.*, 1940, p. 155.
29. Unwin (S.), The Price of Books, p. 15.
30. Findlater (R.), What are Writers Worth?, p. 18.
31. Oxford University, Report of the Committee on the University Press, 1970, p. 71 *n.*
32. Figure supplied by the Library Association.

Index

Authors Quoted

For Product Safety Concerns and Information please contact our EU
representative GPSR@taylorandfrancis.com
Taylor & Francis Verlag GmbH, Kaufingerstraße 24, 80331 München, Germany

www.ingramcontent.com/pod-product-compliance
Lightning Source LLC
Chambersburg PA
CBHW031356210326
41599CB00019B/2783